Contemporary Kantian Metaphysics

Contemporary Kantian Metaphysics

New Essays on Space and Time

Edited by

Roxana Baiasu
Regent's Park College, University of Oxford, UK

Graham Bird
Emeritus Professor, University of Manchester, UK

and

A.W. Moore
St Hugh's College, University of Oxford, UK

palgrave
macmillan

First published 2012 by
PALGRAVE MACMILLAN

Palgrave Macmillan in the UK is an imprint of Macmillan Publishers Limited,
registered in England, company number 785998, of Houndmills, Basingstoke,
Hampshire RG21 6XS.

Palgrave Macmillan in the US is a division of St Martin's Press LLC,
175 Fifth Avenue, New York, NY 10010.

Palgrave Macmillan is the global academic imprint of the above companies
and has companies and representatives throughout the world.

Palgrave® and Macmillan® are registered trademarks in the United States,
the United Kingdom, Europe and other countries.

ISBN 978-1-349-32996-0   ISBN 978-0-230-35891-1 (eBook)
DOI 10.1057/9780230358911

A catalogue record for this book is available from the British Library.

A catalog record for this book is available from the Library of Congress.

10 9 8 7 6 5 4 3 2 1
21 20 19 18 17 16 15 14 13 12

Transferred to Digital Printing in 2012

Contents

Part IV Time

Acknowledgements

This book's project began during Roxana Baiasu's Leverhulme Early Career Fellowship at the University of Sussex. We would like to acknowledge the support of the University of Sussex and the Leverhulme Trust without which this book could not have been published. Between then and now the book has grown as a result of the productive work of the team of co-editors, Roxana Baiasu, Graham Bird and A.W. Moore.

Our sincere gratitude goes to each author who contributed to this book. We would also like to express special thanks to our editor at Palgrave Macmillan, Priyanka Gibbons, for her efficiency, patience and advice. We thank the production team at Newgen Knowledge Works, in particular the Head of the team, Vidhya Jayaprakash, and the anonymous copy editor, for careful attention and support in the final stages of work on this book. We also owe thanks to Coran Stewart for his help in the preparation of the manuscript, and to all those who have supported the project of this book, in particular, to Sorin Baiasu, Liliana Ilie, Stefan Ilie and Doina Baiasu.

We gratefully acknowledge permission to reproduce certain material in this volume, as indicated below.

We thank the editors of *Kantian Review*, including the guest editors of the special issue *Kantian Review* 15 (2011), Sorin Baiasu and Michelle Grier, for permission to reprint A.W. Moore's essay 'Bird on Kant's Mathematical Antinomies'.

In his essay, 'Kant Speaks to Stephen Hawking', Leslie Stevenson reproduces material from chapters 4 and 5 of his book *Inspirations from Kant* (New York, Oxford University Press, 2012). We are grateful to the press for permission to reproduce this material here.

Françoise Dastur's chapter is an augmented version of an earlier essay ('L'idée d'une "chronologie phénoménologique" et la première interprétation de Kant', in J. F. Courtine (ed.) *Heidegger 1919–1929: De l'herméneutique de la facticité à la métaphysique du Dasein* (Paris, Vrin, 1996)). We thank Librairie Philosophique J. Vrin, Paris (http://www.vrin.fr) for permission to reproduce the article in this book.

Contributors

Paul Abela is Associate Professor in Philosophy at the University of Acadia, Canada. He is the author of *Kant's Empirical Realism* (2002). His most recent publications include 'The Demands of Systematicity: Rational Judgment and the Structure of Nature' in *Companion to Kant* (2006) and 'Kant's Philosophy of Religion' in *Companion to the Philosophy of Religion* (2007).

Lucy Allais is Senior Lecturer in Philosophy at the University of Sussex, UK and Associate Professor in Philosophy at the University of the Witwatersrand, South Africa. She has published in the area of Kant's metaphysics; her recent publications include 'Kant's Idealism and the Secondary Quality Analogy' in *Journal of the History of Philosophy* (2007), 'Kant, Non-Conceptual Content and the Representation of Space' in *Journal of the History of Philosophy* (2009), and 'Kant's Argument for Transcendental Idealism in the Transcendental Aesthetic,' *Proceedings of the Aristotelian Society* (2010); 'Transcendental Idealism and Metaphysics,' *Kantian Yearbook* (2010).

Pamela Sue Anderson is Reader in Philosophy of Religion at the University of Oxford and Fellow in Philosophy and Ethics at Regent's Park College. She has published extensively in the area of metaphysics and epistemology of the philosophy of religion in the Kantian tradition, including continental and feminist philosophy. She is the co-author of *Kant and Theology* (with J. Bell, 2010), *A Feminist Philosophy of Religion: The Rationality and Myths of Religious Belief* (1998) and *Ricoeur and Kant: Philosophy of the Will* (1993).

Roxana Baiasu is an Associate Member of the Philosophy Faculty, University of Oxford and a Member of Regent's Park College, Oxford. She has published in the areas of post-Kantian philosophy (Wittgenstein, Heidegger and Merleau-Ponty), epistemology and philosophy of religion. Her recent publications include: 'Being and Time and the Problem of Space', *Research in Phenomenology* (2007), 'Bodies in Space: Transcendence and Spatialisation of Gender' in Pamela S. Anderson (ed.) *New Topics in Feminist Philosophy of Religion,* Springer-Kluwer (2009), and 'Puzzles of Discourse: Minding Gaps in Understanding", *International Journal of Philosophical Studies* (2009). She held a Leverhulme Early

Carreer Fellowship for a research project to which this volume is linked. She is the founder and principal organiser of the Forum for European Philosophy in Oxford and a member of the Editorial Board of the journal *Studia Phaenomenoloica*.

Graham Bird is Professor Emeritus at the University of Manchester. He is Honorary President and founder of the UK Kant Society. His publications include *Kant's Theory of Knowledge* (1962) and *The Revolutionary Kant* (2006). He is the editor of *A Companion to Kant* (2006) and co-founder and co-editor of the journal *Kantian Review*.

John Campbell is Willis S. and Marion Slusser Professor of Philosophy at the University of California at Berkeley. He is the author of *Past, Space and Self* (1994), *Reference and Consciousness* (2002) and numerous articles in the area of metaphysics.

Steven Crowell is Joseph and Joanna Nazro Mullen Professor of Philosophy at Rice University, Texas. He is the author of *Husserl, Heidegger, and the Space of Meaning: Paths toward Transcendental Phenomenology* (2001) and of numerous essays in phenomenology and transcendental philosophy. He is editor of *Transcendental Heidegger* (with Jeff Malpas, 2007) and *The Prism of the Self: Philosophical Essays in Honour of Maurice Natanson* (1995). He is co-editor of *Husserl Studies*.

Françoise Dastur is Honorary Professor of Philosophy attached to the Husserl Archives of Paris (ENS Ulm), a research unit affiliated to the French National Centre for Research (CNRS). She is the Honorary President of the Ecole Française of Daseinsanalyse, of which she was the founder in 1993. She has published many articles in French, English and German on Husserl, Heidegger, Merleau-Ponty, Ricoeur, Derrida and so on. She is the author of several books in French. Some of them have been translated into English; these are *Death, An Essay on Finitude* (1996), *Heidegger and the Question of Time* (1998) and *Telling Time, Sketch of a Phenomenological Chronology* (2000).

Michael Inwood was formerly Fellow and Tutor in Philosophy, Trinity College, University of Oxford. He is the author of *Hegel* (1983, 2002), *A Hegel Dictionary* (1992), *A Heidegger Dictionary* (1999) and *Heidegger* (2000), and is the editor of Hegel's *Philosophy of Mind* (2007).

Jeff Malpas is Professor of Philosophy at the University of Tasmania, Hobart, and Distinguished Visiting Professor at LaTrobe University, Melbourne. He is also an ARC Australian Professorial Fellow and Visiting Distinguished Professor at LaTrobe University, Melbourne. He is the author of *Donald Davidson and the Mirror of Meaning* (1992), *Place and Experience: A Philosophical Topography* (1999), *Heidegger's Topology: Being, Place, World* (2006) and numerous articles linked to Kantian transcendental traditions (in both analytic philosophy and Continental thought). He has edited *Death and Philosophy* (with Robert C. Solomon, 1999), *Heidegger, Authenticity, and Modernity* and *Heidegger, Coping, and Cognitive Science: Essays in Honor of Hubert Dreyfus*, 2 volumes (with Mark Wrathall, 2000), *Gadamer's Century: Essays in Honor of Hans-Georg Gadamer* (with Ulrich Arnswald and Jens Kertscher, 2002), *From Kant to Davidson: Philosophy and the Idea of the Transcendental* (2002) *and Transcendental Heidegger* (with Steven Crowell, 2007).

A.W. Moore is Professor of Philosophy at the University of Oxford and Tutorial Fellow at St Hugh's College, Oxford. He has held a Leverhulme Major Research Fellowship. He is the author of *The Infinite* (1990; 2001), *Points of View* (1997), *Noble in Reason, Infinite in Faculty: Themes and Variations in Kant's Moral and Religious Philosophy* (2003) and *The Evolution of Modern Metaphysics: Making Sense of Things* (2012).

Søren Overgaard is Associate Professor of Philosophy at the University of Copenhagen. He is the author of *Husserl and Heidegger on Being in the World* (2004) and *Wittgenstein and Other Minds* (2007), and a co-editor of *The Routledge Companion to Phenomenology* (2011).

Leslie Stevenson is Honorary Reader of Philosophy at the University of St Andrews, Scotland. His publications include *The Metaphysics of Experience* (1982), *Ten Theories of Human Nature* (with David L. Haberman, 5th edn, 2008), and *Inspirations from Kant* (2011). He is author of many articles on Kant, language, mind and science.

Dan Zahavi is Professor of Philosophy at the University of Copenhagen and Director of the Danish National Research Foundation, the Centre for Subjectivity Research, University of Copenhagen. He has published extensively in the area of phenomenology. His books include *Self-Awareness and Alterity: A Phenomenological Investigation* (1999), *Husserl and Transcendental Intersubjectivity* (2001), *Husserl's Phenomenology* (2003, 2006), *Subjectivity and Selfhood: Investigating the First-Person Perspective* (2005) and *The Phenomenological Mind* (with Shaun Gallagher, 2008). He is co-editor of the journal *Phenomenology and the Cognitive Sciences*.

Günter Zöller is Professor of Philosophy at the University of Munich. He has published widely in the area of German philosophy. He is the author of *Fichte's Transcendental Philosophy: The Original Duplicity of Intelligence and Will* (1998, 2002) and *Theoretische Gegenstandsbeziehung bei Kant: Zur systematischen Bedeutung der Termini 'objektive Realität' und 'objektive Gültigkeit' in der 'Kritik der reinen Vernunft'* (1984). He edited numerous volumes of Fichte's and Kant's works and essay collections, including *Figuring the Self: Subject, Individual, and Others in Classical German Philosophy* (with David Klemm, 1997).

Introduction

Roxana Baiasu, Graham Bird and A.W. Moore

This volume includes newly written essays in metaphysics which share a strong engagement with the Kantian tradition, and are linked to issues concerning space and time. The volume has been designed to respond to two perceived needs in the literature.

First, a powerful trend in contemporary metaphysics in the Anglophone literature assumes that reality is spatio-temporally organized independently of us, the creatures who make sense of it; by contrast, the volume is prepared to question this assumption in its concerns with the relationship between things in time and space, on the one hand, and the epistemic agents who make sense of them, on the other. The volume thus examines the connections which metaphysics and science have to epistemic agency, its cognitive powers and limits. It is in similar terms that Kant described what is generally taken to be his revolutionary contribution to philosophy in the combined theories of empirical realism and transcendental idealism, which he outlined most clearly and directly in his investigations concerning space and time.

The volume's first aim is, therefore, to draw attention to this distinctive approach to metaphysics and to break new ground by broadening the scope of recent discussions in the metaphysics of space and time. The Kantian tradition represents a rich source of ideas and philosophical arguments which has not been sufficiently explored in the Anglophone literature. The volume explores this insufficiently tapped philosophical resource and offers answers to topical questions in the area.

Second, contemporary Kantian philosophy is currently pursued along two distinct lines. These two lines have developed to a large extent apart from one another in the so-called analytic, Anglo-American tradition and European philosophy. The first trend has tended to give priority to space and the constitution of objectivity, whilst the latter has focused more on time and the constitution of subjectivity. The second aim of the volume is, thus, to offer a comprehensive treatment of the issues at stake by pursuing both these trends.

This volume's essays clarify or question main presuppositions and methods of the two approaches and bring their distinct claims into a productive, critical dialogue on the relation between metaphysics and epistemology. The volume includes original, informative discussions of topical issues such as: cognition and action, particularly in relation to perception and embodied existence; receptivity and normativity; the constitution of, and relation between, subjectivity and objectivity; the conceptual and non-conceptual content of experience; and the limits of knowledge.

Part I, on Perception, consists of four chapters. The first two are directly concerned with Kant's *Critique of Pure Reason*. The other two engage with the issue of perception from two different post-Kantian perspectives: John Campbell's approach is primarily epistemological and defended against alternative contemporary accounts; Steven Crowell's inquiry is phenomenological – it focuses on Husserl's theories of perception and considers their links to contemporary debates. The first two chapters, from Paul Abela and Lucy Allais, both address issues about Kant's way of integrating space and time into our general representational capacities. They both discuss the ways in which space and time figure in Kant's account of the representations of the senses (intuitions) and of the understanding (concepts). They consider how Kant's treatment of those representations relates to contemporary debates about non-conceptual content.

The general issue is highlighted by Kant's claim that space and time belong to the senses, as intuitions, and not to the understanding, as concepts. Such a claim might seem to commit Kant to a belief in non-conceptual content, but this is not Abela's view. Throughout his chapter he defends a view of Kant in which all mental content depends on our ability to make judgements, which in turn rests on our exercise of concepts. It is a central claim in his chapter that receptivity, 'openness to the world', is not a mere passive record, as empiricists might claim, but an active engagement inseparable from our conceptual and judgemental abilities. This point stands in an interesting relation to Kant's own belief that space and time are not only 'intuitive' but also '*a priori*', that is, not derivable from *a posteriori* sense experience.

In pursuing these ideas, Abela considers two parts of Kant's account: first the Schematism and second the mathematical principles in the Analytic of Principles. The former seeks to explain how *a priori* concepts, categories, can have application to *a posteriori* experience, while the latter illustrate the necessary connection between those categories and our sensory intuition. In considering the first of these, Abela sets aside a number of well-known criticisms of the apparatus of schematism. Kant's account is represented, rather, as a reflection of the need to appeal to concepts and judgements in formulating the instantiation and meaning conditions for categories. The mathematical principles, the Axioms of Intuition and the Anticipations of Perception, provide an illustration of the detailed working out of the general claim. Abela provides a comprehensive account of the argument in these sections which confirms his (and Kant's) claim that even at the most primitive perceptual level our engagement with the world involves a conceptual structure, and operates, as some recent commentators have it, within the space of reasons.

In the concluding section Abela addresses four potential objections to his view. He argues that to ascribe such views to Kant is not anachronistic. He insists that Kant is not committed to non-conceptual content. He denies that the possibility of alternative cognitive structures (which Kant clearly admits) conflicts with his reading of Kant. And he rejects any substantive role for 'things in themselves' (noumena) in the account of receptivity; hence the absence of references to this notion in his discussion of Kant's account is not an omission but, he argues, is justified.

Lucy Allais addresses similar issues about Kant's distinction between intuition and concepts. Although she agrees with Abela that with this distinction Kant opposes, rather than endorses, Cartesianism, she sees a different role for intuitions from that which Abela canvasses. For her the contribution of the senses is to some degree independent from that of the understanding and cannot be subordinated, as Abela claims, to the roles of judgement and understanding. There is, as she shows, considerable textual support for the claim in the *Critique* that the senses provide such a separate contribution. But, although Kant says, or implies, that intuition distinctively gives us particulars he also, notoriously, asserts an intimate and necessary dependence between sensibility and understanding; the familiar claim that 'thoughts without content are empty; intuitions without concepts are blind' (B75) could be read as expressing this dependence relation between sensibility and understanding.

Allais's task is, then, to reconcile and explain the apparently different accounts Kant offers of the dependence and independence between sensibility and understanding. Her resolution of this problem turns on the distinction between our perception of distinct particulars and a full cognition of some object. The former can be achieved in sensibility, but the latter requires the apparatus of the understanding. She notes that Kant's occasional references to animal perception support the belief that even that limited ability allows perception of distinct particulars, with the resulting behavioural consequences. She does not deny that, in general, a normal adult human experience requires a conceptual element, but distinguishes that requirement from the claim that in every case of perceiving a distinct particular such a conceptual element has to operate.

Such a view has consequences for our understanding of Kant's transcendental idealism and of the relation between the Aesthetic, which deals with sensibility, and the Deduction, which concerns understanding. She notes that, just as Kant's account of the relation between sensibility and understanding involves both a dependence and an independence between them, so his transcendental idealism, whether understood in an epistemological or a metaphysical way, involves both a dependence and an independence between physical reality and the mind. Her basic thesis also entails a specific account of the comparison and relation between the Aesthetic and the Deduction. Because she holds that the senses provide an independent contribution, those two sections identify different requirements for our experience, which, nevertheless, need to be jointly satisfied for a full human experience. The former provides for a basic intentionality in perception, that is, in our perceiving distinct particulars, while the latter trades on this in providing for our ability to ascribe properties to what we perceive. Concepts themselves do not account for the intentionality in perception.

To the question as to what the character of the first, sensory requirement is, she answers in terms of the view that the Aesthetic identifies *a priori* forms of intuition which organize our manifold perception and experience. She draws attention to the arguments in the Metaphysical and Transcendental Expositions of the Transcendental Aesthetic which claim to establish that view. In the concluding part of the chapter, Allais offers a detailed account of Kant's argument for the apriority of space in the Metaphysical Exposition. She reconstructs the argument as consisting of ten complex steps. Each of the steps and the upshot of the whole argument are examined closely. Kant himself did not write the argument in such a form, but the reconstruction aims to make explicit how, on her interpretation of it, such an argument might be formulated. It makes clear what are the advantages and disadvantages of Kant's position, so understood, and clarifies some of the difficulties in following his own text.

Like Abela, John Campbell focuses on the perceptual cognition of *objects*, but he approaches it in relation to contemporary discussions of the topic. He looks closely at the issue of whether spatial awareness is required for the perception of objects. By spatial awareness Campbell means conscious perception of spatial properties, such as volumetric properties (e.g., shape, size and solidity) and location. Campbell engages in current debates on the topic by considering certain post-Kantian perspectives in contemporary analytic philosophy as well as results of recent experimental work in psychology. In relation to the latter, he agrees with Lynn Robertson that visual spatial awareness is necessary for visual object perception; with regard to the former, he shares with Quassim Cassam the view that someone who is incapable of spatial perception in general would be incapable of perceiving objects.

Campbell sets himself to develop a radical view on the necessity of spatial awareness for object perception. He argues that a rather implicit grasp of spatial features or a conceptual understanding of space is not sufficient for object perception: this requires explicit spatial awareness. He offers a strong argument and defence of this radical view against scepticism about the role of spatial *awareness*. He pushes such scepticism as far as it can go and considers its various forms. Some of these involve naturalistic approaches. One general point that such approaches share is the view according to which *awareness* is an epiphenomenon, which has no explanatory value but, rather, needs to be explained. Campbell also refers to a more specific naturalistic objection which draws on recent, experimental research arguing that visual perception of objects does not require visual spatial awareness. Campbell argues that this objection misses the target. He concedes, however, that the position in favour of which Robertson argues is open to the other, general sceptical point mentioned above, according to which spatial *awareness* is an epiphenomenon with no explanatory value. Campbell deals with this point later in the chapter.

He also considers another set of sceptical objections which are no longer formulated in naturalistic terms but are, rather, raised on conceptual grounds. He considers in this context certain scenarios or 'thought experiments' which support a line of thinking according to which someone could have a conception or theory of space but no sensory perception of space, and could still perceive objects. In particular he considers the case of someone who has only non-spatial auditory perception, but comes up with a theory about a kind of space corresponding to the space we experience and are aware of.

To respond to the general points raised by the two forms of scepticism about spatial consciousness mentioned above, Campbell looks more closely at the notions of object and causality. To perceive an object, rather than sensory features or bundles of such features, one has to grasp that the object's earlier properties causally influence its later properties. This is essentially Shoemaker's idea that objects are internally 'causally connected'. There is at work here, then, a transmission of causal influence. In Campbell's view, an account of the object's internal causal connectedness in terms of counterfactuals about how the later properties depend on the earlier properties of the object is unsatisfactory. He argues that the grasp of internal causality requires a grasp of the mechanism operating the transmission of causality. He points out that the mechanism by which causal influence is transmitted over time is the identity of the object; and the mechanism by which causal influence is transmitted through space is the object's movement. He argues that the grasp of these mechanisms requires spatial awareness. In the absence of spatial awareness, manifest, for example, in the case of the subject with non-spatial perception and a theoretical grasp of a kind of space, the subject can have an understanding of the relevant counterfactuals, that is, a grasp of how earlier changes would have made a difference in the later condition of the object, but cannot have an understanding of the mechanisms transmitting causal influence (that is, the objects themselves and their movement). It is in terms of the latter that the former is to be explained, and not the other way around. Only if one has spatial awareness of volumetric properties and locations can one perceive objects, and grasp their persistence and movement as mechanisms transmitting causal influence over time and/or through space, from one location to another.

In response to the first, naturalistic form of scepticism concerning spatial awareness, Campbell argues that spatial awareness is not an epiphenomenon but has an important epistemic function. More specifically, spatial awareness plays a significant explanatory role in relation to our grasp of certain aspects of perception which cannot be accounted for by theories about how the brain works. In response to the second form of scepticism, formulated by means of certain thought experiments and conceptual analysis, Campbell proposes what he calls a 'stronger conclusion' of his argument about the necessity of spatial awareness for object perception. On his account, spatial awareness of the object's volumetric properties and location provides a 'canonical' form of object identification. This idea implies that medium-sized objects constitute prototypes of mechanisms of transmission of causal influence. The stronger conclusion Campbell proposes puts forward a condition for non-spatial perception of an object: this consists in one's capacity to recognize a correct paradigmatic identification of the object in question. As he puts it at the end of Section 4: 'If one is to be said to be perceiving the thing itself non-spatially, one has to be capable of recognizing the correctness of a canonical identification of that thing.'

As a final point, Campbell notes that his approach emphasizes the epistemic role of spatial awareness. He contrasts his approach with a Nagelian perspective on the matter: on Campbell's account, the role of spatial awareness is not conceived in terms of knowing 'what it is like' for the mind to perceive things spatially, but is understood as providing one with 'knowledge of what the world is like'.

The view that consciousness in perception plays an epistemic role involves, more or less explicitly, a notion of normativity. In his contribution to the volume, Steven Crowell engages with this issue from a phenomenological perspective. Crowell shares with Abela and Allais a concern for the question whether perception is necessarily structured conceptually even at its most primitive level. He approaches this topic through a discussion of certain important post-Kantian moments in the history of this debate. He focuses on the twentieth-century phenomenological tradition, and more specifically on Husserl's philosophy, making links with recent debates on perception, between philosophers such as John McDowell, Hubert Dreyfus and Alva Noë. Crowell enquires, from this perspective, into the independence of sensibility, and supports the view, also endorsed by Allais in her reading of Kant, according to which intentionality in perception does not necessarily have a conceptual structure. Crowell argues for this in the context of his discussion of the normative in perception.

This emerges as an issue in relation to the problem of perception as a warrant for empirical judgements. Perception, considered as an experience, can offer justification for empirical judgements only if it is itself responsive to norms. These norms can be understood as rules by means of which one can recognize success or failure of perception. Crowell addresses three interrelated main questions concerning perceptual normativity. First, what does the normative in perception consist in? Second, what makes perception responsive to norms? And, finally, how do norms in perception come to be established?

With regard to the first question, Crowell takes the norms operative in perception as implicit, organizing and unifying principles which constitute an optimal way of experiencing things. On the basis of such principles it is possible to recognize what counts as an adequate, coherent experience of some aspect of reality, and to identify success and failure in perception. Concerning the second issue as to what makes perception responsive to norms, Crowell mentions two other positions before engaging in a detailed discussion of Husserl's views on the issues under consideration. There is, first, the Kantian position, according to which space and time function normatively in the way they structure perception. Crowell notes that this is not sufficient when the perception of *objects* is what is at issue. The pure concepts of the understanding are needed for the normative constitution of object perception. But, he notes, this position is faced with the difficulty of accounting for the relation between the two types of norms (spatio-temporal and conceptual) which are taken to structure perception. The second position is that of McDowell, who argues that conceptual capacities or structures are operative in perception and account for its norm-responsiveness. But how are such capacities and structures at work in perception? Phenomenology, Crowell points out, engages with questions which the two positions mentioned here do not address. The approach to such questions is informed by a distinctively phenomenological view, according to which that which makes perception norm-governed is, at the most basic level, pre-conceptual.

Thus, although Crowell is concerned with the three main questions mentioned earlier, he focuses on the third one, concerning the origin of normativity in perception, since, on his view, phenomenology can offer a very significant contribution to ongoing debates related to this issue. More specifically, as already mentioned, he examines the Husserlian legacy on the matter. Husserl attempts to address the questions about perception raised earlier along the lines just mentioned, that is, by identifying non-conceptual but norm-governed aspects of perception. However, Crowell believes that he fails in his attempt to carry out this phenomenological task. On Crowell's reading, Husserl's early theory of perception uses a conceptualistic model – which brings Husserl's theory close to McDowell's position. But the use of this conceptualistic model makes Husserl's position problematic. Husserl's mature account of perception is developed in terms of passive synthesis. This is understood as a pre-conceptual, yet intentional, primitive aspect of perception. This conception seems more promising, but, Crowell argues, it too fails to account for the origin of normativity, due to its taking over some elements of the earlier account.

Nevertheless, there is, especially in Husserl's mature work, the beginning of a more adequate approach to what is at issue. Crowell points out that this approach to perception emphasizes the role of time consciousness and of the lived body in the constitution of perceptual responsiveness to norms. But, as he notes, Husserl's prioritizing of time and his view that the awareness of the lived body is ultimately constituted in the temporality of appearances seem to be part of what is problematic in Husserl's account. However, both its failure and its opening up of a novel way of thinking about the body can be fruitfully used to develop a more promising approach to the issue of perceptual normativity.

Crowell puts forward the main elements of such an approach. The background of his analysis is the post-Husserlian inheritance in twentieth-century philosophy (Heidegger and Merleau-Ponty) and in contemporary thought (Dreyfus). This background also includes interesting links to Noë's account of perception. Crowell argues that a perceptual optimum is constituted through bodily movement and engagement in contexts of action. He thus proposes an account of the origin of normativity in terms of a central role for the body. Norms in perception are established through the 'perceptual practice' in which we are constantly engaged in accordance with our bodily skills, abilities and tasks. Thus, the origin of normativity in perception can be understood in terms of bodily skills and practices. This challenges the idea of the priority of time. Some of these issues, and in particular the idea of the priority of time, are further discussed in Part IV, which deals with crucial moments and aspects of the phenomenological tradition that are relevant to the volume's overall topic.

In Part II the concern shifts from philosophical reflection on our capacities of cognition and action to philosophical engagement with the sciences in relation to more or less neglected aspects of Kant's philosophy and of its significance for contemporary scientific concerns. Graham Bird considers the relation between Kant's philosophy of space and time and his account of mathematics. Leslie Stevenson focuses on Kant's discussion in the cosmological antinomies of spatio-temporal features of the physical universe as a whole and on a debate with contemporary cosmology. Jeff Malpas and Günter Zöller examine the general character of Kant's critical project in relation to the geographical, cartographic and navigational metaphors which he uses to describe it.

Since the early twentieth century, under the influence of logicism, Kant's philosophy of mathematics has been widely regarded as fundamentally mistaken. It has been argued that Kant's account makes an essential reference to our perceptual – what Kant calls 'intuitive' – capacities in classifying most mathematical propositions as 'synthetic *a priori*'. A prevailing logico-empiricist account, by contrast, treats such propositions as analytic or logical, and holds that pure mathematics neither can nor should appeal to psychological features such as perception. The question which Graham Bird puts in his chapter is whether, in the light of these strong objections, Kant's account of mathematics has any merit at all.

The qualified but affirmative answer given in the chapter draws on two resources, one from Kant's own discussion and another from contemporary structuralist accounts of mathematics. The former stresses Kant's belief that the whole of our experience is governed by a structure of *a priori* principles. In the light of this general claim, it is natural to regard the *a priori* propositions of mathematics as providing a parallel structure for our experience, including natural science. The latter appeals to the belief, canvassed by structuralists such as Paul Benacerraf and Stewart Shapiro, that mathematical propositions, such as arithmetical or geometrical propositions (for example, about numbers or spatial points), do not refer to distinctively mathematical objects but express only formal relations between the members of suitable structures. The chapter argues that such a structuralist account, supplemented with an appeal to Carnap's criticism of traditional debates about the real existence of numbers and abstract objects, offers a defensible account both of mathematics and of Kant's account of mathematics. Kant's rejection of Platonism in mathematics (though not in morality), his belief in general *a priori* principles which provide a structure for experience, and his specific treatment of natural numbers and geometrical points, all indicate a form of structuralism in mathematics which fits naturally into those recent structuralist accounts.

Kant's interest in space and time in the first *Critique* concerned not only their role as essential aspects of our experience but also the traditional controversies that had arisen over the large-scale spatio-temporal features of the physical universe as a whole. No indisputable way had been found of answering questions about the spatial extent or temporal origin of the physical universe, and Kant identifies these disputes as a mark of the difference between straightforward scientific and related philosophical questions. One of Kant's central motives in writing the *Critique*, as he makes clear in the Prefaces, was to analyse the character of these long-running disputes and to resolve them, in order to understand better the dividing line between empirical science and philosophy. But, just as the basic questions about the extent and origin of the physical universe have generated controversy, so has Kant's claimed resolution of that controversy. Leslie Stevenson's chapter addresses these issues both in scientific cosmology and in Kant's philosophical analysis of the traditional debate. He argues that, although Kant's analysis might be thought inadequate in the light of contemporary scientific cosmology, this is not so. He claims that Kant's discussion makes points about the limitations of such theoretical enquiries which might be directed even to a contemporary scientist such as Stephen Hawking.

This is not to say that Kant's own position is entirely clear, and the chapter begins by clarifying some of the central concepts in Kant's analysis. Primary among these are the Kantian notions of 'synthesis' and 'the given', both of which contain significant ambiguities. Since Kant's resolution of the Antinomy turns on his claim that we can never be 'given' in experience any access to features of the physical universe as a whole, these ambiguities compromise his account. Stevenson also criticizes the aspiration of scientists to what they have sometimes called a 'theory of everything', and he sets limits to our grasp of any ultimate origin of the physical universe. He points out that scientists themselves sometimes recognize such limits in the restrictions they place on understanding a 'singularity' such as the posited 'Big Bang' origin of the physical universe. In the conclusion the further Kantian question is raised about how the resolution of the Antinomy relates to Kant's transcendental idealism. It is made clear that, contrary to the views of some commentators, Kant does not accept a verificationist account of meaning. His view is that there are important limits to our understanding of claims about the spatio-temporal character of the physical universe as a whole, but not that such claims are meaningless because we cannot verify them.

Malpas and Zöller stress the role of Kant's topographical imagery in his outlines of the general project in the first *Critique*. Kant appeals not only to a wide range of such spatial metaphors but also to a general description of 'allocating' the principal elements in our experience to their rightful places in relation to one another and to our cognitive powers. More generally, as they point out, Kant's philosophical goal can be seen as an attempt to situate humankind, its concepts, practices, and cognitive powers, in the diverse traditional metaphysical accounts of reality. Kant's general aim might be expressed as that of 'providing a picture of human being and its place in the world'. Among those alternative metaphysical accounts, Kant indicates something of his own preferences in describing Hume as the celebrated 'geographer of human reason' (B788).

The authors note, however, that Kant's project, so understood, has two significantly different but related aspects. On one side it situates our experience 'transcendentally', while on the other it examines 'empirically' the diversity of human populations distributed over the planet. The former transcendental project is carried out in the three *Critiques*, while the latter empirical enquiry is reported in the lectures on anthropology and physical geography. In that latter context the authors consider Kant's views on the influences of climate, race, history and purpose. It is made clear that there are important links, and not necessarily any conflict or tension, between the transcendental and empirical accounts. The authors outline those connections and identify some limitations in Kant's discussion. Kant notoriously never ventured far from Königsberg and relied on others' testimony about populations in distant parts of the world. His view of the relations between the human species and its environment suffered from an inevitable ignorance of a Darwinian account of species mutability and evolution. The authors underline these limitations and point particularly to what they regard as a 'shortcoming' in the empirical enquiry highlighted by the more philosophical, transcendental, account. Throughout their survey of Kant's general account, they emphasize the crucial role of space as an 'objective' aspect of reality and use this to show complexities in the simple contrast between what is 'subjective' and what is 'objective'. In the conclusion they make clear that such considerations have important implications for our understanding of Kant's idealism.

A significant feature of Kant's transcendental idealism which has continued to preoccupy thinkers in the post-Kantian tradition is the concern with the bounds of experience. The three contributions from Pamela Sue Anderson, Roxana Baiasu and A. W. Moore which form Part III of the volume address this concern from three different perspectives. Like Malpas and Zöller, Pamela Sue Anderson has a special interest in Kant's metaphors of spatial location. However, Anderson's main interest is different from theirs. Her critical concern is how to maintain Kant's distinction between boundaries (*Grenzen*) and limits (*Schranken*). Anderson focuses on metaphors of space and spatial location in Kantian thought, in order to address a series of questions concerning the space of the unknowable, the space of the knowable and the boundary separating them. Baiasu and Moore focus more on the knowable and its bounds.

In her contribution to the volume, Anderson confronts an ethical question concerning the space of the unknowable and its boundary. Does treating a limit of knowledge as if it were a boundary constitute a cognitive prohibition? In other words, is a knower prevented from claiming new knowledge when a limit is wrongly understood as an unalterable boundary? Anderson contends that such a misunderstanding undermines the epistemic confidence of a knower who is silenced by this prohibition. Her contention is meant to address debates concerning the ethics of cognition. Maintaining the correct distinction between unmovable boundaries and movable limits of knowledge would have both an ethical and an epistemological impact on cognitive development.

Anderson confronts another question concerning Kant's account of space as an *a priori* form of sensibility and thus as one of the boundaries of empirical knowledge. How do we make sense of space as a boundary of the knowable, while also speaking of 'the space' of the unknowable? Space as a boundary excludes, while the unknowable includes, the fundamental judgements of morality and speculative metaphysics. Anderson contends that metaphors of spatial location can point to the unknowable beyond the boundary of the *a priori* form of sensibility, but that we must 'enlarge' thought when it comes to the unknowable. For this enlargement, Anderson draws on Michèle Le Doeuff's account of the philosophical imaginary and on Hannah Arendt's account of analogical thinking. Le Doeuff helps to underline difficulties and dangers in restricting Kant's space to a boundary; Arendt describes a possible movement across the sensible and the conceptual to the non-sensible space of reasons.

With this philosophical support, Anderson proposes an alternative to the two-world interpretation of Kant's transcendental idealism. This proposal is explored in relation to Kant's central metaphor of an island, 'enclosed by unalterable boundaries' and surrounded by 'the broad and stormy ocean' as 'the true seat of illusion'. This philosophical imagery portrays the dangers of conflating the literal with the metaphorical – a conflation which has served to support a sharp separation of the sensible world from the intelligible world. Anderson argues that confusion of the literal with the metaphorical leads to an epistemic dead end and to the injustice of prohibitive practices, inhibiting confidence and so access to the space of reasons. Kant's own ambivalence with regard to thinking ideas what cannot be known is portrayed metaphorically as the danger of venturing beyond the secure 'land of truth'. The question therefore arises: how it is possible to make sense of this ambivalence without appealing to sensible and intelligible worlds? Anderson suggests that Arendt's reading of the third *Critique*, especially Kant's reflective judgements, provides a form of analogical thinking that moves from particular to universal. Such thinking, as in Kant's use of metaphors of spatial location, provides new possibilities for the enlargement of thought within the shared and shareable space of reasons.

In her contribution to the volume, Roxana Baiasu is concerned with the process of the enlargement of understanding to embrace an extreme form of objective understanding, namely, what is sometimes called 'absolute' thinking about reality. However, the inquiry is confined to an investigation into the enlargement of understanding within the realm of the knowable and within sensible boundaries, including the boundaries drawn by space. More specifically, the question of this chapter is whether objective, possibly absolute, thinking could be disembodied. Baiasu offers an argument in favour of a negative answer to this question, which is developed through an inquiry into spatial awareness. To formulate the argument, Baiasu draws on certain post-Kantian discussions in both contemporary analytical thought and the twentieth-century phenomenological tradition. The discussion of objective understanding and its extreme form, absolute thinking, refers to the accounts of these issues offered by Bernard Williams, Thomas Nagel and A.W. Moore. The approach to embodiment takes over and further develops relevant ideas put forward by Husserl, Heidegger and Merleau-Ponty. A starting point for the argument is the claim that spatial awareness involves a sense of proximity and also a sense of distance in relation to what we come across in the world. These basic elements of spatial awareness are necessarily related to one another. Baiasu argues that the extreme forms (or limits) of the sense of proximity and of the sense of distance are enacted by embodiment and by objective, possibly absolute, thinking, respectively. Since embodiment and absolute thinking enact such limits of spatial awareness, they must be linked to each other. Objective, absolute thinking cannot be but embodied.

Moore, in his contribution, considers Graham Bird's treatment of Kant's mathematical antinomies in *The Revolutionary Kant*, Bird's recent commentary on the *Critique of Pure Reason*. Kant's mathematical antinomies consist of two pairs of arguments concerning the age, extent and composition of the physical universe. The first pair comprises an argument that the physical universe is both finitely old and finitely big, coupled with an argument that it is both infinitely old and infinitely big. The second pair comprises an argument that whatever is composite in the physical universe consists of simple parts, coupled with an argument that the physical universe contains no simple parts. Kant thinks that each of these arguments has considerable appeal. His aim is to resolve the resultant conflicts by providing a diagnosis of the appeal, and by saying what attitude we should take to the issues concerned once any relevant errors have been exposed.

On Bird's interpretation, Kant thinks that the principal error is as follows: we wrench certain *a priori* concepts from a perfectly legitimate use in addressing issues about the structure of physical reality and use them instead to raise issues about the experience-transcendent limits of physical reality, issues that we then fancy ourselves capable of settling by pure reason. In fact, not only are we not capable of settling these issues by pure reason, we are not capable of settling them at all. For, given the underlying misappropriation of the *a priori* concepts in question, they constitute what Bird calls an 'erroneous and undecidable' pseudo-discipline.

Moore offers a different interpretation, on which Kant does not deny that we can settle these issues. In fact, the arguments in the antinomies themselves help us to settle them – not by 'pure' reason, admittedly, but by an exercise of reason involving *a priori* intuition. On Moore's interpretation, our principal error is to presuppose that the concept of the unconditioned has application to physical reality. Once this presupposition has been abandoned, what remains in each case is a perfectly sound argument, not for the view that was originally being defended but against the opposed view. This is unproblematic, because, although the views in each pair are incompatible, there is no reason why they should not both be false. (Thus, if there is no such thing as the physical universe as a whole, then it is both false that the physical universe is finitely big and false that it is infinitely big.) Moore concludes his contribution with some suggestions about how this exegetical disagreement between him and Bird relates to some broader differences between their respective understandings of Kant. A critical response from Bird to Moore's views has been published in a recent issue of *Kantian Review* (16(2), July 2011, 274–80).

Part IV of the volume is devoted to the discussion of space and time in the post-Kantian phenomenological tradition. More specifically, the contributions to Part IV deal, in one way or another, with the problem of the centrality of time characteristic of certain major movements within this tradition. Heidegger is perhaps the most prominent thinker in the history of philosophy, for whom time played a crucial role in shaping the orientation of his thinking. To support the exceptional significance of time within his account of our relation to the world (at least in his early philosophy), Heidegger appeals to Kant. Whilst he also engages with Husserl and Aristotle, Kant is (arguably) more important for the early Heidegger. Why is time central for Heidegger? And why is Kant so important for him? These questions, which are interconnected, are addressed by Michael Inwood and Françoise Dastur, respectively.

Inwood's interpretation of the centrality of time in Heidegger's early thought and Dastur's reading of his indebtedness to Kant complement each other. Dastur points out that Kant was an important precursor of phenomenology, and notes the importance of reading Aristotle and Husserl in order to understand Heidegger's relation to Kant. These considerations are developed in some detail by Inwood. Inwood's reading of the priority of time in Heidegger and his relation to Kant is framed historically through a discussion which critically engages with Aristotle and Husserl. Inwood notes that the influence Kant exerted on Heidegger was crucial for the development of Heidegger's ontology, and raises a question concerning idealism. These topics are addressed by Dastur in her reading of Heidegger's interpretation of Kant, which focuses on Heidegger's discussion of the relation between time and subjectivity. These two chapters by Inwood and Dastur thus clarify Heidegger's reasons and motivations for regarding time as fundamental. The centrality of time is challenged by Zahavi and Overgaard through a discussion of Heidegger as well as of Bergson and Husserl on the relation between time and space.

Inwood approaches the question 'Why is time so important to Heidegger?' by pointing out Heidegger's ontological concern with the question of Being and his critique of traditional metaphysics. In particular, Heidegger thinks that part of the task of dealing with this issue is a critical engagement with what he takes to be the traditional conception of time, the origin of which is, in his view, Aristotle's conception of time. Inwood discusses certain significant aspects of the Aristotelian conception and contrasts these with the Husserlian conception, which, in Inwood's view, is anticipated by Kant, and which has influenced Heidegger. This is the conception of a more basic experience of time, which Husserl accounts for in terms of the unity of time-consciousness. In this context, Inwood raises the question of the priority of time over space in Kant and in Heidegger's interpretation of Kant, and looks into the reasons and motivations for this priority.

On Inwood's reading, the turn to subjectivity which distinguishes the Kantian and Husserlian positions from the Aristotelian approach undergoes a significant change in Heidegger: the human being is no longer conceived as a knower or an observer of nature, but primarily as an agent involved in the world (Heidegger calls this entity engaged in the world, and for which Being is an issue, 'Dasein'). Corresponding to this change there is a shift in the way in which time is conceived. Heidegger emphasizes the significance of the future for the agent concerned with his or her decisions and projects in the world. This contrasts with the priority of the present enacted by epistemic comportments of knowing or observing nature. The different temporal ways of being of Dasein are, however, constituted by the unity of the tenses. Inwood points out that a distinctive thesis of Heidegger's thinking is the claim that Dasein is temporal through and through. The condition of possibility of all human comportments is, for Heidegger, primordial temporality. Inwood ends with a question concerning Heidegger's conception of time relevant for a discussion of Heidegger's indebtedness to Kant: Is time, for Heidegger, ideal? What is the relation between Dasein and time?

These questions are taken up by Dastur; more precisely, she is concerned with the issue of the relation between time and subjectivity as this is approached by Heidegger in his reading of Kant. Her interpretation is meant to answer the question concerning the significance of Kant for Heidegger. She focuses on certain aspects of Heidegger's discussion of Kant in the 1925–6 winter semester lecture course, published under the title *Logic: The Question of Truth,* and contrasts Heidegger's ontological concerns with the neo-Kantian, epistemologically oriented reception of Kant. Her approach to the question of the relation between time and subjectivity is meant to show that what is at stake is the unity of subjectivity and, more precisely, of sensibility and understanding. Dastur points out that, on Heidegger's reading, these are irreducible to one another, but necessarily linked to one another within the experience of the world. She takes Heidegger to argue, in opposition to the neo-Kantian approach, for the necessity of the transcendental aesthetic and its irreducibility to the analytic of the understanding.

The inquiry into time (which is called 'phenomenological chronology' in the 1925–6 lecture course) is concerned with the ultimate conditions of possibility of our comportments and faculties. Dastur notes that this investigation is meant to show that truth has a temporal foundation, and attempts to shed light on the question of the relation between truth and Being, on the one hand, and time, on the other. This is a question that Heidegger raises in connection with his engagement with Aristotle. But how is this inquiry related to his reading of Kant? Why does phenomenological chronology necessitate a discussion of the *Critique of Pure Reason*? Dastur points out that the reason for this is Heidegger's concern with a new conception of time as a structure of Dasein, a conception which, however, is not subjectivist. Like Inwood, Dastur contends that Heidegger sees Kant as a precursor of phenomenology, and, in particular, as anticipating – especially through the theory of the schematism of the understanding – a conception of temporality as a feature of consciousness. However, as Dastur notes, in Heidegger's view, Kant also inherits elements of a tradition of metaphysics with which Heidegger takes issue. Dastur also focuses on another aspect of Kant's thought which Heidegger believes provided an insight into the temporality of our existence. This is Kant's understanding of time as self-affection. Kant says that the pure intuition of time is formed by the mind affecting itself by its own activity. But the mind's activity always involves a relation to the object. This conception of time is, thus, not a subjectivist one. This is how, on Dastur's reading, Heidegger interprets Kant's account of the way in which thinking and the subject are temporal. On this reading, time is the condition of possibility of the 'I think,' and makes possible the unity of subjectivity.

Heidegger's interpretation of Kant often goes far beyond what Kant said. Dastur notes that Heidegger himself acknowledged that his interpretation was informed by the aims pursued in *Being and Time* – the primary one being to establish the claim that time is *the* condition of possibility of what Heidegger calls Dasein's 'Being-in-the-world'.

This claim and, more specifically, the priority given to time over space by most influential approaches in the phenomenological tradition are challenged by Zahavi and Overgaard in their chapter on 'Time, Space and Body in Bergson, Heidegger and Husserl'. Through an engagement with these philosophers, they point out the role of embodiment, understood as a basic form of spatiality, in the formation of our relation to the world. The discussion is thematic, rather than historical. Zahavi and Overgaard start from Bergson's critique of the understanding of consciousness in terms of temporal successions of mental states. In *Time and Free Will: An Essay on the Immediate Data of Consciousness* (1910), Bergson argues that this understanding involves a misguided projection of spatial characteristics of the external world onto consciousness. As the authors point out, Bergson argues that the lived time of the flow of consciousness, which he calls 'pure duration', cannot be properly understood in spatial terms. Bergson considers here a certain conception of space: space as a homogeneous, divisible medium of external reality. Zahavi and Overgaard draw attention to certain limitations of Bergson's account of consciousness, and of his approach to space. They point out the lack of a proper, phenomenological analysis of lived space in Bergson's philosophy. This dissatisfaction makes them turn to Heidegger.

They see Heidegger's phenomenological analysis of spatiality in *Being and Time* as providing a correction to the Bergsonian approach. Heidegger distinguishes the existential spatiality of the agent involved in the world from the Euclidean, three-dimensional space of the knowing subject. This account of space is structurally similar to Heidegger's discussion of world-time. As we have seen, Inwood interprets world-time as the time of the agent, and as constitutionally different from the time of the knowing subject. Zahavi and Overgaard take issue with the notion of the priority of time and, more specifically, with the understanding of time as the most fundamental transcendental structure, and with the priority of time over space. They stress the implausibility of Heidegger's claim in his early philosophy that existential spatiality can be ultimately accounted for in terms of temporality; as they note, Heidegger himself later rejected this *subordination*. They draw attention to an insight Heidegger had before *Being and Time* concerning the embodiment of our existence, which functions as a hidden, neglected presupposition of Heidegger's project. The authors point out that even later, in the *Zollikon Seminars*, Heidegger's position remains more or less unchanged. On Zahavi's and Overgaard's reading, the reason for Heidegger's reluctance to assign a more important role to the body is the attempt to avoid a mind/body dualism. Nevertheless, as they point out, a proper approach to the body can overcome this dualism, and would have made it possible for Heidegger to avoid the subordination of space to time.

This line of thought is further pursued through a discussion of Husserl's approach to perception, which is meant to lay out some of the elements of a phenomenological account of the basic role of the body in the constitution of our relation to the world. Perception is perspectival. It is constituted from the spatial location of the embodied perceiver involved in action. The authors link the Husserlian understanding of perception as interconnected with action to Noë's enactive conception of perception. Their main point in this context is that perception, for Husserl, requires embodied awareness. The unity of consciousness and the identity of an object can be understood in terms of time consciousness. But, whilst the analysis of time can offer an account of formal aspects of perceptual intentionality, the content and concreteness of what is given through perceptual intentionality can be properly understood in terms of an analysis of the basic spatiality of the lived body. This implies that temporality and embodiment are equally fundamental in the constitution of perception. This reading of Husserl emphasizes the view that space and time, although irreducible to each other, are intimately linked. Bergson had some insights into the former aspect of this view, whilst Heidegger attempted to think the latter; however, on Zahavi and Overgaard's reading, both philosophers failed to carry out a proper phenomenological analysis of time and space, elements of which can nevertheless be found through a return to Husserl.

Hence, this volume pursues various considerations about time and space which take us to the heart of recent debates about the nature of cognition and perception, the receptivity and normativity of the senses, the conceptual and non-conceptual content of experience, the bounds of experience, and the nature and role of embodiment and agency.

Part I
Perception

1
Kant on Receptivity and Representation

Paul Abela

Introduction

If Kant offered a comprehensive theory of receptivity, it is unknown.[1]

That anything in Kant is unknown may beggar belief. From the earliest period of the *Critique of Pure Reason*, writers such as J.S. Beck and K.L. Reinhold surveyed, and gently pressed, Kant on his treatment of receptivity.[2] The rather oblique discussions of receptivity among contemporary Kantians tend to range through theories of noumenal causation, two-worlds ontologies and variations on standpoint perspectives. Standing outside the in-house discussions, John McDowell's recent work has rekindled interest in the larger community of epistemologists concerning available resources within the Kantian tradition.[3]

What follows offers a modest sketch of two elements of Kant's treatment of receptivity – no more than a first step in a worked-out Kantian theory. The first deals with the general aims of the Schematism. The second drills down to the specifics of the discursive character of receptivity as articulated in the much neglected first half of the Analytic of Principles – the Axioms of Intuition and the Anticipations of Perception. Taken together, the chapter aims to direct attention to the abiding arc of Kant's treatment of receptivity: establishing the basic contours of Kant's discursively driven approach and identifying the distance between that approach and non-conceptualist readings.

In both areas, a common target of the chapter concerns the distorting impact of the empiricist epistemic template: an influence that frequently obscures an informed reading of these sections. As I have offered a detailed account of the debilitating influence of the empiricist prejudice elsewhere, I omit that task here.[4] Nonetheless, when discussing Kant's account of receptivity, it will be necessary, at times, to make reference to the empiricist model, in particular the privileged position it grants to given mental content and the allied thought that we should model receptivity as evidencing belief ultimately by a notionally separable contribution beyond the boundary of judgement. As I read Kant, he is a fox among the chickens when it comes to the import of his transcendental challenge to this received view. I hope to highlight the mistake of attempting to graft the head of the fox onto the body of the chicken; a feat not altogether foreign to some of the more Dr Moreau-like readings of Kant's treatment of receptivity.

The questions that occupy the Kantian account of receptivity are geared to a different set of problems than one finds under the received view. As the representation of determinate mental content is an achievement, the product of both intuitions and concepts, the Kantian account of receptivity settles naturally on issues related to how judgement is implicated at the lowest level of cognitive engagement with objects. Openness to the world is not a passive relation, but is instead actively informed by categorial forms of judgement operating under restricting conditions enforced by our forms of intuition (space and time). As such, the Kantian account of receptivity grapples with how the conditions of primitive judgement (the categories) are manifested sensibly through empirical intuitions.

The chapter is developed in three sections. Section 1.1 looks to the Schematism as the place where Kant offers his first pass, in its most general form, at the problem of receptivity. Gaining a firm grip on the aims of this much maligned section is crucial in exorcizing the empiricist afterimage that motivates the not uncommon dismissal of the Schematism. In Section 1.2 I turn to the Axioms of Intuition and the Anticipations of Perception as the natural centre of gravity for Kant's treatment of receptivity. It is here that Kant offers his detailed account of the interplay of judgement and intuition in the emergence of empirical intuition – how we come to have the sensations. In the final section, I canvass four potential worries prompted by the proffered reading.

1.1   Receptivity and the schematism

The Schematism is a famously dense section of the *Critique*. It has provoked diverse appraisals ranging from fatuous and ill-conceived to deep and penetrating. To some degree, this distinction has mirrored the division between Anglo-American scholarship and the continental reception of Kant's work. Early analytic approaches marshalled by Prichard in the beginning of the twentieth century, and later in the period by

Bennett, Strawson, Walker and others, tended to view this section with suspicion, regarding it as either unnecessary, or, if necessary, then unconvincing. The giants of continental philosophy of the nineteenth and twentieth centuries, Hegel and Heidegger, both regarded the section as a model of clarity and fundamental to Kant's analysis of representation. More recently, even in the Anglo tradition, the Schematism has won, perhaps grudging, respect.[5]

As I read the Schematism, it is fireworks throughout – Guy Fawkes meets the Fourth of July. If Kant had offered nothing more in this section than the idea that concepts are best understood as rules for the production of images, the section would mark, just in that shift alone, a major transformation of the epistemological tradition: on a par with Quine's Two Dogmas and offering a stark reminder to modern readers that Wittgenstein did not spring from Zeus's head fully formed. Surprisingly, Kant throws that bomb in almost as an aside, setting it off from the real prize of the section. That prize is an account of how the intellectual conditions of judgement can have application to the intuitive grounds of representation, considered in its most general form. As Kant puts it in his characteristic dense manner:

> In all subsumptions of an object under a concept the representation of the former must be **homogenous** with the latter … Now pure concepts of the understanding, however, in comparison with empirical (indeed in general sensible) intuitions, are entirely unhomogeneous, and can never be encountered in any intuition. Now how is the **subsumption** of the latter under the former, thus the **application** of the category to appearance possible … This question, so natural and important, is really the cause which makes a transcendental doctrine of the power of judgment necessary, in order , namely, to show the possibility of applying **pure concepts of the understanding** to appearances in general. (B176–7)[6]

If one may be allowed the occasional conjecture, I suspect that part of the reason the Schematism has fared so poorly in the Anglo-American tradition is that the level of Kant's concern is difficult to discern, particularly with background empiricist prejudices in play. If one thinks of the epistemological project as beginning with determinate empirical content already in place, the problem of homogeneity Kant announces will seem ill-conceived. Surely such determinate content would provide the relevant sensible marks to allow for subsumption under appropriately homogenous concepts. It is not a stretch of the imagination to think that charges that Kant is creating a 'fatuous problem' are, at least in part, an artefact of a failure to grapple with the level of concerns on offer.

A second reason for the otherwise surprising neglect of the Schematism's place in some of the secondary literature is due to Kant's rather artificial (or at least, very abstract) description of the task at hand. The introductory paragraphs (B176) cast the problem in terms of how two heterogeneous elements (intellectual rule-determined representations and intuitive representations) can be brought into coordination. The 'third thing' motif Kant introduces early in the section (B177) encourages, I think, the false view that the driving issue concerns a problem of integration; the Schematism as a type of clutch plate between the discursive engine of cognition and the sensory road below. This can naturally lend support to the thought that perhaps Kant is looking for a mode of linkage between spontaneity in acts of judgement and self-standing content delivered from outside the boundary of the conceptual.

A better rendering of the general aim of the Schematism looks to how receptivity actively instantiates rule-determined judgement. While it is true that transcendental schemata are distinguishable from both pure concepts and the pure forms of intuition, they are not so unrelated as to count as a separable 'third thing'. Better is to think of the task at hand as answering the question of how rule-determined judgement expressed in the categories can be made manifest through the limiting conditions found in receptivity. While 'manifestation condition' is a rather overused label, here it captures the role of transcendental schemata quite precisely. As experience for Kant is an accomplishment – the product of judgement – the problem the Schematism sets out to address concerns how the structures of receptivity are implicated *through* judgement. The non-discursive character of the forms of receptivity is not a marker for locating its determinative role outside the activity of judgement. The elements of concept and intuition are separable analytically, but the resulting two-stemmed structure of cognition is *realized* entirely within the activity of judgement.

At the outset it is also important to keep in mind that the goal of the section concerns receptivity in the context of the application conditions of pure concepts rather than either empirical concepts or pure sensible concepts. While Kant's treatment of the application of these latter concepts keeps to the same template as transcendental schemata – regarding concepts as rules that, in these cases, delineate objects (empirical or pure sensible objects) in conformity with the structures of receptivity – what differentiates the problem of transcendental schemata from empirical concept application is that the pure concepts yield no images. The empirical concept of a dog offers a rule-determined schema that allows for the cognition of all objects that can fall suitably under that construction – from Jack Russells to Great Danes. The empirical schema is sufficiently flexible to express the range of possible images while sufficiently tight to exclude similarly sized cats, ferrets etc.

The problem at hand is that pure concepts yield no images. As such, they pose a monstrous problem: how can the conditions of receptivity be implicated in such judgements when subsumption involves (purportedly) no sensibly expressed content; no perceptual content apparently being framed as it is in the case of the instantiating conditions for dog or circle?[7]

Kant's response is well-motivated and direct. The application of such concepts requires an expression that is pure, intellectual and sensible:

> Now it is clear that there must be a third thing, which must stand in homogeneity with the category on the one hand and the appearance on the other…This mediating representation must be pure (without anything empirical) and yet **intellectual** on the one hand and **sensible** on the other. Such a representation is the **transcendental schema**. (B177)

The requirements of being pure, intellectual and sensible have driven many readers and commentators to blink, perhaps more than once. The rarefied discussion that has marked much secondary literature here inclines me to navigate some of the following discussion with the late John Mortimer's Justice Oliver Oliphant's doctrine of British common sense in play – one concession to empiricism I'm willing to make. I think if, again, we do not regard the task as the introduction of some foreign template that might serve to link disparate domains, but instead view the problem as that of looking for instantiation conditions for categorial concepts, then the aggregate demand of pure, intellectual and sensible becomes less threatening.

By pure, Kant intends a contrast with empirical. Whatever else transcendental schemata are, they cannot be empirical, because all empirical representations are particular. In the same way as the pure sensible schema of a circle is not tied to a circle of any particular diameter, so, too, transcendental schemata cannot be tied, either in origin or expression, to any one empirical representation. The temporal/experiential structures the Schematism enforces, as constructions rooted in pure forms of intuition (time), have, by their nature, the promise of appropriate context independence. Temporal structures are context-neutral; they add no context-specific content to the object represented.

Concerning the twin requirements of being intellectual and simultaneously sensible, these demands appear self-cancelling. If the third thing is genuinely intellectual, it can't be sensible. And, if sensible, it can't be intellectual.

On the proposed reading, the twin demands of intellectual and sensible find their footing in a description of how instantiation conditions are made possible. We can see this most clearly with some of the more straightforward transcendental schemata. Consider, for example, the case of what the receptivity condition looks like for the pure concept expressed in the hypothetical form of judgement 'If A, then B.' The intellectual component is constituted by the relation of logical dependence. This ground/consequent relation expresses the purely discursive (intellectual) aspect that the schemata must capture. This is the rule that the concept embodies. On the sensible side, the form of intuition (time) expresses the ground/consequent relation in accordance with the ordered relation of temporal succession: that there is a necessary objective temporal order to which all objects of representation are subject. Kant puts the two points together as follows:

> The schema of the cause and of the causality of a thing in general is the real upon which, whenever it is posited, something else always follows. It therefore consists in the succession of the manifold insofar as it is subject to a rule. (B183)

This is not a new 'third thing' being gingerly inserted between the discursive and intuitive domains. It is, rather, a non-discursive enabling condition, making judgement meaningful insofar as it restricts judgement to the intuitional form (time) of inner sense. In restricting the expression of the logical relation – binding it down in the unique *temporal* expression of objective succession – receptivity secures significance in the act of realizing objects of cognition. Kant closes the Schematism with this theme in mind, reminding the reader that '[t]his significance comes to them from sensibility, which realizes the understanding at the same time as it restricts it' (B187).

The idea that meaning is realized under a restricting condition is no more mysterious than the idea that the meaningfulness of language operates under the enabling constraint of grammatical structure. As such, it is not that the Schematism restricts cognition to phenomena, but rather that the cognition of phenomena first becomes possible through the restriction imposed on judgement by the pure structures of receptivity. This is the most general lesson of the Schematism as it concerns receptivity.[8] It also marks the Schematism as the centre of gravity for Kant's account of mental content in its most abstract formulation.

As my second, more particular, aim in this chapter concerns how Kant models receptivity in terms of the emergence of empirical intuition (sensation), I pass over going through the other transcendental schemata here, leaving the particular schemata of number and reality that instantiate the judgements of quantity and quality for the extended discussion taken up below. Nonetheless, I hope it is obvious that it is no accident of logic, and no matter of cooking the books, that we should expect schemata for all of the pure concepts. And I hope that it is equally plain that receptivity considered in its most general form concerns, for Kant, how the formal structures of intuition (temporal structure) supply the basis for meaningful judgement. The sensible bearing of thought to the world is not to be found among the usual suspects in the Transcendental Aesthetic. The Schematism is ground zero.

1.2   Receptivity and empirical intuition

In the second portion of the Analytic of Principles, Kant moves from the general formula of each transcendental schema to the application of judgement directed to spatial/temporal objects. As part of that discussion, the Analogies tend to garner the most interest among commentators. As I am interested in receptivity as it relates specifically to the Kantian view of the conditions for realizing empirical intuition, I concentrate instead on the first two principles: the Axioms of Intuition and the Anticipations of Perception. The Axioms and Anticipations, as they deal directly with the application of judgement at the level of the emergence of empirical intuition, are central to explicating how Kant models the idea of receptivity as openness to the world.

As we tend to view receptivity in terms of passivity, openness to the world, so conceived, naturally looks to stimuli, or patterns of stimuli, as the ultimate evidential basis for belief. Receptivity on this view serves to anchor representation by effectively welding mental content to the causal impacts that are viewed as their source (taken either individually or as a corporate body). Even Quine, that great slayer of empiricist prejudice, doggedly defended an evidential role for observation sentences.[9]

Kant's challenge to this view follows directly from his distinctive positioning of receptivity within the sphere of the conceptually imbued.

The Axioms and Anticipations constitute Kant's alternative to the empiricist theory of ideas and mental content: a direct challenge to the affective, non-discursive model of impressions and corresponding ideas. The emergence of empirical intuition, for Kant, is secured *through* acts of judgement, hence the positioning of this discussion in the Analytic of Principles rather than the Transcendental Aesthetic. Moreover, the Kantian analysis of receptivity, suitably invested with discursive features, provides a ready bridge for explaining how the deliverances of receptivity can serve higher-order truth-preserving inferences: the everyday inferences we make when we interrogate our initial picture of the world. As such, this active conception of receptivity provides the basis for explicating how receptivity operates within the space of reasons and hence is answerable to the demands of rational reflection.[10]

How, then, do the Axioms and Anticipations frame the discursive aspect of receptivity? Given that sensation, in Kant's technical sense, is no more than the 'effect of an object on the capacity for representation insofar as we are affected by it' (B34), how does Kant develop the argument that our most primitive engagement with the world is laden with discursive structure?

Beginning with the Axioms, Kant notes that the schematized form of judgement at work is the concept of number. By number, Kant means 'a representation that summarizes the successive addition of one (homogeneous) unit to another. Thus number is nothing other than the unity of the synthesis of the manifold of a homogeneous intuition in general' (B182). While the notion of number is obviously crucial to Kant's account of the possibility, through pure intuition, of mathematics (arithmetic and geometry), it is also fundamental to understanding how mindfulness is implicated in the rendering of empirical intuition.

Kant announces the framework of this rendering of empirical intuition in the principle of the Axioms: 'All intuitions are extensive magnitudes' (B202). This principle applies to all intuitions, pure and empirical.

The manner in which the schematized concept of number underwrites the rule-determined activity that yields extensive magnitude is structurally parallel to the way in which the representation of any discrete quantity (a number of objects represented as an aggregate) involves the idea that the whole is constituted by its parts. It is the same activity of judgement at work when we assert pure mathematical propositions as when we make empirical judgements concerning grouped objects. Kant's novel claim is that the same discursive activity is in play – spontaneously, without reflective deliberation – when our cognitive capacities are prompted into action in acts of immediate sensory engagement with nature. This recalls the general lesson of the understanding and its categories: that the 'same function that gives unity to the different representations in a judgement also gives unity to the mere synthesis of different representation in an intuition' (B104–5).[11] Here the judgement form is quantity, the schematized judgement form is number, and the application to intuition (and objects) is magnitude expressed through the idea of a whole made up of parts (extensive magnitude).

The architecture underwriting judgements of extensive magnitude, under the restricting condition of receptivity (time and space), is the part/whole relation.[12] As much as any quantity of time or space is represented as an aggregate of homogeneous units (five minutes, five metres, etc.), so too, in the act of realizing our sensory engagement with the world, intuitional content is made manifest by means of representing presence as distributed over successive spatial locations. The extended patch of redness in one's visual field that a parked Mini might stimulate is realized in receptivity as an aggregate of sensory influences distributed from parts to a whole. In other words, the *extendedness* of the patch of redness is a product, composed of parts that collectively realize the whole: the temporal schema of number making manifest the aggregate nature of the sensible colour representation with spatial form instantiating this aggregate presence. The sharp edge of this claim is that this part/whole architecture of empirical intuition reflects a discursive contribution, realized as a quantity (extension) under the restricting condition manifested with specific reference to our forms of receptivity (spatial *qua* extension, temporal *qua* the successive character of the aggregate magnitude).

At times, Kant frames the issue somewhat obliquely when he opts to stress the 'process' dimension of sensory representation, highlighting how the whole is a product of a temporally iterated activity. The take-home lesson, though, is not so much about process as it is about structure. The architecture of empirical intuition is realized in the part/whole relation manifested in receptivity at the intersection of judgement and the forms of intuition:

> I call an extensive magnitude that in which the representation of the parts makes possible the representation of the whole ... I cannot represent to myself any line, no matter how small it may be, without drawing it in thought, i.e., successively generating all its parts from one point, and thereby first sketching this intuition. It is exactly the same with even the smallest time. ... Since the mere intuition in all

appearances is either space or time, every appearance as intuition is an extensive magnitude. (B203–4)

Far from viewing receptivity as passive, a mere conduit for *receiving* determinate content, Kant sees judgement hard at work in our original encounter with the world.

The Anticipations of Perceptions offer the second leg of Kant's discursive treatment of receptivity, supplying the conceptual grounds for the qualitative aspect of empirical intuition. As mentioned in the previous section, the schema of quality coming out of the Schematism is the concept of reality. Reality at this level of representation is not a judgement concerning the actuality of objects or events. Actuality pertains to the existence of an object in a particular temporal/spatial location. It is a judgement of modality, asserting the existence of an object (an object that is more than 'possible' and less than 'necessary'). Reality, by contrast, pertains to the presence of intuitional content, instantiated to a determinate degree of presence, realized in the act of apprehension.

The principle announced in the Anticipations of Perception declares that: 'In all appearances the real, which is an object of the sensation, has intensive magnitude, i.e., a degree' (B207). Unlike extensive magnitude, which garners its determinacy in the part/whole relation, intensive magnitude expresses an immediate degree of beingness. We experience the joy of a newborn, not as an aggregate of mild pleasures, but immediately as an intense pleasure. We perceive the dark cherry red of the parked Mini not as an aggregate of many lighter reds, but immediately as a determinate deep shade of red.[13]

In terms of the determining role of receptivity in judgements yielding intensive magnitudes, Kant notes that the instantaneous character of the act of apprehension entails a notion of mental content as the spontaneous filling of a representation. We cognize the character of this magnitude in terms of the *degree* of immediate sensory presence. As such, our sensory engagement with the world is not binary in nature – presence or absence – but is, rather, the representation of sensation up to a limited magnitude. As Kant suggests:

> Now that in the empirical intuition which corresponds to the sensation is reality (*realitas phaenomenon*); that which corresponds to its absence is negation =0. Now, however, every sensation is capable of a diminution, so that it can decrease and thus gradually disappear. Hence between reality in appearance and negation there is a continuous nexus of many possible intermediate sensations. (B209–10)

As with the claim that the extensive magnitude of a sensation is bound up with judgements of quantity, so, too, the representation of the intensive magnitude of sensation is an artefact of a quality judgement: reality realized through an instantiating condition of receptivity – in this case the expression of the degree of saturation of a sensory representation in one moment of time. In this sense, the affective content of sensory representation is not a mirroring, or passive registering, of an exogenous element. No doubt, sensibility is prompted into action by a world of objects as they influence our sense organs. Nothing in that aspect of the Kantian view of sensibility requires the accompanying idea that the content of cognition is determined from outside the sovereignty of the conceptual. Kant's commitment to the discursive character of intensive magnitude should quiet that empiricist impulse.

Taken together, the Axioms and Anticipations constitute Kant's account of how empirical intuition emerges in consciousness. This rendering of sensation, as we have seen, implicates judgement and its manifestation conditions along both extensive and intensive axes. Absent these, receptivity is 'as good as nothing' for us (A111, 112, 120). Receptivity understood as openness to the world is thus nothing like the empiricist dogma of a mere passive registration of determinate sensory content uploaded to higher-order conceptual capacities. On the contrary, the basic components of discursive involvement are written into the fabric of receptivity. Mindfulness reaches as far as receptivity itself.

1.3   Some concluding thoughts

The account of Kant I have offered is consistent with much of the emphasis in post-myth-of-the-given epistemology. I count myself as one of those who see rich connections between Kant's critique of the epistemology of his day and those in the Sellars–Davidson–McDowell tradition who see something fundamentally untenable in the received empiricist model. The priority attached to judgement as the source for ascribable mental content, the denial of the idea of a separable sphere of self-declared sensory reports that can stand in rationally supporting relation to belief, a stress on the role of the constraints afforded by rational reflection as fundamental for possessing a world view, these and other elements offer a wide and deep set of commitments that favour a motivated link between Kant and this contemporary epistemological tradition. The account of receptivity, as it relates to the emergence of empirical intuitions, is just one part of that larger story.

As suggested previously, the extant Kantian literature on receptivity tends to oscillate between rather arid discussions of the plausibility of noumenal resources and accounts that prioritize either competing ontological frameworks or epistemological standpoints as the broad frame of reference for making sense of how receptivity is to be parsed. I have steered clear of these well-worn paths. Nonetheless, sequestering these views entirely is unhelpful. At least four principal areas of concern come immediately to mind.

First is the general concern that one must be attentive to the dangers of reading historical figures through the lens of modern problematics. Kant is not a twenty-first-century epistemologist. Moreover, the history and commitments of empiricism are multifarious, having evolved substantially. An analysis of Kant's treatment of receptivity that stresses the discursive component in the fashioning of sensibility is perhaps guilty of tweaking the enquiry too heavily in favour of modern concerns. While Kant may have something important to offer the contemporary arena, do contemporary concerns offer a helpful window on Kant?

Here I think the grand arc of Kant's approach as it relates to receptivity and representation – that mindfulness is implicated all the way out to the manner in which affective content is realized – anticipates in a rather startling manner the same general lessons that we find in contemporary research. Consider Kant's own critique of radical scepticism – his 'Refutation of Idealism'. This section is the capstone of his critique of the empirical idealist (read 'empiricist') model of mind and world, targeting the idea that our engagement with the world should be framed in terms of a passive affect that (somehow) supports higher-order object-directed inferences. As with many modern 'refutations' of scepticism, Kant considered radical scepticism the bastard child of a false model of mental content, creating a nest of problems largely of its own making, including (1) how we move from subjective private states to judgements about object states of affairs, (2) how we swear epistemic intermediaries to truthfulness, (3) how sensory reports are differentiated from beliefs and (4) how the points of casual contact deliver content (individually or holistically). That Kant's capstone position should align him so closely to modern concerns is evidence, if more were needed, that the Kantian primitive distinction of concept and intuition – now the subject of contemporary epistemological interest – is the right place to situate his doctrine of receptivity.

A second worry that might be prompted by my appeal to the discursive shaping of receptivity concerns the import of involving intuitional features in the account of meaningful judgement. Does Kant's appeal to the non-discursive features of receptivity open up his account to a role for non-conceptual content?

This is a delicate matter, not something I can discharge here, although I hope the direction of response is visible. Given Kant's careful charting of the determining role of judgement acting *through* the (analytically separable) non-discursive forms of intuition, there is no reason to implicate a role for non-conceptual content.[14] If we think, minimally, that assigning a role for non-conceptual content directs us to the idea that experiential judgements garner their *bearing* to the world from outside the discursive sphere, then there is nothing obvious in the fact that the pure structures of intuition are non-discursive that would lead us to regard their involvement as injecting into receptivity any self-standing content.[15] If, as suggested above, their contribution is exhausted in their role as manifestation conditions for judgement, then it is the activity of judgement – realizing a coherent and integrated world view through its rule-determined acts of synthesis – that bears the responsibility for representational assignments and the resulting contents. There is no open path outside the sovereignty of discursive relations that one could invoke as 'grounding content' for the moving picture of the world that the Understanding spontaneously presents and that reflective judgement corrects and refines. In fact, Kant's justificatory thesis is forward-looking, not downward-gazing, as the evidential grounds for the contents of belief are situated squarely in the experiential context of 'the possible progress of experience' (B521). The idea that there can be mental content without discursively driven synthesis is a mistake. One would do as well to imagine a line without extensive magnitude or a colour without intensive degree. The follow-on idea that such contents might act as a transcendental anchor for the bearing of thought to the world merely compounds the error.

The stress I have placed on the determinative structures of receptivity throws into relief a third concern. As previously noted, unlike the pure concepts, there is nothing necessary in the forms of receptivity. As Kant himself speculates, beings on other planets might have quite different modes of receptivity. There is something about our modes of receptivity that is undeniably arbitrary. Hence, the idea of rival ontologies looks like a direct offshoot of Kant's transcendental picture. And, if that is the case, then it appears that the Kantian story countenances the idea of competing representational schemes: something that signals an underlying commitment to some form of scheme/content dualism; an empiricist-minded sequestering of content from judgement that is anathema to the position outlined above.

There are two ways of assessing the import of this worry. First, it is important to be clear about the bearing of the issue. Kant's point, shouted from the height of the transcendental standpoint, is that we cannot rule out the possibility that beings other than ourselves might have different forms of receptivity, with correspondingly different schemata for judgement. Consider, once again, the hypothetical form of judgement. Kant is open to the possibility that the manifestation condition for the relation of dependency (ground/consequence) could be non-temporal: a notion of a relationship of dependency among objects that is made meaningful in a non-successive manner. Now, of course, we cannot assign any significance to that bare possibility. For us, a happening (that something undergoes a change of state) is inherently temporal. Change just is a two-place temporal predicate in which an object moves from one description of its state to a logically distinct state. That we cannot get our heads around timeless change is as it should be; our schema for change makes time the condition of significance for this form of judgement as applied to objects. But we can recognize, in thought, the bare possibility that beings with different forms of receptivity would have different schemata for their judgements, and the resulting content of such judgements would be different; radically different in a way that is, for us, unimaginable, although not unthinkable.

If we carefully restrict the notion of 'competing ontologies' to this thought, there is little that is threatening on offer. Such rival schemes are literally out of this world, with no point of contact with the schematized categories that instantiate the deliverances of our receptivity. In this sense, they are not 'rival' schemes at all. This is entirely different from the operative claim among scheme/content dualists. There the force of the argument is that, at the *empirical level*, the same deliverances of receptivity can yield competing reference relations. What underwrites that view is the guiding thought (mistaken by my lights) that mental content offers a separable, and yet rationally responsive, contribution from outside the sovereignty of any one particular conceptual scheme. On the view I have championed, the transcendental possibility of rival ontologies is not a product of that working model of representation. It comes from a different place altogether. It makes little sense, on the Kantian view, that alternative world views, rooted in different forms of receptivity and informed by the schematized judgements that yield different particular content, could be brought into *competing* rational relations. Absent a shared framework for sensibly expressed judgement, they could no more be rivals than could Manchester United and the Montreal Canadiens. If considered properly from the transcendental standpoint, the recognition of the non-necessary standing of our forms of sensibility serves as an inoculation against the temptation to view sensibility from the transcendental realist perspective. Ours is always a view of the world that begins and ends with the conditions of the possibility-of-experience in play.

The fourth, and final, worry relates to an apparent omission. The sketch of receptivity I have offered above makes no reference to things-in-themselves, or noumena. As mentioned previously, I have deliberately tacked away from that conversation, leading the discussion instead with issues that emerge from the more primitive Kantian point of departure of concepts and intuitions. Beginning there, noumena offer nothing to Kant's doctrine of receptivity. If I am correct in thinking that Kant denies a role to bare givenness at the empirical level, frankly it would be peculiar that he should reintroduce that model, once removed, at the transcendental level. Nonetheless, this view has currency, due, I suspect, to background empiricist considerations, now seductively shifted upward; substituting the idea of transcendental givenness for discredited empirical givenness.

The idea that the content of empirical thought is in fact a passive 'registering' of transcendental objects 'impacting' us in a manner that is independent even of our causal engagement with nature is a non-starter twice over. One could not get any further outside the sphere of experiential judgement and its constituting conditions than to appeal to the 'input' of things-in-themselves. That is as it should be, given all Kant has to say about the only honest role for noumena: the task of reining in the pretensions of theoretical reason and opening up a place for the attribution of moral agency. The import of the representation of noumena in Kant's treatment of receptivity is entirely negative: a reminder that representation is not an unbounded achievement, but one that arises from the rationally responsive activity of judgement that finds its footing in the soil of a conceptually imbued mode of receptivity.

Notes

1. A special thanks for the helpful comments of participants of the Space and Time in Kant and Post-Kantian Philosophy conference at the 2008 UK Kant Society meeting at the University of Sussex. This revised paper reflects the content and tone of that conference presentation.
2. Beck's work, in particular, probes Kant's model of receptivity. For a good example, in miniature, see Beck's letter to Kant of 20 June 1797 in Kant, I. (1999) *Immanuel Kant: Correspondence*, trans. A. Zwieg (Cambridge: Cambridge University Press), letter 192, pp. 512–15. Also see, in same, the

letter of J.H. Tiefrank (letter 200, pp. 529–34) and Kant's illuminating response in same (letter 202, pp. 222–5) for a further early exchange with Kant on the issue of receptivity. F.H. Jacobi and the young J.G. Fichte offer additional important early queries.

3. McDowell offers an astute diagnosis of the deep-seated empiricist prejudices that occupy much of the contemporary backdrop when thinking about receptivity. McDowell's most recent statement, post *Mind and World*, shines light once again on the Kantian role for intuitional content as a way of incorporating the idea that sensibility registers an engagement with objects in a way that acknowledges a determinative role for concepts in fashioning how a picture of the world is realized. See (2009) 'Sensory Consciousness in Kant and Sellars' in McDowell, J. *Having The World in View: Essays on Kant, Hegel and Sellars* (Cambridge: Harvard University Press) for McDowell's most recent, somewhat revised, statements on the Kantian theme of receptivity.

4. See Abela, P. (2002) *Kant's Empirical Realism* (Oxford: Clarendon Press), chapters 1 and 2.

5. In the revised edition of the landmark (2004) *Kant's Transcendental Idealism: An Interpretation and Defense* (New Haven: Yale University Press), Allison regards the section as crucial. It is puzzling, given this commitment, that he omits any discussion of the principles (Axioms and Anticipations) that follow from the schematized categories of quantity and reality. Guyer in (1987) *Kant and the Claims of Knowledge* (Cambridge: Cambridge University Press), and more recently in (2006) *Kant* (New York: Routledge),offers a broadly generous reading of the Schematism. The defects and errors he identifies in the section he believes are made good in the Analogies. This generosity is somewhat blunted insofar as Guyer views the Schematism as, at best, redundant; regarding the Analogies as providing independent support for the time-determinations, and application conditions, of the categories.

6. All references from the *Critique of Pure Reason* are from the second edition, Kant, I. (1999) *Critique of Pure Reason*, trans. P. Guyer and A. Wood (New York: Cambridge University Press).

7. Subsumption by means of transcendental schemata engages a problem not encountered in the McDowell project.

8. The 'figurative synthesis' of section 24 of the Transcendental Deduction should be read with the lessons of the Schematism in mind. Kant is not there developing a separable account of mental content through the transcendental synthesis of the imagination. On the contrary, he is arguing that our two-stem mode of cognition demands giving sensible expression (read 'figure' as pure intuitional structure) to discursive activity. It is worth recalling that 'insofar as its synthesis [imagination] is still an exercise of spontaneity, which is determining and not, like sense, merely determinable... the imagination is to this extent a faculty for determining the sensibility *a priori*, and its synthesis of intuitions, **in accordance with the categories**, must be the transcendental synthesis of the **imagination**, which is an effect of the understanding on sensibility' (B 151–2, emphasis in the original).

9. See Quine's final full-length statement, in print, on the role of observation sentences and the associated conception of 'stimulus meaning' in Quine, W. (1992) *The Pursuit of Truth: Revised Edition* (Cambridge: Harvard University Press). He appears to concede the point to Davidson on the issue

of meaning and its contested relation to truth in the video interview (1997) 'The Quine Discussion: In Conversation with Donald Davidson', Philosophy International, LSE.

10. I do not in this chapter pursue this bridge between receptivity and rational reflection (see *Kant's Empirical Realism*, chapter 5).

11. Judgement in its most general formulation is simply the activity of combination. There are, of course, many instantiations of judgement, including the syntheses involved in pure concepts, empirical concepts, empirical intuitions, pure intuitions and concepts of reflection, among others. For present purposes, taking judgement as 'the action of putting different representations together with each other and comprehending their manifoldness in one cognition' (B 103) captures the relevant intent. What needs to be emphasized is that the activity of rendering empirical intuitions is not a deliberative activity. That view of 'judgement' expresses a very high-order case, at home not in the faculty of the Understanding but rather in the faculty of Reason. The emergence of empirical intuition is a spontaneous, non-reflective, activity of mind.

12. In (1983) *The Structure of Experience* (Chicago: Chicago University Press), chapter 4, Gordon Nagel offers a clear and thorough statement of the part/whole structuring implicated in this discursive contribution of judgement.

13. Although I do not pursue the point here, Kant's treatment of intensive magnitude has a direct bearing upon McDowell's discussion, following on Sellars's work, concerning the manner in which receptivity is implicated in the representation of objective colour properties.

14. See R. Hanna's (2005) 'Kant and Non-Conceptual Content', *European Journal of Philosophy*, 13(2), 247–90 and (2008) 'Kantian Non-Conceptualism', *Philosophical Studies*, 137(1), 41–64, in addition to Lucy Allais's contribution in this volume, for well-crafted defences of the non-conceptualist position.

15. Hannah Ginsborg in a series of thoughtful papers, including (2006) 'Empirical Concepts and the Content of Experience', *European Journal of Philosophy*, 14(3), 349–72 and (2008) 'Was Kant a nonconceptualist?', *Philosophical Studies*, 137(1), 65–77, offers a fine-grained attack on the notion that Kant's treatment of receptivity is best read as non-conceptualist. The thrust of her account, as it bears on sensory representation, follows her general emphasis on the normative aspect of judgement – reading this all the way out to the immediate sensory presentation of objects. As I am dealing in this paper with discursive involvement in the content of sensory representations themselves, I have sidestepped this discussion, although it strikes me as crucial to a fully worked-out account of the possibility of explaining the linkages between receptivity and its rational responsiveness to the demands of reflective judgement. What is surprising in Ginsborg's account is her concession to the non-conceptualist idea that immediate sensory content is instantiated outside the sphere of conceptual involvement: 'No exercise of understanding is required to bring about the unity among her sense-impressions which constitutes them as a perceptual image with intentional content; instead the process is a purely naturalistic one which can be understood on the lines of Hume's association of ideas' ('Was Kant a nonconceptualist?', pp 72–3). Even if Ginsborg's appeal to the normative context for determining the appropriateness of retrieving previous impressions

in this process of representation is correct, the original concession appears unmotivated. A stronger (conceptualist) rendering is available.

References

Abela, P. (2002) *Kant's Empirical Realism* (Oxford: Clarendon Press).

Allison, H. (2004) *Kant's Transcendental Idealism: An Interpretation and Defense* (New Haven: Yale University Press).

Ginsborg, H. (2006) 'Empirical Concepts and the Content of Experience', *European Journal of Philosophy*, 14(3), 349–72.

Ginsborg, H. (2008) 'Was Kant a nonconceptualist?', *Philosophical Studies*, 137(1), 65–77.

Guyer, P. (1987) *Kant and the Claims of Knowledge* (Cambridge: Cambridge University Press).

Guyer, P. (2006) *Kant* (New York: Routledge).

Hanna, R. (2005) 'Kant and Non-Conceptual Content', *European Journal of Philosophy*, 13(2), 247–90.

Hanna, R. (2008) 'Kantian Non-Conceptualism', *Philosophical Studies*, 137(1), 41–64.

Kant, I. (1999) *Critique of Pure Reason*, trans. P. Guyer and A. Wood (New York: Cambridge University Press).

Kant, I. (1999) *Immanuel Kant: Correspondence*, trans. A. Zwieg (Cambridge: Cambridge University Press).

McDowell, J. (2009) 'Sensory Consciousness in Kant and Sellars', in *Having The World in View: Essays on Kant, Hegel and Sellars* (Cambridge: Harvard University Press).

Nagel, G. (1983) *The Structure of Experience* (Chicago: Chicago University Press).

Quine, W. (1992) *The Pursuit of Truth: Revised Edition* (Cambridge: Harvard University Press).

Quine, W. (1997) 'The Quine Discussion: In Conversation with Donald Davidson', Philosophy International, LSE (video interview).

2
Perceiving Distinct Particulars

Lucy Allais

1

Kant is often thought to hold that we cannot perceive distinct particular things without applying concepts to our experience, and, in particular, without applying the *a priori* concepts he calls the categories. I argue that, once we draw a distinction between the *perception* of a distinct *particular* and *cognition* of an *object* in the full-blown Kantian sense of an object, we can allow that Kant does not see concepts as necessary for the basic intentionality of perception – the fact that perception presents us with distinct particular things.[1] Rather, he thinks it is an *a priori* and non-conceptual representation of space which enables us to perceive particulars which are distinct from ourselves and from each other. I argue that this reading straightforwardly makes sense of Kant's account of the separate and essential contribution to cognition made by intuition and concepts, and, in particular, of the contribution made by intuition.[2] I then look at the implications this account has for how we think about transcendental idealism, the relation between transcendental idealism and the Transcendental Deduction of the categories, and Kant's argument for transcendental idealism in the Aesthetic.

Kant says that the categories are *a priori* concepts of an object in general, and in the Deduction he argues that they are conditions of the possibility of experience, and that they are necessary conditions of thinking about objects. The Deduction contains much apparent support for the standard reading of Kant, which sees him as saying that we cannot perceive particular things without applying concepts to our experience. There are a number of places in the text where Kant says that we cannot *experience an object* without both the concepts of an object in general, and the concept of the self. For example, Kant says

41

that the Deduction will show that without the categories 'nothing is possible as object of experience' (A93/B126),[3] and he says that:

> The synthetic unity of consciousness is therefore an objective condition of all cognition, not merely something I myself need in order to cognize an object but rather something under which every intuition must stand **in order to become an object for me**, since in any other way, and without this synthesis, the manifold would **not** be united in one consciousness. (B 138, see also B 137)

These texts might be thought to be unequivocally against the idea that we can perceive distinct particulars without concepts, since they say that without the categories we are not presented with an object. But I think the situation is not so clear. It is crucial to see that, when Kant talks about experience of an object in the Deduction, both 'experience' and 'object' have very specific senses. Kant says that *experience* is empirical knowledge or empirical cognition (A176/B218); it is *not* mere thing-involving perception. And an *object* is something which we recognize as a persisting causal unity, made up of stuff which is conserved, and which is in causal interaction with all other existing objects, which interactions fall under causal laws. In contrast, a distinct visual particular may be a shadow or a patch of light. If the point of the Deduction is that the categories are necessary to cognize an object as an object *in this sense*, then it is far less clear that it is inconsistent with Kant's position to say that perception of distinct particular things is not possible without the categories.

To bring out the difference between experience of an object in the full-blown Kantian sense, and the mere perception of a particular, consider an animal whose actions indicate that it sees a located, relatively spatially unified thing, which it can discriminate from other things, which (following spatial boundaries) it can track, and with respect to which it has some expectations of how it will act. Think, for example, of an animal following a moving insect. What capacities do we need to attribute to the creature? Thinking that it can perceptually discriminate the thing clearly does *not* require thinking that it can *think* of the thing as a persisting and causally unitary substance, that it can make general use of and attribute to other animals thoughts about the thing and its interactions in a general causal order, or that it thinks of the particular it is tracking as being made up of stuff which cannot go out of existence absolutely. Denying that it has these thoughts need not force us to say that the animal does not perceive a spatially bounded and located particular, and that it merely has an inner display of non-intentional, raw sensations, as opposed to being perceptually presented with distinct things.

I am not trying to give an account of how *Kant* thought about the perception of *animals* – this is simply not something about which he says enough to base any interpretation on. But it is worth noting that, in the few places where he does talk about animals, he pretty clearly thinks that they perceive the world at the same time as thinking that they lack concepts. He says that the ox sees the gate, but it does not see it as a gate (FS 2:59). He discusses different levels of cognition and explicitly allows the first three levels to apply to non-human animals, including 'to represent something with consciousness, or to perceive' and 'to be acquainted with something (noserere), or to represent something in comparison with other things both as to sameness and as to difference' (JL64–5). He does not allow to non-human animals the higher levels which include cognizing something 'through the understanding by means of concepts', and says that 'Animals are acquainted with objects too, but they do not cognize them' (JL64–5). He clearly implies that animals have consciousness when he says that they have subjective expectations of necessity (CPR:13), and that they feel pain (MM 6:443). So, although he does *not* have a developed account of animal perceptual experience, neither does he deny that animals are conscious, or that they have intentional perceptual states, and, in his occasional comments on animals, he says the opposite. That said, my aim is not to give an account of how Kant thought about animal perception; my point in thinking about what is involved in a non-concept-having creature perceptually discriminating a particular is to draw attention to the distinction between the mere perceptual discrimination of a distinct particular and cognition of an object in the full-blown Kantian sense. Also, I'm not denying that Kant's view is that our experience of the world is 'suffused' with concepts, and that this changes our experience. Of course, Kant thinks that *our* perception (the perception of creatures with understanding who are capable of empirical knowledge) involves concepts; my point is not to deny this, or to suggest that Kant has a 'two-layer' view of perception, according to which we can distinguish a stage in the formation of perceptual beliefs which does not involve concepts,[4] since I am not arguing for the attribution to Kant of the idea that we can distinguish a pre-conceptual aspect of *our* perceptual experience which is then brought under concepts. Rather, the point is simply to be clear about the respective *roles* played by intuitions and concepts in our cognition, what it is that they each contribute. To say that they depend on each other for full-blown cognition is compatible with saying that they do not depend on each other to make their distinctive contributions to cognition.

Once we draw the distinction between perceptually discriminating a distinct particular and cognizing an object in the full-blown sense, we can see the claims in the Deduction about what is necessary for something to be 'an object for me' as concerned with the conditions of thinking of an object as a persisting causal unity which is made up of stuff which is conserved and which is in law-governed causal interactions with other things. Since this is something much more demanding than the mere perception of a particular, something distinct from other things and distinct from me, it allows us to see Kantian intuition as presenting us with particulars independent of concepts. So, although there is apparent textual support for thinking that Kant is a strong conceptualist, these texts can be read in a way that sees them as not concerned with the basic intentionality of perception. And there is also clear textual evidence for thinking that Kant's view is that intuitions present us with particulars, and that they do not depend on concepts to make this contribution. Kant says that:

> objects can indeed appear to us without necessarily having to be related to the functions of the understanding;(A 89/B 122)
>
> appearances could after all be so constituted that the understanding would not find them in accord with the conditions of its unity... Appearances would nonetheless offer objects to our intuition, for intuition by no means requires the functions of thinking; (B 132)
>
> that representation which can be given prior to all thinking is called **intuition**; (B 132)
>
> Concepts differ from intuition by virtue of the fact that all intuition is singular. He who sees his first tree does not know what it is that he sees. (VL905)

The opposition between intuitions and concepts is fundamental to most of Kant's arguments in the *Critique*. He thinks that we cannot have cognition without both ingredients, and they each play completely distinct, necessary and complementary roles. Kant introduces the two ingredients by contrast with each other, saying that intuition is 'immediately related to an object and is singular', whereas the way concepts relate to objects is 'mediate, by means of a mark which can be common to several things' (A 320/B 377). A clear and straightforward way of understanding these claims is to see intuitions as representations which essentially involve the presence to consciousness of the particular things they represent.[5] He says that 'an intuition is a representation of the sort which would depend immediately on the presence of an object' (P:281). In other words, intuitions represent objects immediately because they *present* the object itself, as opposed to being representations which enable us to think about the object whether it is present or not. *Immediacy* says that an intuition is in fact a presentation to consciousness of that thing (not simply a representation which is caused by a particular thing). And intuitions are *singular* since an intuition presents a particular thing, the particular thing which is present to consciousness (as opposed to concepts which apply to many particulars).[6] So, as Kant introduces the notion, intuitions are singular representations of particulars.

This point neatly fits the *role* for which Kant introduces intuitions: that of ensuring that we are presented with a world, that we can be 'given' objects. He says that 'all thought...must ultimately be related to intuitions, thus, in our case, to sensibility, since there is no other way in which objects can be given to us' (A 19/B 33), and that 'For every concept there is requisite...the possibility of giving it an object to which it is to be related...Not the object cannot be given to a concept otherwise than in intuition' (A 239/B 298). Kant's opponent here is the Leibnizian–Wolffian view that objects are individuated by complete conceptual or intellectual determination, by complete individual concepts. Kant thinks that concepts are essentially general (although they could be used in a singular way) and cannot secure unique objects, and that it is intuition alone which enables us to do this. A concept could, in principle, apply to some other thing, so a concept on its own is never sufficient to guarantee direct reference to an object. Kant thinks that the mistake the Leibnizians make is in not seeing that cognition requires the presentation to consciousness of particulars; they think we can cognize a world through general thoughts, concepts, alone. Kant thinks that concepts alone would not be able to latch onto a world. This is not simply because we need to posit a role for sensation in information processing: we need presentations of individual things to consciousness.

One view of pre-conceptual perception is that it delivers merely a manifold of sensory features; the idea is that we need the application of a concept to draw a boundary around or group together distinct aspects of the manifold. This is not Kant's view. Two points are important here. First, it is crucial here that Kantian intuitions are not *sensations*, and, second, Kant does not think that in the absence of a concept there is nothing that determines how different bits of the sensory manifold might be organized together (a thought which might support thinking that we need the concept of a kind of thing before we can organize the manifold in a determinate way).[7] In contrast, Kant thinks that, independently of the application of concepts, we have ways of organizing the manifold in our *a priori* forms of intuition. In the *Critique*, Kant's dominant view seems to be that sensations are not, on their own, intentional: they do not present us with objects, but, rather, 'refer to the subject as a modification of its state' (A 320/B 376).[8] The difference between intuitions (singular representations that involve the presence of the objects they present) and sensations (which are non-intentional) is *not* that intuitions involve concepts. If it were, they would not be the distinct ingredient in cognition that Kant presents them as being, but, rather, would be dependent on concepts for their distinct contribution. Rather, the difference between non-intentional sensations and intuitions is that intuitions have been ordered according to the *a priori* and non-conceptual representation of space. So, rather than arguing that it is the application of concepts that distinguishes presentations of distinct particulars from sensations, Kant in fact says that it is the *a priori* and intuitive (non-conceptual) representation of space that plays this role: that enables us to be presented with outer appearances, things which are distinct from each other and ourselves. It is the spatiality of perception that is the condition of its intentionality, not the application of concepts. (I am simplifying Kant's view here, and throughout what follows, in that I consider only the *a priori* intuition of space, whereas the complete view also involves the *a priori* intuition of time.) Kant thinks that we perceive located particulars through discriminating spatial boundaries.[9] It is important to stress that saying that we perceive distinct particulars in the sense of located things with spatial boundaries does not imply that the particulars we pick out in perception need be persisting causal unities: the located particulars which preconceptual perception delivers could be shadows, or patches of light, which are clearly not objects in the sense with which Kant is concerned in the Deduction.

An obvious objection to my view is Kant's famous statement that 'intuitions without concepts are blind' (A 51/B 75), which has been taken to suggest that they are not singular representations, or representations of particulars.[10] But in the famous passage Kant is asserting that both intuitions and concepts are necessary ingredients in *cognition*: he is not talking about *perception*. Of course, we do need to give some explanation of what intuitional blindness amounts to, but it clearly cannot be the idea that intuitions are not singular representations, since Kant *defines* intuitions as immediate singular representations. That intuitions are singular is one of Kant's most central claims about them, maintained throughout the critical and post-critical writings and in his lectures on logic.

According to John McDowell's extreme conceptualist reading of Kant, intuitions do not make an 'even notionally separable contribution'.[11] However, a more common, less extreme, but still conceptualist reading would be to say that, although intuitions play an essential and distinct role, their contribution is not realizable in the absence of concepts; this might be taken to be an objection to my view. In the Aesthetic Kant separates out the role of intuition and concepts, but this does not mean that he thinks that these roles are really separable, and, clearly, we do not have the full story about cognition of objects without the Deduction. Thus, it might be thought that in the Aesthetic Kant is making an abstraction which cannot really be made, in order to isolate the different ingredients in cognition. It might be argued that Kant's view is that neither intuitions nor concepts alone can give us a direct perceptual presentation of a particular. The idea could be that in order to perceive a particular we need sensation to provide a given manifold of input, and concepts to carve up and organize this manifold. In other words, the fact that Kant thinks concepts alone cannot supply distinct perceptual particulars does not mean that he thinks intuitions alone could do so either; the point about the mutual dependence of intuitions and concepts could be that both ingredients are necessary. One problem with this is that, as I have argued, it seems to undermine Kant's view that intuitions are direct, singular representations which give us objects. He does not say that the role of intuition is to provide a sensory manifold for concepts to work on, but that it gives us objects, and he says that what enables it to play this role is the representation of space and time.

Against this, it might be pointed out that in the Deduction Kant seems to modify the account of space he presented in the Aesthetic, saying that the representation of space *itself* requires a categorial synthesis, and that this is necessary to bring the representation of space to the transcendental unity of apperception (B160n, B152). This is a point which has been emphasized by Beatrice Longuenesse.[12] This is a tricky issue because, on the one hand, Kant clearly says that the understanding operates on sensibility to generate at least some aspects of our representation of space. But, on the other hand, we have Kant's basic

statement of the fundamental duality and independence of the faculties of sensibility and understanding, and their respective representations, intuitions and concepts. To reconcile both of these, Longuenesse
suggests that, while our representations of space and time as forms in
which sensible manifolds are given have qualitative features that are
entirely independent of any activity of the understanding, they have
other features which are not so independent: specifically, the unity,
unicity and infinity of space, which are necessary for the unity of consciousness, and necessary for thinking of space as the object of study of
geometry.[13] Earlier, I introduced a distinction between the mere perception of a particular and the recognition of an object in the full-blown
Kantian sense. We can make a similar distinction with respect to our
representation of space. On the one hand, space can be seen as merely
the form of intuition which enables us to represent things as distinct
from each other and ourselves, and therefore is what distinguishes non-
intentional sensations from the perceptual presentation of particulars.
On the other hand, for creatures like us, who use concepts and think
about the particulars we perceive as full-blown objects, there is more
to the representation of space, as we can think of it as unified in a way
which is part of our representing the world as objective. So to say that
the representation of space is transformed by the understanding, and
that this is necessary for it to be brought to the unity of apperception,
for thought of an objective world, for self-consciousness, and for thinking of it as an object studied in physics, does not undermine the idea
of our having an *a priori* representation of space as an oriented field or
structure in which particulars are located which is independent of this
work of the understanding.

Paul Abela has argued persuasively that one of Kant's concerns in the
Critique is to reject the Cartesian internalism about mental content, and
my view can be clarified by contrasting it with his.[14] As should be obvious, I disagree with his reading Kant as saying that determinate mental representation requires the application of concepts in judgements.[15]
However, I agree with his view that a central part of Kant's position
is the rejection of the Cartesian conception of experience according
to which mental states of awareness, experience or perception can be
fully characterized in a way which is entirely internal to the subject,
and makes no reference to anything external to the subject.[16] This can
be seen most clearly in Kant's argument against Cartesian scepticism
(B274–279; Bxxxix–Bxli),[17] but it can also be seen in his notion of intuition. Intuitions are representations (mental states), but they are representations which essentially involve the presence to consciousness of

the things they represent. One of Kant's fundamental thoughts is that the kind of direct cognitive contact with objects which involves particular things being present to consciousness is essential for cognition, because it is essential for our thought to have what he calls objective validity: for our judgements to make truth-evaluable claims about the world. Intuition is what links our concepts to the world through directly (immediately) presenting particular (singular) things to our consciousness. Thus, I agree with Abela that Kant thinks, against the Cartesian view, that our experience gives representations which involve the presence to consciousness of the things represented. The disagreement is merely over where this happens: I suggest that it is already the case in Kant's account of intuition, independent of the application of concepts. Kant's position is more complex than one which sees the difference between mere sensation and properly intentional perception as being that the latter involves concepts.

One way in which Abela puts his point is that he thinks, for Kant, determinate mental content requires *reference* relations.[18] One way to put my point is to draw attention to two different things which might be meant by reference. Reference to an object might be taken to mean that a particular thing in the world is present to the consciousness of the subject; the subject is able to attend to a particular thing. On the other hand, it might be taken to mean that the subject is in a position to *think about* the object, to attribute properties to it. On my reading, Kant thinks that concepts are required for the latter, not the former. The Transcendental Aesthetic is concerned with the *a priori* conditions of being presented with empirical particulars in empirical intuition; the Transcendental Deduction is concerned with the *a priori* conditions of being able to apply concepts (attribute properties) to the particulars with which we are presented. Kant does not think our capacity to perceptually pick out a unique particular depends on our ability to bring things under concepts; he thinks that our ability to attribute properties to things depends on our being able to apply the *a priori* concepts of an object in general. If *referring* to an object is a way of *thinking* about an object, then there is a clear sense in which my account is compatible with thinking that we do not have determinate reference to an *object* without the categories. But this does not require thinking that we need the categories to perceive distinct, spatially bounded located particulars, to be presented with things outside ourselves.

It might be thought that allowing intuition to present us with distinct particulars in the absence of concepts leaves no role for the categories in determining which objects we are presented with. On my account, the

Deduction is concerned with something distinct from the conditions of merely perceiving distinct particulars: the conditions of thought or empirical concept application. Kant thinks that, in order to be able to think about the particulars given in perception as *objects*, to ascribe properties to them and investigate them empirically, we need a framework which provides a unity and necessity that govern the ascription of properties to particulars. Since this framework contains necessity, it could not be learnt from experience, and must be *a priori*. Roughly, the idea is that the world does not determine how we ascribe properties, what counts as an object and what counts as a property, so we need a concept of an object in general to govern property ascription. Kant thinks that attributing properties to objects requires having a governing conception of an object in general, which, in abstract terms, requires thinking of objects as subjects of predication, and in terms of ground–consequence relations. These abstract conceptions, for us, must be given a spatio-temporal interpretation according to which the subject of properties is something which persists, and persisting things have causal properties and are subject to causal laws. Kant thinks that these ways of thinking about objects correspond to applying the *a priori* concept of an object in general, and that this is a condition of empirical concept application. To understand the argument of the Deduction, the question is not why perception of a distinct located particular requires *a priori* concepts, but why the attribution of properties in empirical concept application should depend on the kind of unity and necessity that *a priori* concepts involve. Thus, it seems to me that if we allow, as seems straightforwardly compatible with the text, that Kant thinks that perceiving located particulars outside of you requires *a priori* intuition, but is not the same as being able to represent things as objects (persisting causal unities which are thought of as existing unperceived), we get a more interesting view of what concepts add: it is not the basic intentionality of perception, but the ability to attribute properties to the things we perceive.

2

So far I have argued that the idea that intuitions are perceptual presentations of particulars is the most straightforward reading of Kant's claim that they are immediate and singular, and of the role for which he introduces them, that of 'giving' us objects. This would be in tension with Kant's claims in the Deduction that the categories are necessary for something to become an object for me, only if the Deduction is taken to be concerned with conditions of the perception of particulars. I suggest that this is not Kant's concern in the Deduction; the Transcendental Aesthetic discusses what is necessary for the basic intentionality of perception (which, although Kant does not talk about animal perception, animals could have), while the Deduction is concerned with the conditions of applying concepts to the particulars we perceive in such a way that they can be *thought* of as objects. Kant thinks this involves thinking of them as persisting causal unities which are made up of stuff which is conserved and which are in law-governed causal interactions with each other, and he thinks this requires applying *a priori* concepts to them.

I now want to look at how my account relates to Kant's transcendental idealism, both in terms of how we interpret the position, and in terms of Kant's argument for the position. There are two respects in which my argument so far might be thought to be in tension with Kant's transcendental idealism. One is that saying that particulars are immediately presented to us in perception might be thought to imply that these particulars are entirely independent of us. The second is that saying that particulars are presented to us in perception might be said to undermine the role of the categories in the construction of objects, and therefore to lead to an extremely deflationary account of transcendental idealism. I cannot argue for an interpretation of transcendental idealism here; the interpretation I favour is one which I see as a middle road between the deflationary or merely epistemological distinctions, such as that defended by Henry Allison,[19] and the extreme metaphysical view which sees Kant as a phenomenalist and a noumenalist.[20] Rather, I see transcendental idealism as having both epistemological and metaphysical components: on my view, Kant is committed to the existence of an aspect of reality that is independent of us, and more metaphysically ultimate than the aspect which we experience, of which we cannot have knowledge; and he is committed to the appearances of things being mind-dependent in some sense, although not a phenomenalistic sense.[21] However, the only point I want to make about transcendental idealism here is that the account I have given of the role of intuition seems to me to be compatible with both a deflationary and a metaphysical reading of Kant's transcendental idealism. On the reading I have presented so far, empirical intuitions present us with distinct empirical particulars, but the condition of their doing so, according to Kant, is our *a priori* representation of space. Kant thinks that this *a priori* intuition is responsible for ordering the matter of sensation in such a way that it presents us with distinct particulars, and he thinks that this *a priori* structuring intuition does not correspond to some mind-independent reality. If the structure which determines our perception of distinct particulars does not represent a mind-independent aspect of reality, then the particulars thus perceived will be mind-dependent appearances, which do not present us with things as they are in themselves. Notice that, on this reading, the mind-dependence of sensible appearances is fully established in the Aesthetic, which is the way Kant presents it.

Stressing this role for space in the determination of the objects of perception might be thought to undermine the role of the categories in the construction of objects, and this might be thought to be in tension with transcendental idealism. But it is important to notice that, despite the way, in the B preface, Kant presents *a priori* intuitions and *a priori* concepts as making a parallel contribution (Bxvii–xviii), he does not in fact make claims with respect to the categories that parallel his claims with respect to space and time, in terms of their transcendental ideality. While Kant explicitly says that things in themselves are not spatial and not temporal, he does not make parallel claims with respect to causation and substance, and such claims would be considerably more difficult to make sense of.[22] Rather than saying that there is nothing like ground–consequence dependence in reality as it is in itself, he says that we can use these concepts only for knowledge of spatial objects. Immediately following the argument for space and time being merely our forms of intuition, Kant has a discussion in which he states explicitly and repeatedly that space and time represent no properties of things as they are in themselves, and exist only in our possible experience (A42–4/B59–61). In contrast, immediately following the Analytic, Kant clarifies its results in the section 'On the ground of the distinction of all objects in general into phenomena and noumena,' in which he repeatedly and explicitly says that we cannot use the categories for knowledge of things other than appearances: 'the understanding can make only empirical use of all its *a priori* principles' (A238/B297; see also A236/B296, A246/B303). Thus, an alternative to seeing the Deduction as leading to a contribution by mind to the world that exactly parallels that of the Aesthetic is to see Kant's point as being simply that the Deduction is limited by the results of the Aesthetic: the categories can be used only for cognition of things that are given in experience. This would not result in weakening Kant's idealism, because it would still be the case that we have knowledge only of mind-dependent appearances (in whatever sense we want to understand this), and not of things as they are in themselves. We can use the categories only for cognition of what is given in intuition, and what is given in intuition are mind-dependent appearances.

3

I have talked about two respects in which my reading of the Aesthetic relates to the interpretation of transcendental idealism. I now want to look at the way it relates to Kant's argument for his transcendental idealism. One of the many puzzling features of Kant's argument for his transcendental idealism in the Aesthetic is its apparent brevity. This is particularly apparent in the A edition, in which Kant presents five numbered arguments for the claim that our primary representation of space is intuitive and *a priori* (A23–5), and then immediately presents as following from this two conclusions about space itself: a) that it represents no property of or relation between things in themselves, and b) that space is nothing other than merely the form of our intuition (A26). Thus, at least in the A edition, Kant seems to take the claims that space represents no property or relation of things in themselves and that it is nothing other than merely the form of all appearances of outer sense to follow immediately from showing that our primary representation of space is an *a priori* intuition. But, since the immediately preceding arguments concern *our representation* of space, while the conclusions simply concern *space*, it is by no means clear how the latter follows from the former. This gives rise to the famous 'neglected alternative' objection, which says that Kant assumes that space must be either a form of intuition or a feature of mind-independent reality, and neglects the possibility that it could be both. Since conclusions a) and b) concern space itself, while the preceding arguments concern our representation of space, the objection seems fair (but also so obvious that it is hard to see how Kant could have failed to notice it).

Both the idea that there is a step missing in the presentation of the argument, and the idea that Kant has a response to the 'neglected alternative' objection, seem to be supported by the alteration in the presentation of the arguments which Kant makes in the B edition. In the B version, the arguments for the claim that our representation of space is *a priori* and intuitive are grouped under the heading 'The Metaphysical Exposition of the Concept of Space' (A22–5/B37–40), and the third argument in the A version, which concerns geometry, is taken out of this section and is developed at more length in the section called 'The Transcendental Exposition of the Concept of Space' (B40–1), which is placed between the Metaphysical Exposition and conclusions a) and

b) (A26/B42). This suggests that it is the argument from geometry that is supposed to take us from the claim that space is the *a priori* form of our intuition to the conclusion that space is *merely* the *a priori* form of our intuition, and not a feature of reality as it is in itself. Given the way Kant introduces the official argument based on substantive *a priori* cognition in the B preface (Bxvi–xvii), an obvious account of the way the argument from geometry is supposed to establish the ideality of space is through the idea that cognition of the synthetic *a priori* claims made about space in geometry can be understood only by seeing that space is not something independent of us (otherwise they would be inexplicable). However, it is not obvious that this is actually what the Transcendental Exposition argues.

In the Transcendental Exposition, Kant starts by saying that we have synthetic *a priori* knowledge of space, and then asks: 'What then must the representation of space be for such a cognition of it to be possible?' His answer is that it must be a pure intuition (B41). He thinks that our representation of space must be an intuition because (he thinks) geometrical claims are not analytic and so require something which enables us to go beyond what is contained in their concepts; this something is intuition. And, as he argued in argument 3) in the Metaphysical Exposition in A, he thinks that only if this representation is *a priori* can we account for the necessity of geometrical claims. The main difference from the A version is a developed statement of his reason for thinking that our representation of space must be an *intuition* (whereas the A version argues for the need for our representation of space to be *a priori*). Thus, as in the arguments in the Metaphysical Exposition, Kant is arguing for the claim that space is the *a priori* form of our intuition, and his preliminary conclusion again concerns our *representation* of space. Kant then goes on to ask: 'how can an outer intuition inhabit the mind that precedes the objects themselves, and in which the concept of the latter can be determined *a priori*?' He answers: 'Obviously not otherwise than insofar as it has its seat merely in the subject, as its formal constitution for being affected by objects and thereby acquiring **immediate representation** i.e., **intuition** of them, thus only as the form of outer **sense** in general' (B41). Here we have something like the move from substantive *a priori* knowledge to ideality, but we do not have any new account of the argument that is supposed to get us there. That space is the *a priori* form of our intuition, which therefore determines in advance the form of the objects of experience, is something Kant takes himself to have established in the Metaphysical Exposition. The final stage of the argument in the Transcendental Exposition, which asks how this is possible and answers that it requires seeing space as mind-dependent, could just as well be asserted at the end of the Metaphysical Exposition. Thus, the Transcendental Exposition does not obviously introduce a new argument. It says that our geometrical knowledge can be explained only on the assumption that our representation of space is *a priori* and intuitive. It then says that an *a priori* form of intuition cannot correspond to the way things mind-independently are. Instead of presenting a new argument for the claim that space is the *a priori* form of our intuition, the Transcendental Exposition seems to elaborate on reasons for thinking that our representation of space is an *a priori* intuition. This still leaves unanswered the question of how we get from the claim that our representation of space is an *a priori* intuition to the claim that *space* is merely an *a priori* form of intuition.

Kant's official argument for transcendental idealism is that it is the only explanation of synthetic *a priori* knowledge: that we can cognize of things *a priori* only what we ourselves 'put into' them (Bxviii). The simple version of the argument from synthetic *a priori* knowledge says that substantive *a priori* knowledge is mysterious, and can be explained only on the assumption that it is knowledge of something for which our minds are responsible. This argument has obvious problems: in addition to the problem of the neglected alternative, we might wonder why we should have transparent access to the cognitive structure of our minds, and whether the principle is not self-defeating in the same way as the verification principle.[23]

In an extremely helpful account of the argument, Marcus Willashek argues that the reason Kant's transcendental idealist conclusions appear to be insufficiently argued for is that Kant is incorrectly taken as presenting them as following from the Metaphysical Exposition alone, when in fact Kant intends them to follow from the Metaphysical Exposition together with all the previous material introduced in the Aesthetic, including the distinction between intuition and concepts, Kant's view of the nature of intuition, and his reasons for thinking that there must be an *a priori* form of intuition.[24] Willashek argues that in the Aesthetic Kant introduces intuition as an essential ingredient of cognition, and says that it is a kind of representation which is essentially caused by the object it represents. It follows from this that an *a priori* intuition could not represent a mind-independent feature of reality (because, being *a priori*, it could not be caused by such a feature). Although my account is in some respects different from Willashek's causal externalist account of intuition, I agree with his general strategy for making sense of the argument of the Aesthetic, as well as with the idea that an account of intuition according to which intuitions involve the presence to consciousness of the objects they represent is crucial for this. The key point is that, given Kant's account of what intuition is – that it essentially involves the presence of its object – an *a priori* intuition cannot present something mind-independent.[25]

Developing this line of thought, we can present a ten-stage account of Kant's strategy in the Aesthetic. (Note: this is not supposed to correspond to ten steps in an argument; for example, step 6 corresponds to all the arguments in the Metaphysical Exposition). The first five steps in the strategy concern background material which Kant establishes before the Metaphysical Exposition, but which is crucial for seeing how we get from the Metaphysical Exposition to conclusions a) and b). Kant argues that:

1) Cognition or knowledge of an objective world requires both intuitions and concepts.
2) Intuitions are representations which essentially involve the presence of the objects they present.
3) Empirical intuition requires *a priori* intuition, which gives it its order or form.
4) We have an *a priori* form of our intuition.
5) *A priori* intuition could not represent a mind-independent feature of reality (from 2).

1) and 2) simply seem to be asserted by Kant. 3) is argued for extremely briefly: Kant says that:

> I call that in the appearance which corresponds to sensation its **matter**, but that which allows the manifold of appearances to be intuited as ordered in certain relations, I call the **form** of appearance. Since that within which the sensations can alone be ordered and placed in a certain form cannot itself be in turn sensation, the matter of all appearance is only given to us *a posteriori*, but its form must lie reading for it in the mind *a priori*, and can therefore be considered separately from all sensation. (A20/B34)

Kant says that intuitions must be ordered, and that this order cannot be derived from sensation.[26] If he is wrong about this claim his entire argument will collapse, but our concern at this point is not with whether or not his argument is sound, but with why he thinks his conclusions follow at the end of the Metaphysical Exposition, and to understand this we need to see what he thinks he has established in saying that there is an *a priori* form of our intuition. What is significant here, in addition to the claim that the form of intuition is *a priori*, is the role played by the *a priori* form of intuition: without this *a priori* form we would not be presented with particulars in empirical intuition; we would simply have a mass of sensations, not individual particulars. As I argued in section 1, the *a priori* form of intuition plays a particular role: that of structuring the sensory input such that it can represent particulars.

4) follows simply from 3). 5) follows from 2) and 4). 2) says that intuitions are representations which essentially involve the presence to consciousness of the particular things they present. It follows from this that an *a priori* intuition could not represent a mind-independent feature of reality, because an *a priori* intuition must present us with its 'object' (what it represents) independent of experience; its object can be present to us independent of experience. Thus, from 2) and 4) we get 5) *a priori* intuition could not represent a mind-independent feature of reality.

The next step in the argument is to show that our representation of space is an *a priori* intuition, and that our representation of space can be identified with the *a priori* form of our intuition; this is the burden of the Metaphysical Exposition. The Metaphysical Exposition does this in two ways (which Kant does not always clearly distinguish): by arguing that our representation of space must be *a priori* and must be intuitive, and by arguing that space is the form in which particulars are represented – that it fills the role of enabling us to be presented with particulars.

Argument 1 of the Metaphysical Exposition says:

> Space is not an empirical concept that has been drawn from other experiences. For in order for certain sensations to be related to something outside me (i.e., to something in another place from that in which I find myself), thus in order for me to represent them as outside and next to one another, thus not merely different but as in different places, the representation of space must already be their ground. (B38)

Given Kant's concern with conditions of the possibility of experience, and the fact that in the Deduction and the Principles he argues that the categories and principles are *a priori* conditions of the possibility of experience, this passage is sometimes read as arguing that space is a condition of the possibility of representing distinct particulars. However, unlike the Deduction, which gives a detailed argument for the categories being conditions of the possibility of experience, Kant seems simply to *assert* that space is a condition of the possibility of being presented with distinct particulars.[27] Clearly, to say that the aim of the argument is not to establish that the representation of space is necessary for the representation of distinct particulars is not to say that the latter idea plays no role in the argument. On the contrary, it seems to be the key *premise* of the argument. In other words, the idea that space is a necessary condition of individuating or distinguishing objects does play a central role in the argument, but as a premise, not a conclusion. In the passage, Kant claims that the representation of space is necessary:

- to represent things as distinct from and outside me (*etwas außer mir*);
- to represent things as in different places/as spatially located (*als in verschiedenen Orten*);
- to represent things as spatially related (*außer und neben einander*) and
- to represent things as distinct/different from each other (*verschieden*).

Note that Kant says that space is necessary to represent things 'not merely as different' (*nicht bloß verschieden*), which presumably means that, *a fortiori*, it is necessary to represent things as distinct or different. Kant thinks that having, through sensory affectation, a presentation of a particular involves representing a thing which is outside me, is distinct from other things, is located and spatially related to other things. He then says that, *because* the representation of space necessarily grounds these features of representations of things, the primary representation of space must be *a priori*. It is not just because we have a representation of structure which does not depend on the particular locations and arrangements of individuals in the structure, but because (Kant thinks) we could not be presented with distinct (outside me, outside each other, located and spatially related) individuals *at all* without the representation of space, that he thinks that the representation of space cannot be abstracted from our experience of spatial relations between particulars. In step 3) Kant says that an *a priori* intuition is necessary for us to be presented with particular things (empirical intuitions). He now says that space is the way we represent particular things. And in the rest of the sections in the Metaphysical Exposition Kant gives further arguments for the claim that the representation of space must be *a priori* and intuitive. Our representation of space is *a priori* and intuitive, and space is the form of our intuition.

This gives us step 6 in Kant's strategy (a summary of the Metaphysical Exposition):

6) Our representation of space is the *a priori* form of our intuition (from the Metaphysical Exposition).

As we have seen, in the A edition Kant moves immediately from this to his conclusions a) and b), which I will represent as step 7) in the overall argument for transcendental idealism:

7) Therefore our representation of space does not represent a mind-independent feature of reality; it is merely the form of our intuition.

This is the move which appears puzzling if it is taken to follow from the arguments of the Metaphysical Exposition alone, and, as I argued above, the addition of the Transcendental Exposition does not seem to help, as it seems to simply give further argument for the claim that our primary representation of space is *a priori* and intuitive. However, if we put 6) together with 5), we can see why Kant takes his conclusion to follow immediately. If the arguments in the Metaphysical Deduction have succeeded in showing that space is the *a priori* form of our intuition, and we have already shown that *a priori* intuition could not represent a mind-independent feature of reality (1–5), then it immediately follows that 'a) Space represents no property at all of any things in themselves nor any relation of them to each other' and 'b) Space is nothing other than merely the form of all appearances of outer sense, i.e., the subjective condition of sensibility, under which alone outer intuition is possible for us' (A26/B42).

My concern here is with how Kant reaches conclusions a) and b), but it must be noted that this leaves us short of the complete transcendental idealist position. To give Kant's complete argument for transcendental idealism (as opposed to simply for his conclusions with respect to space), we need to generalize the conclusion so that it applies to all objects which we can experience. To get the generalized conclusion we need to add a further step:

8) Since the spatial order which enables us to be presented with things in empirical intuition is a feature only of things as they appear to us, and not things as they are in themselves, the objects which are presented in empirical intuition are only appearances and not things as they are in themselves.

It is arguable that this still does not get us the complete transcendental idealist position, since it has established the mind-dependent nature of spatio-temporal appearances, but not yet ruled out knowledge through concepts alone of things as they are in themselves. It might be thought that Kant needs the argument of the Deduction, with the limitation of the categories to the spatio-temporal objects of our intuition, before he is finally in a position to establish that we have no knowledge of reality as it is in itself. If this is right, then to complete the argument we need two further steps:

9) We cannot have cognition through concepts alone, because we cannot have cognition where there is not something given in intuition (this follows from 1).
10) We cannot have knowledge of things as they are in themselves (from 8 and 9).

The main advantage of this account of Kant's argument in steps 1–7 is that it shows why Kant takes his conclusions a) and b) to follow straightforwardly and immediately at the point at which he states them, without any further argument. On this reading of the argument, a large amount of the work is done by Kant's claim that there must be an *a priori* form of our intuition, for which, as we have seen, he does not provide a lot of argument. However, it is surely an advantage of a reading if the claims which Kant thinks follow from his premises do in fact do so, while the parts which are left unargued are the premises for which Kant does not provide much argument. On this account, if we want to evaluate Kant's argument, the real pressure on the argument is why we should think that there must be such an *a priori* form.

A noteworthy feature of this reading of the argument is that the pressure is not on Kant's beliefs about Euclidean geometry, or even on *a priori* claims about space. It may even be compatible with the argument that it is contingent that we represent space as we do: Kant says that 'for the peculiarity of our understanding, that it is able to bring about the unity of apperception *a priori* only by means of the categories and only through precisely this kind and number of them, a further ground can be offered just as little as one can be offered for why we have precisely these and no other functions for judgment or why space and time are the forms of our intuition' (B145–6, see also A27/B43). Space happens to be the way we represent things as outside us and distinct from ourselves and each other. Kant's argument says that what is a condition of representing things as distinct must be an *a priori* intuition. Since the way we experience things as distinct from us is by experiencing them as in space, space is the *a priori* form of our intuition. If we grant that intuition is a kind of representation that essentially involves the object it presents, we will see that an *a priori* intuition could not represent mind-independent features of reality. But, if this is the case, then the conclusion that space cannot represent a feature of mind-independent reality, and is merely the *a priori* form of our intuition, follows immediately, as Kant seems to think it does.

The version of the argument I have presented is compatible with, but more complex than, the simple version of the argument from synthetic *a priori* knowledge. Rather than simply asserting that synthetic *a priori* knowledge of mind-independent reality is inexplicable, the argument is that it can be seen to be inexplicable because all knowledge requires intuition, intuition requires *a priori* intuition, and *a priori* intuition cannot be of something mind-independent. Once we see that we have *a priori* intuition we can see how *a priori* synthesis is possible, and therefore how synthetic *a priori* judgements are possible: they are possible so long as they are restricted to our form of intuition.

I have suggested that, on Kant's account, concept application is not necessary for the perception of distinct particulars. I argued that this makes sense of the way Kant defines intuition, and the role he allocates to it as one of the distinct and necessary ingredients in cognition. I suggested that, on my account, the issue that is key to understanding the Transcendental Deduction is not the role of concepts in perception, but why Kant thinks that attributing properties to objects, empirical concept application, requires the application of *a priori* concepts. And I have suggested that this account of what intuition is allows us to make sense of why Kant thinks that the transcendental ideality of space follows from the Metaphysical Exposition. I have also isolated what seems to me to be the key claim we need to understand to assess Kant's argument: why he thinks that the basic intentionality of perception requires that the sensory input is arranged in an *a priori* structure, why sensation could not be ordered in a way which enables it to present distinct particulars unless it was ordered in a structure which was not derived from sensation.

Notes

1. Throughout, when I talk about the intentionality of perception, I refer to its object-directed nature, the fact that it presents us with objects. Intentionality

is not understood here in the sense in which the objects of perception are merely intentional, or represent an object whether or not it is present, but rather as concerning the actual presentation of objects to consciousness.

2. I defend this in more detail in my (2009) 'Kant, Non-Conceptual Content, and the Representation of Space', *Journal of the History of Philosophy*. Here my concern is to motivate the view sufficiently to then go on to relate it to the argument for idealism in the Transcendental Aesthetic. For a more extreme non-conceptualist reading of Kant, see R. Hanna (2005) 'Kant and Non-conceptual Content', *European Journal of Philosophy*, 13, 247–90, and for a good representative of the conceptualist reading see H. Ginsborg (2006), 'Empirical Concepts and the Content of Experience', *European Journal of Philosophy*, 14(3), 349–72, and C. Wenzel (2005) 'Spielen nach Kant die Kategorien schon bei der Wahrnehmung eine Rolle?', *Kant Studien*, 96(4), 407–26.

3. For convenience, references to Kant's texts are given parenthetically in the text, following standard practice of A and B referring to the first and second editions of the *Critique of Pure Reason*: Kant, I. (1998) *Critique of Pure Reason*, trans. P. Guyer and A. Wood (eds) (Cambridge: Cambridge University Press). Other Kant texts referred to are abbreviated as follows: CJ: (1987) *Critique of Judgment*, trans. W.S. Pluhar (Indianapolis: Hacket Publishing Company); CPR: (1996) *Critique of Practical Reason*, trans. M.J. Gregor (ed.) (Cambridge: Cambridge University Press); FS: (1992) 'The False Subtlety of the Four Syllogistic Figures', *Theoretical Philosophy 1775-1770*, trans. D. Walford and R. Meerbote (Cambridge: Cambridge University Press); JL: (1992) *Jäsche Logic*, trans. J.M. Young (ed.) (Lectures on Logic, Cambridge: Cambridge University Press); MM: (1996) *Metaphysics of Morals*, trans. M.J. Gregor (Practical Philosophy, Cambridge: Cambridge University Press); P: (2004) *Prolegomena to any Future Metaphysics*, trans. G. Hatfield (ed.) (Cambridge: Cambridge University Press); VL: (1992) *Vienna Logic*, trans. J.M. Young (ed.) (Lectures on Logic, Cambridge: Cambridge University Press). Page references are to the standard Akademie edition of Kant's works.

4. See B. Maund (2003) *Perception* (Chesham, Bucks: Acumen), p. 61 for discussion of two-stage views.

5. M. Willashek (1997) 'Der transzendentale Idealismus und die Idealität von Raum und Zeit', *Zeitschrift für philosophische Forschung*, 51, 537–64, has a closely related position, based on the claim that intuitions essentially involve the subject being affected; he argues that Kant is an externalist about mental content in the sense that he thinks that the causal origin of intuitions is an essential determinant of their intentional content. I want to put the point more strongly, and say that an intuition presents its object to consciousness (rather than that its object plays an essential causal role in determining its content), and, since Kant has a notion of *a priori* intuition, it seems to me that the notion of direct presence is more fundamental to his notion of intuition than that of the causal interactions that are required for us to have empirical intuitions.

6. Arguably, singularity goes beyond immediacy, because it could be that what was immediately present was simply sensation, or an unorganized manifold. In contrast to this, Kant thinks that what is immediately present to us are spatially located things with discriminable spatial boundaries.

7. Further, Kant thinks that the way we use the categories allows us to discover that a perceptual particular which we take to be an object is not in fact an object. The way we use the concept of substance allows us to *discover* that something we took to be (and perceived as) one creature is in fact a host and a parasite. The way we use the concept of substance does not straightforwardly determine which things in the world are in fact persisting causal unities; rather, it enables us to look for persisting causal unities. This suggests that it is not the categories which are determining distinct perceptual particulars.

8. See K. Westphal (2004) *Kant's Transcendental Proof of Realism* (Cambridge: Cambridge University Press), p. 44 and R. George (1981) 'Kant's Sensationism', *Synthese*, 47, 229–55.

9. As Stefanie Grüne points out, Kant thinks that both intuitions and concepts can be distinct, and that they are distinct in different ways. Concepts are distinct when we can divide them into their sub-concepts. We discriminate particulars by discriminating their spatial boundaries, and we perceive them distinctly when we can spatially discriminate their parts (Grüne, 2008; see also CJ 226n43).

10. L. Falkenstein (1995) *Kant's Intuitionism* (Toronto: Toronto University Press), p. 59.

11. J. McDowell (1996) *Mind and World* (Harvard, Massachusetts: Harvard University Press), p. 9.

12. B. Longuenesse (2005) *Kant and the Human Standpoint* (Cambridge: Cambridge University Press),chs. 1–3.

13. Longuenesse (2005), p. 73.

14. P. Abela (2002) *Kant's Empirical Realism* (Oxford: Oxford University Press).

15. Abela (2002), p. 36.

16. See also G. Bird (1962) *Kant's Theory of Knowledge*(London: Routledge & Kegan Paul); A. Collins (1999) *Possible Experience* (Berkeley and Los Angeles: University of California Press); Willashek (1997).

17. It is, of course, controversial how Kant's so-called refutation of idealism should be read. The anti-Cartesian reading of Kant sees him as arguing that being able to have cognition of the temporal nature our own mental states requires our being directly aware of objects outside us. In other words, outer experience is primary; awareness of ourselves as having an inner life depends on our having direct experience of objects outside us.

18. Abela (2002), p. 36.

19. H. Allison (2004) *Kant's Transcendental Idealism*, Revised and Enlarged Edition (New Haven and London: Yale University Press).

20. For example, P.F. Strawson (1966) *The Bounds of Sense* (London: Methuen & Co. Ltd).

21. I develop this kind of account in L. Allais (2007) 'Kant's Idealism and the Secondary Quality Analogy', *Journal of the History of Philosophy*, 45(3), 459–84.

22. The fact that Kant does not claim for the categories a status parallel to that of space and time, in that he does not say that things in themselves do not contain necessity that corresponds to our concepts, follows from a closely related point: the categories are forms of thought for all rational creatures, and they are originally based in logic.

23. This is argued by Lawrence Bonjour, who thinks that Kant's solution undermines itself in a parallel way to that in which the verification principle is self-defeating. If the verification principle claims that all meaning statements are empirically verifiable, it seems to be self-defeating in that it is not itself empirically verifiable. Similarly, Bonjour argues that the claim that we can know *a priori* of objects only what we ourselves put into them is neither analytic nor empirical; it must therefore be synthetic and *a priori*, and therefore Kant must explain it in the only way in which he allows such knowledge to be explicable. However, it is doubtful whether the claim that the cognitive structure of our minds is responsible for the fact that the cognitive structure of our minds is responsible for the structure of objects makes sense, and it generates a vicious regress. L. Bonjour (1998) *In Defence of Pure Reason* (Cambridge: Cambridge University Press).
24. Willashek (1997).
25. This point is also made by Daniel Warren, who argues that 'in general the mere fact that a representation has its origin in us has no idealist consequences. But when that representation is an *intuition*, then, according to Kant, it *does*—and that is because intuition, insofar as it is what Kant calls an "immediate" representation, guarantees the presence of its subject' (Warren (1998) 'Kant and the A Priority of Space', *Philosophical Review*, 107, 179–224, p. 221).
26. Willashek suggests that we understand this claim in the light of the arguments in the Metaphysical Exposition. He argues that the claim that that in which alone sensation can be ordered cannot be given in sensation is justified only if 1) no sensation organizes itself and 2) there are global ordering features which apply to all sensations (Willashek (1997), p. 550). He argues that this is what Kant intends to establish in the Metaphysical Exposition. For example, in the second argument of the Metaphysical Exposition, Kant says that we can abstract what we know about bodies from what we know of space, but we cannot abstract space from our representation of bodies. A problem with this is that, on the face of it, the aim of the Metaphysical Exposition is to establish that space coincides with the *a priori* form of our intuition (taking the existence of the latter to be already established). In other words, the arguments of the Metaphysical Exposition argue for the claim that our representation of space has global structuring features which mean that it is an *a priori* form of our intuition, but not for the prior claim that intuition must have an *a priori* form.
27. Daniel Warren (1998) gives a detailed argument against the readings of this passage which see Kant as trying to show that space is a necessary condition of individuating or distinguishing objects. His argument is targeted on Allison's (1983) account of the argument, which reads Kant as arguing that, in order to be aware of things as numerically distinct from one another, it is necessary to be aware, not only of their qualitative differences, but also of the fact that they are located in different places. Warren questions both the textual basis for this interpretation and the plausibility of the argument it represents. He points out that the *Critique* has an account of how we make judgements distinguishing qualitatively identical objects, in the Amphiboly, that this argument is concerned with the use of concepts, and that it assumes, rather than argues for, the results of the Aesthetic (Warren

(1998),p. 93). Further, he says that the argument would not work, because space is sufficient but not necessary for judging that objects are distinct: the capacity to distinguish objects 'is after all a capacity for making certain kinds of judgments' (Warren (1998),p.192). He argues that we need spatial features to ground such judgements only when we have already run out of other qualitative features. His alternative account of Kant's aim in this section is that it is to argue against Leibniz's view that our representation of space could be derived from our experience of spatial relations; on the contrary, Kant argues, we must have the representation of space to represent things as spatially related.

References

Abela, P. (2002) *Kant's Empirical Realism* (Oxford: Oxford University Press).

Allison, H. (2004) *Kant's Transcendental Idealism*, Revised and Enlarged Edition (New Haven and London: Yale University Press).

Allais, L. (2007) 'Kant's Idealism and the Secondary Quality Analogy', *Journal of the History of Philosophy*, 45(3), 459–84.

Allais, L. (2009) 'Kant, Non-Conceptual Content, and the Representation of Space', *Journal of the History of Philosophy*, 47, no. 3, pp. 383–413.

Bird, G. (1962) *Kant's Theory of Knowledge* (London: Routledge and Kegan Paul).

Bonjour, L. (1998) *In Defence of Pure Reason* (Cambridge: Cambridge University Press).

Collins, A. (1999) *Possible Experience* (Berkeley and Los Angeles: University of California Press).

Falkenstein, L. (1995) *Kant's Intuitionism* (Toronto: Toronto University Press).

Hanna, R. (2005) 'Kant and Non-conceptual Content', *European Journal of Philosophy*, 13, 247–90.

George, R. (1981) 'Kant's Sensationism', *Synthese*, 47, 229–55.

Ginsborg, H. (2006) 'Empirical Concepts and the Content of Experience', *European Journal of Philosophy*, 14(3), 349–72.

Kant, I. (1987) *Critique of Judgment*, trans. W.S. Pluhar (Indianapolis: Hacket Publishing Company).

Kant, I. (1992) 'The False Subtlety of the Four Syllogistic Figures', *Theoretical Philosophy 1775-1770*, trans. D. Walford and R. Meerbote (Cambridge: Cambridge University Press).

Kant, I. (1992) *Vienna Logic*, trans. J.M. Young (ed.) (Lectures on Logic, Cambridge: Cambridge University Press).

Kant, I. (1992) *Jäsche Logic*, trans. J.M. Young (ed.) (Lectures on Logic, Cambridge: Cambridge University Press).

Kant, I. (1996) *Critique of Practical Reason*, trans. M.J. Gregor (ed.) (Cambridge: Cambridge University Press).

Kant, I. (1996) *Metaphysics of Morals*, trans. M.J. Gregor (Practical Philosophy, Cambridge: Cambridge University Press).

Kant, I.(1998) *Critique of Pure Reason*, trans. P. Guyer and A. Wood (eds) (Cambridge: Cambridge University Press).

Kant, I. (2004) *Prolegomena to any Future Metaphysics*, trans. G. Hatfield (ed.) (Cambridge: Cambridge University Press).

Longuenesse, B. (2005) *Kant and the Human Standpoint* (Cambridge: Cambridge University Press).

McDowell, J. (1996) *Mind and World* (Harvard, Massachusetts: Harvard University Press).

Maund, B. (2003) *Perception* (Chesham, Bucks: Acumen).

Strawson, P.F. (1966)*The Bounds of Sense* (London: Methuen & Co. Ltd).

Warren, D. (1998) 'Kant and the A Priority of Space', *Philosophical Review*, 107, 179–224.

Wenzel, C. (2005) 'Spielen nach Kant die Kategorien schon bei der Wahrnehmung eine Rolle?', *Kant Studien*, 96(4), 407–26.

Westphal, K. (2004) *Kant's Transcendental Proof of Realism* (Cambridge: Cambridge University Press).

Willashek, M. (1997) 'Der transzendentale Idealismus und die Idealität von Raum und Zeit', *Zeitschrift für philosophische Forschung*, 51, 537–64.

3

Is Spatial Awareness Required for Object Perception?

John Campbell

Is spatial awareness required for perception of objects? The idea that awareness is required gives a significant epistemological role to conscious experience; it implies that spatial awareness is a way of accessing the world. In contrast, many naturalistically inclined philosophers would take it for granted that an appeal to consciousness can have no explanatory value. Consciousness has to be an epiphenomenon, a puzzle to be explained that can itself have no explanatory role. In this chapter I set out a case for saying spatial awareness is a basic element in our epistemic access to our surroundings. I leave open whether this is a problem for naturalism, properly construed.

3.1 Does visual object perception require visual spatial awareness?

We can distinguish between perception of objects, such as, for example, a blue square, and perception of features, such as blueness or squareness. It's one thing to be able to tell, on the basis of vision, that a blue square is present, and another to be able to tell, on the basis of vision, that a feature such as blueness or squareness is present. These capacities came apart in the case of Lynn Robertson's patient R.M., who had Balint's Syndrome.[1] Presented with an array of colours, and asked whether blueness was present, R.M. was substantially above chance; he could reliably tell, on the basis of vision, whether the display contained blue. Presented with an array of shapes, and asked whether a square was present, R.M. was again substantially above chance; he could reliably tell, on the basis of vision, whether the display contained a square. However, when asked whether a blue square was present, he was at chance; he really had no idea. R.M. was incapable of visual perception of objects, in the following sense: he could not see an object as the possessor of a number of different properties. However, he evidently was capable of visual perception of features.

R.M. had problems with his spatial vision. It is not that no spatial information was available to him visually. On the contrary, he had unconscious or implicit access to a lot of spatial information. Let me give one rather striking example of how much implicit spatial information he did access. R.M. was shown a display with four circles on it, of various colours. This display then was replaced by a display with a single central icon on it. R.M. had two tasks: (1) to press a buzzer the moment he saw the central icon, but only if it was an arrow, and (2), at the end of the trial, to say whether there was a green circle in the initial display. (It was explained to him at the start of the trial that at the end he would be asked to say whether a green one had been present in the initial display.)

The background to this experiment is that it's already known that ordinary subjects will be faster to press the buzzer if the arrow they see points to the position that the green target had occupied. The more the arrow points away from the position previously occupied by the green target, the slower subjects are to press the buzzer. The explanation of this phenomenon is a separate problem. For the moment the point is only that, if your reaction times show this pattern, then there is some sense in which you have spatial vision. You have at least an implicit coding of the spatial relation between the arrow and the remembered green target. Of course, in this test the subject is not being asked to pay attention to spatial relations; not being asked, for example, to say anything about them.

R.M. showed this phenomenon in the trial.[2] It is also true, however, that R.M. had no explicit visual spatial awareness at all. You could show him the arrow and the green target side by side and he would be at chance if you asked him whether the arrow pointed towards or away from the target. Robertson's conclusion is that it is his lack of spatial awareness that explains R.M.'s being incapable of visual object perception. She puts this conclusion in the context of Treisman's notion of a master map of locations.[3] The idea is that in vision the various aspects of an object – its colour, shape, orientation and so on – are all being processed in separate processing streams. This basic level of vision, at which we have only various features being plotted as at this or that location, is largely intact in R.M. There is at least implicit spatial information here, in that each processing stream is constructing a 'feature map' representing the locations of various particular properties. What

R.M. lacks is visual object perception, in that he cannot see that it is one thing that has the various properties identified in the various processing streams: that there is one thing that is blue and square, for example. According to Treisman, what makes this possible for ordinary subjects is their use of a master map of locations. Attention to any one of the locations on the master map allows one to put together all the properties found at that place in each of the various specialized processing streams. It is this master map of locations that is compromised in R.M., according to Robertson. Since what R.M. lacks seems to be specifically conscious spatial perception – as we saw, he has implicit visual spatial information – Robertson proposes that the master map of locations is conscious. It is R.M.'s lack of spatial awareness that is responsible for his being incapable of visual object perception.

I want briefly to mention Zenon Pylyshyn's objections to Treisman's picture here. Pylyshyn has argued that our capacities to keep track visually of four or so moving objects simultaneously show that we can visually lock on to an object without knowing any of its properties, and without representing its location; the suggestion is that the speed of the movements of objects in Pylyshyn's multiple object tracking experiments means that the subject cannot be constantly updating representations of their locations, though at the end of the experiment the subject characteristically is able to identify the target they have been keeping track of.[4] The full analysis of these experiments is a further matter. Here I want only to remark that they cannot of themselves show that object perception does not require spatial awareness. For object perception, in the sense in which I am talking about it, requires the ability to ascribe multiple properties to a single object on the basis of perception. And it is quite consistent with the multiple object tracking experiments themselves that the ascription of multiple properties to a single thing will require knowledge of the location of that thing. Success in the multiple object tracking experiments may show that one has successfully kept track of the initial group of objects, but it does not of itself involve the capacity to ascribe any particular property to any of them.

Even if we accept Robertson's analysis of R.M. and the general moral she draws – that Treisman's master map of locations should be viewed as the basis of spatial awareness – there is still a puzzle about the role of consciousness here. It would be possible to argue that the functional workings of the system could be described without any explicit mention of consciousness at all. Indeed, that is exactly how Treisman set up her theory. So the case of R.M. might indeed suggest that the master map of locations is the basis of spatial awareness. But that may be merely an epiphenomenon. What does the work in the system is the spatial representation. Whether the representation is the content specifically of spatial awareness, as opposed to being a merely implicit or non-conscious representation, may not make any difference to anything else. In that sense, the fact that we are dealing here with spatial *awareness*, even if it is so, may be merely an epiphenomenon.

How should we decide whether that is the right conclusion to draw? The puzzle here is to see what work spatial *awareness* specifically might be doing in vision. After all, you might argue that it would be consistent with Robertson's overall picture to acknowledge the possibility of a subject who had a master map of locations – a spatial representation that had the same functional role as the master map of an ordinary subject – without that master map being the content of consciousness. How could it make a difference to the possibility of object perception whether one has spatial awareness or merely an implicit master map of locations? Or is there some contradiction in the idea of a master map of locations that is not the content of the subject's awareness? This last would seem to make Robertson's appeal to the case of R.M. redundant, for one of the things that the case of R.M. was supposed to establish was that it is specifically spatial *awareness* that makes object perception possible. My aim now is to try to find what work awareness might be doing in our perception of objects.

3.2   Could spatial concepts be entirely theoretical?

I want to push a little further this scepticism about the role of spatial awareness in object perception. You might wonder whether any kind of spatial perception at all is required for object perception. You might press this scepticism while acknowledging that object perception requires that one conceive of the objects one is perceiving as spatially located. Couldn't we have someone who doesn't have spatial perception, but who has elaborated a theoretical conception of space? After all, consider the conceptions of space used in contemporary physics. It can hardly be said that these are in any sense observational concepts; they are formed as elements of theories postulated to explain our observations. Now it's true that these observations are themselves spatial; our perceptions ordinarily involve experience of a three-dimensional space. But couldn't there be someone who does not even have that much by way of spatial perception? That is, couldn't there be someone who doesn't have spatial perception at all? And couldn't such a person nonetheless postulate, say, a three-dimensional space, in order to explain the perceptions they do have? Such a person might form the conception of various particular spatial objects in their surroundings. When one of them makes a noise, our subject might hear and say, 'That's the steam-roller starting up!', for example. This person could, on the face of it, be said to hear the steamroller, even in the absence of spatial perception. To fill out the picture here a little, consider the following analogy for ordinary hearing, given by Bregman in a book on the psychology of hearing. Suppose you are on the edge of a lake and a friend challenges you to play a game:

> The game is this: Your friend digs two narrow channels up from the side of the lake. Each is a few feet long and a few inches wide and they are spaced a few feet apart. Halfway up each one, your friend stretches a handkerchief and fastens it to the sides of the channel. As waves reach the side of the lake they travel up the channels and cause the two handkerchiefs to go into motion. You are allowed to look only at the handkerchiefs and from their motions to answer a series of questions: How many boats are there on the lake and where are they? Which is the most powerful one? Which one is closer? Is the wind blowing? Has any large object been dropped suddenly into the lake?[5]

Bregman's point is not that this task is impossible but only that it is, obviously, quite difficult; and it is his analogy for the task faced by the auditory system in recovering information about the world from sound. If you just watched the movements of the handkerchiefs closely, you could in principle recover quite a lot of information about what is happening on the lake. You know, on the basis of prior perception of it, that there is a lake there and the kinds of things that are likely to happen on it; the data from the handkerchiefs allow you to narrow the possibilities further. If the analogy is good, the task must be possible, since, after all, in hearing we do manage to recover a lot of information about what is happening around us. This depends on our having some idea of what kind of environment we're in and what kinds of things are likely to happen in it, just as in the case of the lake. And ordinarily we have a lot of this information from vision and touch. Suppose now, though, that we set aside this use of auxiliary perceptual information. Consider someone who is only watching the movements of the handkerchiefs, but has no idea that there are such things as lakes or boats. This subject simply observes the movements of the handkerchiefs and has to explain them somehow. This is a much more difficult task, and most of us would not naturally come up immediately with the 'lake and boats' theory. But suppose many people carried out the observations, over many centuries, with lots of theories being formulated and refuted. Here it does not seem at all impossible that people would eventually arrive at the theory of lakes and boats. But, if many people could do it over a long time, in principle it would be possible for one person to do it in a lifetime, supposing them to be reasonably diligent. Isn't something similar possible for hearing? Consider someone who has no spatial perception, and no prior conception of space, only non-spatial auditory perception. This person has a lot of work to do to explain what they hear. But, though the task is not easy, they could eventually come up with the 'space and objects' theory: that they live in a space occupied by various objects that are making the noises they hear. In fact, we could make the task easier than this. We could suppose that we have a subject who has some innate tendency to postulate the 'space and objects' theory. There would still be all the work of articulation and confirmation to do, for the subject. But it could be that this subject formulates and establishes the correctness of the space and objects theory without ever having spatial perception.

Suppose someone lives an ordinary life, perhaps working as the operator of a steamroller, until a disaster in middle age, when they lose all spatial perception. Perhaps this person has only non-spatial hearing left. At this point, people they know well might speak to them; the old steamroller might be operated in their vicinity. On hearing her old friend Ralph speak, our subject enters into conversation and reminiscence. It seems compelling to say she hears Ralph, and not just some sounds. When the steamroller is driven past, our subject not only hears it but recognizes it. Suppose now that our subject was born without spatial perception, but, perhaps exploiting some innate tendency to form such a theory, arrived at the 'space and objects' theory of her surroundings, including such details as the presence of a steamroller and of other people. When people talk in her vicinity, she can presumably be said to be hearing them, and not just sounds they make. When the steamroller drives past, she hears it, and not just noise emanating from it. When you think of this case, it is hard to see why spatial awareness would be needed for object perception. Spatial perception is not needed for object perception.

In *The Possibility of Knowledge*, Quassim Cassam considers the case of someone who is altogether incapable of spatial perception: this person has no experience of location or spatial relations, and no perception of the volumetric properties of objects, such as shape and size. Such a person, Cassam says, would be incapable of perceiving material objects. Of course, a bell might toll in the hearing of our subject. But there would be no reason to say that our subject had heard the bell, as opposed to the sound made by it. Cassam says, '[T]here would be no justification for saying that someone who is simply incapable of perceiving properties such as shape, size and solidity is nevertheless capable of perceiving material objects.'[6] Indeed, suppose that there is no such thing as hearing the volumetric properties of objects. Then 'a being with hearing but no touch or vision would be incapable of perceiving material objects.'[7] If the line of argument I have just sketched is correct, however, it is possible that someone could have the conception of space while being incapable of spatial perception; and, in that case, it seems entirely possible that they could perceive objects while being incapable of spatial perception.

3.3 Causality

If we are to do justice to the question of whether spatial awareness is required for perception of objects, however, we really have to look further at the question of just what work spatial awareness might be doing in perception of objects. I began with Lynn Robertson's idea that spatial awareness may be what makes it possible for vision to identify objects as the bearers of multiple visible properties. I remarked that Robertson and Treisman may be right that spatial perception is required for object perception, and yet it could still be that the fact that the spatial perception here is conscious is epiphenomenal. We have to understand what work the consciousness of spatial perception could be doing in object perception. I have just remarked, moreover, that it may be that Robertson's point is quite specific to vision; it may be that, in general, spatial perception is not required at all for perception of objects, so long as the subject has at any rate the conception of space and objects. To make further progress, I think we have to look more critically at the notion of object than I have done so far.

The core idea we need here is the notion of objects as internally 'causally connected', in Shoemaker's phrase.[8] I will argue that it is the demands of the notion of objects as internally causally connected that make it plausible that spatial awareness is required for object perception. To set out the case here, I have first to say something about the notion of 'internal causal connectedness'. We tend to think of causality as involving interactions between objects. For one thing to strike another, and thus make a difference to it, is our prototype of causation. Suppose a motorcycle strikes a barrier, bending it. The way the barrier is after the collision depends partly on the kind of thing that struck it, and how it was behaving at the time. But the way the barrier is after the collision also depends, in part, on its own properties. The way the barrier was before the collision will affect how it is after the collision. That is why it is worth putting some thought into exactly how to construct a barrier – what to make it of, what structure to give it, and so on. Its earlier properties are one of the determinants of its later properties. So here we have a kind of causality that is, as it were, internal to the object. And this internal or 'immanent' causality ticks away within the object even when it is not engaged in collisions or any interactions with other objects. If the object is stable, the reason it has its later properties is that it had those very properties earlier. If the object is unstable, still its having the properties it does later is a consequence of its having had the particular properties it had earlier. In general, an object's later properties are causally affected by its earlier properties.

We can put the question of whether spatial awareness is required for perception of objects as the question of whether spatial awareness is required for one to grasp the internal causal connectedness of perceived objects. Someone who only perceives sounds has no need to grasp the internal causal connectedness of anything. Robertson's patient R.M. had no grasp of an internal causal connectedness relating to the features he observed. But someone who hears a steamroller has to have some grasp of the causal dependence of the way the thing is later on the way the thing was earlier. Someone who hears a person talking has to have some grasp of how the way the person is later depends on the way the person was earlier. Otherwise, there really is no point to saying that we have here perception of a material thing. Without spatial awareness, could one have a grasp of the internal causal connectedness of what one perceives?

What does it come to, that one has this grasp of the internal causal connectedness of what one perceives? One answer is that it is a matter of knowing what difference a change in the way the object was earlier would make to how the object is later. If the barrier had been made of stronger material, it would not have bent. If it had been made of more brittle material, it would have broken. And so on. Knowing what difference interventions earlier might have made to how the object is later is an aspect of one's knowledge of its internal causal structure.

So there are these counterfactuals about how the later condition of the object depends on the earlier condition of the object. But, when causal influence is transmitted over time like this, we can always ask the following question: what is the mechanism by which causal influence is being transmitted here? To take a parallel case, suppose we establish that the water supply is a key element in public health. We say that the way the water supply is earlier affects how public health is later. If the water supply is chlorinated earlier, then there will be a difference in the levels of various diseases later, for example. When we have this counterfactual connection, we can ask: what is the mechanism by which causal influence is being transmitted here? The idea that disease spreads through the operation of miasmas is one theory as to mechanism; the germ theory is another. Now consider the case of the barrier again. We say: the way the object is earlier influences the way the object is later. For example, the fact that the barrier was painted earlier affects what colours it has now. And now we ask: what is the mechanism by which causal influence is being transmitted here? And an element in the answer will be: the sameness of the object itself. Physical objects themselves are the basic mechanisms by which we think of causal influence as being transmitted from earlier to later.

This is vivid if we consider the transmission of causal influence from place to place. Suppose, for example, that we take a blowtorch to the barrier, and heat it up. So now it's warm where the barrier is, at the side of the road. Now we move the barrier, still warm, to a backyard. It's now warm at that particular place, in the backyard. If we hadn't applied heat at the side of the road, it wouldn't now be warm in the backyard. So how has causal influence been transmitted from one place to another? What's the mechanism? The basic answer is the movement of the object. The movement of the barrier is the mechanism by which heat has been transmitted from one place to another. It's because the barrier was moved that we don't have here a case of action at a distance. This is, of course, a very simple case, much simpler than the transmission of disease. The case in which we appeal to object identity as our mechanism is the prototype of many other cases.

The point here is quite general. Sameness of the object over time is the prototypical mechanism by which causal influence is transmitted over time. Movement of physical objects is the prototypical mechanism by which causal influence is transmitted from place to place. These facts about the causal role of physical objects cannot be explained in terms of counterfactuals concerning how things would have been different at the later time if they had been different at the earlier time. They cannot be explained in terms of counterfactuals concerning how things would have been different at one place if they had been different at the other place. These facts about the causal role of physical objects cannot be explained in terms of these counterfactuals, because they have to do with the role of physical objects as the mechanisms that make these counterfactuals true. You might just as well hope to explain facts about the mechanisms by which diseases are generated and transmitted in terms of counterfactuals about how disease levels depend on the purity of the water supply. The facts about mechanisms explain these counterfactuals. They cannot be reduced to them.

So what does it come to, that we have this understanding of physical objects as the mechanisms by which causal influence is transmitted over time and from place to place? This, if anywhere, is where we find the role of spatial awareness. Suppose we go back to our hypothetical subject, who has only non-spatial perception and a purely theoretical grasp of the 'space and objects' hypotheses as to the causes of what she is hearing. Could this subject have an understanding of physical objects as the primitive mechanisms by which causal influence is transmitted over time, or from place to place? Certainly this subject could grasp counterfactuals about the dependence of things at one time on how things were at an earlier time, or the dependence of how things are at one place on how things were at another place. But, lacking spatial awareness, could this subject have an understanding of physical objects as the mechanisms by which causal influence is transmitted? We can certainly suppose that she uses the form of words 'physical objects are mechanisms', but it is hard to see what it could possibly add to the mere counterfactual connections themselves. Our subject has no grasp of the mechanistic explanation of these counterfactuals.

Consider, in contrast, the situation of a subject who does have spatial awareness. To make the point vivid, suppose we stay with our subject who has only non-spatial perception and a purely theoretical grasp of the 'space and objects' hypothesis. Let us suppose that our subject does have a very fully elaborated and well-confirmed version of the hypothesis. We can suppose, in fact, that it is structurally very similar to the picture that you and I have of the world we inhabit. And suppose, now, that one day things change for our subject. In some way that we need not go into, she achieves ordinary spatial awareness of her surroundings. In vision and touch in particular, she now has awareness of shapes and sizes and locations. What, if anything, will she learn?

I think it is just obvious that she will learn something, and that what she will learn is something about the world she inhabits. It is not as if all that she will learn here is something about her own or other people's mental states. We might suppose that our subject has very little interest in the psychological life as a topic for reflection. Her attention is firmly on the material world; in that sense, she is a material girl. Still, when confronted for the first time in her perceptual experience with all these shapes, sizes and locations, she is learning something new, something she did not know before. She is learning about the categorical objects and properties around her: the categorical objects whose persistence and movement are the mechanism by which counterfactual influence is transmitted over time and from place to place.

3.4 Does consciousness explain or is it only explained?

There is a basic split in how people currently think about sensory experience. On the one hand, it seems common sense that sensory experience plays a big role in our cognitive lives. It is because we have sensory experience of our surroundings that we know what is going on around us. Even more fundamentally, it is only because we have sensory experience that we have any ideas of the things and properties around us. Consider how we think about blindsight patients. Such patients can become remarkably fast, fluent and reliable at guessing what is in their blind field. No matter how well they do, however, we still say that they are 'guessing'. The patient doesn't have non-inferential perceptual knowledge of what's in the blind field. At best, the patient might construct an argument from her own inclination to make a particular guess as to what's in the blind field, together with background knowledge of the general reliability of her guesses in such contexts, to arrive at knowledge of what is in the blind field. Consciousness makes a difference. In the ordinary case, where one does see what's in front of one, one does not need this kind of inference to achieve knowledge. Because of the absence of sensory experience of the blind field, the blindsight patient does not have immediate perceptual knowledge of what's there.

We usually take it that sensory experience makes a difference to what knowledge we have. We also usually take it that sensory experience makes a difference to our grasp of concepts of the medium-sized world. In the absence of experience of colour, for example, you don't know what the colours are.

In contrast, though, many scientists and many philosophers working on perception take it that consciousness of itself makes no difference to our cognitive lives. The study of the brain systems that respond differentially to various external stimuli can, and generally does, proceed without any explicit notice being taken of phenomena of consciousness. And, when the topic of consciousness does become the focus of study, it is usually regarded as a somewhat puzzling phenomenon that has to be explained. It is not usually supposed that consciousness itself does any epistemological work. The idea is that our cognitive contact with our surroundings can be explained entirely in terms of brain mechanisms that are differentially sensitive to one or another aspect of our surroundings. Consciousness is an epiphenomenon in this process, something to be explained, but which itself explains nothing.

The role I have been setting out for spatial awareness belongs firmly with the first approach; it implies that there is significant epistemic work being done by sensory experience, that it makes a difference to our knowledge of our surroundings. My argument has been that there is more to our knowledge of the causal significance of concrete objects than counterfactuals relating what would have happened later to what might have happened earlier. We think of medium-sized objects as the prototypical mechanisms by which causal influence is transmitted from one time to another, or from one place to another. And a mere responsiveness of brain systems to external stimuli cannot explain how we have that conception. If we think in functional terms of the role of brain systems in cognition, we can explain only our knowledge of functional aspects of our surroundings. We cannot explain our having knowledge of concrete objects as the mechanisms that underlie these functional connections.

If this is correct, then spatial awareness is indeed required for perception of objects. In fact, a somewhat stronger conclusion than this seems implied. I want to approach the point by taking up a loose end I left dangling in Section 3.2. There I discussed the possibility of a 'purely theoretical' understanding of space, and I talked about someone who thinks in terms of a 'space and objects' theory postulated to explain their entirely non-spatial perceptions. I said that, if this makes sense, then we would have the right to say that this person does perceive spatial objects, even though they do not perceive their volumetric properties or locations. For example, if this person has non-spatial hearing, they can be said to be hearing people, or bells, rather than merely the sounds they produce.

One response to this argument would be to say that this subject is in fact hearing only sounds, rather than material objects; it is just that they have a theory about the causes of the sounds they hear. Now, I have said that, in fact, possession of such a theory would not of itself amount to a grasp of the idea of concrete objects as mechanisms by which causal influence is transmitted. To explain our grasp of that idea, we have to appeal to spatial awareness. But there is a parallel question here too. Consider a subject who has spatial awareness, but who is currently in the vicinity of an audible object. Is this subject hearing only the sound, but possessed of the conception of the kind of thing that could make such a sound? Or is this subject hearing the thing itself?

The distinctions we ordinarily draw here may not all bear much weight. But I think there is one condition we can say is required for someone to be said to have non-spatial perception of a concrete object. We can think of spatial awareness of an object – that is, a sensory perception in which one is aware of the volumetric properties of the thing and its location – as giving us a canonical identification of the object. If one is to be said to be perceiving the thing itself non-spatially, one has to be capable of recognizing the correctness of a canonical identification of that thing. For example, suppose I am listening to a pneumatic drill operating. I may hear it without being able to say even in what direction the thing is, and my hearing is not giving me information about the size and shape of the thing – if it turns out to be a quite non-standard size and shape, I can't say that I have been subject to an auditory illusion. But, if I am presented with the thing visually, I have to be capable of recognizing that this is the thing I heard. There has to be that specific connection between my non-spatial perception of the thing and a canonical identification of the thing for me to be said to have heard it, rather than merely a sound it produced.

3.5   Knowing what the world is like

I began with Lynn Robertson's point that the master map of locations, fundamental to object perception, to our ability to ascribe multiple properties to one and the same thing, seems to be the basis of our explicit spatial awareness. For disruption of spatial awareness disrupts this capacity for object perception, to see one thing as having multiple properties. I said, though, that this point would be consistent with thinking of awareness as an epiphenomenon in object perception, something that accompanies the process but plays no role in it. If the account I have set out is correct, however, spatial awareness does do work in our canonical identifications of concrete objects as the prototypical mechanisms for the transmission of causal influence. It is not a wheel that turns nothing.

This kind of approach, emphasizing the epistemic role of consciousness, is opposed to an approach to consciousness that emphasizes 'what it is like' to have one type or another of consciousness, in Nagel's famous phrase.[9] On the approach I am recommending, the role of spatial awareness is to provide one with knowledge of what the world is like. If I know that you have spatial awareness of your surroundings, that means in the first place that I know something about your cognitive access to the world. I know that you are in a position to grasp the idea of concrete objects as mechanisms for the transmission of causal influence.

Supposing that we should think of knowledge of another's conscious experience in terms of 'knowing what it is like' for that person does not give enough weight to the transparency of experience. It suggests that we can think of the other person's experience as being, as it were, something that is insulated from the world, as if I could access what your experiences are like without accessing your surroundings. But, of course, that is not true. Knowing what spatial awareness is like is, first and foremost, a matter of knowing what concrete objects and spatial relations are like. It is because spatial awareness gives us this epistemic access to the way the world is that it is required for perception of objects.

Notes

1. L. Robertson (2004) *Space, Objects, Minds and Brains* (Hove, East Sussex: Psychology Press).
2. Ibid., pp. 172–7.
3. A. Treisman (1988) 'Features and Objects: The Fourteenth Bartlett Memorial Lecture', *Quarterly Journal of Experimental Psychology*, 40A, 201–36.
4. Z. Pylyshyn (2007) *Things and Places: How the Mind Connects with the World* (Cambridge, MA: MIT Press), p. 34.
5. A.S. Bregman (1994) *Auditory Scene Analysis* (Cambridge, MA: MIT Press), pp. 5–6.
6. Q. Cassam (2007) *The Possibility of Knowledge* (Oxford: Oxford University Press), p. 120.
7. Ibid.
8. S. Shoemaker (1979) 'Identity, Properties and Causality', *Midwest Studies in Philosophy*, 4(321–42),246.
9. T. Nagel (1974) 'What is it Like to be a Bat?', *Philosophical Review*, LXXXIII, 435–50.

References

Bregman, A.S. (1994) *Auditory Scene Analysis* (Cambridge, MA: MIT Press).
Cassam, Q. (2007) *The Possibility of Knowledge* (Oxford: Oxford University Press).
Nagel, T. (1974) 'What is it Like to be a Bat?', *Philosophical Review*, LXXXIII, 435–50.
Pylyshyn, Z. (2007) *Things and Places: How the Mind Connects with the World* (Cambridge, MA: MIT Press).
Robertson, L. (2004) *Space, Objects, Minds and Brains* (Hove, East Sussex: Psychology Press).
Shoemaker, S. (1979) 'Identity, Properties and Causality', *Midwest Studies in Philosophy*, 4, 321–42.
Treisman, A. (1988) 'Features and Objects: The Fourteenth Bartlett Memorial Lecture', *Quarterly Journal of Experimental Psychology*, 40A, 201–36.

4
The Normative in Perception
Steven Crowell

4.1 Perception as epistemic warrant

Suppose I tell a friend that the rose bush on my front porch is in bloom. If he wonders how I know such a thing, I might respond that I saw it as I left for work this morning. If pressed, I might invite my friend home so he can see the bush for himself. What is supposed to be served by my report of what I saw? It is supposed to provide justification for what I say by grounding it in what I see. But what does 'grounding' mean here? My claim about the rose bush is a claim about an entity in the world, and I assume that looking at such an entity warrants the claim, that perceiving it underwrites the truth of what I say. Sceptics have often questioned this assumption, pointing out that perception can be deceptive in many ways; indeed, we may have no good reason for holding that any perception delivers the world as it is. When I make a judgement, the object about which I judge becomes a standard against which the judgement may be measured: if the object is as I say it is, then my judgement is true (i.e., does what it is supposed to do as this judgement); if not, not. But the sceptic reminds us that the fact that the *object* is a norm for judgement does not entail that *perception* can serve as warrant for judgements. Only if perception provides reliable access to objects can it serve this role. To show that it does, one might try to establish a connection between the content of perception and a causal process running from the object to the brain. But this has the disadvantage of severing ties between justification and the first-person experience of 'getting it right'. Whether this is a price we are willing to pay for an answer to the sceptic is something that others will have to decide. The sort of approach that interests me here, a phenomenological one, looks for the connection between perception and epistemic warrant in first-person experience.

Even in first-person terms, however, there are ways of describing the content of perception that make it hard to see how perception could serve as any kind of warrant for judgements.[1] One is to take it as what Hume called 'impressions of sense', a kind of sensuous givenness entirely distinct from our capacity to judge, reason, and use concepts – part of our 'sentience', as Robert Brandom puts it, not our 'sapience'.[2] As Wilfred Sellars argued, the deliverances of such a pre-rational system cannot hook up in a *justificatory* way with the conceptually formed content of judgements. If perception is to provide justification, it must afford access to what is referred to in the judgement in a form compatible with the content of the judgement– namely, as something that has a meaning. Thus not only the judgement, but also the perception, must be assessable in terms of possible success or failure. Perception itself must be beholden to norms.

A judgement's beholdenness to norms is inscribed in the act of predication. In saying something about an object, in characterizing it *as* something, predication establishes the object as a norm of attribution. It is this orientation toward a norm that distinguishes predication from mere combination and makes up an essential aspect of the judgement's meaning. In Husserl's terms, it is what makes the judgement an 'expressive' rather than an 'indicative' sign.[3] An indicative sign is causally related to what it signifies, as smoke indicates fire or a footprint indicates an intruder. But an expressive sign characterizes its signified in a determinate way, that is, it establishes conditions of satisfaction that can either meet or fail the object as it is. If perception is to provide warrant for our judgements, it too must have meaningful content, provide access to the object *as* something; it too must entail conditions of satisfaction that 'set up' or 'posit' (*Setzen*) its object as a norm. The question that requires phenomenological elucidation, then, is this: What is the normative *in* perception, and how does it come to be established?

It may be helpful here to recall Kant's two-tiered answer to this question. First, perception is receptive – that is, it involves sensibility – and is thus necessarily structured by the *apriori* forms of sensibility, space and time. To say that perceptual content is necessarily spatial and temporal is to say that space and time are normative for perception, that is, that they help establish what *counts* as perceptual content. Space and time do not suffice to account for perceptual content, however, since we do not perceive sensations but *things*, 'objects'. Perception thus involves those norms that establish what counts as an *object* – namely, the *apriori* 'categories' or 'concepts of objects in general'.[4] But what is the connection between these two norm-types? Are they independent of one another? Does one arise from the other? Is one reducible to the other? A phenomenology of perception should answer this question.

That this is an important question for phenomenology is clear from the fact that phenomenology holds perception to be the root form of *Evidenz*, the self-givenness of the 'things themselves'.[5] But interest in it is not restricted to phenomenology. Recently, John McDowell has argued that the connection between perception and justification can be preserved only if we acknowledge that what one 'sees' and what one 'judges' can be the same, namely, '*that* things are thus and so'.[6] So, for instance, I judge that 'my rose bush is in bloom', and when I look at it I do not merely see a rose bush; I see that my rose bush is in bloom. My perception, and not just my judgement, has a meaning, and this meaning has a structure identical to that of the corresponding judgement, namely, a *conceptual* structure. McDowell seems to hold that perceptual content must have a conceptual structure since only predication, an operation with concepts, establishes the object as a norm, places it in the space of reasons. But just this point makes McDowell's position elusive, for in perception no such predication takes place. In Kantian terms, perception is 'receptive': I simply open my eyes and look around. How, then, does conceptual normativity get a foothold in perception? Whence the suspension between success and failure that would allow us to ascribe a meaning or content to perception? McDowell's answer is mysterious: conceptual capacities are not merely exercised *upon* the givens of perception; rather, 'the relevant conceptual capacities are drawn on *in* receptivity.'[7] Perception has content because it belongs to creatures who have the capacity to reason, even though that content does not arise through explicit reasoning.[8]

McDowell is relatively uninterested in explaining how conceptual capacities can be drawn on in receptivity. His aim is therapeutic rather than constructive. But phenomenologists concerned with the question of the normative in perception have tried to go further. Daniel O. Dahlstrom, for instance, argues that 'Husserl's analyses of passive syntheses' provide a 'neglected alternative' between conceptualists like McDowell and information-semanticists like Fred Dretske or Pierre Jacob: 'His alternative is not, as it is for McDowell, to extend conceptuality to all levels of intentionality, but instead to identify levels of intentionality in the pre-conceptual yet indicatory syntheses constituting sensory fields.'[9] In other words, Husserl's analyses of passive synthesis should explain how perceptual content comes to be norm-governed independently of conceptual capacities and inferential relations. To this extent, Husserl tries to achieve in a transcendental *aesthetic* at least part of what Kant sought in transcendental *logic*. Indeed, Husserl himself in several places refers to the phenomenology of passive synthesis as a 'transcendental aesthetic'.[10] In this he stands directly opposed to neo-Kantians such as Paul Natorp, who, in Hegelian fashion, deny that sensibility can supply any norms distinct from logical (conceptual) ones. McDowell, in contrast, might be seen as a neo-Kantian in the Marburg tradition.[11]

In what follows I will touch upon the question of whether a phenomenology of perception shows that the content of perception can be both non-conceptual and yet responsive to norms. I say 'touch upon' because the phenomenological literature on perception is vast, and I will be restricting myself merely to a few central elements of Husserl's phenomenology that pertain to the issue of normativity. Beginning with Husserl's early account of perception, I argue that it conforms, in spite of some of its tendencies, to McDowell's idea that our conceptual capacities account for the normative moment in perception. I then consider whether Husserl's later genetic phenomenology, with its analysis of passive synthesis, uncovers a non-conceptual, yet normatively responsive, perceptual content, arguing that it too falls short.[12] In a final section, then, I argue that accounting for the normative in perception requires a shift of focus from the temporality of consciousness to embodied agency – a shift characteristic of post-Husserlian existential phenomenology that has been taken up recently by a number of phenomenologically oriented philosophers.[13]

4.2   Husserl's early (1893–1912) theory of perception: the primacy of the conceptual

I see a candle – a fat cylinder recently lit – burning on a stand on my dining room table. I see a bit of melted wax run down its side, which, I know, is blue but now looks almost black in the shadowy room. I move to get a closer look at where the wax has dripped, to see whether it is dripping uniformly on the side that is currently turned away from me. There look to be no drips on that side, while the blue colour stands out more clearly thanks to the light that shines on it from the kitchen. I turn away for a moment to check the source of the light and then resume my inspection of the candle, considering whether it is suitable for the arrangement of the table for dinner later that evening.

If we may take this description as typical of an act of perception, we may remark a few important features. First, perceiving is a temporally extended process that involves what might be called different 'moments': the candle seen now from this side, now from that, as I move about it. These moments do not distinguish themselves as individual 'pieces' that are simply strung together; we cannot think of them as a series of 'snapshots'.[14] Rather, they are subordinated to – they are what they are only within – the unity of the temporally extended perceptual act. Second, this unity has, as its correlate, an individual thing given meaningfully *as* something: a candle. Perceiving has intentional content. Third, the candle is there 'in person', in contrast to the way it would be present in memory or imagination, despite the fact that it has aspects and properties which are not currently in view. It is given throughout as itself, as continually one and the same thing. Fourth, the candle is seen to be qualitied in various ways – a specific shade of blue, a distinct cylindrical shape of a definite size – and, like the candle itself, these qualities are there objectively, that is, experienced as belonging to the candle independently of the current perceptual act. Fifth, each property is perceived as constant throughout the act, though it is seen from different spatial locations and thus appears differently. To adapt Charles Siewert's formulation: the cylinder appears differently from here than it does from over there, but it never appears otherwise than as a cylinder.[15] In Husserlian terms, the candle and its properties appear in 'profiles' or 'adumbrations' (*Abschattungen*), which change without our perceiving the candle or its properties as having changed.

From this we can also see something of the role that norms play in perception. For perception's temporally extended grasp of an identity in a manifold – whether it be the identity of the candle as its unseen sides become visible and the previously visible ones fall out of view, or the constancy of its properties in their changing profiles – presupposes something like an *ordering principle*, a norm, that establishes that later temporal moments are 'of the same thing' rather than of some newly appearing thing. Of course, we can also perceive the emergence of some new thing – the little Santa Claus that was hidden behind the candle now comes into view – but this itself presupposes that perceiving involves a norm by which we determine that the Santa Claus is not itself part of the candle. Thus, in perceiving the candle I must *perceptually* be able to determine that the back side, which shows itself to have no drips when I move to view it, belongs to the candle I was previously viewing.

Reference to the norm that governs such belonging is implicit in the act's content. The meaning of my act makes a kind of claim on the world, sets it up as a norm under something like a description, such that my perception is veridical *if* the world includes a candle just as I take it in my perception. But this 'taking' is more complicated than in the case of judgement, with its explicit predicative structure. To perceive something as a blue candle is to hold that the world contains this candle not only just as I take it in my perception, but also just as it *would* show itself if I moved around to view it from another angle. The normative in perception supports a peculiar sort of counterfactual, one that is both more familiar and also more obscure than the sort sustained by what is logically entailed by the judgement, 'This is a candle.' The difference lies in the fact that what is 'entailed' by the content of a perceptual act is not inferred, but *perceived*. As Alva Noë puts it, you have a 'perceptual sense' of the unseen backside; you don't *see* the backside, but the candle *looks* to have one; it is 'present now' in what you see. But this is quite different from 'thinking that' it has a backside.[16] If such a *perceptual* sense of the backside belongs to the intentional content of my perception, then, it can only be because that content responds to a norm that operates within perception itself.

Similarly, my experience of the candle as having an objective property – this particular blue colour – is governed by a norm, namely, by an 'optimal' way for the colour to appear. When I see the colour in shadow I grasp it as the very blue of the candle, even though the blue appears differently from here than it does from across the room. And when I move to the back where the lighting is different I get a *better* look at it, and eventually an *optimal* view: the real blue, the real cylinder. But this is not to say that the previous views did not see the blue itself; rather, the optimally appearing blue serves as a norm for what it itself *should* look like from here or there, in these or those lighting conditions, and so on. Our question is thus: what is the phenomenological basis for the presence of such normativity within perception?

Beginning in 1893, and continuing through 1905, Husserl sought to account for these features of perception by means of a kind of form/content schema. Though he modified certain aspects of this view after he introduced the phenomenological reduction in 1907, these changes did not affect his approach to the normative in perception. Only in the early 1920s, with the development of genetic phenomenology, did a new approach emerge. It is important, then, to consider Husserl's earlier position in some detail.

Husserl begins by linking the 'in person' character of the perceived object to the fact that it is given sensuously. To do so, however, he believes he must distinguish between the sensations themselves (*präsentierende Empfindungskomplexe*) and the quality of the perceived thing (*die präsentierte Bestimmungen*).[17] Sensations are not themselves intentional objects; sensing is an *Erlebnis* but not an *Akt* (Hua (38), pp. 23, 25). Thus, sensations by themselves cannot 'present' anything. To present some quality – the blue of this candle – they require an 'interpretation' (*Deutung*), which is achieved through the perceptual act's way of apprehending (*Auffassung*) the sensations *as* something – namely, as presentative of properties of the intentional object, 'this candle' (Hua (38), p. 27). Perceptual apprehension, then, includes a meaning, the *Auffassungssinn*, which remains the same through the changing *Empfindungserlebnisse*. Thanks to this meaning, the thing is not merely there in person but there in a *determinate* way, *as* something, as an object of a particular type.

Husserl's descriptions of perceptual intentionality all draw upon normative vocabulary: perception is not a mere succession of changing sensations but a kind of synthesis that has a 'distinctive and particular character' (Hua (38), p. 47); in perceptual experience one set of sensations does not merely replace another but provides a 'more perfect view' of the object; the object is 'given more clearly, richly, visually more adequately' (Hua (38), p. 144). The perceptual intention is characterized by a 'felt approximation' (*fühlbare Annäherung*) to a 'complete' perception (Hua (38), p. 145). The perception as a whole, and in each of its determinations, tends toward a 'maximum', an 'adequate construction' (*angemessene Abbild*) of the thing or quality in which we attain 'not merely an appearance of it' but 'the thing itself' (Hua (38), pp. 146, 213, 209, 254). All these descriptive terms presuppose a standard against which relative richness, completeness, clarity, and adequacy can be measured. Now, the defining feature of Husserl's early approach to such normativity is its dependence on tools borrowed from his analysis, in the *Logical Investigations*, of the way a *signifying* intention – paradigmatically, a judgement – relates to the perception in which the object it signifies is given. Husserl writes: 'We find between the elements [of perception] a peculiar descriptive relation, which I touched upon in another context, where I denoted it as the relation between intention and the *fulfillment* of the intention' (Hua (38), p. 144). Thus, Husserl takes a logical relation between concepts and intuitions as his model for the normative in perception.

The first thing to note is that this extension of the notion of fulfilment to perception is not at all obvious. Significative intentionality is general, symbolic and predicative. Thus, we can readily understand what would fulfil a judgement – say, 'The moon is at the horizon' – since the concepts involved determine what sorts of experience *could* establish the success or failure (truth or falsity) of the judgement. Perceptual intentionality, however, is individual, non-symbolic and pre-predicative. It is, thus, not immediately clear where the relation of fulfilment can get a foothold. How can fulfilment in perception provide 'the unity-constituting moment in the succession' of perceptual acts of one and the same thing? For instance, how can the experience of the candle I have from over here count as a 'better' look at it, or as 'fulfilling' something 'entailed' in an earlier moment of the perception? Why is it not merely something that *follows upon* that earlier view? Husserl wants to describe the kind of normativity that is indigenous to perception, but it might appear that he has merely smuggled in such normativity by his use of logical vocabulary to describe the perceptual process.

To test this suspicion we must consider, more particularly, how the intention/fulfilment structure is supposed to work in the case of perception. According to Husserl, the distinction between empty and fulfilled intentions maps onto a descriptive feature of all perception: every perception consists of some determinations that are 'directly' or 'authentically' presented and others that are only 'indirectly' or 'inauthentically' given (Hua (38), pp. 152–5, 210). For instance, the front side of the candle is directly presented by means of the current complex of sensations, while the back side is only indirectly presented. In the course of my perceiving, the indirectly given aspects of the object can come to be directly given and so partially fulfil the anticipation of completeness inherent in the perception as a whole. But *which* determinations are indirectly presented, and *how* do they come to be so?

What makes the case of perception interesting is, as Husserl points out, the fact that, while what is indirectly given – the back side of the candle, say – is 'indeterminate' (*unbestimmt*), this 'does not mean that it lacks determination'. The peculiar indeterminacy is not a featureless void but an 'incomplete determinacy' (Hua (38), pp. 58–9). The incompleteness in question is not to be measured against the idea of the complete *objective* determination of the thing, the thing with all its properties, whether known, unknown or even unknowable (Hua (38), pp. 26, 148). The molecular structure of the candle is not presented or intended, even indirectly, in my perception of it. Nor does the incompleteness refer to my *knowledge*, to what I might subjectively be said to know or think about the candle. The incomplete determinacy of the hidden side is, as Husserl puts it, neither a 'fantasy' nor 'conceptual thought'– neither an instance of imagining what it is like nor an instance of judging what it is like (Hua (38), pp. 150–1). The determinations are there, intended, in a way peculiar to *perception*. In Noë's terms again, we have a 'perceptual sense' of the back side. Thus, extending the intention/fulfilment structure to perception is plausible only if our perceptual sense of the emptily intended hidden side is *determinate enough* to support the idea of being fulfilled or unfulfilled (confirmed or disconfirmed) by subsequent perceptual experience. But *any* degree of determinateness involves a norm that establishes what the determination is *supposed* to be. Husserl suggests that the incomplete determinacy of the indirectly presented back side is 'mediated' by the directly presented perceptual properties (Hua (38), pp. 153–4). If this is so, then these properties must provide the standard for determining what is indirectly presented. How do they do this?

Husserl's answer is that the presentative contents – the directly experienced sensation-complexes – do not merely *display* (*darstellen*) the corresponding properties of the object but also serve 'a referential [*hinweisende*], symbolizing function'; they 'appear in a way analogous to that of *signs*'– not signs for one particular determination but for a delimited range of *possible* determinations (Hua (38), pp. 41, 37, 155, 60). Husserl knows that it could be misleading to speak of 'signs' here, since sensation-complexes are not themselves 'objects' that 'point toward something' (Hua (38), p. 36). Nevertheless, he argues that they exercise a 'symbolizing' function insofar as they operate according to the principles of 'similarity' and 'contiguity' (Hua (38), pp. 33). What is directly sensed – this blue sensation – primarily displays the objective blue of the candle, but 'mediately' it refers to, indicates or indirectly presents the hidden side through the principle of contiguity, and presents it, emptily, as blue through the principle of similarity. Thus, the applicability of the intention/fulfilment structure to perception turns on the claim that sensations can signify what they do not directly present, thereby opening up the possibility of further fulfilment – a better, richer, more complete look at the thing – by following up what the principles of similarity and contiguity enable us to anticipate.

Despite its initial plausibility,[18] there are obvious problems with such a view, and Husserl himself notes the most important one: even if we accept the idea that sensations can function analogously to signs, 'there is nothing that predestines the sensations for such a role' (Hua (38), p. 35). We are thus left to wonder what allows them to signify in the first place. Without an answer to that question we do not know how normativity gets a foothold in perception.

As mentioned earlier, for Husserl it is the 'apprehension-meaning' (*Auffassungssinn*) of the act of perceiving that allows sensations to signify by subjecting them to a particular 'interpretation' (Hua (38), pp. 27,

150). This apprehension-meaning is supposed to be pre-judicative, something distinctly perceptual, but even Husserl wonders what a distinctly perceptual meaning might be: 'Is it not the case that every apprehension is simultaneously an apprehension of a *conceptual* sort?'(Hua (38), p. 192). In some respects the apprehension-meaning seems to have the character of a concept: 'That which makes fulfillment possible ... is the generic form [*gattungsmäßig Form*],' a form that includes 'all' the perceptual object's determinations within itself, whether directly or only indirectly presented (Hua (38), pp. 61, 31). In other places, however, Husserl denies that it is conceptual: perceptual fulfilment, the 'closer determination' of the object, 'involves nothing of the conceptual' (Hua (38), p. 62). The perception of an object 'can be linked' in many ways with 'judgment (cognition) by means of general, conceptual representations'; nevertheless, 'not everything in the perception is judging in this sense.' When I perceive something as a candle, for instance, I 'apprehend what is there just as it is, without continually having to classify it', subsume it under a concept in an act of judgement. But here Husserl seems to waver: 'Isn't individual apprehension always a cognition, the apprehension of something thus and so determined, of such a type, etc., even if it is not expressible and no subordination (classification) has taken place?'(Hua (38), pp. 195–6).[19]

We have already seen one reason for doubting that the apprehension-meaning is conceptual. Our concept of a house consists of everything necessary for something to be a house, including many things that cannot be presented in perception at all, whether directly or indirectly – for instance, the property of being a dwelling-place. The *Sinn* of a perception, on the other hand, includes only perceptual features, both directly and indirectly presented. Perceiving a house from here is said to 'imply' (*impliziert*) what can only be seen from there: the roof, the back door, and so on. But such 'implication' is not supposed to be a matter of what can be inferred from something's being a house (Hua (38), p. 200). Further, in the course of an ongoing perceptual episode in which I successively transform indirectly presented determinations into directly presented ones, Husserl claims that 'a cognizing apprehension is carried out' to the extent that the whole process is governed by the 'type' (*Art*) contained in the apprehension-meaning. But, Husserl insists, this is 'cognizing, interpretive apprehension in another sense' than that which is governed by logical or inferential rules (Hua (38), pp. 192–3). It is 'another sense' since thinking, judging and cognizing are syntheses in which, as Husserl puts it, the ego is *actively* engaged, whereas perceiving does not involve this sort of mental activity.

Thus, the apprehension-meaning accounts for something like a type, a 'moment of universality' (standard, rule), in the act of perception, but it is not exactly conceptual, since perceiving does not actively subsume anything under a concept.[20] Further, the kind of articulation that belongs to judgement is absent in perception: my perception of a house 'includes' perception of its roof and windows but cannot be described as perceiving *that* it *has* these parts. These categorial structures are at most 'implicit' in the perception, and only with the judgement does the 'fact that' the roof is 'part' of the house become a phenomenological datum (Hua (38), pp. 199–200).

In his early phenomenology of perception, then, Husserl does not unambiguously answer his own question: 'Isn't every apprehension simultaneously apprehension of a *conceptual* sort?' For he has not clarified the nature of the universality that belongs to such apprehension, and with it the normative in perception.[21] Everything he says about it is compatible with McDowell's proposal that in perception conceptual capacities are receptively 'drawn into operation', since even McDowell denies that perception involves active judgement, the *exercise* of our conceptual capacities. Further, since Husserl, like McDowell, thinks that perception provides evidentiary warrant for our judgements – fulfils them – there must be some sense in which, for Husserl too, perception can be described as seeing '*that* things are thus and so'. My judgement that 'the house has a tiled roof' is justified not merely by seeing its tiled roof but by seeing *that* the house has a tiled roof.[22] This suggests that Husserl's early position does not succeed in clarifying a kind of perceptual meaning that would be governed by normative relations that are not themselves conceptual or inferential. And, since an account of our 'perceptual sense' of what is currently out of view but indirectly presented by what is directly in view depends on how apprehension-meaning is understood, one cannot unambiguously ascribe a phenomenology of non-conceptual perceptual content to Husserl's early work. But is such a clarification perhaps to be found in his later approach to perception as passive synthesis?

4.3 Passive synthesis, association and the genesis of meaning

Husserl's mature analysis of perception is found within his larger project of uncovering the transcendental 'genesis' of logic. Logic is understood as 'the general science of reason'; that is, the science that studies those laws holding among concepts and judgements which flow from their assessability in terms of truth and falsity. An analysis of perception belongs here, because logic is not the *source* of these normative distinctions. Rather, because 'consciousness contains a meaning within itself, relates itself…to objectivities, that is, relates itself to something identical', the question of whether such a relation is a 'rational or an irrational one' arises *prior* to conceptual activity (Hua (XI), p. 253). Thus, the phenomenological question is: 'What characterizes consciousness (and the meaning immanent to it) in each case as something that bears within itself truth and true being?'(Hua (XI), p. 254). Before it relates itself to things in a conceptual manner through judgements, consciousness is already attuned to the normative distinctions that logic will thematize explicitly. A phenomenology of logic, then, has the 'transcendental' task of 'illuminating' the 'originary sources' of the norms of truth-functionality 'all the way down to the bottom' in the 'passive syntheses' of consciousness – that is, to syntheses that do not require active stand-taking or predicating on the part of the ego (Hua (XI), p. 256). If, in Husserl's genetic phenomenology, perception is understood as that from which conceptual operations emerge, the phenomenology of perception as passive synthesis must already illuminate how normative relations get established among the intentional contents of consciousness. Here, then, if anywhere, one should find intentional content that is both meaningful and (as the *origin* of conceptual, logical relations) non-conceptual.

In the present context it is impossible to do justice to the way Husserl's genetic phenomenology both continues and revises his earlier approach to perception. We must content ourselves with noting two significant departures. First, in his early theory Husserl conceived the sensuous aspect of perception as a *non*-intentional stratum of 'sense-complexes', but genetic phenomenology conceives it as an at least *proto*-intentional field of 'appearance-systems' (Hua (XI), p. 11). And, second, Husserl's early theory was a static analysis of the relation holding between a given apprehension-meaning and its sensuous fulfilment. But, because genetic phenomenology makes explicit the *temporal* dimension of the intention/fulfilment schema, it thematizes the *origin* of such intentional content or meaning. On the basis of these innovations Husserl purports to uncover a 'primordial conformity to law' (*Urgesetzmäßigkeit*) already in perception, one that grounds the laws of logic without being identical to them (Hua (XI), pp. 319–20). In examining these innovations, then, we need to see whether the phenomenology of passive genesis really overcomes the weak point in Husserl's earlier theory – namely, that the supposedly pre-conceptual normativity in perception was traced to the suspiciously conceptual apprehension-meaning. Does the new analysis really show how logical laws arise from 'a primordial conformity to law' at the level of perception that is both genuinely intentional – that is, assessable in normative terms –and yet non-conceptual?

Husserl's later work abandons the idea of apprehension-meaning. The intentional object of perception is an 'objective meaning' (*gegenständlicher Sinn*), but this meaning does not arise through an apprehension that interprets meaningless elements of sense. Rather, it is now seen to arise from the interplay between anticipation and fulfilment among pre-objective, but proto-intentional, 'systems of appearance'. These are 'referential systems' (*Hinweis-systeme*) that operate not only at the level of perception proper – thus constituting the inner and outer horizons of perceptual objects – but now also at the sub-perceptual level of internal time-consciousness (Hua (XI), pp. 5, 11). The latter are particularly important for Husserl, since they provide the basis for the former. For instance, the referential system that allows us to perceive a thing as the bearer of determinate properties (e.g., the way in which the changing colour-adumbrations of the objective property, blue, are seen to 'belong' to the identical candle) is grounded upon a sub-perceptual referential system in which the entire temporally flowing visual field is organized according to what stands out, gets 'noticed', recedes, and so on. This involves a kind of proto-intentionality, since the temporality that belongs to the flow as such is not a mere succession of data but is structured in such a way that what is experienced 'now' is always accompanied by a 'retention' of the now just past and, on that basis, a 'protention' or anticipation of what is to come.

In his later theory, Husserl also introduces the term 'apperception' to designate what he previously called 'incomplete determinacy'– namely, the way the hidden aspects of a perceived object are nevertheless present in perceptual experience. 'Apperceptions are intentional experiences that have in themselves a consciousness of something perceived but which is not self-given in them' (Hua (XI), p. 336). As an example of the 'laws of genesis' he mentions the laws that regulate the 'formation of apperceptions', that is, the formation of meaningful intentional content. Among these is a law of 'motivation', in which what is self-given in the perception does not merely contain that which is not self-given, but, rather, '*refers* to this other as belonging to it' (Hua (XI), pp. 338). But how can what is self-given motivate some *specific* range of further content such that a meaningful whole or identity is constituted – that is, so that we can speak of 'fulfilment' or its failure? What defines the scope of an apperception, establishing what would *count* as coherent (*einstimmig*) further experience?

One answer would be: the conceptual rule governing the type of object given in the perception. But Husserl is committed to the idea that perceptual content at the level of passive synthesis is non-conceptual. A different answer might be sought in genetic phenomenology's deeper understanding of the body's role in perception. By means of the covariance relation that obtains between my bodily movements and the appearances that accompany them, something like a non-conceptual norm is established, a perceptual optimum that grounds our perceptual anticipation of an incompletely determinate range of further experiences of the same thing.[23] But, for Husserl, this is only the beginning of an answer. In *Ideas II*, for example, he first describes how 'in all experience of spatio-temporal thingly objects, *the body* [*Leib*] "is involved" as the perceptual organ of the experiencing subject.'[24] But, on his view, the body is not an *irreducible* aspect of perceptual experience. Instead, 'we must investigate the constitution of this corporeality' itself, an investigation that fixes upon the phenomenon of 'localization': when I touch my left hand with my right, for example, I do not merely discover tactile properties of the left hand (smooth, soft) but also experience sensations of being touched, 'localized' in the left hand. It is by means of sensations of this latter kind (as well as the closely related 'kinaesthetic' sensations that accompany my bodily movements) that the body is constituted for consciousness *as* the living body (*Leib*): '[It] is not that the physical thing is now richer, but instead *it becomes body*, it senses' (Hua (IV), pp. 145/152). Husserl thus believes that, to explain the normative in perception, it is first necessary to show how the body is constituted in the *temporality* of the appearance-systems or referential systems themselves. Before we can assess the potential found in Husserl's phenomenology of embodiment, then, we must examine this idea.

To account for the norms governing apperceptions, Husserl reflects on the constitution of sensory fields prior to the emergence of object-constituting apperceptions. At the level of the temporal organization of a sensory field – the 'lowest level of passivity' – he purports to find a kind of 'coherence of meaning-giving' that underlies the perceptual genesis of 'objective meaning' (Hua (XI), p. 254). These are nothing but the sub-perceptual 'referential systems' we noted earlier, the saliences that emerge within the temporally flowing visual field as a whole prior to its constitution as a field of things with properties. Dahlstrom summarizes what he (and Husserl) believes to be accomplished by this move, namely, identification of genuinely 'non-conceptual yet intentional contents of experience' in which 'sensory fields come to be constituted passively (preconceptually) yet with an intentional and, to that extent, epistemically normative structure.'[25] But what provides the normative moment here? As Dahlstrom puts it: 'How do these sensory fields manage to be informative and thus have an intentional or proto-semantic character?'[26] It is not enough to appeal to the 'retention–protention' structure of the temporality of consciousness, since the point here is to explain how the protention or immanent anticipation of something *definite* can arise *within* this structure. What is it about what *appears in* the temporal flow that allows protention to involve an anticipation 'of' something particular, that is, to have a 'proto-semantic' character?

Disappointingly, Husserl's answer appeals to 'laws of association'. To be sure, such laws are not psychological: 'For us the term association designates a form and conformity to law of immanent genesis that belongs continually to consciousness in general – not, however, as for the psychologists, a form of objective, psychophysical causality' (Hua (XI), p.117). From causal laws no meaningful content could arise. Yet associative laws are not supposed to be conceptual either. At the level of passive genesis, 'talk of universality is merely a crutch for an indirect description that points toward the phenomenon itself. For one may not think here on logical concepts, on classifying or generalizing universalities' (Hua (XI), p. 40). Of what sort, then, are the phenomenological laws of association that generate intentional content? Again, Husserl's answer is a familiar one. As Dahlstrom explains: 'What makes association a theme for phenomenology and not merely for objective psychology ... is [its] "indicatory" character.'[27] And, when Husserl specifies what kind of indication is meant here, we find that we have come full circle: association involves relations of 'similarity', 'contiguity', 'contrast' and so on.[28]

The problem, of course, is that this indicatory structure is no different from what we encountered in the earlier 'sign' theory of sense-complexes, in which the latter were held to indicate by means of similarity and contiguity. There Husserl admitted that 'nothing predestines the sensations' to play a signifying role and was forced to invoke the apprehension-meaning to explain how sensations are subordinated to the normativity constitutive of perceptual intentionality. The supposed indicatory character of sensations could not *account* for the normative in perception, nor was Husserl able to articulate an unambiguously non-conceptual, purely perceptual, notion of apprehension-meaning. In his later genetic phenomenology Husserl holds that appearance-systems, unlike sensation-complexes, are proto-intentional. But if what makes them so is their indicatory character, and if this is traced to the very same associations that proved insufficient in the earlier account, little progress has been made. Thus, it is hard to see how the claim that sensory fields have an 'epistemically normative structure' is supported by Husserl's actual analyses of passive synthesis. In Kantian terms, the syntheses of 'apprehension' and 'reproduction' do not add up to *perceptual* content; it is only with the 'synthesis of recognition in a concept' that we can speak of a normativity other than the spatio-temporal sort that governs *sensations*.[29]

Even if there is a pre-conceptual level of consciousness where concatenations of sensory fields emerge through associative syntheses of similarity, contrast and contiguity – and even if all higher-order conceptual syntheses (such as judgement) presuppose such an organized 'pre-given' sensory field – we still do not know how such association can admit of normative assessment, without which talk of 'intentionality' is empty. Association is, at best, a necessary condition of perception. Even if it is not conceived psychologically or causally, association is not the sort of thing that can be said to succeed or fail: contents just are or are not associated as similar, contiguous or whatever, and by itself this cannot lead to 'anticipations' that might or might not be fulfilled. Thus, though the sensory fields to which association gives rise are supposed to play an indicatory role, we still have no idea how they can do so.[30]

4.4   Sensorimotor knowledge and non-conceptual normativity

At this point we should return to the suggestion that the normative in perception is grounded in our bodily engagement with the world. In his early theory Husserl made reference to a 'maximum' appearance of something, the perspective which provides the standard for what counts as a better – richer, fuller – view of the thing. But the earlier theory could not explain how this optimal view of the thing's shape or colour managed to establish itself *as* optimal, *as* a norm within perception. In genetic phenomenology Husserl believes he can address this issue by appeal to the body. We recall that Husserl described one's ongoing experience of perceptual aspects as guided by a *'felt* approximation' to a 'complete perception' (Hua (38), p. 145). It is this idea – namely, that the standard of wholeness does not govern the process conceptually but *feelingly* – which Husserl's later theory links to the body: 'The qualities of material things as aestheta, such as they present themselves to me intuitively, prove to be dependent on my qualities, *the make-up of the experiencing subject*, and to be related to *my Body and my "normal sensibility"* ' (Hua (IV), pp. 56/61).

As this reference to 'my "normal sensibility"' suggests, however, Husserl does not trace the normative in perception to the body's movements *per se* but to the correlation between one set of appearances (the 'kinaesthetic sensations' that are the conscious *traces* of such movements) and another (the sensations that adumbrate the properties of the perceived thing). He thus remains within a temporal analysis of consciousness. But we have already encountered reasons to think that this 'felt approximation' to a norm – and so also the origin of perceptual meaning – cannot be grounded in consciousness alone, at least if consciousness is understood as a monadological 'absolute' temporal flow. Such a perspective inevitably elides the role of the body and its responsiveness to those norms that define our capacity to *act*, and I shall argue that it is in these practical capacities that standards for what counts as successful perception find their ground.[31]

Husserl's analysis turns on a distinction between 'presenting acts of sensation' (those sensations whose destiny is to adumbrate objective qualities of the thing) and the 'series of kinaesthetic sensations' upon which the former are 'dependent...as motivated' (Hua (IV), pp. 56/61). This motivational dependency consists in the following: the kinaesthetic awareness of my bodily movements (including the movement of my sense organs) makes up a 'system' of sensations that admits of a distinction between 'normal' functioning –'systems of orthoaesthetic perceptions'– and abnormal functioning (Hua (IV), pp. 58–75/63–80). Instances of the latter include the kinaestheses belonging to my sense of touch when I have burned my finger or tongue, or the feeling of restricted control in my arm when it has 'fallen asleep'. Here 'normal' simply means what is regular or usual; what normally happens. But this provides the basis for a normal appearing of *things*, since kinaesthetic sensations are conditionally related to a second system of sensations, which present objective qualities: '*If* the eye turns in this way, *then* so does the "image"' (Hua (IV), pp. 58/63). The normal kinaesthesis of eye movement 'motivates' a series of sensings of the thing in an ordered way: if I move my eyes this way, then the candle will (i.e., *ought to*) appear in just that way.

According to Husserl, the 'ought' here derives from the fact that a normally functioning kinaesthetic system constitutes, as its correlate, a second 'system of orthoaesthetic perceptions', namely, the normal appearings of things and their properties. An objective world is possible only if 'the subject has its system of orthoaesthetic experiences and has thereby, continuously over against itself, the one spatio-temporal causal nature. This again presupposes that its Body is constituted in

systems of orthoaesthetic perceptions: thus the Body cannot be patho-
logical throughout …' (Hua (IV), pp. 74/79).[32] Looking at the candle, I
have a 'perceptual sense' of the back side because I am feelingly aware
of the conditional relation between the kinaesthetic referential system
and the system of adumbrative appearances of the thing motivated by
it. And within this system, Husserl argues, 'there stands out … the "optimal givenness" in which the thing comes to the fore along with the
properties that "befit it itself" '– that is, the thing seen 'in sunlight, on
a clear day, without the interference of other bodies that might affect
the colour-appearance'; seeing it 'in air' rather than through water, and
so on (Hua (IV), pp. 80/75, 65/60). Normal experience establishes for
itself an optimum, a kind of standard of variation: the cylinder appears
like this from here and like that from there because these appearings
are ordered variations of how it appears optimally, that is, from the *best*
angle and in the *best* lighting conditions. Thus, there is a kind of norm
in perception itself.

Husserl here touches on what Noë calls 'sensorimotor knowledge': 'We
experience the presence of what is out of view by understanding, implicitly, that our relation to what is in view is such that movement of the eyes,
or of the body, brings it into view, and such that movements of the thing
itself make a sensory difference to what we experience.'[33] What Husserl
saw as the relation of conditional motivation between two 'orthoaesthetic
systems of sensation' is, for Noë, a 'sensorimotor coupling': there is a perceptual sense of the hidden sides (and *pari passu* the normally expected
appearing of qualities like colour or shape in these or those conditions)
'because we are coupled with [those hidden sides] in a special, immediate, familiar sensorimotor manner'.[34] Such coupling is norm-governed:
getting a *better* look at something depends on knowing *how* to look – that
is, being skilled at bringing oneself into the circumstances that will allow
the optimal look to emerge. As Charles Siewert glosses it: 'To get a better
look at something is to do something, to look at it better – it is to exercise
relevant sensorimotor skills. Thus what it is for perspectivally varying
appearances to be "appropriately related" amongst themselves so as to
constitute the appearance of a constant object is something understood
only by exercising or enacting these skills.'[35]

In his frequent references to the 'I can,' Husserl clearly recognizes
this aspect of what we might call 'perceptual practice'. But, as we saw,
he held that the relevant normativity arose from the co-ordination of
kinaesthetic with presentative sensations. Practices and abilities like
walking around a candle or playing tennis or typing, however, are *bodily*
skills that cannot be reduced to covariance relations between systems of

appearances in consciousness. The body cannot itself be constituted as a function of temporal associations, nor can the norm of proper functioning relevant to bodily skills be understood as arising from a system of kinaesthetic sensations. For a skill (sensorimotor knowledge) gains its normative sensitivity from its being 'out for' something, its trying to accomplish a task, and *trying* is not any kind of sensation. The task in question need not be conceptually mediated – my concept of walking is not involved in my exercise of that skill – but any such task must be responsive to the distinction between success and failure. Thus, while sensorimotor knowledge does involve the body's sense or 'feeling' of itself as being appropriately situated within its project, the normative concept of the 'appropriate' does not arise from the feeling but from the body's own *way of being*.[36]

It is true that I feel movement toward the optimum, toward the better look. The norm is not established by the *feeling*, however – nor by any other kinaesthetic sensation or system of sensations – but by the practice itself: it is the skill or ability, and not the feeling which accompanies it, that contains success conditions, even if the skill in question is only that of being able to walk or control one's eye movements. The success conditions for such abilities (looking, walking) – unlike those for games like tennis or practices like using a microscope – are tied to the *facticity* of the body; its feeling of 'equilibrium' is keyed to specific contingent features of its make-up: its upright posture, its bi-symmetry, its eyes in front, and so on.[37] The baseline of perceptual normativity lies here, and not in the feeling of striving for or of having sustained that equilibrium, or in the 'orthoaesthetic' sensations that accompany the successful exercise of bodily skills.

To contrast the responsiveness to norms of bodily skills with our responsiveness to conceptual norms, Hubert Dreyfus distinguishes between 'success conditions' and 'conditions of improvement'.[38] Whereas success conditions require a concept – that is, a conception of the end to be achieved by a certain series of bodily movements – conditions of improvement require no such concept. They pertain to a level of bodily comportment (skills and abilities) that is usually bound up with action that is explicitly goal-directed, instrumental and conceptually mediated, but the kind of normativity involved at that level does not *derive* from the success conditions of the action. Phenomenological description of such skilful coping shows that 'the body of the performer is solicited by the situation to perform a series of movements that *feel appropriate*, without the agent needing in any way to anticipate what would count as *success*.'[39] In playing tennis, for instance, the player's skill consists in his body's ability to seek and maintain a kind of equilibrium or 'optimal gestalt' throughout a rally, reaching to attain optimal contact at the sweet spot, moving effortlessly toward the appropriate position for the next shot, and so on. But 'the tennis player cannot represent the optimal gestalt that, nonetheless, directs the movements of his body.'[40] In contrast to Husserl's account, in which perceptual normativity is grounded in the normal kinaesthetic sensations that motivate our perceptual sense of what is to come, Dreyfus sees the motivation moving the other way: the body responds to 'affordances' in the total situation as it attempts to maintain its equilibrium.

The optimal gestalt that serves as a norm or condition of improvement for such ubiquitous behaviour is not a visual gestalt that is displayed *for* consciousness but a gestalt that holds between the body and its world (situation). And, for this reason, bodily responsiveness to such conditions of improvement is also the source of a pre-conceptual *perceptual* normativity. As Merleau-Ponty describes it: 'The distance from me to the object is not a size which increases or decreases, but a tension which fluctuates around a norm. An oblique position of the object in relation to me is not measured by the angle which it forms with the plane of my face, but felt as a lack of balance, as an unequal distribution of its influences on me.'[41] As Wakefield and Dreyfus write, 'our bodies have a capacity to respond to moment-to-moment stimulation in a way which tends to promote an optimal fit between perception and action.'[42] This explains how a perceptual optimum can emerge, because it contextualizes the mere feeling of equilibrium by reference to the improvement conditions of a practice, bringing with it an optimum for the *things involved* in that practice. The perceptual optimum of a tennis ball in flight is relative to the 'best' place for my body to be in order to return it; the optimal view of a painting depends on whether my perceiving it is embedded in the practice of aesthetic appreciation or in that of the restorer interested in its facture; and the kind of optimum that Husserl focuses on – the view of the 'real' colour or the 'real' shape of a thing – belongs, as we saw, to the exercise of those skills and abilities keyed to the body's 'default' state of equilibrium: upright, bi-symmetrical, forward-looking view, and so on.[43] What Merleau-Ponty calls 'motor intentionality',[44] then, is the source of the *'fühlbare Annäherung'* to which Husserl refers: perception is feelingly guided by an optimum because it takes place in the context of practices in which the body seeks to improve its stance in, and by means of, its dealings with things in the world.

Of course, much more needs to be said about how specific normative or conceptual aspects of the perceptual object (e.g., its characteristic of being a thing-with-properties) emerge from such practical coping or 'trying'. But, if an approach such as this is on the right track, then we must, I think, conclude that, though Husserl's account of the body opened the door to an understanding of a distinctive kind of normativity in perception, it was left for later phenomenologists like Heidegger and Merleau-Ponty, who emphasize the primacy of practical engagement with the world, to show us how we ought to walk through it.[45]

Notes

1. Here I mean by 'content' only that which, in the mental process picked out by the term 'perceiving', is (in Locke's phrase) 'before the mind'. As will be clear in what immediately follows, the notion of content must actually be restricted to something that has a semantic structure, a meaning. It is not necessary to defend this restriction here, since I am not considering third-person accounts of perception, but only first-person ones, in which perception is always 'intentional', that is, *of* something *as* something.
2. R. Brandom (1994) *Making it Explicit* (Cambridge, MA: Harvard University Press), pp. 275–7.
3. E. Husserl (1970) *Logical Investigations*, Vol. I, trans. J.N. Findlay (London: Routledge and Kegan Paul), pp. 269ff.
4. I. Kant (1968) *Critique of Pure Reason*, trans. N.K. Smith (London: Macmillan), p. 126 (A93/B126).
5. Husserl's own theory of *Evidenz* – of epistemic warrant – required him to 'give the name "perception" to each fulfilling act of confirmatory self-presentation, to each fulfilling act whatever the name of "intuition", and to its intentional correlate the name of "object"'. I will here ignore this aspect of Husserl's theory and deal exclusively with *sense*-perception. See E. Husserl (1970) *Logical Investigations*, Vol. II, trans. J.N. Findlay (London: Routledge and Kegan Paul), pp. 764–5, 785.
6. J. McDowell (1994) *Mind and World* (Cambridge, MA: Harvard University Press), p. 9. In (2009) 'Avoiding the Myth of the Given', *Having the World in View: Essays on Kant, Hegel, and Sellars* (Cambridge, MA: Harvard University Press), pp. 256–72, McDowell modifies his views somewhat to make room for content that 'is not propositional but intuitional' (p. 260) – distinguishing between content that has the form of a judgement and 'intuitional' content that does not, where the former is 'discursive' or 'articulated' and the latter is not (p. 262). Both kinds of content remain conceptual, however. Thus, since our concern is with phenomenology and not primarily with McDowell, we shall leave this otherwise welcome clarification out of our account.
7. McDowell, *Mind and World*, p. 9.
8. McDowell attributes the meaningful character of perception to our capacity for language, to our general *Bildung*, not to reason as such. But the salient aspect of language and *Bildung* here lies in its introduction of the possibility of *inferential* relations, that is, reason. Thus, there is a sense in which even McDowell's distinction between 'propositional' and 'intuitional' content retains a *certain* rationalistic tenor, since intuitional content is still 'content' only by virtue of its potential connection with inferential norms.

9. D.O. Dahlstrom (2007) 'The Intentionality of Passive Experience: Husserl and a Contemporary Debate', *The New Yearbook for Phenomenology and Phenomenological Philosophy*, VII, 1–18; here pp. 5, 18. See also W. Hopp (2008) 'Husserl on Sensation, Perception and Interpretation', *Canadian Journal of Philosophy*, 38(2), 219–46; and W. Hopp (2008) 'Conceptualism and the Myth of the Given', *European Journal of Philosophy*, 17(3), 363–85.

10. See, for instance, E. Husserl (1966) *Analysen zur passiven Synthesis (1918-1926)*, Husserliana Bd. XI, M. Fleischer (ed.) (The Hague: Martinus Nijhoff), p. 295. Henceforth cited in the text as Hua (XI).

11. See S. Crowell (2010) 'Transcendental Logic and "Minimal Empiricism": Lask and McDowell on the Unboundedness of the Conceptual', in R. Makkreel and S. Luft (eds) *Neo-Kantianism in Contemporary Philosophy* (Bloomington: Indiana University Press), pp. 150–74.

12. But see T. Mooney (2010) 'Understanding and Simple Seeing in Husserl', *Husserl Studies*, 26(1), 19–48, for a nuanced account of the conceptual and non-conceptual aspects of perception in Husserl; and Hopp, 'Husserl on Sensation, Perception and Interpretation,' for a different approach to the question of '*how* perceptual experience can transform a mere thought into knowledge' (p. 219).

13. See, for instance, A. Noë (2004) *Action in Perception* (Cambridge, MA: The MIT Press); E. Thompson (2007) *Mind in Life* (Cambridge, MA: Harvard University Press); S. Kelly (2000) *The Relevance of Phenomenology to the Philosophy of Language and Mind* (New York: Routledge).

14. For a critique of the 'snapshot' idea, see Noë, *Action in Perception*, pp. 35–73.

15. See C. Siewert (2006) 'Is the Appearance of Shape Protean?', *Psyche*, 12(1), 1–16; http://www.theassc.org/vol_12_2006 (last accessed November 23, 2011).

16. A. Noë (2006) 'Experience of the World in Time', *Analysis*, 66(1), 26.

17. E. Husserl(2004) *Wahrnehmung und Aufmerksamkeit: Texte aus dem Nachlass (1893-1912)*, Husserliana Bd. XXXVIII, T. Vongehr and R. Giuliani (eds) (Dordrecht: Springer), p. 152. Henceforth cited in the text as Hua (38).

18. Even Noë ('Experience of the World in Time', p. 29) uses the language of referring, indicating and implying. Of the perceptual grasp of an event, he writes: 'In this way, what is present, strictly speaking, *refers to* or is *directed toward* what has happened and what will happen. Just as in a way the front of the tomato is directed toward the back – indicates the space where the back is to be found – so the present sound implicates a temporal structure by referring backwards and forwards in time.'

19. Foreshadowing his later theory, Husserl speculates that what is needed is an entirely new concept of *Sinn*: in one case, the (non-conceptual) *Sinn* governs the fact that a multitude of perceptual 'appearances' belong to one and the same object; in another direction, (conceptual) *Sinn* governs the 'full determinateness' of the (perceptual) object (Hua (38), p. 31n).

20. In his later phenomenology of perception Husserl will develop the concept of type (*Typus*) as a way to mediate between passivity and activity. We cannot enter into the details of that account here, but see D. Lohmar (2008) *Phänomenologie der schwachen Phantasie*, Phaenomenologica 185 (Dordrecht: Springer), especially pp. 103–46.

21. For the same reason, the notion of 'noematic meaning', introduced in 1913, does nothing to alter the picture, for it too is ambiguous between a conceptual and a non-conceptual interpretation. This ambiguity has given rise to a lively debate, which can be reviewed in J. Drummond (1990) *Husserlian Intentionality and Non-Foundational Realism* (Dordrecht: Kluwer).

22. See Husserl, *Logical Investigations Vol. II*, pp. 773–8 and 782–4 on categorial intuition and perception of 'states of affairs'. For an argument that the *Logical Investigations* contains ambiguities on this point that are clarified in Husserl's later work, see Mooney, 'Understanding and Simple Seeing in Husserl'.

23. For a Husserlian analysis along these lines, see J. Drummond (1979–80), 'On Seeing *a* Material Thing *in* Space: The Role of Kinaesthesis in Visual Perception', *Philosophy and Phenomenological Research*, 40, 19–32. Husserl's approach is brought into dialogue with McDowell in M. Barber (2008) 'Holism and Horizon: Husserl and McDowell on Non-conceptual Content', *Husserl Studies*, 24(2), 79–97.

24. E. Husserl, *Ideen zu einer reinen Phänomenologie und phänomenologischen Philosophie, Zweites Buch*, Husserliana Bd. IV, Marly Biemel (ed.) (The Hague: Martinus Nijhoff), pp. 144–5; English translation (1989) *Ideas Pertaining to a Pure Phenomenology and to a Phenomenological Philosophy, Second Book*, trans. R. Rojcewicz and A. Schuwer (Dordrecht: Kluwer), p. 152. Hereafter cited in the text as Hua (IV), with German pagination followed by the pagination of the English translation, for example, here (Hua (IV), pp. 144/152).

25. Dahlstrom 'The Intentionality of Passive Experience', pp. 16, 17.

26. Dahlstrom, 'The Intentionality of Passive Experience', p. 14.

27. Dahlstrom, 'The Intentionality of Passive Experience', pp. 14–15.

28. The clearest discussion of these issues is in E. Husserl (1973) *Experience and Judgment*, trans. J.S. Churchill and K. Ameriks (Evanston: Northwestern University Press), pp. 74–5: 'It is the phenomenon of associative genesis which dominates this sphere of passive pregivenness, established on the basis of syntheses of internal time-consciousness....That association can become a general theme of phenomenological description and not merely one of objective psychology is due to the fact that the phenomenon of *indication* [*Anzeige*] is something which can be exhibited from the point of view of phenomenology.'

29. Kant, *Critique of Pure Reason*, pp. 130–1 (A97).

30. Husserl makes much of the phenomenon of temporally emergent contrast – an unexpected noise, for instance, that stands out from an ongoing background of silence. For him, such contrasts underlie the constitution of what 'belongs' and what does not, and are thus the basis for subsequent perceptual *object*-identification. We cannot examine this suggestion fully here, but it should be clear that, taken by themselves, such 'contrasting' sensations – that is, *differences* within the sensory appearance-systems – can be seen to 'indicate' something only if the ongoing 'undifferentiated' flow is *already* indicative, that is, does not merely flow but 'points' to 'more of the same'. But the question was precisely how it is able to do this.

31. As Joseph Rouse has argued, however, this move, rather than establishing the idea that perception is pre-conceptual, might force us to revise what

'conceptuality' itself *is*: by 'taking more seriously the worldly and bodily character of language, and the linguistic character of thought', we would not need 'to place limits upon the conceptual domain, but to recognize it as a finite, embodied worldly capacity all the way up.' J. Rouse (2005) 'Mind, Body, and World: Todes and McDowell on Bodies and Language', *Inquiry*, 48(1), 38–61, p. 40.

32. Here Husserl makes plain that this system is not just part of the body, but *constitutes* it *as* 'living body'. Thus, as we noted earlier, embodiment is not primordial but arises from temporal associations within consciousness.

33. Noë, 'Experience of the World in Time', p. 26.

34. Noë, 'Experience of the World in Time', pp. 26–7.

35. Siewert, 'Is the Appearance of Shape Protean?', pp. 14, 15. For a fuller elaboration of this view, see C. Siewert (forthcoming) 'Intellectualism, Experience, and Motor Understanding', in J. Schear (ed.) *The Myth of the Mental?*

36. In (2006) 'Aesthetic Judgment and Perceptual Normativity', *Inquiry*, 49(5), 403–37 – an important article that deserves more discussion than we can give it here – Hannah Ginsborg draws upon Kant's notion of aesthetic judgement to introduce a concept of 'perceptual normativity' that is close to what we are examining in this paper. The idea is that 'perceptual experience…involves the awareness of its own appropriateness with respect to the object perceived'; or, in Kantian terms, that perception is characterized by a consciousness of *exemplarity* – one's ability to take oneself 'to be perceiving an object as [anyone] ought to perceive it' (p. 403). For Ginsborg, such normativity is not to be traced to our conceptual capacities; it is 'primitive'. But, as I will suggest below, we must take the analysis of perceptual normativity back to our ability to be norm-responsive as such – an analysis that leads first to our bodily skills and practices but ultimately to our nature as (in Heidegger's phrase) 'beings in whose being that very being is an *issue*'. The argument for this can be found in S. Crowell (2007) 'Conscience and Reason: Heidegger and the Grounds of Intentionality', in S. Crowell and J. Malpas (eds) *Transcendental Heidegger* (Stanford: Stanford University Press), pp. 43–62.

37. Hubert Dreyfus notes the implications of this for the project of AI: 'Merleau-Ponty's and Freeman's account of how we directly pick up significance and improve our sensitivity to relevance depends on our responding to what is significant for *us* given our needs, body size, ways of moving, and so forth. … If we can't make our brain model responsive to the *significance* in the environment *as it shows up specifically for human beings*, the project of developing an embedded and embodied Heideggerian AI can't get off the ground.' H. Dreyfus (2007) 'Why Heideggerian AI Failed and how Fixing it would Require making it more Heideggerian', *Philosophical Psychology*, 20(2), 247–68.

38. H. Dreyfus (1999) 'The Primacy of Phenomenology Over Logical Analysis', *Philosophical Topics*, 27(2), 6.

39. Dreyfus, 'Primacy of Phenomenology', 6.

40. H. Dreyfus (2000) 'Response to Searle', in M. Wrathall and J. Malpas (eds) *Heidegger, Coping, and Cognitive Science. Essays in Honor of Hubert Dreyfus*, Vol. 2 (Cambridge, MA: The MIT Press), p. 331.

41. M. Merleau-Ponty (1962)*The Phenomenology of Perception*, trans. C. Smith (London: Routledge and Kegan Paul), p. 302.

42. J. Wakefield and H. Dreyfus (1993) 'Intentionality and the Phenomenology of Action', in E. Lepore and R. van Gulick (eds) *John Searle and his Critics* (Oxford: Blackwell), p. 264.
43. This, of course, implies that were our bodies different our perceptual experience would involve different norms.
44. Merleau-Ponty, *The Phenomenology of Perception*, p. 138.
45. Versions of this chapter were presented in Tokyo at the PEACE Conference on Perception, Science, and the Lifeworld (September 2006), in Baltimore at an APA Symposium on Phenomenology and Philosophy of Mind (December 2007), and at the University of Sussex during the Annual Conference of the UK Kant Society (August 2008). I am grateful to the organizers of these events for the chance to present my work in progress, and to all those in attendance, in discussion with whom the chapter was significantly improved. In particular, I want to thank Charles Siewert for helping me to appreciate the inherent normativity of our factic bodily stance.

References

Barber, M. (2008) 'Holism and Horizon: Husserl and McDowell on Non-conceptual Content', *Husserl Studies*, 24(2), 79–97.

Brandom, R. (1994) *Making it Explicit* (Cambridge, MA: Harvard University Press).

Crowell, S. (2007)'Conscience and Reason: Heidegger and the Grounds of Intentionality', in S. Crowell and J. Malpas (eds) *Transcendental Heidegger* (Stanford: Stanford University Press).

Crowell, S. (2010) 'Transcendental Logic and "Minimal Empiricism": Lask and McDowell on the Unboundedness of the Conceptual', in R. Makkreel and S. Luft (eds) *Neo-Kantianism in Contemporary Philosophy* (Bloomington: Indiana University Press).

Dahlstrom, D.O. (2007) 'The Intentionality of Passive Experience: Husserl and a Contemporary Debate', *The New Yearbook for Phenomenology and Phenomenological Philosophy*, VII, 1–18.

Dreyfus, H. (1999) 'The Primacy of Phenomenology Over Logical Analysis', *Philosophical Topics*, 27(2).

Dreyfus, H. (2000) 'Response to Searle', in M. Wrathall and J. Malpas (eds) *Heidegger, Coping, and Cognitive Science. Essays in Honor of Hubert Dreyfus, Vol. 2* (Cambridge, MA: The MIT Press).

Dreyfus, H. (2007) 'Why Heideggerian AI Failed and how Fixing it would Require making it more Heideggerian', *Philosophical Psychology*, 20(2), 247–68.

Drummond, J. (1979–80)'On Seeing *a* Material Thing *in* Space: The Role of Kinaesthesis in Visual Perception', *Philosophy and Phenomenological Research*, 40, 19–32.

Drummond, J. (1990) *Husserlian Intentionality and Non-Foundational Realism* (Dordrecht: Kluwer).

Ginsborg, H. (2006) 'Aesthetic Judgment and Perceptual Normativity', *Inquiry*, 49(5), 403–37.

Hopp, W. (2008) 'Husserl on Sensation, Perception and Interpretation', *Canadian Journal of Philosophy*, 38(2), 219–46.

Hopp, W.(2008) 'Conceptualism and the Myth of the Given', *European Journal of Philosophy*, 17(3), 363–85.

Husserl, E. (1966) *Analysenzurpassiven Synthesis (1918-1926)*, Husserliana Bd. XI, M. Fleischer (ed.) (The Hague: Martinus Nijhoff).

Husserl, E. (1970) *Logical Investigations*, trans. J.N. Findlay (London: Routledge and Kegan Paul).

Husserl, E. (1973) *Experience and Judgment*, trans. J.S. Churchill and K. Ameriks (Evanston: Northwestern University Press).

Husserl, E. (1989) *Ideas Pertaining to a Pure Phenomenology and to a Phenomenological Philosophy, Second Book*, trans. R. Rojcewicz and A. Schuwer (Dordrecht: Kluwer); *Ideenzueinerreinen Phänomenologie und phänomenologischen Philosophie, Zweites Buch*, Husserliana Bd. IV, Marly Biemel (ed.) (The Hague: Martinus Nijhoff).

Husserl, E. (2004) *Wahrnehmung und Aufmerksamkeit: Texte aus dem Nachlass (1893-1912)*, Husserliana Bd. XXXVIII, T. Vongehr and R. Giuliani (eds) (Dordrecht: Springer).

Kant, I. (1968) *Critique of Pure Reason*, trans. N.K. Smith (London: Palgrave Macmillan).

Kelly, S. (2000) *The Relevance of Phenomenology to the Philosophy of Language and Mind* (New York: Routledge).

Lohmar, D. (2008) *Phänomenologie der schwachen Phantasie*, Phaenomenologica 185 (Dordrecht: Springer)

McDowell, J. (1994) *Mind and World* (Cambridge, MA: Harvard University Press).

McDowell, J. (2009) 'Avoiding the Myth of the Given', *Having the World in View: Essays on Kant, Hegel, and Sellars* (Cambridge, MA: Harvard University Press).

Merleau-Ponty, M. (1962)*The Phenomenology of Perception*, trans. C. Smith (London: Routledge and Kegan Paul).

Mooney, T. (2010) 'Understanding and Simple Seeing in Husserl', *Husserl Studies*, 26(1), 19–48.

Noë, A. (2004) *Action in Perception* (Cambridge, MA: The MIT Press).

Noë, A. (2006) 'Experience of the World in Time', *Analysis*, 66(1).

Rouse, J. (2005) 'Mind, Body, and World: Todes and McDowell on Bodies and Language', *Inquiry*, 48(1), 38–61.

Siewert, C. (2006) 'Is the Appearance of Shape Protean?', *Psyche*, 12(1), 1–16; http://www.theassc.org/vol_12_2006 (last accessed November 23, 2011).

Siewert, C.(forthcoming)'Intellectualism, Experience, and Motor Understanding', in J. Schear (ed.) *The Myth of the Mental?*

Thompson, E. (2007) *Mind in Life* (Cambridge, MA: Harvard University Press).

Wakefield, J. and Dreyfus, H. (1993) 'Intentionality and the Phenomenology of Action', in E. Lepore and R. van Gulick (eds) *John Searle and His Critics* (Oxford: Blackwell).

Part II
Sciences

5
Is There Any Value in Kant's Account of Mathematics?

Graham Bird

5.1   Introduction

Kant's account of mathematics in the *Critique* is not confined to his discussion of space and time in the Aesthetic; it is outlined also in the Analytic and in the Methodology. But the link in Kant's account between mathematics on one side and space, time, and perception on the other is one reason for my raising the question in this context. In whatever way his account of space and time relates to our phenomenology and perception, it includes also an account of an objective, *a priori*, mathematics. Another reason lies in my response to a common conviction nowadays that Kant's account of mathematics is so outdated that it has no value at all. Though the account I offer at some points goes beyond what Kant actually says, I want to explore aspects of it which have some connection with contemporary debates and may still have some value.

I have, however, to start by making a proviso recognizing that two substantial obstacles stand in the way of finding *any* value in his account of mathematics. There is, first, the widespread belief that what is sometimes called 'logico-empiricism' has finally provided the truth about mathematics; and there is, second, the conviction, which I share, that, if Kant is taken to be a traditional idealist despite his frequent and vehement disclaimers, then his position is hopeless both in general and in relation to mathematics.

I take 'logico-empiricism' to hold that all determinate propositions (truths) are either analytic (logical) or synthetic (empirical) and that mathematical propositions (truths) fall into the former class. That doctrine by itself does not entail the logicist doctrine that mathematics can be reduced to logic, but the latter can be regarded as a strong version of the former generic view. Both doctrines, however, are clearly incompatible with Kant's view: formally because he rejects an exclusive 'analytic/synthetic' distinction and classifies some mathematical propositions as 'synthetic *a priori*'; materially because he thinks that mathematics, along with the whole of our experience, rests on certain non-analytic but *a priori*, transcendental principles which determine the character of that experience. Anyone who accepts 'logico-empiricism' (in either strong or weak form) will naturally take Russell's view that Kant's account of mathematics contained disastrous mistakes.[1]

In a similar way, anyone who interprets Kant as a traditional idealist will naturally find it hard, even impossible, to defend his account of mathematics. I take traditional idealism to hold that all our knowledge depends on, and is somehow constructed out of (analytically reducible to), subjective (mental) representations. But, just as, in general, such a dependence, and such a construction (reduction), have never been adequately explained, so the related account of mathematics is similarly questionable. It seems to turn mathematics into a private, idiosyncratic exercise which neither allows an objective character to the discipline (cf. B206) nor explains the public, communal practices of mathematicians. It is open to the charge of 'psychologism', which, since Frege, has come to be regarded as the original sin in philosophy of mathematics.[2]

I shall evade both of these obstacles in what is perhaps too summary a way. With regard to the first, I note only that many contemporary philosophers of mathematics regard 'logico-empiricism' as at best controversial and at worst inadequate. Such views rest on queries about the logical or analytic character of the foundations of mathematics. They question whether it has been demonstrated that all mathematical principles (e.g., the Peano axioms for arithmetic, or Euclidean postulates for geometry) depend for their truth solely on the meanings of their constituent terms (or are derivable, as Frege claimed for arithmetic, purely from logical principles[3]). In recent times this particular query has issued in extensive controversy about the character of Hume's principle, as a replacement for (or in relation to) Frege's Basic Law V – the number of Fs is the same as the number of Gs iff there is a one–one correlation between the members of F and G.[4] They question whether the appeal to set theory in founding mathematics can be properly regarded as an appeal solely to logic, and whether existence claims in mathematics, or logic, can be regarded as analytic truths. So far as I can judge, these are not just minor cavils but grounds for at least suspending belief in the logico-empiricist view. Anyone who has Quinean or Kripkean qualms about the analytic/synthetic distinction can add this to these doubts.[5]

With regard to the second obstacle, I don't attempt to defend traditional idealism against the objections; instead I deny that Kant is committed to such a doctrine. I have offered support for that denial[6] and won't rehearse those grounds here. But it *is* evident that Kant himself wished to outline a non-standard, non-traditional form of idealism; the only question is how such a form should be understood and how far it deviates from the traditional varieties. My assumption is that Kant's position cannot be regarded as a traditional idealism of the kind summarized above, and that he consequently avoids the immediate objections to that doctrine. In particular, I take it that Kant regarded mathematics as an objective, but *a priori*, discipline (B206), accepted the communal public practices of mathematicians, and so is not obviously open to the charge of psychologism.[6] Anyone who regards Kant as a traditional idealist, therefore, should take it that my argument is hypothetical in form. It says that if Kant is *not* interpreted as a traditional idealist then his position can be understood in the following ways.

These summary points allow me at least to consider alternatives to a logico-empiricism about mathematics and to Kant's alleged traditional idealism. Accordingly, in Section 5.2, I outline a very general alternative, 'structuralist' picture of Kant's metaphysical position in the *Critique*, and then apply it to his account of mathematics. In Section 5.3 I consider some contemporary structuralist views about mathematics and finally, in Section 5.4, compare those accounts with Kant's position in more detail.

5.2 An alternative Kantian structuralist account of mathematics

Kant's general strategy in the first *Critique* and *Prolegomena* is to identify from our experience those elements which are *a priori* and, in the fundamental, transcendental cases, govern the most general character of that experience. That same strategy can, I believe, be extended to cover more specific regions of experience as well as experience as a whole. So psychology as well as physics (*Prolegomena*§15), morals as well as mathematics, aesthetic appreciation as well as teleological and religious belief, can all be seen as subject to underlying *a priori* principles. In some cases a full account of the discipline needs to include some *a posteriori* elements, for example in a reference to 'matter' in empirical physical science (*Metaphysical Principles of Natural Science*, Introduction), but that proviso is not necessary in the case of disciplines, such as mathematics, which are themselves *a priori*.

Two lines of thought then converge on a general Kantian thesis about mathematics. One is that Kant, as he says in the *Critique* and *Prolegomena*, bases his philosophical programme on the known examples of accredited science, such as mathematics and physics. So the structure of Euclidean geometry with its fundamental *a priori* principles (postulates) provides a very general picture of the way in which experience as a whole is structured by more fundamental *a priori*, transcendental principles. That general picture, however, can easily be misunderstood, and I forestall two such misunderstandings. Kant also wishes, very firmly, to distinguish mathematics and metaphysics (in the Doctrine of Method, The Discipline of Pure Reason in its Dogmatic Employment, B740–66); he plainly does not believe that his reformed metaphysics can be conducted along the axiomatic, deductive lines of Euclidean geometry. Such a procedure, *more geometrico*, would be more in line with the rationalist antecedents whose methods are decisively rejected in the Critical philosophy.

A further difference is that Kant regards metaphysics as a 'conceptual' exercise, while mathematics is not because it can appeal to intuition and to construction in intuition. That difference allows mathematics, but *not* metaphysics, to be properly dogmatic. These claims, too, are open to misunderstandings. Kant evidently does not think that metaphysical claims are 'conceptual' in the contemporary sense, that is, analytically true. Rather, his caveat for metaphysics is that the discipline is, or should be, undogmatic by trading in concepts which by themselves do not directly *establish* any corresponding reality. That is why transcendental proofs, and transcendental deductions, are needed for Kant's chosen fundamental concepts and principles. The motivation derives primarily not from the external pressure of philosophical scepticism, as is often supposed, but from Kant's own 'internal' understanding of the character of the two disciplines, viz. metaphysics and mathematics.

The second part of the convergence looks at the relation of metaphysics and mathematics, as it were, from the *other* side; considering not how metaphysics might both be modelled on, and yet differ from, mathematics, but rather how metaphysics throws light on the character of mathematical systems such as Euclidean geometry, and their application in experience. The proofs in the Metaphysical Expositions of the Aesthetic are designed to show how certain central *a priori* features of space (three-dimensionality, infinitely given magnitudes) lead to their more systematic development in Euclidean geometry. In the Transcendental Expositions the idea is that those earlier proofs underpin the claim that such a system is itself universal, necessary and *a priori*. In the later Analytic of Principles Kant attempts further to show how transcendental principles of the understanding make possible both mathematics and its application to appearances. Without considering at all how successful these attempts are, I want to suggest that these ideas point towards the following picture. Just as, for Kant, the *a priori* transcendental principles provide a formal *structure* governing the whole of our experience, so the *a priori* (but *not* transcendental) principles of mathematics in Euclid and in what Kant calls 'the general doctrine of motion' provide the formal *a prioristructure* of space and motion, that is, the translation of appearances in space over time. Understood in these terms, Kant's account of mathematics can quite naturally be labelled 'structuralist'.

Such philosophical labels are unclear and misleading without some more specific grasp of what they signify and which other theories they are designed to exclude. The very notion of a 'structure' is itself vague and questionable. The general intention in a structuralist theory is to represent the essential, contested items (e.g., numbers, or geometrical points) not as objects or contents but rather as forms in which other, more manageable and less mysterious objects are captured or embedded. But our ordinary use of 'structure' does not always conform to this intention, when, for example, we describe a building as a structure, or as both 'being' and also 'having' a structure. So in arithmetic, for example, the leading idea would be that numbers (specifically the natural numbers) provide a structure in which items of various sorts can be counted or measured. In one version[7] there is nothing more to the distinctive character of any particular number than its relations to other numbers, including its specific location in the number series. But beyond that there is evidently the danger of triviality in regarding mathematics, as some have put it, as 'the science of patterns'.[8] Plainly more needs to be said to spell out how such conceptions of a 'pattern' or a 'structure' function in the meta-mathematical context; and this requirement holds just as much of the recent structuralists as of any such theory ascribed to Kant.

In Kant's case, such a theory has to forestall at least the following two objections. If his view is that mathematics provides the abstract, formal structure of presented appearances in experience, then it is natural to object that mathematics must be derivable, abstracted, from those *a posteriori* appearances. But then the abstracted mathematical concepts so derived would themselves be *a posteriori* and not, as Kant accepts, *a priori*. Kant would be in serious danger of canvassing an empiricist, Mill-type account of mathematics, which he plainly rejects (cf. the comments on Hume at B793–4). The objection can be easily dealt with. Although the bare theory may allow the possibility of such empiricist abstraction, there is no necessity to accept such an operation.[9] Kant provides arguments to indicate that this is not feasible in the case of mathematics (specifically geometry), since the discipline is *a priori* and contains both general features (priority, infinite magnitude) and more specific features (three-dimensionality), which *cannot* be empirically abstracted from *a posteriori* experience and still preserve their *a priori* status. To disregard these would be to beg the question against Kant's position.

It might also be objected that such a picture of Kant overlooks the fact that he regards it as necessary to prove that mathematics has, even must have, an application to appearances. But two responses can be made to diminish the significance of that objection. One is that I am not, at this stage, claiming the success (particularly the soundness) of Kant's arguments, but only rehearsing the way in which his arguments are elaborated in the Aesthetic and elsewhere. The *a priori* character of mathematics, and the structural account of the transcendental principles, rest on the arguments in the Aesthetic and Analytic, but I am not claiming that they all succeed. The other point is to insist again that Kant's account of the relation between mathematics and *a posteriori* experience is not intended to rebut a scepticism about mathematics. Kant makes it plain that mathematics needs no such support from metaphysics (B119–20). His arguments are designed to show, given his account of the structure of experience and of mathematics, how it is possible for mathematics to have such an application. They are not designed to guarantee that application, or the truth of mathematics; in his view there is no guarantee, and certainly metaphysics in any case could not supply one. As before, the primary motive comes not from external, sceptical pressure, but from Kant's internal requirements.

5.3   Recent structuralist accounts of mathematics

Recent 'structuralists', such as Paul Benacerraf, Stewart Shapiro, Geoffrey Hellman and Michael Resnik, often refer to Dedekind as an ancestor of their own views.[10] I do not consider the important connection to Dedekind, but note only that his discussion evidently forms a historically interesting bridge between Kant and the more recent philosophers.

Those more recent accounts are not by any means the same, and the individual theorists have not always consistently adhered to the doctrine – Benacerraf in particular offered some extensive modifications of his original view[11] (as I later indicate). However, their structuralist principles can be given a general characterization and, with some provisos, they share similar motivations for adopting such views. Shapiro, for example, offers such a general characterization in the following:

> Structuralism is a variant on the realist theme...arithmetic is not about a particular realm of abstract objects, the natural numbers. Rather the subject-matter...is the natural-number-structure, the form common to any infinite system of objects with a distinguished initial object, which plays the role of zero, and a successor relation satisfying the (mathematical) principle of induction....Mathematics is to material reality as pattern is to patterned.[12]

The account identifies the characteristic aspects of the Peano axioms as the defining features of the relevant structure, often summarily referred to as an 'ω-sequence'. It focuses primarily on arithmetic rather than other branches of mathematics, such as geometry, but it suffers from some of the vagueness and incipient triviality noted earlier in appealing to the notion of a 'structure' or 'form'. We might wonder, if numbers amount to nothing more than a structure, whether it can be right to talk of zero as an initial 'object'; or why Shapiro seems to restrict the application of mathematics to 'material' reality, as if it's impossible to count headaches. It might also be asked what is meant by calling the account 'realist', but that seems to trade on a natural distinction between a 'Platonism' committed to the unqualified existence of abstract objects such as numbers and a 'realism' which endorses only a determinate, and mind-independent, truth or falsity for mathematical propositions. Some of these queries can be resolved by considering Benacerraf's original argument.

In that argument Benacerraf begins by considering Frege's problem about delimiting the range of objects over which numbers range. The point was put, strikingly, in Frege's anxiety that nothing in the characterization of number established whether, for example, Julius Caesar might be a number. Frege's problem arose just because he took the view that numbers are objects (abstract objects), which committed him to a Platonist view open to familiar difficulties.[13] One of these is the epistemological difficulty of explaining how we can know truths about such objects when they occupy no spatio-temporal position and have no causal properties, and in particular have no causal relations to subjects who might access them. Benacerraf's response is plainly motivated by a wish to evade such Platonist consequences, but his argument continues with a related problem about the set theoretical foundations for arithmetic. Essentially it rests on the idea, exploited also by Quine,[14] that set theory can provide such a foundation, with several different, but equivalent, ways of characterizing the natural numbers.[15] Benacerraf's central point is that in that case there is no way in which the natural numbers can actually be identified with any specific set. Though different versions of set theory can adequately provide the basis for natural number arithmetic, they do not allow us to identify any such number with any specific set. The consequence is that no identity of the form 's = n', where 's' names a set and 'n' a natural number, can be accepted. This encourages Benacerraf towards the drastic solution of claiming that numbers cannot be objects at all, specifically that they cannot be sets, and that Frege's original problem was a pseudo-problem.

The natural numbers, then, are not objects but only a structure in which objects of some kind can be configured. Benacerraf captures these conclusions and a central argument for them in the following:

> Under our analysis any system of objects that forms a progression of a recursive sort...must be adequate...To discover that other systems do the job properly cannot be to discover what numbers are.[16]
> ...that any recursive sequence whatever would do suggests that what is important is not the individuality of each element but the structure which they jointly exhibit.[17]

Benacerraf uses the point to explain the puzzle he started with:

> Why there are so many interpretations possible of number theory without any being singled out is obvious...there is no unique set of objects which are the numbers...Number words do not have single referents.[18]

The conclusion is importantly modified in the following Carnapian way:[19]

> They think that numbers are really sets of sets while, if the truth be known, there are no such things as numbers; which is not to say that there are not at least two primes between 15 and 20.[20]

Benacerraf in that passage indicates an implicit distinction, of the kind Carnap drew, between an external, metaphysical question and an internal, mathematical question about the existence of numbers. The suggestion is that the Frege problem is an 'external' question which either is meaningless or else has no answer, while the practice of mathematicians continues without these metaphysical anxieties in allowing the 'internal' existence (in arithmetic) of two primes between 15 and 20.

The more general argument for these conclusions can be summarized in the following two passages:

> The pointlessness of trying to determine which objects the numbers are thus derives directly from the pointlessness of asking the question of any individual number. For arithmetical purposes the properties of numbers which do not stem from the relations they bear to one another in virtue of being arranged in a progression are of no consequence whatever.[21]

He argues that if there were such objects they:

> would need independent characterisation; but that's just what can't be provided for numbers.[22]

Consequently:

> Arithmetic is the science that elaborates the abstract structure that all progressions have in common in virtue of being progressions.[23]

I note, finally, that Benacerraf was encouraged to express his view in what he later recognized to be extravagant ways. Of the central argument he later said:

> Section III of 'WNCNB' does 'argue' that not only could numbers not be sets, they couldn't even be numbers.[24]

He notes that the section in the original paper was entitled 'Way Out', which he took to be an indication of a rather 'wacky/off-beat' conclusion, but which was widely misunderstood instead as '*The* Way Out', that is, as a straightforward resolution of the original problem. He said in that later passage:

> Although I am still persuaded that there is something right about it, it is so dialectically hobbled by the conceptual baggage it carries. Believing it has to be an auto da fe.[25]

More soberly, we have to ask what can be made of this whole line of thought. There is undoubtedly something persuasive in the idea that numbers have their significance just through their mutual relations and hence through the structure, and the salient features of the structure, which they inhabit. How else *could* numbers be characterized?[26] The seemingly obvious answer that they can be characterized as sets runs against two decisive objections: first, that set-characterization rests on the features of the structure they exhibit; second, that if there are diverse, equally adequate, ways of formulating the relevant sets then we cannot simply *identify* any number with any particular set.

On the other hand, these plausible points do not *establish* the conclusions that numbers *cannot* be regarded as 'objects', that we *cannot* regard number terms as having single referents, still less (of course) that we cannot regard them as *numbers*. There is also something seriously odd about an argument which assumes that structures need objects (to structure), takes it that numbers cannot be characterized independently of their structure, and then infers that, therefore, numbers themselves cannot be the objects of such mathematical structures. Does it not seem more plausible to argue that numbers are essentially the objects for such structures just because they cannot be identified independently of it? Perhaps it could be replied that they are 'formal' or 'internal' objects for such structures, but this Carnapian response raises other queries.

For it might be asked how Benacerraf's account fares with regard to the semantics of number statements. If that account is 'realist', and insists on a determinate truth or falsity for such statements, how can we give an account of their truth conditions when there are no objects for the relevant predicates to satisfy? It seems as though, without numbers as objects, and without numerals as singular referring terms, there will either be no viable semantics for number statements or else none that requires such referents with properties to satisfy the truth values of those statements. The position might be thought still further obscure because, although Benacerraf denies that there are such things as numbers, he accepts as true statements to the effect that there are two primes between 15 and 20. The Carnap interpretation of that last claim indicates a distinction between what we can say 'externally' (metaphysically) of numbers and what we can say 'internally' (mathematically) of them. But Benacerraf neither makes this clear nor indicates how we might devise an 'internal' semantics for arithmetic.[27]

There is, finally, a general anxiety about one central motivation for structuralism and its success in achieving it. The suggestion was that structuralism aims to evade any temptation towards a Platonist commitment to existent abstract objects such as numbers, but critics have pointed out that structures are themselves just such abstract objects.[28] To aim to avoid Platonism about numbers by reinstating such a doctrine about structures does not look like a convincing strategy. Some structuralists have offered explicit responses to this question, in particular Hellman in his 'modal-structural' rewriting of Peano arithmetic. He aims to avoid Platonism in a two-step strategy which represents any arithmetical truth T as a consequent in a modal hypothetical of the form 'Necessarily if X is any ω-sequence (i.e., meets the requirements of the Peano axioms), then T.' Such a reformulation is designed deliberately to avoid quantification over structures and over objects.

Hellman is forced by his strategy to abandon a possible worlds semantics for mathematics despite the fact that its statements make hypothetical claims about possibilities in mathematics. He envisages a straightforward 'satisfaction' semantics for arithmetical statements, so long as it is understood that appealing to 'objects' as satisfying propositional functions is in the context only a 'façon de parler'.[29] His approach is not an analytic reduction of arithmetic to modal logic, but only a procedure for rewriting arithmetic which avoids any formal commitment to, or quantification over, the dubious existents. Evidently such a procedure is both modest and defensive. The claim is not that the reformulation provides a more perspicuous analysis of mathematics, still less an accurate description of mathematical procedures, but only that it preserves everything that is needed in Peano arithmetic while avoiding any dubious Platonist or meta-mathematical commitments. Whether Hellman's approach succeeds or not, it requires that we accept a purely formal resolution of the issue, and this has seemed unsatisfactory to some critics, such as Dummett.[30] There is no doubt that structuralism faces problems, but also that there are resources available at least to begin to resolve them.

5.4 A Kantian version of structuralism in mathematics

The remaining question is whether, and how far, Kant's account of mathematics, and space and time, can be compared with these more recent structuralist views. I note finally and summarily some of the points to be made in such a comparison, moving, as the discussion goes on, further and further from Kant's own explicit claims.

(i) Kant does not have the problem, noted in Benacerraf, that structures need objects (to be structured), that numbers are not objects, and yet that they are what the mathematics structures. For Kant there are only appearances in our properly cognitive experience, and so it must be *those* objects which are mathematically structured. The point is well made by Friedman:

> pure mathematics is not a body of truths with its own peculiar subject matter for Kant. There are no 'mathematical objects' to constitute this subject matter, for the sensible and perceptual objects of the empirical world (that is 'appearances') are the only 'objects' there are. For this reason pure mathematics is not, properly speaking, a body of knowledge (cognition).[31]

The picture, conformably with the Kantian background, is that appearances, the objects of outer and inner sense, are the objects structured according to the principles of Euclidean geometry or arithmetic. That evident advantage, though, has to be weighed against obvious disadvantages, namely, that appearances are given *a posteriori* while mathematics is *a priori*; and given appearances are only finite in our experience, while mathematics has, and needs, reference to infinite magnitudes.

(ii) That Kantian restriction of genuine knowledge to appearances conforms to another of his claims about mathematics, not so far noted, namely that a Platonist account of mathematics and the (abstract) objects of mathematics is unacceptable. Kant makes the point in a particularly forceful way by referring to Plato's account as 'mystical':

> He even extended [his concept] to mathematics although the object of that science is nowhere to be found except in possible experience. In this I cannot follow him any more than in his mystical deduction of these ideas or in the extravagances whereby he, so to speak, hypostatised them – although, as must be allowed, the exalted language which he employed...is quite capable of a milder interpretation that accords with the nature of things. (B371n.)

Kant's anti-Platonism is associated in this way with his rejection of any genuine knowledge of noumena (things in themselves). In line with that rejection, mathematics, though *a priori*, has in some way essentially to deal with appearances (phenomena).

(iii) Kant's suggestion that Plato might be interpreted in a 'milder' way prompts a further speculation, though Kant himself does not specify any further what such a modified Platonism might be. We might, with one proviso, distinguish, as Kant seems to do, between a 'strong' and a 'weak' form of Platonism. The former, committed straightforwardly to the existence of abstract objects, satisfies the general requirement for providing a formal semantics for mathematical statements by admitting the existence of numbers, sets and other abstract items. If Kant and modern structuralists reject any such admission, then they face the problem of explaining how they can provide any such formal semantics in terms of 'objects' satisfying the predicates, the propositional functions, employed in mathematics. A weaker form, however, which offers the prospect of providing such a semantics would use such a model of objects satisfying predicates so long as it was understood that there was no definite commitment to the actual existence of the 'objects'. Such an account would conform generally to Hellman's claim, noted above, that this involves only a 'façon de parler'. It would be, as other commentators have suggested, like offering a semantic account of the propositions in a Sherlock Holmes story in just those terms, while accepting that the objects, the characters, exist only as elements in the story, that is, *as* 'fictions'. In the same way, although Kant had no idea of constructing a formal semantics, or of the logical background to contemporary accounts of formal semantics, he would surely have been sympathetic to the idea of providing such a semantics for abstract and fictional discourse *'as if'* the singular terms named actual existents.

I do not think it is a serious objection to this that mathematics is not a 'fiction' at all. There may be many contexts for such a non-committal formal semantics which would not represent the 'objects' just as 'fictions' exactly like a story. Such contexts as moral, aesthetic or even religious (supernatural) discourse would provide examples. Such models would not be committed either to the existence of the relevant objects or to their simple non-existence as 'fictions'. Whether such cases qualify as genuine *fictions* is determined not by their formal semantics but by their functional uses. We rightly think of mathematics as having a function quite different from that of fictional entertainment (especially in its application to accessible phenomena), and would reject any such assimilation as an absurd devaluation of mathematics (perhaps of fiction too). But the differences we rightly insist on are a matter of function, not formal semantics. To avoid 'fictional' status consequently we do not *need* to, are not *forced* to, accept the unqualified existence of such things as numbers in a strong Platonism.

(iv) A corollary of that quasi-Kantian position, closer to Kant's text, concerns Carnap's similar account of what might be called 'weak' and 'strong' Platonism. Carnap, like Benacerraf, allows as meaningful an 'internal' question about the existence of numbers, whose answer is trivially provided by accepted claims in arithmetic, such as that there are two prime numbers between 15 and 20. What Carnap regarded as meaningless were 'external' questions which claimed to raise a more profound question about whether numbers *really* exist, rather than trivial questions about whether they exist 'in arithmetic'. Because those external questions had never been provided with an adequate criterion for the new form of 'real' existence, Carnap believed that their apparent greater profundity was an illusion. Although Kant does not make these points in his own text, he has some apparatus which allows him to do so. His distinction between 'empirical' and 'transcendental' enquiries, which cannot be identified with the contrast between what is '*a priori*' and what is '*a posteriori*',[32] parallels Carnap's contrast between internal and external questions. For Kant, 'empirical' enquiries are those which raise questions internal to some discipline (or *within* experience), even when the discipline is, like mathematics, itself *a priori* (cf. B80–1). 'Transcendental enquiries', by contrast, raise higher order questions about the discipline itself (or experience as a whole). Kant's distinction has evident parallels with Carnap's and allows him, with one proviso, to make the points that Carnap made in his terms.

The necessary proviso is that Kant, unlike Carnap, did *not* regard all transcendental ('external') questions as meaningless or spurious. He did regard the 'transcendent' *sub-class* of transcendental enquiries as spurious, though generally not meaningless. But, so long as those transcendental questions were *immanent* and *not transcendent*, he believed some were meaningful, in principle answerable, and indeed answered, by the Critical philosophy. Nevertheless, Kant also held that the metaphysical urge to ask transcendental questions led inexorably to the construction of spurious issues of the *transcendent* kind. His link between the transcendental and the transcendent, as well as the division between genuine and spurious transcendental questions, allows him to provide a similar diagnosis of philosophical error to that of Carnap.

(v) A different, but related, aspect of Kant's text reinforces his anti-Platonism. For, when he comes explicitly to treat abstract items such as points in geometry, instants in time, or numbers in arithmetic, he recognizes their ambiguous status as *seeming* to designate particular objects and yet not genuinely doing so. Points and instants are represented as intersections of line segments, or as limits of spatial or temporal regions. More precisely, Kant rejects the idea that there are smallest possible, 'simple', spatial or temporal parts, since space and time are 'quanta continua'(B211). Each part of space and time is itself a space and a time, so that points and instants are merely 'positions' which limit space and time, but out of which space and time cannot be constructed (B211–12: 'out of mere positions neither space nor time can be constructed'). Such an appeal to 'positions' in some wider manifold, or progression, provides a further tie with the recent structuralist account of natural numbers.

Numbers, for Kant, depend essentially on schemata which are not images designating actual objects. Schemata relating to number, for example, represent an operative procedure such as that formulated in the Peano axioms for successive addition, or in what Benacerraf calls a 'progression', or Hellman an 'ω-sequence'.

> The pure schema for magnitude is number, a representation which comprises the successive addition of homogeneous units. (B182)

5.5 Conclusion

These points indicate that Kant's account of mathematics can rightly be called 'structuralist', even though he does not elaborate the account in the ways recent structuralists have done. Kant does not provide in the *Critique* the same amount of detail as those recent structuralists, but his account of mathematics, understood in these ways, undoubtedly points in the same direction. His repudiation of a strong Platonism coupled with his rejection of simple atoms, points and instants, out of which mathematical objects might be composed; his belief that the only 'objects' at issue in relation to mathematics are appearances, structured in accordance with mathematical principles; his conception of *a priori* principles as providing a structure which governs our experience and its specific, for example scientific, branches; and a philosophical apparatus marking the distinctions between immanent, transcendent and transcendental principles which has a clear parallel with Carnap; all point in the same 'structuralist' direction. They provide a ground for regarding Kant, as well as Dedekind, as an ancestral founder of such structuralist theories.

It is, of course, also true that Kant's account, at least as much as the recent theories, is open to serious queries and leaves significant gaps.[33] Among the latter, perhaps the most notable is the way in which he accommodates appeals to infinite magnitudes in arithmetic, geometry and calculus. Although he makes allowance for such appeals, he might be thought simply to help himself to these notions by indicating that formally space, for example, is given as an infinite magnitude (B39–40), or that time's limitlessness is established by recognizing its presented limits (B47–8). Other structuralist accounts recognize difficulties in this area, but the problems are greater for Kant in the light of his belief that the objects structured are appearances, that is, experienceable items in both outer and inner sense. For no sequence of these items can plausibly be presented in that infinite given way. There can consequently be no serious suggestion that Kant answered, or even directly faced, these outstanding issues, but the direction of his theory, understood in these ways, importantly qualifies Russell's dismissal of his views.

Notes

1. Russell wrote: 'I found that many of the stock philosophical arguments about mathematics (derived in the main from Kant) had been rendered invalid by the progress of mathematics...'(Russell, B.(1956) *Logic and Knowledge*, R. Marsh (ed.), London: G. Allen and Unwin, pp. 324–5). He cites such developments as non-Euclidean geometry and the work of Weierstrass, Cantor and Frege as demonstrating the fundamental errors.
2. Michael Dummett outlines this original sin in (1991) *Frege: Philosophy of Mathematics* (Cambridge, MA: Harvard University Press), pp. 13–19, ch. 2 and pp. 76–83).
3. Michael Dummett, op. cit., pp. 3, 43–6 makes clear the particular sense in which Frege held that mathematics was derivable from logical principles.
4. The issue has been discussed in: Boolos, G. (1993) 'Basic Law (V)', *Proceedings of the Aristotelian Society*, LXVII, 213–34; Stirton, W.R. (2000) 'Hale's Weak Sense is Just too Weak', *Proceedings of the Aristotelian Society* C, 209–13; Potter, M. and Smiley, T. (2001–2) 'Recarving Content: Hale's Final Proposition', *Proceedings of the Aristotelian Society* CII, 351–4; Hale, B. (2007) 'Neo-Fregeanism and Quantifier Variance', *Proceedings of the Aristotelian Society*, CVII, 375–85.
5. Quine's rejection of a standard 'analytic/synthetic' distinction won't help Kant in the end, since it rejects also Kant's conception of mathematics as containing synthetic *a priori* propositions. Kripke's account is closer to Kant, since it admits classifications of propositions as 'necessary *a posteriori*' and 'contingent *a priori*', which echo Kant's 'synthetic *a priori*' classification. See Bird, G. (2006) *The Revolutionary Kant* (Chicago: Open Court), pp. 77–82.
6. A traditionalist interpretation of Kant claims that the explanation of the synthetic *a priori* character of mathematics rests on his belief that all knowledge is 'mind-dependent' in a straightforwardly idealist way. It is this interpretation of Kant which I question in Bird, op. cit., ch. 1, and later reject.
7. Benacerraf, P. (1983) 'What Numbers Cannot Be', in Benacerraf and Putnam, *Philosophy of Mathematics*, 2nd edn (Cambridge: Cambridge University Press), pp. 272–94.
8. Shapiro, S. (1995) 'Problems in the Philosophy of Mathematics', in T. Honderich (ed.), *The Oxford Companion to Philosophy* (Oxford: Oxford University Press), pp. 535–9.

9. Michael Dummett, op. cit., pp. 83–94, comments on the dangers and errors of appealing to the notion of abstraction in mathematics. His objections are, however, not to operations of 'abstraction' as such, but to a particular doctrine that might be called 'abstractionism', captured in the apparently absurd claims that '[if] we pay no attention to their [objects'] colour, they become colourless'; or '[if] we take less notice of a property it vanishes'. Later (op.cit., p. 216) the abstraction operator is allowed to introduce 'new objects'.

10. Benacerraf, P. 'What Numbers Cannot Be', in Benacerraf and Putnam, op. cit., pp. 272–94; Benacerraf, P. 'Mathematical Truth', in Benacerraf and Putnam, op. cit., pp. 403–20; Benacerraf, P. (1996) 'What Mathematical Truth Could Not Be - I', in Morton and Stich (eds), *Benacerraf and his Critics*(Oxford: Blackwell), pp. 9–59; Shapiro, S. (1983) 'Mathematics and Reality', *Philosophy of Science*, 50, 523–48; Shapiro, S. (1995) 'Problems in the Philosophy of Mathematics', in *The Oxford Companion to Philosophy*, T. Honderich (ed.) (Oxford: Oxford University Press), pp. 535–9; Resnik, M. (1981) 'Mathematics as the Science of Patterns: Ontology and Reference', *Nous*, 15, 529–50; Resnik, M. (1982) 'Mathematics as the Science of Patterns: Epistemology', *Nous*, 16, 93–105; Hellman, G. (1989) *Mathematics without Numbers* (Clarendon Press, Oxford); Dedekind, R. (1888) 'Was sind und sollen die Zahlen?', translated as 'The Nature and Meaning of Numbers' in (1963) *Essays on the Theory of Numbers* (New York: Dover), pp. 31–115.

11. See Benacerraf in Morton and Stich, op. cit., pp. 23–5.

12. In *The Oxford Companion to Philosophy*, p. 536.

13. Michael Dummett, op.cit., especially pp. 157–61, 209–14, has an extensive discussion of this issue.

14. W.V.O. Quine (1960) *Word and Object* (Cambridge, MA: MIT Press), p. 263.

15. The two most commonly specified ways of associating natural numbers and sets are those of Zermelo/Fraenkel and von Neumann. These are outlined as part of Benacerraf's original argument.

16. Benacerraf and Putnam, op. cit., pp. 289–90.

17. Ibid., p. 290.

18. Ibid., p. 291.

19. Carnap drew the fourfold distinction between theoretical and practical internal and external existence questions in Carnap (1950). Since Carnap's famous distinction between internal and external questions has been claimed to be inadequate, I offer a summary criticism of one such strong claim in Hale(1987), pp. 5–8. A more extensive defence of Carnap is given in my two papers on Carnap's distinction in my (2003) 'Carnap's Internal and External Questions' in *Language, Truth, and Logic*, T. Bonk (ed.) (Amsterdam: Kluwer), ch. 7. Hale's central argument goes like this: Carnap's external theoretical questions can be identified with his external practical questions, but then it is just an error to think that the latter have no 'ontological commitments'. If I decide practically to accept a framework then it is epistemically trivial that its fundamental objects exist (internally). Carnap's mistakes are to confuse epistemic and ontological triviality, and to rely on a distinction between internal and external (theoretical) questions which remains opaque. We should just accept that there are genuine internal theoretical existence questions which cannot be regarded as peculiarly philosophical. But Hale's argument

is seriously vulnerable to the following points. (1) Hale follows Quine (op. cit., p. 271) in identifying external theoretical and practical questions, but Carnap does not *identify* these questions. The former, but not the latter, are at best unclear and at worst meaningless. (2) Hale's unqualified appeals to 'ontological commitment' and to 'ontological triviality' are liable to beg the question against Carnap, since his interest is precisely in elucidating the different questions that might be asked under the description 'ontological'. (3) In any case, the practical decision to accept a framework does not *guarantee* the existence of its fundamental categories. All it can do (if the framework is properly constituted) is to provide criteria with which to determine answers to internal theoretical questions. There will be differences between internal theoretical questions in logical and factual frameworks, since in the latter, but not in the former, the questions require empirical investigation, but Hale disregards these points. (4) It is quite unsurprising that external theoretical questions remain opaque, since that was precisely Carnap's basic conclusion. When Hale concludes that there are legitimate, clear, internal theoretical questions he is not disagreeing with, but accepting, Carnap's basic point.

20. Ibid., p. 294.
21. Ibid., p. 291.
22. Ibid., p. 291.
23. Ibid., p. 291.
24. Morton and Stich, op. cit., p. 23.
25. Ibid., p. 25.
26. Michael Dummett (op. cit., p. 53) has an apparently strong argument against this view, in which he insists that the number 3 cannot be adequately characterized just by its location in a progression, because its location in such a progression will vary according to the starting point.
27. An attempt to meet the requirements of providing such an 'internal' semantics for number statements is an underlying goal in Wright, C. (1983) *Frege's Conception of Numbers as Objects* (Aberdeen: Aberdeen University Press), but Wright, like Hale, does not accept Carnap's argument (see note 14).
28. Chihara, C. (1990) *Constructibility and Mathematical Existence* (Oxford: Clarendon Press), pp. 126–45, has an extensive discussion, and criticism, of the attempt to make the notion of 'structure' fundamental in an account of natural numbers.
29. Geoffrey Hellman, op. cit., p.28.
30. Michael Dummett's objection (if it is directed at Hellman) seems to be that the proposal simply evades, and does not resolve, the basic issue (Dummett, op. cit., pp. 304–5).
31. Friedman, M. (1992)*Kant and the Exact Sciences* (Cambridge, MA: Harvard University Press), p. 94.
32. The point is made in Bird, *The Revolutionary Kant*, ch. 5 (especially pp. 89–96).
33. One query, inevitably, will concern the extent to which Kant's (transcendental) idealism makes his account vulnerable to the charges of 'subjectivism' or 'psychologism' in mathematics. I have chosen to set aside that aspect of Kant's overall position, and the way it affects his views of mathematics, but even so there remain residual problems. Even if Kant is not canvassing a straightforwardly idealist reduction of mathematical (and other) concepts to personal and private 'ideas', still there is a question about his

less straightforward way of representing such concepts as *a priori* and so as dependent (in some way) on features of our minds.

References

Benacerraf, P. (1983) 'What Numbers Cannot Be', in Benacerraf and Putnam, *Philosophy of Mathematics*, 2nd edn (Cambridge: Cambridge University Press), pp. 272–94.

Benacerraf, P. (1996) 'What Mathematical Truth Could Not Be - I', in Morton and Stich (eds), *Benacerraf and his Critics* (Oxford: Blackwell), pp. 9–59.

Bird, G. (2003)'Carnap's Internal and External Questions', in *Language, Truth, and Logic*, T. Bonk (ed.) (Amsterdam: Kluwer).

Bird, G. (2006) *The Revolutionary Kant* (Chicago, Open Court).

Boolos, G.(1993) 'Basic Law (V)', *Proceedings of the Aristotelian Society*, LXVII, 213–34.

Carnap, Rudolf (1950), 'Empiricism, Semantics, and Ontology', *Revue Internationale de Philosophie*, 4.

Chihara, C. (1990) *Constructibility and Mathematical Existence* (Oxford: Clarendon Press).

Dedekind, R. (1888) 'Was sind and sollen die Zahlen?', translated as 'The Nature and Meaning of Numbers' in Dedekind, R. (1963) *Essays on the Theory of Numbers*(New York: Dover), pp. 31–115.

Dummett, M. (1991) *Frege: Philosophy of Mathematics* (Cambridge, MA: Harvard University Press).

Friedman, M. (1992) *Kant and the Exact Sciences* (Cambridge, MA: Harvard University Press).

Hale, Bob (1987), *Abstract Objects*, Blackwell, Oxford.

Hale, B. (2007) 'Neo-Fregeanism and Quantifier Variance', *Proceedings of the Aristotelian Society*, CVII, 375–85.

Hellman, G. (1989) *Mathematics without Numbers* (Oxford: Clarendon Press).

Honderich, T. (ed.) (1995) *The Oxford Companion to Philosophy* (Oxford: Oxford University Press).

Potter, M. and Smiley, T. (2001–2) 'Recarving Content: Hale's Final Proposition', *Proceedings of the Aristotelian Society*, CII, 351–4.

Quine, W.V.O. (1960) *Word and Object* (Cambridge, MA: MIT Press).

Resnik, M.(1981) 'Mathematics as the Science of Patterns: Ontology and Reference', *Nous*, 15, 529–50.

Resnik, M. (1982) 'Mathematics as the Science of Patterns: Epistemology', *Nous*, 16, 93–105.

Russell, B. (1956) *Logic and Knowledge*, R. Marsh (ed.)(London: George Allen and Unwin).

Shapiro, S. (1983) 'Mathematics and Reality', *Philosophy of Science*, 50, 523–48.

Shapiro, S. (1995) 'Problems in the Philosophy of Mathematics', in Honderich (ed.),*The Oxford Companion to Philosophy*(Oxford: Oxford University Press), pp. 535–9.

Stirton, W.R. (2000) 'Hale's Weak Sense is Just too Weak', *Proceedings of the Aristotelian Society*, C, 209–13.

Wright, C. (1983) *Frege's Conception of Numbers as Objects* (Aberdeen: Aberdeen University Press).

6
Thinking of Everything? Kant Speaks to Stephen Hawking

Leslie Stevenson

Theoretical physicists have recently described themselves as aspiring to a 'theory of everything'. But more than two centuries ago Kant offered in the Dialectic of his *Critique of Pure Reason* a systematic diagnosis of a certain kind of transcendental illusion about absolute totalities, an illusion to which we are prone whenever we try to think about the world as a whole. I propose to look afresh at Kant's thought and ponder its implications for contemporary cosmological theorizing, and, conversely, to ask whether modern science can throw any light on his dark musings.[1]

6.1 Theoretical reason and Kant's first antinomy

In the Introduction to the Transcendental Dialectic, Kant describes the operation of our faculty of reason. He tells us that it has a valid use in seeking to organize and unify our scientific knowledge of the world:

> in inference reason endeavours to reduce the varied and manifold knowledge obtained through the understanding to the smallest number of principles (universal conditions) and thereby to achieve in it the highest possible unity. (A305/B361)

Later on, Kant remarks that human reason is by nature architectonic, in that it regards all our knowledge as belonging to a possible system (A474/B502). But he holds that the systematizing use of our reason has a distinctive way of leading us astray. If we have explained a fact p by another fact q, we may then seek to explain q by some further condition r, and so on: as Kant puts it, 'the condition of the condition must be sought whenever practicable.' But we tend to assume that there must be

an endpoint to this process, and Kant offers a grand-sounding formulation of this assumption behind our naïve thinking:

> the principle peculiar to reason in general, in its logical employment
> is: – to find for the conditioned knowledge obtained through the
> understanding the unconditioned whereby its unity is brought to
> completion. (A307/B364)

What he seems to have in mind is an ultimate premise which can serve
to explain everything else, but does not itself need explanation, or can
be shown not to be susceptible of any further explanation: that is, not
just an unexplained explainer, but an inexplicable explainer –perhaps
even a self-explanatory explainer.

However, to search is not necessarily to find: people can look for
something that does not exist (like the Yeti), or even for something that
cannot exist (e.g., a geometrical construction to square the circle). Kant
goes on to say:

> this logical maxim can only become a principle of pure reason
> through our assuming that if the conditioned is given, the whole
> series of conditions, subordinated to one another – a series which is
> therefore itself unconditioned – is likewise given, that is, is contained
> in the object and its connection. (A307–8/B364)

Yet he finds this assumption deeply problematic, as we will see below.

At the beginning of the Antinomies chapter, Kant claims that our
naïve reasoning leads us into apparently *contradictory* claims. (Much
of the discussion in this lengthy chapter can be understood without
appeal to what comes earlier in the *Critique*, and Kant himself once
said in a letter that it might have been better to start the book with the
Dialectic.) In this chapter I will focus on the First Antinomy. Here are
the contradictory propositions, with a brief summary of the arguments
for them that Kant presents.

Theses:

(A) *The world has a beginning in time*: for otherwise there would have
    been infinitely many events before the present, but an infinite
    series 'can never be completed through successive synthesis' (A426/
    B454).

(B) *The world is limited in space*: for if one is to think of an infinite whole
    'the successive synthesis of the parts of an infinite world must be

viewed as completed, that is, an infinite time must be viewed as having elapsed in the enumeration of all coexisting things' (A428/ B456) – but that is impossible.

Antitheses:

(A′) *The world has no beginning in time*: for there cannot have been a first event, for 'no coming to be of a thing is possible in an empty time', since there would be no reason why the world should start at that time rather than at any other (A427/B455).

(This is an appeal to the Principle of Sufficient Reason espoused by Leibniz, applied to Newton's concept of absolute time.)

(B′) *The world has no limits in space*: for there cannot be a sphere in space outside which there is no matter, for a relation of the whole material world to empty space would be 'a relation to no object, and such a relation ... is nothing' (A429/B457).

(This is Leibniz's rejection of Newton's concept of absolute space in favour of the view that space consists only in the spatial relations between material objects – A431–3/B459–61.)

Kant is here thinking not so much of a succession of pure temporal moments –'times' in the abstract, as it were –but of the series of all *events*, that is, changes in material objects and states of affairs. And, similarly, his topic is not spaces considered merely as mathematical segments of infinite empty space, but rather the matter that occupies portions of space. This Antinomy concerns *the whole material world*, that is, the universe, the sum total of all the matter and energy in space and all the changes in them occurring in time.

There is some ambiguity between ontology and epistemology in Kant's presentation of the supporting arguments. Is he concerned with the conceptual and/or metaphysical conditions for something to *be* the case, or about the epistemic conditions for our *knowing* it? The argument for (B) refers to conditions for our *thought* (representation) of the past (in the talk of 'successive synthesis'); but the other arguments may appear at first sight to concern pure ontology. Interpreted as such, the support for (B′) may seem particularly weak, for what is the problem about the mere *conception* of a finite amount of matter existing in infinite space? But, as we will see, much depends on how we interpret 'synthesis'.

Having presented this clash of arguments, Kant goes on to claim that only his Critical solution can pinpoint where we are led astray, and his diagnosis of the first two Antinomies is that the rival conclusions are dialectical, rather than analytic, contradictories; that is, they can't both be true, but they can both be false. That is because they rest on a questionable assumption about the universe as a complete totality, and a resulting ambiguity between taking it as phenomenon or noumenon, appearance or thing in itself. Now I propose to approach this topic while postponing as long as possible any consideration of Kant's obscure and controversial doctrine of transcendental idealism, despite the fact that in section 6 of the Antinomies chapter he presents that doctrine, which he claims to have already proved earlier in the *Critique*, as the key to the solution (see A491–507/B519–35). My justification for such blatant disregard for that bit of the text is that in the very next section Kant claims that the antinomies provide 'indirect proof of the transcendental ideality of appearances - a proof which ought to convince any who may not be satisfied by the direct proof given in the Transcendental Aesthetic' (A506/B534). Since many readers may remain unconvinced by that direct proof from Kant's initial treatment of space and time, my hope is that careful examination of issues raised by the antinomies may throw some light on transcendental idealism, rather than the other way round.

6.2   An approach to Kant's solution of the first antinomy

As he begins his elaborate diagnosis of what goes wrong in our cosmological thinking, Kant draws a sharp distinction between empirical science, where 'in the explanation of natural appearances... much must remain uncertain and many questions insoluble', and transcendental philosophy, in which 'no question which concerns an object given to pure reason can be insoluble' (A477/B505). In science we can always say that we do not yet know the answer to some question, and must await further evidence. In fact, at every stage in the progress of science, we have to say something of this form. But for metaphysical issues, like those we are dealing with here, Kant boldly says: 'it is not permissible to plead unavoidable ignorance; the solution can be *demanded*.' This does not mean that we are forced to choose between the antinomial alternatives; rather, we have to take a conceptual step backwards to a position from which we can see that both sides are wrong. Sometimes the only correct answer to a badly formed question is that there is no answer. No new evidence or experience is needed to solve *philosophical* problems: all the relevant parts are already before us; the difficulty is to see how they fit correctly together, and to arrive at 'a perspicuous representation' (to echo the thought of Wittgenstein, who also sharply distinguished philosophy from science at all stages of his philosophizing). As Kant puts it:

> the answer to the transcendent cosmological question cannot lie anywhere else save in the idea. We are not asking what is the constitution of the object in itself... (A479/B507)

He is not merely being agnostic about whether the world is finite or infinite in space and time. There is a *conceptual* problem, which, if we are careful, we can diagnose and remedy *a priori*, before we appeal to any *a posteriori* scientific investigation of the world. (But this opposition between 'conceptual' and '*a posteriori*' should not be identified with the standard empiricist opposition between 'analytic' and 'synthetic'. There is a special Kantian conception of the 'conceptual', which includes, besides the analytic, the synthetic *a priori* conditions for experience.)

Kant's main point here is that, when we try to theorize about the universe as a whole (the cosmos), we run into special problems about the relation between our concepts and their supposed object:

> The cosmological ideas alone have the peculiarity that they can presuppose their object, and the empirical synthesis required for its concept, as being given. The question which arises out of these ideas refers only to the advance in this synthesis, that is, whether it should be carried so far as to contain absolute totality - such totality, since it cannot be given in any experience, being no longer empirical. (A479/B507)

This is not the most limpid of sentences! Its meaning will depend crucially on what Kant means by 'given' and 'synthesis', so I will devote some time to each. Let us consider synthesis first. His official definition of it came much earlier in the *Critique*:

> By *synthesis*, in its most general sense, I understand the act of putting different representations together, and of grasping what is manifold in them in one act of knowledge. (A77/B103)

Synthesis seems to be a task or process that we perform, something that thus takes a certain amount of time. What is it that is synthesized? Kant is not thinking of material processes in factories or kitchens, producing cars or toys or synthetic cream. Kantian synthesis does not literally synthesize *objects*; it is *we* who synthesize our *representations* of objects (or, more precisely, it is our conscious or unconscious mental processes that do so). Our perceptions are themselves processes taking place in time. There are very rapid syntheses taking place whenever information is processed through our sense organs and brain (psychologists measure reaction times and brain-processing in fractions of a second). But, in the case of a large object which cannot be surveyed in a single glance, the perception of the whole of it may take rather longer; for example, inspecting a house could take several minutes (which is Kant's example at A193/B238). On a larger scale, circumnavigating Australia could take weeks.

In the Antinomies section, Kant seems more concerned with scientific research than with simple perception. His talk of a regress of conditions (see, e.g., A331–2/B388–9) involves a series of 'Why?' or 'What before?' questions, so 'synthesis' here seems to refer to the process of reaching answers to such questions by inquiries in history, archaeology, biology, geology and cosmology. Such research involves much more than the syntheses involved in perception (though, of course, it all ultimately depends on perception): it is a temporal process, but it is social rather than individual, and it takes much longer. The elaboration, testing and confirmation of a scientific theory can take decades; the building up of a collective body of human knowledge in geography, history, geology and scientific theory (and its passing on by education) involves most of human history.

So much for synthesis, for the moment. Let us now ask what Kant means by 'given'? This is a very ordinary word (*gegeben* in the German), which seems to take on more than ordinary depths of meaning in Kant's philosophy. Maybe a little old-fashioned linguistic philosophy will help. We can talk of something being 'given' in several different ways:

(i) actually perceived by a certain observer ('given to the senses')
(ii) perceivable by any observer who is, was, or will be in the right place at the right time ('given to the senses' in an extended sense)
(iii) known to exist, even if not presently perceivable (e.g., 'Given that there is an island to the west, as the map shows ...', or 'Given that the colonel was knifed in the back ...' or 'Given that uranium has an isotope ...'). In such cases the speaker is appealing to empirical knowledge of the world that has already been established, ultimately on the basis of many observers' perceptions

(iv)   merely conceived of (e.g., 'Given five people, and a boat that takes only two, how would you get them all across the river?', 'Given Hamlet's situation, what would you do?', 'Given a prime number, prove that there exists a bigger one')

Representations of type (iv) differ from the others in that they are not about any particular facts in the actual world; this is a purely abstract or imaginative sense of being 'given'. Amongst our representations that *are* of facts in the world, some are based on present perceptions, some on memory of previous perceptions, and some on testimony, that is, on what one has learnt from other people. We each acquire most of our historical, geographical and scientific knowledge in this second-hand way, but, if it *is* knowledge, some people must have justified the relevant claim by perception, or by reasoning based on perception. Theoretical science thus claims to justify our belief even in *im*perceptible entities such as elements, atoms, chemical bonds, genes, the collapse of wave functions, and black holes, as the best explanation of observed phenomena.

It would seem to be primarily sense (iii), to do with human knowledge, that Kant has in mind when he talks of 'the given' in these passages. He says as much himself:

Nothing is really given us save perception and the empirical advance from this to other possible perceptions. (A493/B521)

It seems that to be 'given' means, for him, for the relevant claim to be justifiable on the basis of perception, directly or indirectly. At A412/B439 he says: 'in conformity with the idea of reason, past time, as condition of the given moment, is necessarily thought of as being given in its entirety.' Despite Kant's wording, I suggest that he is not thinking of mere instants or stretches of time, but of events occurring in time. Of course, there is no question of the entirety of past events being perceived, or being perceptible by any one observer, so (i) cannot apply. And (ii) applies to past and *future* events equally, for they all count as perceivable by an observer who is in the right place at the right time, yet Kant sees an asymmetry between past and future in respect of being 'given':

Thus we necessarily think time as having completely elapsed up to the given moment, and being itself given in this completed form. This holds true, even though such completely elapsed time is not determinable by us. But since the future is not the condition of our attaining to the present, it is a matter of entire indifference, in our comprehension of the latter, how we may think of future time, whether as coming to an end or as flowing on to infinity.

...I must presuppose the first series [of all past events] in order to be able to regard [the present] as given. ... This latter series [of all future events] may not therefore be regarded as given, but only as allowing of being given.(A410–11/B437–8).

His point is presumably that we are entitled to think of there being a vast multitude of facts about the past, which the various disciplines of history, archaeology, geology, palaeontology and cosmology can in principle tell us about, whereas we are not entitled to think of there being a similarly determinate set of facts about the future. (There was once a fad for a supposed new discipline called 'futurology', but so far as I know it has not caught on, and no university has such a department.)

This is not yet to solve the First Antinomy. In outline, it looks as if Kant's proposal is going to be that we can be 'given' (i.e., acquire by 'synthesis' empirical knowledge of) lots of particular facts about the contents of space and time (past time, at least), but we can never be 'given' empirical knowledge of the whole universe as a complete totality. But at this point I propose that we give ourselves a short break from Kant and take an amateur look at some relevant science, before returning to the peculiarly Kantian mysteries.

6.3   Reinterpreting Kant in light of the progress of science

Let me now try to relate Kant's highly abstract philosophizing to our scientifically informed contemporary views. Let us take a concrete example, to clarify our thinking. Consider the birth of a baby, a tender event that can be perceived by those privileged to be there. But we know that the mother must herself have been born of another mother. Thus a regress starts, and we are led to say that there must have been a whole series of ancestors, going back into the mists of prehistory. But there is no corresponding pressure to say that there *must* be a series of *descendants* of today's baby: for there can be no guarantee that it will live long enough to have progeny, or choose to have any. Indeed, humans as a species could even become extinct (God forbid). (The example is, in effect, Kant's own at A512–13/B540–1, though to allow for contemporary sensibility I have added the bit about birth and motherhood.) This confirms that sense (iii) of 'given' yields the asymmetry between past and future events that Kant is talking about. We know that our ancestors must have existed, even if we know nothing specific about them (which is presumably what Kant meant by the phrase 'not determinable by us'). But future generations are not yet known to exist, and in this contingent and climate-changing world there is no guarantee that they will.

I have been proceeding cautiously, holding on to the leading strings of common sense. But conceptual problems lurk. When we talk of 'the whole series' of ancestors that have led up to the newborn baby before us, what do we mean? In what sense can such a series be a *whole*? The regress of ancestors soon disappears into the unknown mists of past time. Of course, it is logically possible to stop the regress with a postulated first pair of humans, as is the view of those who take traditional Creation stories such as those in *Genesis* literally. Actually, that would imply serious inbreeding from the third generation onwards, but perhaps the Creator could turn the trick again, and enhance the gene pool by creating occasional new people (or arranging virgin births?). For those of us who hold that the laws of biology allow no such miraculous exceptions, the regress may seem mind-bogglingly infinite (do we have to believe that it is humans 'all the way down'?). But, if we really want to know anything about the distant past, we will have to take on board some serious science.

In the early nineteenth century, geology made a revolution in the prevailing worldview that literal readers of the Bible found deeply disturbing, for it involved recognizing that our earth has had a hugely longer past than anyone previously imagined. (Kant himself made an early contribution to the scientific study of the remote past, with his nebular hypothesis about the formation of the solar system.) The geological revolution provided enough past time for the evolution of new species by natural selection (Charles Darwin presupposed Charles Lyell). Biology now believes neither in a first human, nor in an infinite series of past humans, but rather that we have evolved from creatures that were not human, and ultimately not even mammals. But, if all humans are born from humans, how can humans have evolved from something else? A Sorites paradox threatens here, but it can be seen off by the Darwinian reflection that species are mutable, so that species terms are vague in their application over evolutionary time. There was no first pair, yet we can put a temporal lower bound on *homo sapiens*: there have *not* been infinitely many humans (you may be relieved to know!), but there hasn't been any determinate finite number of them either.

This solution to what we might call 'the Human Antinomy' takes the logical form Kant envisaged for his first two Antinomies, namely, the rejection of both alternatives. It is not a *sceptical* solution: there is no fact of the matter that lies beyond our ken. It is a *critical* solution in the sense that it involves conceptual considerations that show why we should reject both alternatives. Of course, Kant himself, writing in the century before Darwin, did not have those theoretical resources, so this is not a Critical solution. (And he may have been inhibited from voicing doubts about the existence of a first human pair by awareness of the theological opprobrium that this would have brought down upon his head.) However, I suggest it is illuminating to compare it with what he does have to offer.

It may be said at this stage that these evolutionary considerations only push the problem further back, for we now have to extend the series of our ancestors through an even longer series of life forms on earth. But, if a living thing can only come from another living thing, how did life get started? To suggest that it may have come from elsewhere in space (as Fred Hoyle used to do) only puts the question back a further stage: how did extraterrestrial life get started? There may be a scientific stop to this regress, if it can be shown that simple forms of life can emerge from inanimate matter in certain conditions. And, besides, there may be some conceptual vagueness and elasticity about what exactly to count as life, and whether there are borderline cases.

But we are in a metaphysical frame of mind here, and we can hardly confine our thought to biology. Even if science does lead us to believe that there was a first emergence of life from inorganic matter, this would not be conceived of as creation *ex nihilo*. Nothing can come of nothing –so a very ancient thought goes. (Kant argued for it transcendentally in his First Analogy.) In the envisaged scientific account of the origin of life, what we are imagining is one special kind of organic structure with self-maintaining and self-replicating powers being produced out of a rich chemical soup. Yet in any such set of chemical reactions we believe that at least the atoms themselves are conserved: exactly as many atoms of each element must come out of the process as went into it.

But are the atoms themselves eternal? The ancient Greeks thought so, and so did most chemists (though not the alchemists) until the advent of atomic theory. Since then physicists have told us that protons, neutrons and electrons are themselves composed of still smaller and more mysterious entities rejoicing in the names of quarks and bosons, which hardly count as 'particles' at all. And we are now reliably informed that all the contents of the whole universe originated in a mathematical singularity, the 'Big Bang', which occurred a finite time ago. I have now gone far beyond common sense, but I have still been holding the hand of science. But let us try and see what bearing Kant's philosophical considerations have on these cosmological issues.

6.4　Stephen Hawking speaks to Kant – and Kant answers back

We have seen how we can get an empirical grip, so to speak, on some very large totalities of past entities. Evolutionary theory enables us to put a lower bound on our human ancestors. For the origin of life itself, physics and chemistry may one day show how that was possible. For the origin of the observed material universe, our best contemporary theories and observations enable us to extrapolate back to a mathematical point of origin some very large, but finite, time ago. In each case, there is no question of anyone ever *perceiving* such huge totalities, or their limiting points, so they can never be 'given' in sense (i) or (ii) above. But (so we are told) we can get to know something about them by indirect means, since the scientific theories we appeal to are well confirmed by a variety of observational evidence; if so, these totalities are 'given' in sense (iii).

It may, therefore, sound very much as if contemporary cosmology has now provided scientific justification for the *theses* of the First Antinomy –that the universe has indeed had a beginning in time, and presumably has had a finite extent in space at each stage of its expansion. So have Kant's elaborate philosophical reflections simply been outdated by scientific progress? Certainly, theoretical physics has gone way beyond anything that he conceived of. We have got used to hearing of non-Euclidean space, of space–time as a four-dimensional continuum, of curvatures in space–time itself, and even of space–time itself being finite but unbounded –though hearing is one thing, and understanding is another! We also hear confident predictions from theoretical physicists like Stephen Hawking that they are getting close to a Grand Unified Theory, covering both the very large and the very small, and uniting the four fundamental forces in a so-called Theory of Everything. It would be easy to conclude that Kant's discussion in the Antinomies chapter is of merely historical interest. However, I beg leave to question that, though doing so may strain my limited understanding of modern physics to breaking point.

In the first place, a paradox lurks behind the tempting phrase 'a Theory of Everything'. Suppose at some stage physicists come up with some single formula –no doubt very complex in its meaning and its implications –which they claim is the Ultimate Law of Nature, the explanation of everything (Kant's 'unconditioned'). Then each particular event (or total state of the universe) could be explained in terms of this Ultimate Law, applied to the conditions preceding that event. What, then, about explaining those preceding conditions? That sets us off on a familiar regress. We are told that we can now take the regress back to a singular first event, the Big Bang. Physicists say that the laws of nature break down at a singularity: when there is infinite density and zero size, nothing can be predicted. But, in that case, we do not have a theory that explains literally *everything*.

Theologians tend to take a metaphysical jump here, and say that it is God who decided on the Creation, and lit the touch-paper for the Big Bang, as it were. But that just moves the regress further back –or, rather, *sideways*, into a different kind of theorizing or language-game. For we can ask *why* God created the universe, particularly such a universe as we have been burdened with –but it is not at all clear how such questions can be answered, except by appeal to theological authority.

Maybe the latest theory of space–time as finite but unbounded will allow us to sidestep such awkward questions about the causation of a *first* event –but if mathematical singularities such as black holes occur at various places within the universe, it still seems that the laws (or Law) of physics will break down at those points. And, even if such singularities can be avoided, the Ultimate Law will still surely be an *a posteriori*, not an *a priori*, truth. Its epistemological role is to explain all the other empirical truths, including all the observed ones –and to be supported by the fact that it explains all observations so far. There lies an inductive rub, for we can never exclude the logical possibility that new observations may one day turn up that will *not* fit our so-called Theory of Everything. Of course, if centuries had passed without our finding any such counter-evidence, we would say that it had been proved beyond all reasonable doubt. But the logical fact would remain that even such an extremely well-evidenced theory could not explain *itself*: it could not be literally a theory of *everything*. It would remain open for new generations of ambitious young physicists to ask why the so-called Ultimate Law takes the form it does, and to search for a deeper level of physical theory to provide an explanation of it. If they succeeded, that would invite yet further regress. I submit that the continual search for explanations is fine, but the thought that there is a particular place where it must stop is not. And this is very much what Kant said:

> The principle of reason is thus properly only a *rule*, prescribing a regress in the series of the conditions of given appearances, and forbidding it to bring the regress to a close by treating anything at which it may arrive as absolutely unconditioned. (A509/B537)

And perhaps there is still more to be learnt from Kant. In my amateur attempt to review contemporary cosmology, I was careful to use the phrase 'the whole *observed* material universe', and I suggest that there remains a crucial gap between that and the whole material universe, period. Cosmologists tend to be silent about what (if anything) happened before the Big Bang. Some of them may say that the question makes no sense, since time itself began with the Bang. That invites a counter-question: what sense does it make to talk of time *beginning*? And, if piles of stuff can fly out from the initial singularity, a mathematical zero-point in the equations, couldn't stuff stream *into* such a point, too? (Isn't that what is supposed to happen in black holes?) It may be replied that no structure, and hence no information, can survive a Big Bang, so that, if the universe has had a pre-Bang history, we can never know about it. So how can empirical science ever be in a position to say anything about the *whole* history of the *whole* universe? It looks as if the synthesis cannot be completed, as Kant said.

I suggest that Kant's instinct was right, even if some of his details are outdated or dubious. Despite the confidence of Stephen Hawking and his ilk, it is not clear that anyone could ever be in a position to make claims about 'the whole universe' as a totality, a completed whole. This is not merely a contingent limitation on our knowledge; it is not something that might be overcome by the progress of science and technology. When physicists talk, with their sublime arrogance, of 'a Theory of Everything', I make bold to suggest that they do not literally mean what they say. It is not part of the ambition of physics to explain why Mozart's Piano Concerto no. 21 is so ravishing, why Hitler rose from the gutters of Vienna to become Chancellor of Germany, or why Asha eventually consented to marry Ahmed. Physics abstracts in its lordly way from all such wonderful or terrible details of the world. Physical theories are not about such humanly important stuff, but about measurable quantities of mass, length, time, charge and radiation.

And, even when confined to such physical facts, there are still deep problems in the notion of a Theory of Everything. A scientific theory, as Hawking himself admits, is a humanly constructed model which exists only in our minds, but tries to economically explain a large class of past observations in terms of a small number of assumptions, and to accurately predict future observations(*A Brief History of Time*, updated edition, Bantam Press, 1998, p. 11). Up till now, all physical theories have been partial; they have only tried to explain a large but limited class of physical phenomena. Moreover, the computing of the observational implications of a physical theory always involves making approximations and simplifying assumptions, as Hawking also concedes (pp. 187, 204). Adjudicating the fit or lack of fit between a theory and reality always seems to be a somewhat messy business, both conceptually and technologically. Is there, then, any real possibility of a theory that is complete rather than partial, and which fits observations exactly rather than approximately?

Hawking famously concluded his best-selling book with the line that, if we ever find out why it is that we and the universe exist, we would know the mind of God. But the word 'why' is ambiguous – are we talking of causes, or of purposes? But purposes, intentions, values and humanly intelligible meanings lie completely outside the domain of physics. No doubt Hawking just wanted a memorable, resonant phrase to end his book. But, if we really assumed that there must be a single true answer to the question about causes, a theory of everything waiting to be discovered by sufficiently clever scientists, an ultimate truth that is already known to God in His Omniscience, then we would be committed to that theocentric transcendental realism which Kant did so much to undermine.

6.5 Does all this throw any light on Kant's transcendental idealism?

Kant's transcendental idealism is too large and controversial a topic to be dealt with in the last section of this chapter. But I hope my reflections may cast a *little* light on it. We have found reason to doubt that any race of finite beings, however intelligent and technologically sophisticated, could ever get an empirical grip, in terms of well-confirmed scientific theory, on the universe as a whole. If so, the universe cannot be given in sense (iii). But now we meet some classic issues of Kant-interpretation. If he is not saying that the universe has an age and a size but we can never know it, is he saying that these questions *are not even meaningful*?

In twentieth-century terms, if he is not an epistemically pessimistic realist, is he a verificationist?

Paul Guyer has argued that Kant is a verificationist in the *Critique*, though at earlier stages of his thinking he had restricted himself to epistemic modesty. As we have seen, Kant's arguments for the thesis and antithesis of the First Antinomy are essentially epistemic, since they rest on the possibilities of synthesis, which I have interpreted in terms of our processes of getting to know about things. Guyer argues that an explicitly verificationist premise is needed to derive the conclusion that there can be no fact of the matter about the age and size of the universe, and he concludes that, since Kant fails to justify verificationism, he fails to support his metaphysics of transcendental idealism.[2]

I suggest, however, that this misses something vital in Kant's thought. Of course, there are plenty of cases in which epistemic modesty is the right attitude to take: we do not know whether there is intelligent life elsewhere in the universe, though it is a perfectly realistic possibility (Kant himself allowed the empirical hypothesis that the moon is inhabited, at A493/B521). We might find evidence of alien intelligence by picking up meaningful radio signals, or one fine day bug-eyed creatures might drop by in their spaceships; though we could never have such decisive proof of the negative claim that there is *no* intelligence anywhere else. It is important to note, however, that epistemic modesty about a proposition involves a conceptual presumption about its determinacy of sense. To say that there may be life elsewhere is to presuppose that we know what would *count* as life in all manner of exotic locations, that is, that *our* concept of life would have determinate application, true or false, to whatever strange stuff there may be out there.

But in some other cases we can see that our lack of knowledge is not merely contingent. When we discussed whether there has been a finite or an infinite series of human ancestors, we concluded that there is no fact of the matter either way, since we have had to reconceptualize our understanding of species terms as involving vagueness of application over long periods of evolutionary time. We now realize that in the evolution of primates there will have been many hominoid creatures about which there is no determinate fact of the matter whether they count as human beings. Our concept of humanity does not reach out with clean-cut application into the deep past. (And our concept of a *person* might get similarly stressed by whatever alien life forms there may be in deep space.)

Analogously, but perhaps more radically, Kant's diagnosis of the First Antinomy would seem to be that there is a *conceptual* defect in the very idea of the universe as a complete totality, of which it would make sense to say that it must be either finite or infinite, even if we can never know which. For example, at A506–7/B534–5 he says it is 'false that the world (the sum of all appearances) is a whole existing in itself'. Here Kant may sound like a verificationist. Yet there remains for him some sense in which we *can* meaningfully talk about the whole universe. And this is a point where his notorious distinction between appearances and things in themselves comes in. Remember his 'principle of reason' that generates all this trouble:

> the principle that if the conditioned is given, the entire sum of conditions, and consequently the absolutely unconditioned (through which alone the conditioned has been possible) is also given. (A409/B436)

At A498–9/B526–7 he says that, if the conditioned and its conditions are understood as things in themselves, then if the former were given, so would the latter be. But if the conditioned is only an appearance, given only in an empirical synthesis in space and time, a regress to the conditions is not given, but only set as a task:

> if the conditioned as well as its condition are things in themselves, then upon the former being given, the regress to the latter is not only set as a task, but therewith *already really given*. ... The synthesis of the conditioned with its condition is here a *synthesis of the mere understanding*, which represents things as they are, without considering whether or how we can obtain knowledge of them.
>
> ... If, however, what we are dealing with are *appearances* ... I cannot say, in the same sense of the terms, that if the conditioned is given, all its conditions (as appearances) are likewise given ... The appearances are in their apprehension themselves nothing but an *empirical synthesis* in space and times, and are *given only in this synthesis*. (A498–9/B526–7 [my italics])

The first part of this passage allows that there is after all a sense in which the whole universe can be given, but only by a synthesis *of the understanding*, not empirical synthesis involving sensibility. (Kant's terminology tends to wobble in the struggle to include all the conceptual complexities into his system.) In terms of the varieties of 'the given' that I distinguished above, we can say that the universe can be given to thought only in sense (iv), not (i)–(iii). As Kant puts it: 'we can have the cosmic whole only in concept, never, as a whole, in intuition' (A519/B547). Yet he does *not* say that all talk of the cosmic whole is meaningless: he was not an eighteenth-century logical positivist (Hume is a better candidate for that label).

The concept of the whole universe, the sum total of all matter and events, is a paradigm case of what Kant calls a transcendent 'idea', something that can be conceived of, but cannot be exemplified in experience. There is no corresponding completed, synthesized total-ity of which we can have any empirical knowledge. So there is no fact of the matter about whether the universe has a definite size or temporal extent, whether finite or infinite. Here is one last Kantian quotation:

> Since the world does not exist in itself, independently of the regres-sive series of my representations, it exists *in itself* neither as *infinite* whole nor as a *finite* whole. It exists only in the empirical regress of the series of appearances, and is not to be met with as something in itself. (A505/B533; see also A518/B546ff)

This is one of those Kantian sayings that raise hackles in realists (which means most of us, most of the time), and leads many readers to interpret him as a Berkelean idealist. His use of the singular posses-sive pronoun 'my' (yes, it is there in the German) makes it sound as if he were saying that the world does not exist outside his mental states, which would make him Master of the Universe in a sense that not even Stephen Hawking would aspire to! He should surely have used the *plural* pronoun 'our', for we have seen how his notion of synthesis implicitly embraces our collective knowledge-gathering. But that still leaves him open to the robustly realist objection that the physical world is not a product of our scientific activity (after all, it long pre-dated the advent of humans). I suggest that Kant had better mean only that *our conceptions of the world* are a product of human cognitive and scientific activity, and I make so bold as to propose rewriting the pas-sage as follows:

> Any conception of the world is a product of our human cognitive activ-ity; and any theory about the universe is a result of science as it has progressed in terms of theory and observational evidence up to that

time, so it will be fallible and incomplete. We can never arrive at a theory that represents the world exactly as it is ('in itself') –that is an impossible ideal. In particular, our conceptions of finitude and infinity depend for their application on principles of individuation and counting, which have changed in the progress of science, and may change again. So we cannot claim that the whole universe itself is finite, or infinite, only that some of our fallible theories represent it as such.

Notes

1. I use material from this chapter in Chapters 4 and 5 of my book *Inspirations from Kant* (New York, Oxford University Press, 2011).
2. Guyer, P. (1987) *Kant and the Claims of Knowledge* (Cambridge: Cambridge University Press), ch. 18, pp. 407–9.

References

Guyer, P. (1987) *Kant and the Claims of Knowledge* (Cambridge: Cambridge University Press).
Hawking, S. (1998) *A Brief History of Time* (London: Bantam Press).
Kant, I. (1781/1933) *Critique of Pure Reason, translated by Norman Kemp Smith* (London: Macmillan).
Stevenson, L. (2011) *Inspirations from Kant* (New York: Oxford University Press).

7
Reading Kant Topographically: From Critical Philosophy to Empirical Geography

Jeff Malpas and Günter Zöller

7.1 Transcendental and empirical place

The idea that the Kantian philosophy could be read 'topographically' – that is, in a way that takes it to be centrally concerned with the deline-ation of a certain *topos* or place (*Ort, Stelle*)[1]– is suggested by the very terminology that Kant uses in the development and articulation of his work, and by the ideas and images that he frequently deploys – both in the critical works and elsewhere.[2] Perhaps nowhere is this more vividly apparent than in the famous metaphor, in chapter III of the 'Analytic of Principles', in which he describes his project as one of surveying the 'land of truth'– a land that turns out to be an island surrounded by dangerous and deceptive seas.[3]

Kantian topography, however, takes two forms: the first is what we might call a *transcendental* topography,[4] in which the focus is on the exploration of the place that reason itself occupies (and so also on the delineation of the bounds and limits of that place);[5] the second is an *empirical* topography that takes as its focus the specific character of human being in its relation to climate, geography and culture. The first project is pursued in Kant's critical works, most paradigmatically in the *Critique of Pure Reason*, while the second is undertaken in his *Anthropology*, and also, of particular importance here, in his *Lectures on Physical Geography*.

One might be tempted to suppose that these two projects would be in tension with one another, for surely recognition of the empirical differ-ences between the ways in which human beings find themselves on the earth would tend to undermine the pretensions of the transcendental project to uncover the structures that obtain irrespective of empirical situations. Certainly some writers have suggested as much.[6] Yet, although it is possible that the fact of diversity would incline one towards the abandonment of any notion of an over-arching transcendental structure, there is surely no necessity about this. Indeed, in the sense in which Kant employs the notion of the transcendental, there are no empirical facts that could undermine its claims to universality or necessity. Empirical investigation might reveal the inadequacy of some particular construal of the transcendental, but it cannot imply the necessary abandonment of the transcendental as such.

In fact, the empirical and transcendental projects are closely related. Not only does the transcendental project aim at establishing how it is that empirical inquiry can itself be possible, thereby also establishing the proper bounds of that inquiry, but the empirical project provides both the motivation as well as the material on which the transcendental project builds. In this latter respect, the transcendental project can be said to find its own possibility in the empirical, but the empirical also depends on the transcendental for its own self-understanding. Indeed, the idea of *topos* itself provides the unifying conception that enables us to grasp the interconnection between the transcendental and the empirical here, since the place that is investigated transcendentally is nothing other than the structure that is also empirically instantiated in diverse forms – there is no *topos*, no place, that stands behind or apart from the place and places in which human beings find themselves.

Reading Kant topographically, then, enables us to think of the transcendental and empirical projects in an integrated fashion, not as in tension, but as approaching the place of human being from two different directions, and in a way that avoids any overstepping of the proper bounds of that place. Moreover, as the discussion here unfolds, it will also become evident that understanding the specifically topographical character of Kant's transcendental project may actually provide the means to identify a significant shortcoming in Kant's own understanding of the place-bound character of human being as it is empirically instantiated.

7.2   Place and space

Our being in place is not some merely accidental feature of our empirical situation. On Kant's view, the experience of which finite beings such as ourselves are capable is always based on the deliverances of sensibility – on our receptivity – and so can be said always to be dependent on the *place* in which we are empirically located, although the point is not one to which Kant himself draws attention. Moreover, the locatedness at issue here is both our own locatedness and the locatedness of the sensible entities that we encounter. As Edward Casey points out in his account of the philosophical history of place, 'Kant insists that sensible things must occupy particular places: we cannot perceive them, much less know them, except in such places ... bodiless beings are unimplaced, sensible bodies (i.e., bodies perceivable by our own bodies) are inherently implaced entities'.[7] Place and the very possibility of sensibility are thus bound closely together.

Now, in order for human beings and other beings to be in one place or another, there has to be a place or places to be in – in the first place, as it were. But, according to Kant, this in turn presupposes the prior presence and original involvement of the very being that is to be or find itself in place. Only because place is basically, originally or, as Kant's terminology has it, 'transcendentally' in us (human beings), can we (human beings) find ourselves subsequently, derivatively and contingently, or 'empirically', in one place or another. Empirical placement presupposes transcendental placing. On Kant's account, then, we are as much in place (empirically) as place is in us (transcendentally). We can thus understand the Kantian project as already taking its primary orientation from the focus on the placed character of experience, and thus also from the way that place is essentially constituted in relation to the human subject, just as the human subject, in virtue of being a finite sensing being, is itself constituted in relation to place.

Although it might seem a somewhat tendentious contrast, this approach, when read in the topographical fashion suggested here, bears comparison with Heidegger's much later emphasis on the notion of being-in-the-world as the basic characterization of the essence of human being that is *Dasein*. While it is usual to view Kant's more 'subjectivist' orientation as marking his position off from that of Heidegger (and being viewed so by Heidegger himself), this may be to prejudge the way subjectivity figures in Kant's thought, and to neglect the way in which the Heideggerian notion of being-in-the-world is already to some extent prefigured in Kant's topographical orientation – albeit understood as based in what can now be thought of as the topographical structure of subjectivity. Indeed, the topographical reading of Kant's project may suggest a greater continuity between the Kantian position (and perhaps also that of German idealism) and Heidegger's existential phenomenology than might ordinarily be assumed.

The account of space (*Raum*) that underpins the way of understanding place sketched out here is one of Kant's most important and innovative ideas. Kant argues that space, along with time, is neither a self-subsisting thing nor a substance (Newtonian absolute space) nor an adhering relational order among originally non-spatial (and non-temporal) substantial unities or monads (Leibnizian relative space).[8] On Kant's account, as first presented in the Inaugural Dissertation of 1770 (*On the Form and Principles of the Sensible and Intelligible World*) and restated, a 'silent decade' later, in the 'Transcendental Aesthetic' of the *Critique of Pure Reason* (1781), space – along with time – is the a *priori* subjective form of all empirical *intuition* (*Anschauung*) – of outer intuition in the case of space and of inner intuition in the case of time. Moreover, on Kant's analysis (itself understood as an *Erörterung* or 'elucidation', literally a 'placing'), space – along with time – is not only the pure, non-empirical form of empirical intuition but an intuition in its own right, more precisely a purely sensible, non-empirical intuition.[9]

The original nature of Kantian space as intuitive, and not as conceptual or discursive, affects both the ontology and the epistemology of space with regard to the latter's infinitely many possible determinations into plural spaces. Ontologically considered, all such distinct spaces are dependent on finite, receptive subjectivity and therefore restricted to the 'human standpoint' (*Standpunkte eines Menschen*).[10] Epistemically considered, all such spaces are grasped, in their original form, directly and immediately ('intuited'; *angeschaut*) and not by means of representations of general features of concepts (*Begriffe*; *Allgemeinbegriffe*).

With respect to places, understood as determined locations in space (or rather locally determined space itself), the ontologically anthropocentric and epistemically immediate or felt character of space means the following: places are, and are to be ascertained as, regions of an oriented space, the coordinates of which are established by reference to inwardly felt basic differentiations such as those between left and right, up and down, forward and backward. Kant deals with the phenomenon of space's orientedness and the resulting orientations of space in several of his writings, typically citing the evidence from the phenomenon of incongruent counterparts or so-called *enantiomorphs*. Kant points to the paradox that two objects, such as a hand and its mirror image, may be identical in their spatial properties and yet not be able to be mapped onto each other, each being side-reversed in relation to the other. On Kant's analysis, the phenomenon of incongruent but otherwise spatially identical objects is due to the oriented nature of space and the objects

in it, which in turn is owed to the dependency of space on human sensibility. Spatial objects are not located in a neutral spatial net, but are
placed in an oriented space, the basic topological feature of which is the
distinction between right and left.[11] On Kant's account, then, all places
are human places; places can be established and grasped only from the
human standpoint, and are deeply informed by this standpoint.

Although the oriented character of space is already given in space as
such, we only have a sense of the basic orientation of that space through
the sense we have of the orientation given in our bodies. Thus, while
the orientedness of space belongs to space as such, our grasp of that
orientedness, and so our grasp of the externality of space, is dependent
upon our sense of ourselves – upon our own subjectivity – and so upon
the grasp of our own internality. Since the form of inner sense is time,
this means that the grasp of space is dependent upon our grasp of time.
In part, this merely reflects the Kantian point that all our representations, both inner and outer, are subject to a temporal ordering. It also
reflects the way in which our own being oriented in a space involves
more than just a basic sense of the orientedness of space itself, but also
requires the connecting of features of that space to the possibilities we
have for action. In this way, to be oriented in a space is actually for our
inner experience to be coordinated with our outer surroundings.

Kant himself has much to say about the way in which our sense of
ourselves, and so what is given in inner sense, is dependent upon what
is given externally. As is well known, Kant's argument against material
idealism depends on the argument, in summary form, that subjectivity is dependent upon objectivity. Since Kant also argues that objectivity is itself tied to space, so the subjective can also be seen to depend,
if indirectly, on the external and the spatial. In fact, the relationship
of dependence here is reciprocal, and the other side of this reciprocity
(which might be also described in terms of a bilateral asymmetry) is
partly what is expressed in the insistence on the temporal ordering of
all representations. When considered in relation to the structure of that
being in place that is fundamental to the possibility of experience (at
least of the sort of which we are capable), this means that place always
comprises both externality and internality (in a way that concurs with
the phenomenal experience of being in a place) as well as both subjective and objective components. Consequently, we can say that not only
does the sensible world come to appearance in place, but it is only in
place that we encounter ourselves.

Moreover, on a Kantian account of matters, original space and its local
counterpart, prior place, are identical across the plurality and indeed

infinity of human beings – past, present and future. The 'human stand-point' underlying space and place and their determinations to spaces and places is one and the same across human individuals. Transcendental space-place is one, and this proto-space and proto-place is not so much a particular first space and place but the principal ground, basis or root of all spaces and places. Given the unity of space, and so the implicit communicability between places, our being tied to place does not clo-seoff dialogue between finite sensing beings such as ourselves, but actu-ally makes it possible. The possibility of such dialogue does not depend, moreover, on a single space that is everywhere experienced as the same. The unity of space allows for (we might even argue that it requires) plural determination in terms of particular spaces and places, and, as such, it also allows for communicability across difference – to be located or spatially oriented is always to be located and oriented in a way that allows connection to other spaces and places,[12] and so also allows com-munication across those spaces and places.[13]

7.3 Place and geography

Kant is not only the transcendental theoretician of the unity and dif-ference of space and place and of the dialogic interplay of places – of interlocation and interlocution, as we might put it. Kant is also the empirical investigator of the many places that human beings have occu-pied as individuals and in groups of all sizes – over time as well as in current times. Kant pursued this second major topographical interest over several decades in his regular university lectures on physical geog-raphy. In fact, he was the first academic teacher to introduce this sub-ject matter into the curriculum of the University of Königsberg (today's Kaliningrad). From the summer semester of 1756, when he was still an unsalaried lecturer (*Privatdozent*), through the summer semester of 1796, he offered the lecture course on 'physical geography' (*Physische Geographie*) almost every year (nearly fifty times), eventually alternating it with his other academic innovation, the lecture course in anthropol-ogy, which he regularly offered every winter semester.

Unfortunately, as has been pointed out by a number of recent commentators,[14] the version of Kant's *Physical Geography* that was pub-lished under his name in an edition by Friedrich Theodor Rink in 1802 is a compilation, loosely based on Kant's lecture materials which are no longer extent. While the work in this form had been included, some-what unjustifiedly, among Kant's own publications in the Academy edition,[15] the proper place for the edition and publication of the

surviving texts from Kant's lectures on physical geography is the fourth
section of the Academy edition, containing the transcripts of Kant's
lectures. After more than a century since the inception of the Academy
edition, the publication of representative lecture transcripts of Kant's
physical geography lectures is finally scheduled to complete this part
of the Academy Edition in the near future.[16] This edition will finally
make available extensive previously unpublished and even unavailable
texts documenting almost four decades of Kant's continuing work on
the geographical unity as well as diversity of the earth's places and their
inhabitants, human as well as non-human.

For Kant, geography is the strictly empirical and hence descriptive
counterpart to the scientific, mathematically based study of nature
undertaken by physics. Moreover, the empirical cognition of nature
as the comprehensive object of outer sense (geography) has its counterpart in the empirical cognition of human being, or rather of the
human 'soul' (*Seele*), as the comprehensive object of inner sense
(anthropology).[17] The joint object of geography and anthropology is
the 'world' (*Welt*),[18] with the latter term not only referring to a domain
of objects to be studied with a theoretical, purely cognitive intent, but
also indicating the ulterior pragmatic purpose of such cognition in the
context of the human ability to interact with nature and with other
human beings. The word 'world' in this second, pragmatic sense designates the 'place for the display of our skilfulness' (*Schauplatz, auf dem
das Spiel unserer Geschicklichkeit vor sich geht*).[19] Kant regards nature in
us and outside us as the theatre for human action of all kinds, and he
considers geography and anthropology, which he initially presented
jointly before according each one its own lecture course, as the propae-
deutic for a life that is informed, enabled and enhanced by knowing
the ways of the world.

Due to the fact that cognition of remote places is as hard to come by
on one's own as cognition of remote times, Kant stresses the need to
rely on 'reports' (*Nachrichten*) to extend personally limited experiences,
including his own, to encompass, indirectly, the experiences made by
others, especially those laid down in written form. Kant divides all
such 'foreign experience' (*fremde Erfahrung*) modally into 'narration'
(*Erzählung*) and 'description' (*Beschreibung*), with 'history' (*Geschichte*)
forming the object of narration and 'geography' (*Geographie*) that of
description.[20] To be sure, the narration of nature's past may also include
the latter's geographical shape, as it developed over time. Accordingly,
Kant's conception of a strictly descriptive geography refers specifically
to the earth in its current shape. Any account of its inhabitants that

goes beyond the present time is not a description but a narration: more precisely, it is not a 'description of nature' (*Naturbeschreibung*) but a 'natural history' (*Naturgeschichte*), which does not form part of Kant's presentist program of geography.[21]

Kant further divides geography's constitutive concern with the earth's many places into 'topography' (*Topographie* – this being intended in a much narrower sense than we have employed in our own discussion) or 'the description of a singular place of the earth' (*die Beschreibung eines einzelnen Ortes der Erde*[22]), 'chorography' (*Chorographie*) or the 'description of a region' (*Gegend*), 'orography' (*Orographie*) or the 'description of this or that mountainous region' (*Gebirge*), and 'hydrography' (*Hydrographie*) or the 'description of bodies of water' (*Gewässer*). While the term 'place', when taken in a larger, *topological* sense, encompasses spaces of all shapes and sizes that serve the purpose of localization, 'place' in the narrower meaning of the term refers to a particular, geographically limited place of the earth, such as the point of confluence of two rivers or the point at which a valley cuts through a mountain range.

A further, in our terms, 'topographical' taxonomy underlying Kant's concept of geography is the distinction between the foundational discipline of physical geography (*physische Geographie*), which provides 'a general sketch of nature' (*allgemeiner Abriß der Natur*), and the 'possible geographies' (*mögliche Geographien*) established on that basis, in particular 'mathematical geography' (*mathematische Geographie*) or the study of the shape, size and motion of the earth, 'moral geography' (*moralische Geographie*) or the study of the different customs and characters of human beings in accordance with the different regions, 'political geography' (*politische Geographie*) or the study of the laws of a civil society in their relation to the physical condition of the soil as well as the inhabitants, and 'theological geography' (*theologische Geographie*) or the study of theological principles in their relation to the condition of the soil.[23]

Accordingly, the text of Kant's physical geography – in Rink's compiled edition – consists of 'mathematical preliminary concepts' (*mathematische Vorbegriffe*),[24] followed by a first, general part on physical geography proper, dealing with the earth's component parts – water, land and atmosphere – and an account of the great changes that the earth has been and is still undergoing;[25] a second, special part on the 'earth's creatures' (*Erdgeschöpfe*) or on what the 'surface of the earth' (*Erdboden*)[26] comprises – the human being in its different 'formation' (*Bildung*) and 'colour' (*Farbe*),[27] the animal kingdom, the plant world and the mineral world;[28] and a third, final part that deals with the most

remarkable natural peculiarities of all countries according to 'geographical order' (*geographische Ordnung*), ranging from Asia through Africa
to Europe and concluding with America, with no mention made of
the fifth continent.[29] In this final part Kant combines physical, moral,
political and theological geography in a geoanthropological general survey listing different countries and peoples, with the section on Europe
the most sketchy, presumably because Kant's parallel lecture course and
publication on anthropology contained extensive material on European
national characters.

7.4   Place and purpose

The anthropological, moral and political scope of Kant's geography
lectures, which is not limited to Rink's edited version but can also be
observed in the extant lecture transcripts from the 1750s through the
1790s, puts into perspective the more narrow focus of Kant's publications
in moral philosophy from the 1780 and 1790s, which seem to forego
entirely empirical considerations in the 'foundation' or 'groundwork'
(*Grundlegung*) of the metaphysics of morals as well as in its twofold elaboration as 'Metaphysical First Principles' (*metaphysische Anfangsgründe*) of the
doctrines of law and virtue (*Rechtslehre, Tugendlehre*). The very specifica-
tion of those works as involving the 'foundations' or 'principles' of human
conduct already indicates that a more completely elaborated picture of
human being and its place in the world might well involve cognitions
of the self and world that lie beyond the domain of *a priori* concepts and
precepts. To be sure, on Kant's view, the multiple, indeed infinitely many,
empirical manifestations of human life have no bearing on the validity
of the unconditional norms of legal and ethical conduct. However, they
serve to document the range of the factual in relation to which those
very norms need to establish themselves in processes of instantiation and
exemplification. One might say, then, that the surveying of the empirical
field of human life as it is known *a posteriori* is a necessary counterpart to
any attempt to delineate the *a priori* grounds and limits of that field.

But Kant not only juxtaposes the *a priori* and the *a posteriori* by way
of developing parallel lecture and publication series in pure philosophy
('transcendental philosophy' and 'moral philosophy') and empirical
philosophy ('geography' and 'anthropology'). He also seeks to address
the forms and conditions for the transition between the two sets of disciplines and their respective object domains. In particular, Kant attempts
to identify a procedure for ascertaining or establishing lawfulness even
with regard to what is contingent in the natural as well as the social (or

human) world. The principle of the lawfulness of the contingent as such is that of the teleological order of nature and culture.

To be sure, the 'use' or 'employment' (*Gebrauch*) of teleological principles in philosophy – to cite the title of Kant's pioneering essay from 1788 (*Über den Gebrauch teleologischer Principien in der Philosophie*),[30]which prepares the systematic account of the forms and conditions of 'purposiveness' or 'finality' (*Zweckmäßigkeit*) in the *Critique of the Power of Judgment* (1790) – is not 'constitutive' but 'regulative', and not 'determining' (*bestimmend*) but 'reflective' (*reflektierend*). Natural and historical phenomena are to be regarded 'as if' (*als ob*) they had their ultimate causal origin in some being endowed with the ability to set and pursue 'ends' or 'purposes' (*Zwecke*). The point of this fictitious or hypothetical mode of thinking about the natural and social world is the unity it is able to bring out in apparently diverse and unrelated phenomena. By means of reflective teleology, Kant extends the feature of *a priori* regularity that pertains to nature and morals due to the legislation of the understanding and (practical) reason, respectively, to encompass the quasi-legislation of nature and culture through the principle of reflective judgement, which unifies the manifolds of both natural and cultural phenomena through the notion of purposive unity.

While the main areas to which Kant applies teleological thinking in the *Critique of the Power of Judgment* are aesthetics and biology (subjective or aesthetic and objective or logical purposiveness, respectively), the beginnings of Kant's critical or reflective teleology lie in natural history and physical geography and involve the role of place in the differentiation of animal and human life. In particular, Kant manifests a strong methodological and conceptual interest in the geographically distributed differentiation of the human species. While Kant shares the pre-Darwinian belief of his time in the constancy of biological species, understood as immediate products of divine creation, he also partakes in the contemporary project of natural history (*Naturgeschichte, histoire naturelle*), that is, the hypothetical reconstruction of the development of the current state of nature across time.

Under the strictures of species constancy and divine creation, the historical account of nature, specifically of animal and human nature, envisioned by Kant is, in essence, the twofold history of individual or *ontogenetic* generation and growth concerning the single living being and the collective or *phylogenetic* generation and growth of a given species into classifications of various levels. Moreover, for Kant, ontogenetic generation serves as the model for phylogenetic generation; the development of the species into classes and subclasses is construed along the lines of the generation and growth of an individual living being from some original unarticulated but differentiable unity into a fully formed adult being. In his transposition of ontogenetic formation onto phylogenetic formation, Kant draws on the most advanced biological theories of his time.[31] In particular, he rejects the position of ontogenetic preformationism, which regards the coming about and maturation of a living being as the successive unfolding and growing into proper size of an already fully articulated miniature living being. The philosophical basis for this biological theory had been Leibniz's phenomenal infinitesimalism joined with his noumenal monadism. Metaphysically speaking, all past, present and future human beings, along with their fates and fortunes, were contained in the first human being. On the preformationist view, development is but the unfolding or 'evolution' (*Evolution*) of the encased but fully formed 'educt' (*Edukt*).

Kant rejects genetic preformationism early on, maintaining instead the 'epigenesis' (*Epigenesis*) of new life or the genuine arising of a previously non-existing individual on the basis of 'germs' (*Keime*) and 'predispositions' (*Anlagen*) that do not preform the future individual but contain both the generic enabling grounds and the limiting conditions of its individual formation.[32] On the epigeneticist view, which had been developed by Albrecht von Haller based on his study of the intraovular formation of the chick and had been propagated by Caspar Friedrich Wolf (*Theoria generationis*, Halle, 1759; *Theorie der Generation*, Berlin, 1764), an individual living being is not a preformed educt but an originally and newly formed 'product' (*Produkt*). The development of individual life is not an unfolding or 'evolution' (*Evolution*) of some being that is already fully formed *en miniature*, but involves the bringing about of diversity, indeed of infinite variety, on the basis of a prior unity (germ, disposition) that provides the necessary but not the sufficient condition of biological formation.

A key factor in the epigeneticist account of the formation of living beings (their origination as well as gestation and maturation) is the formative role of factors outside the living beings themselves. More specifically, the germinal or predispositional unity undergoes differentiation at the instigation of conditions that are specific to the *place* in which the beings find themselves or into which they relocate, in case of locomotive living beings or animals. The formative factors of the habitat include, in the first instance, the climate of the region of the earth, but also the latter's soil condition, and so on. On Kant's account, place as a formative factor in the development of living beings provides a further necessary condition for generation and growth. Jointly, *germs* and *predispositions*, on the part of the living beings, and *place*, on the part of the surrounding world, constitute the principal sufficient conditions for animal life, and the character of such life is worked out through their combined interaction.

7.5 Place and race

The intrinsic linkage between natural history and geography established by epigeneticism in biological matters governs not only the formation of living individuals but also the life – or, shall we say, the quasi- or hyper-life – of the species. For Kant, the classificatory differentiation of a given species into subspecies, varieties, families, kinds, and so on occurs on the basis of a purposive interaction between the 'hidden', as yet unfolded, germs and predispositions of the species, which are present and passed on ('inherited'; *anerben*) in each of the species' exemplars, and the place of sojourn in which individual members of the species find themselves over long periods of time.

The 'adaptation' (*Anartung*) of the living being to its climate is an extended process, over the course of which a selective actualization of the germinal or presdispositional (epi-)genetic potential occurs. Put in terms of the causal theories prevalent in post-Leibnizian German philosophy, the place factor exercises the role of an 'occasioning cause' (*Gelegenheitsursache*) that provides the external cue for an otherwise entirely internal development. Yet, unlike its characterization in Malebranche's occasionalist metaphysics of exclusively divine causation, the agency behind generation and growth is not a single divine being but each living being, which is therefore to be regarded as a substantial being in its own right. To put the matter in Leibnizian terms, on the epigeneticist account, living beings are independent, even if not entirely self-sufficient, entities that operate autonomously on the basis of external stimuli. Living beings are monads with a window on their *place*.

Kant develops his epigeneticist account of the internal differentiation of the species primarily, and problematically, with regard to the human species. Throughout he maintains the unity of the human species and its natural-historical origin in *one* biological entity ('phylum', *Stamm*). In particular, Kant defends radical monophyleticism against the assumption of plural and unrelated original human populations– theologically put, plural local creation (polyphyleticism) – which was prevalent in the racial discourse of the time and advocated against Kant by the South Sea explorer Georg Forster, with whom

Kant entered into an extended published dispute about the matter.[33] On Kant's view, the unfailingly inheritable characters that justify a classification of the one human species into plural subspecies do not establish an original diversity among the human species but are the result of the differentiation of an original, unitary formation under the influence of different climates as a result of the population of the earth.

But the differentiation of the species under the influence of the climate, and hence of place, is not unlimited. There is a fixed set of differential characteristics that are brought out by climatic factors. In the human species, according to Kant, this is primarily the colour of the skin, which he therefore takes as a criterion for intraspecies inheritable differences constituting a finite number of subspecies or races (*Racen*). Moreover, the adaptation of the skin colour to the climatic condition over long periods of time is, on Kant's view, not a reversible process, and not an indefinitely continuing one either. For Kant, in any given population adaptation occurs once, as the gradual differential actualization of generic potentialities under condition of the habit of the first long-term transplanting. With this first diversification the adaptive potential of the species in the given place-specific population is exhausted.

Any relocation that is subsequent to the emergence of the racial differentiation does not affect the racial characteristics as such. According to Kant, it leads only to superficial effects, such as the colouration of the skin through exposure to the sun, and not to the deeper, if only skin deep, change of the skin's pigmentation. For Kant, the constancy of the species has its counterpart in the constancy of the developed subspecies, although this constancy obtains only with respect to what Kant identifies as the four basic skin colours.

7.6 Place and history

The racial theory that emerges in Kant's empirical topography presents many problems from a contemporary perspective – most of which cannot be addressed adequately here.[34] So far as the inquiry into Kantian topography is concerned, however, it is particularly notable that Kant's account gives a determining role to *place* in the racial differentiation of the human species. While Kant's assertion of the original differentiation of the human species into climatically adapted subspecies can be seen as the natural-historical equivalent of the divine command to human beings to populate the earth, the locking-in of a given subspecies into its climatic zone suggests a view of the world as originally divided among the different human subspecies in accordance with properties of place. Kant thus holds to a fairly straightforward geographical determinism.

The Kantian teleology of the natural history of the human species envisions the population of an originally uninhabited earth to the point of a perfect match between place and people. It does not, however, address the subsequent voluntary or involuntary relocations from a given first habitat to another place that might well be geographically different. We might say that Kant's natural history of the human species is limited to its prehistory, to a natural history before or outside history proper. We might add that what Kant neglects is the possibility of variability that is independent of race, or, indeed, the possibility that race might represent a more malleable and less significant point of human differentiation than he assumes.

Moreover, this is not only tied to an assumption of the determination of the human by the geographic, but also involves an assumption of a determinacy of the geographic, or, more particularly, of place, that is the basis for the determination of the human. Such a conception is in marked contrast to the view of place, and the relation between subjectivity and place, that emerged in our discussion of Kant's transcendental topography above. There the empirical subject emerges only in relation to, and reciprocally with, its external surroundings as these are constituted within the over-arching structure of place, and there is no simple relation of determination between one element and the other. Moreover, the way in which place emerges as transcendentally understood within Kant's Critical philosophy points to an essential reciprocity between outer and inner sense, and so between space *and* time, that implies a much more dynamic structure to place than is evident in Kant's empirical geography. One might say that, while Kant's transcendental topography is already, in a fundamental sense, 'historical' (in that it recognizes the way in which cognition is worked out in and through the temporal as well as the spatial), Kant's empirical topography remains narrowly 'geographical'.

Significantly, it is on just this point that Kant's empirical geography stands apart from the developments in geographic thinking that arose in the latter half of the nineteenth century and continued into the twentieth. Those developments emphasize not the simple determination of human being by the geographic as statically conceived, but, rather, the dynamic character of the relation between human life and its physical environment.[35] Thus, geography comes to be seen as essentially historical, even as history is understood as necessarily geographical. Significantly, such geographic 'possibilism' (as opposed to geographic

'determinism') can be seen to be opposed to those static conceptions
of human being that focus around the concept of race exemplified
in Kant.[36] Rather than Kant's empirical topography undermining the
transcendental, then, it seems that the transcendental brings into
sharp relief the shortcomings of the empirical. Moreover, one might
argue that it does so through exhibiting *topos* as itself a reciprocal and
dynamic structure that encompasses both the temporal and the spatial,
the human and the environmental, and so stands opposed to any simple 'reductionist' or determinist conception of human being.

7.7   Place and philosophy

Kant famously characterized his own thinking in terms of a 'Copernican
Revolution,' which, as he presents it, consists in a shift from the assumption that our cognition must conform to its objects to the assumption
that objects must conform to our cognition.[37] There is, however, a more
direct and immediate sense in which Kant's project is Copernican in
character – one that draws explicitly on the topographical reading
sketched here: what lies at the heart of the work of both Copernicus and
Kant is the idea that the appearing of things is always a function of our
own location and orientation. If we are to investigate the very structure
of such appearing, as Kant attempts, then we must look to the structure
of the place in which such appearing occurs and in which we find ourselves. Since we are ourselves inextricably bound up with that place, so
we may say that the investigation of that place is also an investigation
of the structure of our own *subjectivity* (a structure in which, of course,
objectivity is also entangled).

The investigation of the place, the *topos*, that is at issue here is a project
that can be undertaken empirically *and* transcendentally, and Kant, as
we have seen, attempts both. Yet Kant's empirical inquiry seems not to
heed one of the key lessons to be drawn from the *transcendental* investigation, namely, that the structure of place depends, at a fundamental
level, on the mutual interplay between the elements that are constitutive of it, and especially on the interplay between the spatial and
the temporal. As a result, Kant's *empirical* topography is dominated by
a narrow and static conception of the spatial that in turn leads to a
deterministic conception of human being. If we do indeed read Kant
topographically, and so take seriously the dynamic character of place
as revealed through the transcendental investigations of the Critical
philosophy, then Kant's empirical geography must appear as itself topographically inadequate.[38]

The topographical framework within which Kant's project can be read not only provides a way of exploring the shortcomings of the empirical aspect of that project, but also enables us to consider its transcendental side anew. In particular, the way in which place and subjectivity are brought together in Kant – so that the inquiry into the structure of subjectivity is also an inquiry into the structure of place and placedness – not only reinforces the special character of Kant's own 'transcendental idealism' as distinct from 'empirical' or Berkleyan idealism, but also indicates the need to rethink what might be involved in the notion of subjectivity itself. Rather than understanding the structure of subjectivity in 'subjectivist' terms, Kant may be read as opening up the possibility of understanding the subject through the notion of *topos*– and so as essentially entangled with place.

Indeed, one might argue that the topographical reading of Kant can also be applied to the broader German idealist tradition that develops after him. That tradition is one in which the focus on the actual places and spaces of human existence – as worked out through the geographical and anthropological – continues in close conjunction with the inquiry into the transcendental place that can itself be seen to constitute the structure of human subjectivity. Thus, the work of Herder and Fichte, and even Hegel, can be seen as allowing a similarly topographic reading to that which can be applied to Kant, although with important differences in the way that reading is worked out. Rather than see the German idealist tradition as characterized only by its focus on the *subject*, then, it may be just as accurate, and perhaps more illuminating, to see it as characterized by a continuing and pervasive preoccupation with *place*.

Notes

1. Kant's concern with place is both methodological and substantive. It implies a method of approach that looks to employ spatial and topographical tropes and figures in the exploration and elaboration of the issues that it takes up, and that construes the overall problem to be addressed analogously with the task of terrestrial surveying or mapmaking. But it also implies a thematization of space and place as themselves objects of inquiry. Kant thus provides an account of space and place at the same time as he deploys concepts of space and place as key elements in his analysis.
2. The idea of a 'philosophical topography' is developed in Jeff Malpas (1999) *Place and Experience* (Cambridge: Cambridge University Press); see also Malpas (2006) *Heidegger's Topology* (Cambridge, MA: MIT Press).
3. Kant (1781/1789) *Critique of Pure Reason*, A235/B294– A260/B315; English translation used throughout is Kant (1999)*Critique of Pure Reason*, edited by Paul Guyer and Allen W. Wood (Cambridge, Cambridge University Press).

4. Kant himself makes use of the idea of 'transcendental place' in the 'Amphiboly of the Concepts of Reflection' in the *Critique of Pure Reason*, A268/B324, to refer to 'the position (*Stelle*) that we assign to a concept either in sensibility or in pure understanding'. Clearly this should be distinguished from the sense of 'transcendental place' that is implied in talk of transcendental topography as used throughout much of this essay. Here, as elsewhere, *topos* and 'topography' turn out to be terms that allow of many different applications.

5. For more on the nature of such a topography, discussed via the way the geographic may be understood to play a key role in Kant's Critical project, see Jeff Malpas and Karsten Thiel (2010) 'Kant's Geography of Reason', in S. Elden and E. Mendieta (eds), *Reading Kant's Geography* (Albany, NY: SUNY Press).

6. See, for instance, David Harvey (2007) 'The Kantian Roots of Foucault's Dilemmas', in Jeremy W. Crampton and Stuart Elden (eds), *Space, Knowledge and Power* (Aldershot: Ashgate), pp. 41–8. Harvey suggests that the tension here is one that Foucault identifies as a result of his reading of Kant's *Anthropology*. Harvey cites a passage from Amy Allen: 'Kant's system contains the seeds of its own radical transformation, a transformation that Foucault will take up in his own work: namely the transformation from the conception of the a priori as universal and necessary to the historical a priori; and the related transformation from the transcendental subject that serves as the condition of possibility of all experience to the subject that is conditioned by its rootedness in specific historical, social and cultural circumstances' (Amy Allen (2003) 'Foucault and Enlightenment: A Critical Reappraisal', *Constellations*, 10, 180–98).

7. Edward Casey (1996) *The Fate of Place* (Berkeley: University of California Press), p. 204.

8. It should be noted that David Harvey's repeated assertion (see, for instance, Harvey, 'The Kantian Roots of Foucault's Dilemmas', pp. 44–5) that Kant was firmly Newtonian in his view of space is a serious misreading of the Kantian position.

9. On Kant's discovery of non-intellectual, sensible intuition, see Günter Zöller (1984) *Theoretische Gegenstandsbeziehung bei Kant. Zur systematischen Bedeutung der Termini 'objektive Realität' und 'objektive Gültigkeit' in der 'Kritik der reinen Vernunft'* (Berlin/New York: Walter de Gruyter), pp. 31–46.

10. *Critique of Pure Reason*, A26/B 42.

11. For Kant's presentation and analysis of incongruent counterparts, see Kant (1900–) *Kant's gesammelte Schriften* (Berlin: Königlich Preußlische Akademie / later, Berlin and New York: Reimer / later, Berlin: de Gruyter), 2:380–3 and 4:285f. For English translations, see 'Concerning the Ultimate Ground of the Differentiation of Directions in Space', in Immanuel Kant (1992), *Theoretical Philosophy, 1755-1770*, trans. and edited by David Walford in collaboration with Ralf Meerbote (Cambridge: Cambridge University Press), pp. 364–72, and Kant (2004) *Prolegomena to Any Future Metaphysics That Will be Able to Present Itself as Science. With Two Early Reviews of the* Critique of Pure Reason, edited by Günter Zöller (Oxford: Oxford University Press), pp. 92f.

12. Kant's insistence on the unity of space is often viewed as unsustainable and readily refuted – see especially Anthony Quinton (1962) 'Spaces and Times',

Philosophy, 37, 130–47. Viewed topographically, however, the unity of space (as well as of time) is tied to the necessary unity of subjectivity, such that, to put the matter briefly, those examples that might be taken to demonstrate a failure in the unity of space usually also imply a problematic failure in the unity of subjectivity.

13. The idea that understanding depends, not on the sharing of what is every-where and determinately the same, but rather through participation in a structure of interconnection and engagement is a key idea for which Malpas has argued independently of the particular Kantian context at issue here – see, for instance, Jeff Malpas (2011) 'What is Common to All: Davidson on Agreement and Understanding', in Jeff Malpas (ed.), *Dialogues with Davidson* (Cambridge, MA: MIT Press).

14. See, for instance, Stuart Elden (2009) 'Reassessing Kant's Geography', *Journal of Historical Geography*, 39, 3–25.

15. *Kant's gesammelte Schriften*, 9:151–436.

16. We are here reporting on this matter from Günter Zöller's perspective as a member of the Kant Commission of the Berlin Brandenburg Academy of Sciences. The edition of the student transcripts of Kant's lectures on physical geography is undertaken by Werner Stark.

17. *Kant's gesammelte Schriften*, 9:156.

18. Ibid., 9:155.

19. Ibid., 9:158.

20. Ibid., 9:159.

21. Ibid., 9:159–62.

22. Ibid., 9:159.

23. Ibid., 9:164f.

24. Ibid., 9:166–83.

25. Ibid., 9:183–308.

26. Ibid., 9:312.

27. Ibid.

28. Ibid., 9:309–76.

29. Ibid., 9:377–436.

30. Ibid., 7:157–184. For a recent translation into English, see note 33.

31. On Kant's acquaintance with contemporary biological theories and the use to which he put them in his epistemology, see Günter Zöller (1988) 'Kant on the Generation of Metaphysical Knowledge', in Hariolf Oberer and Gerhard Seel (eds), *Kant: Analysen - Probleme - Kritik* (Würzburg: Königshausen & Neumann), pp. 71–90.

32. In Kant's usage, 'germ' designates the ground for the qualitative develop-ment of particular parts and 'predisposition' the ground for the quantitative development affecting the size and relation of particular parts. See *Kant's gesammelte Schriften*, 2:434 ('*Von den verschiedenen Racen der Mesnchen*').

33. The texts of that dispute, virtually unknown in the English-speaking world, have now been made available as part of the Cambridge Edition of Work of Immanuel Kant in Translation, in the volume Kant (2007) *Anthropology, History, and Education*, edited by Günter Zöller and Robert B. Louden (Cambridge: Cambridge University Press), pp. 145–59 ('Determination of the Concept of a Human Race') and pp. 195–218 ('On the Use of Teleological Principles in Philosophy'). See also the third of Kant's essays on the topic

of race, in the same volume, pp. 84–97 ('Of the Different Races of Human Beings').

34. But see Robert Bernasconi (2001) 'Who Invented the Concept of Race? Kant's Role in the Enlightenment Construction of Race', in Robert Bernasconi (ed.), *Race* (Oxford: Blackwell), pp. 145–59.

35. See Jeff Malpas (2008) 'Heidegger, Geography, and Politics', *Journal of the Philosophy of History*, 2, 185–213, for a discussion of this issue in relation to Heidegger as well as the geographers Friedrich Ratzel and Paul Vidal de la Blache. There Malpas opposes the 'possibilist' approach with the subjectivist neo-Kantianism exemplified in the work of Jakob von Uexküll. From the perspective of the current inquiry, the argument of Malpas's earlier essay would need to be modified slightly to take account of the topographical reading of the Kantian transcendental project proposed here, and to more clearly distinguish the original Kantian project from von Uexküll's neo-Kantianism. See also Malpas (2012) 'Heidegger, Space, and World', in Julian Kiverstein and Michael Wheeler (eds), *Heidegger and Cognitive Science* (London: Palgrave Macmillan).

36. David Harvey also sees such 'determinism' as evident in Kant's geographical thinking (see Harvey, 'The Kantian Roots of Foucault's Dilemmas', pp. 42–3), but is less clear on the extent to which a 'possibilism' might be operative within the Kantian transcendental project.

37. *Critique of Pure Reason*, B xvi.

38. One might argue that the shortcomings evident in Kant's empirical topography are addressed in different ways in some of the thinkers who come after him – both Herder and Fichte, for instance, adopt much less deterministic conceptions of the relation between human beings and their physical environments, even while one can nevertheless also discern a similar focus on of the topographic. The way in which specifically geographic thought develops in later part of the nineteenth century and into the twentieth also includes a trend towards more interactive conceptions of place (notably in the work of the French geographer Paul Vidal de la Blache), although more deterministic tendencies also continued, especially in German geographic thought as it developed under the influence of Nazi ideology in the 1930s.

References

Allen, A. (2003) 'Foucault and Enlightenment: A Critical Reappraisal', *Constellations*, 10, 180–198.

Bernasconi, R. (2001) 'Who Invented the Concept of Race? Kant's Role in the Enlightenment Construction of Race', in R. Bernasconi (ed.), *Race* (Oxford: Blackwell).

Casey, E. (1996) *The Fate of Place* (Berkeley: University of California Press).

Elden, S. (2009) 'Reassessing Kant's Geography', HYPERLINK "http://www.sciencedirect.com/science/journal/03057488" *Journal of Historical Geography* 39, 3–25.

Harvey, D. (2007) 'The Kantian Roots of Foucault's Dilemmas', in J. W. Crampton and S. Elden (eds), *Space, Knowledge and Power* (Aldershot: Ashgate).

Kant, I. (1900-) Kant's gesammelte Schriften (Berlin: Königlich Preußlische Akademie / later, Berlin and New York: Reimer / later, Berlin: de Gruyter).

Kant, I. (1992) Theoretical Philosophy, 1755–1770, trans. and edited by D. Walford in collaboration with R. Meerbote (Cambridge: Cambridge University Press)

Kant, I. (1999) Critique of Pure Reason, trans. P. Guyer and A. W. Wood (eds) (Cambridge: Cambridge University Press).

Kant, I. (2004) Prolegomena to Any Future Metaphysics That Will be Able to Present Itself as Science. With Two Early Reviews of the 'Critique of Pure Reason', Günter Zöller (ed.) (Oxford: Oxford University Press).

Kant, I. (2007) Anthropology, History, and Education, G. Zöller and R. B. Louden (eds) (Cambridge: Cambridge University Press).

Malpas, J. (1999) Place and Experience (Cambridge: Cambridge University Press).

Malpas, J. (2006) Heidegger's Topology (Cambridge Mass.: MIT Press).

Malpas, J. (2008) 'Heidegger, Geography, and Politics', Journal of the Philosophy of History 2, 185–213.

Malpas, J. (2011) 'What is Common to All: Davidson on Agreement and Understanding', in J. Malpas (ed.), Dialogues with Davidson (Cambridge, MA.: MIT Press).

Malpas, J. (2011) 'Heidegger, Space, and World', in J. Kiverstein and M. Wheeler (eds), Heidegger and Cognitive Science (London: Palgrave Macmillan).

Malpas J. and K. Thiel (2010) 'Kant's Geography of Reason', in S. Elden and E. Mendieta (eds) Reading Kant's Geography (Albany, NY: SUNY Press).

Quinton, A. (1962) 'Spaces and Times' Philosophy, 37, 130–147.

Zöller, G. (1984) Theoretische Gegenstandsbeziehung bei Kant. Zur systematischen Bedeutung der Termini 'objektive Realität' und 'objektive Gültigkeit in der 'Kritik der reinen Vernunft' (Berlin/New York: Walter de Gruyter).

Zöller, G. (1988) 'Kant on the Generation of Metaphysical Knowledge' in H. Oberer and G. Seel (eds), Kant: Analysen – Probleme – Kritik, (Würzburg: Königshausen & Neumann).

Part III
Limits of Experience

8
Metaphors of Spatial Location: Understanding Post-Kantian Space

Pamela Sue Anderson

Abstract

This chapter argues that the nature and function of spatial location and corresponding metaphors in Kant's first *Critique* have crucial implications for post-Kantian debates about the space of the knowable, the space of the unknowable and the boundary between them. Of course, on Kant's account, one of the boundaries between the knowable and the unknowable is precisely space as a condition of possibility of cognition belonging to sensibility. The chapter addresses questions about space considered both as an *a priori* form of sensible intuition and as a metaphor for what, in Kant, is non-sensible, but thinkable, in particular, the ideas of freedom, immortality and God. Thinking these ideas of reason, as regulative ideals, involves acts of the imagination and provides an alternative to the two-worlds reading of Kant. Crucially, this reading resists any fundamental ontological distinction between the spatio-temporal, knowable world and the noumenal, unknowable world. Instead, it offers a critical approach to the Kantian locations of reason, their sensible and non-sensible boundaries. The critical challenge is twofold: first, to try to avoid contradictions and ambivalences concerning the limits and boundaries of space; and, second, to try to expose the epistemic injustice of taking metaphors literally, in order to bolster one's own, however self-deceptive, confidence.

8.1 Introduction

'The philosopher's island is not to be found on any map. Yet [it] is far from vanishing: its evocative power, its representational flexibility, has scarcely been exhausted.'[1]

The argument of this chapter is that understanding the nature and function of spatial location in the *Critique of Pure Reason* is crucial to post-Kantian debates about the limit(s) of human knowledge and the boundary between the knowable and the unknowable. By calling these debates 'post-Kantian', I mean that they explore and often alter Kantian metaphors concerning locations within or beyond the one general knowable space. Here 'spatial location' will include locations both literally understood and metaphorically understood. For example, I will consider a now classic philosophical account of the island which cannot be found on any map, but whose metaphorical power evokes analogical relations between empirical and non-empirical space, northern and southern islands, secure land and insecure seas. I will also draw out the relations between the three standpoints of (i) the conceptual space of the autonomous knower; (ii) the extended space of shared or 'enlarged' thought; (iii) the space of reasoning consistently from (i) to (ii) and, so implicitly, across conceptual and non-conceptual locations.

I will argue that adequate understanding of the role of metaphors about spatial location enables the thinker better to grasp the limits (*Schranken*) within which we have knowledge and the boundaries (*Grenzen*) beyond which lies the humanly unknowable.[2] For Kant, 'space' itself is both a boundary on what we know and a metaphor for what we can never view 'from above' (the boundary and its two sides). Of course, with Kant, we can constantly increase our knowledge, pushing further out the limit of what we know as, for example, new scientific knowledge is acquired. The real philosophical danger is confusing limit and boundary. When philosophers after Kant claim to know spatial location from above, as if gazing on the *boundary* and the locations on either side, they succumb to transcendental illusion.[3] They transgress the boundary of human knowledge by wrongly treating it as if it were a limit.

Locating Kant's spatial metaphors within the history of Western philosophy is also helpful for recognizing his radically new manner of imagining parts of empirical space, their limits and boundaries. In turn, this history is taken up by subsequent philosophers who follow Kant by either bringing back earlier metaphorical stories about land and sea or transforming the philosophical significance of 'his' spatial imagery. As will be discussed in this chapter, Kant's central metaphor of 'the land of truth' in the first *Critique* recalls, not only Francis Bacon's imagery in the *New Atlantis*, but Plato's and Rousseau's uses of island imagery; and there will be other philosophers who could be named for their examples of islands and of ships on the wide-open sea.[4] Kant is clearly not the first Western philosopher to draw on spatial metaphors in the history of the philosophical imaginary.[5] But it can be enlightening to consider in more detail Kant's descriptions of the island surrounded by 'a broad and stormy ocean', with 'a fog bank', and of the philosopher who, after 'another glance at the map of the land', imagines that 'we venture out on this sea' as we leave the island at the end of the 'Transcendental Analytic', in Kant's *Critique of Pure Reason*.[6] In this way, Kant pushes at the frontiers of philosophy, employing and transforming well-known metaphors, in order to move from a secure location of pure reason to another space of reason; that is, to the insecure location of reason's dialectics. Although this conceptual location seems uncertain, a new world of possibilities for practical reason and for reflective judgement is imagined but, also, hoped for.

8.2 Boundaries and limits: Kant's concepts and metaphors

To preface my discussion of boundaries and limits, it is helpful to consider the spatial imagery of island and sea in a pivotal passage from Kant's *Critique of Pure Reason*.

> We have now not only traveled through the land of pure understanding, and carefully inspected each part of it, but we have also surveyed it, and determined the place for each thing in it. This land, however, is an island, and enclosed in unalterable boundaries [*unveraendliche Grenzen*] by nature itself. It is the land of truth (a charming name), surrounded by a broad and stormy ocean, the true seat of illusion, where many a fog bank and rapidly melting iceberg pretend to be new lands and, ceaselessly deceiving with empty hopes the voyager looking around for new discoveries, entwine him in adventures from which he can never escape and yet also never bring to an end. But before we venture out on this sea, to search through all its breadth and become certain of whether there is anything to hope for in it, it will be useful first to cast yet another glance at the map of the land that we would now leave, and ask, first, whether we could not be satisfied with what it contains, or even must be satisfied with it out of necessity, if there is no other ground on which we could build; and, second, by what title we occupy even this land, and can hold it securely against all hostile claims.[7]

In the above, Kant employs his island imagery to represent the space of the knowable which is secure within carefully drawn-out boundaries.

He also imagines venturing off this island of sensible intuition, or land of understanding, to the unknowable. For this unknowable space of freedom, i.e., `a property of being to which I ascribe effects in the world of sense', Kant stipulates critical distinctions as follows:

> I cannot **cognize** freedom as a property of any being to which I ascribe effects in the world of sense, because then I would have to cognize such an existence as determined, and yet not as determined in time (which is impossible, since I cannot support my concept with any intuition), nevertheless, I can **think** freedom to myself, i.e., the representation of it at least contains no contradiction in itself, so long as our critical distinction prevails between the two ways of representing (sensible and intellectual), along with the limitation of the pure concepts of the understanding arising from it, and hence that of the principles flowing from them. (Kant, Bxxviii, p. 116)

Kant seeks to locate morality in the space of reason outside the boundary of the pure concepts of understanding. Here, I suggest, whereas sensibility is specifically human, the pure concepts of the understanding are not. Instead, the latter are limited, that is, restricted, by sensibility; and our human employment of pure concepts has space as a boundary. In other words, human knowledge requires both sensibility and understanding, but remains limited by what a human subject can know within (conceptual) space. Kant, then, argues that we *think*, rather than cognize or *know*, freedom. He energetically defends what is required for morality in the following terms:

> for morality I need nothing more than that freedom should not contradict itself, that it should at least be thinkable (Kant, Bxxix, p. 116).

Ultimately, for Kant, it is only from a distinctively human standpoint that space can be known as both that which limits empirical, or scientific, knowledge and points beyond metaphorically, or analogically, to freedom and to hope of God and of immortality. The critical point appears to be simple:

> We can accordingly speak of space, extended beings, and so on, only from the human standpoint. (Kant, A26 / B42, p. 177)

Yet it is much less simple to explain how, from this human stand-point, we can speak literally of space as a boundary without contradiction. With 'space as a boundary' of 'the human standpoint' there is a danger of illusion, or of self-deception; the danger would be in failing to treat space literally as a boundary, as if it were a mere metaphor for what can be transgressed by the ideas of freedom, God and immortality. To stop any cognitive claim from transgressing the human standpoint, it is necessary to maintain that these three ideas of reason are not constitutive of knowledge. Instead, they are regulative ideals; that is, the ideas of freedom, God and immortality guide moral action and practical reason. In addition, the full extent of Kant's thinking beyond constitutive knowledge relies upon the imagination which, as will be seen in discussion of Hannah Arendt (below), develops analogical thinking. At this stage, in also drawing from Michèle Le Doeuff's conception of the philosophical imaginary, I insist that Kant's acts of the imagination clearly engage with a stock of metaphors and images (e.g., about an island and the sea) from the history of Western philosophy, even while transforming them.[8]

Elsewhere, my work on islands, Kant and the philosophical imaginary has focused on the manner in which limits are taken literally and treated as a form of prohibition.[9] For example, social and material characteristics (or 'markers') of the knower can adversely affect (her) epistemic confidence on certain matters of knowledge.[10] A knower may possess knowledge but be confused into believing she could not have this, because of her social location. This lack of confidence in one's own knowledge can arise when social and material limits (*Schranken*) are imposed upon her understanding as if they were boundaries (*Grenzen*). In the first *Critique*, it is the (unalterable) boundary of sensible experience in general that renders impossible any claims to knowledge beyond the *a priori* intuitions of sensibility and the pure concepts of understanding. However, this impossibility is not because of particular social or material restrictions. Instead, epistemic limits can change whenever new empirical knowledge is acquired. While Kant gives a central role to space as a boundary, he distinguishes space in general from particular locations in space. As already explained, boundary[11] itself can function as a metaphor of space when it functions like a horizon of human knowledge and for what is definitely beyond all human knowledge. However, as I am seeking to demonstrate here, the salient epistemological distinctions between the space of the knowable, the space of the unknowable and the boundary between them are necessary in order to understand the philosophical issues in post-Kantian debates about space and metaphors of spatial location.

Epistemic confidence requires (at a minimum) that subjects understand the nature and function of both the limits and the boundaries of knowledge. Subjects who try to go beyond the boundaries of sensible experience by treating them as limits suffer from an illusory 'overconfidence' in claiming to know more than is humanly possible. But the reverse danger would be to treat a limit (i.e., *Schranken*, which is moveable as long as empirical knowledge increases) as if it were an unmovable boundary (*Grenzen*), resulting in a loss of epistemic confidence. Le Doeuff argues that this loss of confidence can result in a 'cognitive blockage', and that a block to the acquisition of knowledge becomes effectively a 'prohibition' of philosophy. The critical question is whether Le Doeuff is correct that to prohibit women from doing philosophy is to block their thinking and undermine their knowing.[12]

For Kant at least, the ability to '*think* freedom' continues beyond cognition. Thinking, but not knowing, freedom can generate hope that from reason's practical standpoint the autonomous subject has an infinite worth. In other words, the unknowable redirects the thinker to the moral law, that is, 'to a destination which is not restricted to the conditions and limits of [worth in] this life.'[13]

Hannah Arendt interprets Kant's 'boundary' as a metaphor, functioning to 'generate an analogical movement across the known to the unknowable'.[14] According to Arendt's definition, 'metaphor...achieves a carrying over of a genuine and seemingly impossible transition from one state to another'.[15] So, she interprets the Kantian boundary-metaphor as an analogy which moves thought to a new conception of the space of reason. Arendt also employs her idea of metaphor as an analogical movement to explain the significant extension of thinking made by Kant's creative acts of reflective judgement; she finds this latter extension of reflection from particulars to universal as 'an analogical movement' in aesthetics. I will return to Arendt's (post-)Kantian account of reflective judgement in later sections of this chapter.

8.3 'The philosophical imaginary': Le Doeuff and Kant

In this section, I would like to propose that Kant be read explicitly with the help of the Le Doeuffian philosophical imaginary.[16] In other words, we should assess the metaphors and accompanying images which make up the imaginary dimension of Kant's philosophical texts. In the previous section, we read his account of the philosopher's island, but we will also find that Kant's metaphor of an island of understanding has an implicit relation to other locations in space, such as an island of bliss in the South Seas.[17] In fact, some readers – like Le Doeuff – find Kant suggesting that we imagine the philosopher venturing off the security of the land of truth, in *The Critique of Pure Reason*, onto the stormy seas and to other metaphorical islands in other philosophical texts. My contention, supporting the main argument of this chapter, is that the function and nature of spatial location are necessary for understanding the shape and structure of Kant's philosophical positions in the three *Critiques*, but also his relation to a philosophical tradition. It could be said that his use of the philosophical imaginary holds his theoretical, practical and reflective positions, with their various spatial metaphors, together. Yet the ability to avoid contradictory claims, when the use of metaphors is ambiguous, is still not simple, especially when Kant's Enlightenment metaphors are compared to more ancient island-metaphors.

Perhaps unwittingly, Kant's texts teach us a lesson concerning the function of metaphors in the history of philosophy. Subsequent philosophers struggle with Kant's distinctive metaphors because of the metaphor's epistemic power to direct and control conceptual thinking; this power can become an ethical and a political matter of control. For instance, as already mentioned, feminist philosophers have contended that 'the bounds of sense'[18] could have been employed to prohibit certain subjects from being acknowledged as knowers. After Kant, the boundary of space has represented the horizon of human knowledge. However, the question is whether we can *know* when a limit is treated as a boundary, and not as a limit. Following Le Doeuff, I have argued elsewhere that imaginary restrictions (with real implications) against women philosophers surface in, for example, Kant's seductive, spatial imagery of, on the one hand, sensible nature's secure enclosure and of, on the other hand, thought's wide-open space.[19] According to Le Doeuff, prohibitions lurk near the seductive and ambivalent imagery of the traditional 'bounds' of sense.[20] The space of new possibilities – that is, of new worlds and new knowers – is associated by Kant with thinking freedom. But can we locate the standpoint of freedom? The critical problem is how (if it is locatable) we can make sense of locating this unknowable standpoint beyond sensible knowledge. A range of spatial imagery can easily generate a highly significant debate about the nature of the knower's locations in space. Of course, following Kant, we can never, as spatio-temporal subjects we can never know, or apply the concepts of understanding to, anything outside or beyond the boundary of space.

So, how the unknowable can be thought as a space of reasons and, in some sense, as spatially locatable remains a critical problem for post-Kantian philosophers. Kantian debates concerning the nature of space often focus on the sharp distinction between 'the *ideality* of space in regard to things when they are considered in themselves through reason, i.e., without taking account of the constitution of our sensibility' and 'the *reality*...of space in regard to everything that can come before us externally as an object'.[21] The ideality and reality of space as an *a priori* form of pure intuition would seem to make up Kant's conception of space as 'outer sense'. And yet, although what we know depends upon both the ideality and the reality of space, we have knowledge only of 'whatever can be presented to us outwardly as object' and not of 'things when they are considered in themselves through reason'. Moreover, although concepts require intuitions for empirical knowledge, thoughts can be entertained which are empty of sensible intuitions. The critical question for Le Doeuff is whether the philosophical imaginary does in fact convey these critical distinctions concerning space with (the aid of) metaphors of spatial location.

Consider another significant spatial metaphor employed by Kant to represent the boundary of sensible experience; that is, the flat surface of the earth. This metaphor may help us to grasp the fine distinctions between limits and boundaries. In this case, human knowledge of the world of sense appears as a flat surface. Given our limited acquaintance with the flat surface of the earth, we do not know how far it extends, but we do know that it extends further than we have managed to voyage. Here the critical problem is captured by A.W. Moore as follows:

> If we *can* only know how things are on the surface, then our knowledge is limited to two dimensions. This does not preclude our determining the extent of what we can know. But it does preclude our determining its [boundaries], or even acknowledging that there are any. To do this we should need access to another dimension.[22]

It is worth remarking again that common images like the flat surface of the earth, or an island surrounded by a stormy sea, have accompanied the contested concepts at the heart of philosophical debates about space. It will be clear by this stage that a shared stock of imagery and metaphor is what Le Doeuff means by 'the philosophical imaginary'. And yet, can we see the philosophical imaginary at work in a shared stock of metaphors which, perhaps unwittingly, structure the texts and arguments of the philosopher? In the central case of the present chapter, the imagery of limits (*Schranken*) and boundaries (*Grenzen*) has not been easy to keep distinct. It has been difficult at times to distinguish literal from metaphorical uses of the terms. The German terms may help distinguish them better than the English translations, but the philosophical distinction between *Grenzen* and *Schranken* remains both subtle and significant.

Post-Kantian debates about the space of philosophical prohibitions and of freedom are paradigmatic of other theoretical issues. We remain deeply indebted to Kant's use of the philosophical imaginary as material for new thinking about space. What would we do without Kant's 'land of pure understanding'? It gives security 'if there is no other ground on which we could build'.[23] Le Doeuff equally connects this imagery to a more ancient philosophical hope (than Kant's) concerning the sensual bliss of an island paradise. Kant's northern island (i.e., the land of understanding) calls to mind the island in the South Sea which, Le Doeuff insists, exists in Kant's own imaginary. He does, after all, anticipate both the danger of seduction in being enticed towards a blissful paradise (to the warmer lands beyond the seas, even at the risk of possible death at sea) and the necessity in being drawn off the secure island to speculate, with empty concepts. In fact, these 'concepts' are, as Kant stipulates, the 'regulative ideals' of God, of immortality and of freedom. In the *Critique of Practical Reason*, each of these regulative ideals becomes necessary to make sense of moral experience. In the second *Critique*, Kant also points to 'the starry heavens above' and 'the moral law within',[24] suggesting that the latter not only fills him with awe, but extends our thinking to 'the one fact of pure practical reason'.

Morality is not part of the empirical knowledge of the well-mapped-out island. Yet, even though Kant speaks metaphorically of two worlds, that of the knowable and that of the unknowable, morality is not merely in one world and knowledge in another. In this chapter I am treating 'the worlds' as a metaphor, conveying the 'two-aspects'[25] of Kantian space. We can learn from these Kantian metaphors of spatial location, especially if we do not too quickly dismiss the role of the philosophical imaginary in addressing the antinomies and contradictions of Kant's dialectics of pure speculative reason, as well as the subtext of island pleasures which could go unnoticed. The next question is whether spatial metaphors generate not just ambivalence but contradiction. For a Kantian, there cannot literally be more than one space, but there is a range of spatial locations.

8.4 Kant's spatial metaphor: ambivalence and contradiction

Generally speaking, philosophers resist admitting contradictions into their thinking and ambivalence into their reflections. However, we must admit that our philosophical debt to Kant's spatial metaphors crucially includes not only his antinomies of pure reason but a characteristic, Kantian sort of ambivalence. For example, if we ask why Kant draws the bounds of sense where he does, there may not be an answer; or, perhaps, not an answer which can be conceived without the use of metaphors about space. In fact, this must be so precisely because of the ambivalence in Kant's epistemological account of 'the territory of pure understanding' in the 'Analytic of Principles', in the *Critique of Pure Reason*. This is the point in his text where Kant reflects back upon what his 'Transcendental Analytic' both adds to the earlier 'Transcendental Aesthetic' and anticipates in his 'Transcendental Dialectic'.

At this pivotal point in the first *Critique*, Kant's highly distinctive metaphorical narrative about truth, the knowable and the unknowable, portrays caution, possibly hesitation, in any move beyond the security of the spatial location on an island, in the North Seas, which has been carefully mapped out. Nevertheless, this ambivalence does not prevent Kant from either traversing the boundaries of the mapped-out land to the Transcendental Dialectic or extending the limits of his Transcendental Analytic. As his readers move into the Transcendental Dialectic, they follow Kant in addressing crucial contradictions like that between the causal laws of nature and the freedom of thought over and against these laws. Furthermore, following the first *Critique*, Kant's second and third *Critiques* continue to address possible contradictions and ambivalence on matters of morality, history, aesthetics, religion and politics.[26] In the range of his writings, Kant confronts unanswerable questions about non-sensible reality, God, the highest good, the kingdom of ends. But this confrontation does not mean making claims to know the unknowable. Instead, it means that reason is impelled across space towards the unconditioned.

Kantian ambivalence could be read as an attempt to avoid contradictory claims (and illusion), with the contrasting images of land and sea, of foggy skies and clear horizons, of cold northern and warm southern islands, of the heavens above and the law within. The metaphors accompanying expressions of Kant's conceptual knowledge remain unavoidable. Central Kantian metaphors of spatial location point to significant epistemological and ontological tensions in Kant's transcendental idealism, especially his transcendental philosophy's relation to naturalism.[27] Twentieth-century philosophers after Kant, from Wittgenstein to significant Anglo-American philosophers, including, for example, W.V. Quine, John McDowell, Mark Sacks, John Campbell and A.W. Moore, have employed metaphors in their expressions of both conceptual knowledge and non-conceptual thinking, notably, in conveying critical issues concerning worlds, minds and spatio-temporality. At the same time, other philosophers after Kant on the European Continent, like Hans Blumenberg, Arendt and Le Doeuff, have explicitly focused on, and freely played with, spatial metaphors as intertextual links within the history of Western philosophy. Le Doeuff points out that an often ignored critical task would aim to tease out salient philosophical connections between, for example, philosophers at sea and philosophers on land; the resultant imaginative insight contributes to the activity of the Western philosophical imaginary.[28]

Crucially, Kant's land of pure concepts of understanding is structured by both empirical and pure *a priori* concepts; but it is equally, so to speak, unbounded by non-sensible ideas such as freedom. Concepts beyond the bounds of sense would be empty; intuitions without concepts would be blind. Yet freedom, immortality and God can still be thought as ideas of reason. Arguably, this movement across Kant's *Critiques* depends to some degree on imaginative insight. Discovery of the space of the regulative ideals, or practical ideas, of reason enlarges our thinking. The extension both of thinking and of practical reason beyond Kant's empirical standpoint is inevitable (for him), even though it creates highly significant philosophical problems; and these problems are increased by those who struggle with Kant's transcendental idealism, especially the tension between the 'two worlds'. This metaphor of 'world(s)' alone creates philosophical questions for the first and second *Critiques*, but also for *Religion within the Boundaries of Mere Reason*.[29] To repeat, the extension of Kant's own thinking places Kantian and post-Kantian philosophers in a situation where they cannot express the exact bounds of sense in empirical terms. Nevertheless, they may think that they can place themselves, or imagine their location, in thought on the other side, on these non-empirical, and so sensibly un-locatable, standpoints.

The post-Kantian philosophers who have interested me most show us how expressions of conceptual knowledge are accompanied by specific dimensions of the philosophical imaginary, especially spatial metaphors.[30] For example, Arendt explains the role of metaphor in Kant's account of boundaries and reason in the first *Critique* as follows:

> reason's need transcends the boundaries of the given world and leads us on to the uncertain sea of speculation where 'no intuition can be given which shall be adequate to [reason's ideas]'. At this point

metaphor comes in. The metaphor achieves the 'carrying over' – *metapherein* – of a genuine and seemingly impossible *metabasis es allo genos*, the transition from one ... state ... to another ... by *analogies*.[31]

We will return to this account of the analogical movements in Kant's philosophy.

8.5   Standpoints in Kantian philosophy

Reason's persistent drive to embark on the sea of illusion, in order to address the dialectical questions raised by reason's own purity, becomes a critical focus of Kant's Transcendental Dialectic in the first *Critique*. This rational pursuit also raises the question about what philosophers refer to (perhaps variously) as the conceptual space of reasons in the second and third *Critiques*. Turning to Kant's principles of human thought, from the *Critique of Judgment*, we find that three principles make communication from our different individual standpoints possible. These are: (1) to think for oneself, which is a necessary standpoint for any thought; (2) to think from the standpoint of everyone else, which is necessary for 'an enlarged mind', for having shareable thoughts; and (3) to think consistently (i.e., in accord with oneself) as 'the maxim of reason' to be attained with the effort of bringing the other two standpoints together.[32] These standpoints are not without their own problems. Yet these extend our account of spatial location, metaphorically at least.

As a Kantian or (depending on one's reading of Arendt on Kant) a post-Kantian political thinker, Arendt also questions Kant's three principles of shared human thought. How does the standpoint from which one thinks work with the standpoint of everyone else? How does Kant conceive of this third principle of consistency? Whatever the philosophical questions we may have about the nature of a standpoint, Arendt for her part introduces the standpoint of 'the spectator' to help make sense of Kant's standpoints. She describes the role of the spectator for Kant as follows:

> The spectator's verdict, while impartial and freed from the interests of gain or fame, is not independent of the views of others – on the contrary, according to Kant, an 'enlarged mentality' has to take them into account. The spectators, although disengaged from the particular characteristic of the actor, are not solitary.[33]

Once again (above), Arendt finds Kant – this time with his three principles of thought – employing new spatial metaphors. The spectator in
Arendt[34] is not a particular person. Instead, Arendt seeks to imagine the
way in which metaphor – for example, of a spectator – helps us to think
something beyond the boundaries of sensible reality, or the 'world of
appearances'. Yet she still insists we cannot leave this world behind in
moving metaphorically beyond it, in thinking. In Arendt's words,

> If the language of thinking is essentially metaphorical, it follows that
> the world of appearances inserts itself into thought quite apart from
> the needs of our body and the claims of our fellow-men, which will
> draw us back into it in any case. No matter how close we are while
> thinking to what is far away and how absent we are from what is close
> at hand, the thinking ego obviously never leaves the world of appear-
> ances altogether. The two-world theory, as I have said, is a metaphys-
> ical delusion although by no means an arbitrary or accidental one; it
> is the most plausible delusion with which the experience of thought
> is plagued. Language, by lending itself to metaphorical usage, ena-
> bles us to think, that is, to have traffic with non-sensory matters,
> because it permits a carrying over, *metapherein*, of our sense experi-
> ences. There are not two worlds because metaphor unites them.[35]

Arendt is bold in her critical statement (above) about a 'two-worlds'
interpretation of Kant. I am not going to critically engage with Arendt's
account in relation to Anglo-American two-world theory. The crucial
point is that Arendt raises the right questions for us here about Kant's
thinking and about the two-world theory. In addition, she provokes
us to treat the non-sensible 'world' as a metaphor, in order to avoid
the contradiction in the conception of the philosophical knower/agent;
contradiction seems evident if assuming that the one subject literally
knows and acts in two distinct worlds.

Arendt certainly accepts Kant's distinction between the sensible
and the intelligible worlds. Yet she seems to support rejection of this
as an ontological distinction. She claims that the distinct conscious
acts of knowing and thinking, seeing and not seeing, are – somehow – united by metaphor. Or perhaps her metaphorical language
anticipates the possibility that judging (in Kantian philosophy, at
least) brings together, imaginatively and reflectively, two distinct
terms by finding unacknowledged relations between the two.[36]
Arendt herself brings out the significance of thinking, even without a

direct intuition, which must be communicable; and, according to her reading of Kant, this communication is ultimately achieved by analogy transferring the reflection upon an object of intuition to a new (empty) concept; that is, moving from the particulars by the power of reflective judgement.[37] As Kant states in his third *Critique*, reflective judgement is under obligation to ascend from the particular in nature to the universal. Or, in the words of Paul Guyer's translation: 'If, however, only the particular is given, for which the universal is to be found, then the power of judgement is merely reflecting.'[38] For Kant – and for Arendt – this reflecting (or, depending on the translation, reflective) power of judging is creative.

8.6   Ontological distinctions and North–South Sea Islands

This section focuses on 'the space of reasons', questioning whether this spatial metaphor requires an ontologically distinct space, different from the reality of our sensibility. A temptation exists to answer this question in the affirmative, while locating freedom in this so-called space of reasons. If so, then 'the logical space of reasons', or simply 'conceptual space', could emphasize the distinction between the space of reason and that of nature. Yet is this Kant's distinction? Certain post-Kantian philosophers (at least) in talking about the space of reasons are alluding to the conceptual in general.

The previous section prepares the ground for showing that 'the conceptual' is not an ontologically distinct location. Kant himself extends conceptual knowledge without either leaving his (particular bodily) sensible space or being able to locate any fixed sensible limit. Yet, as we have seen, the sensible is a boundary for Kant. His extension in thought includes most notably the idea of freedom as a regulative ideal which can be viewed both from the standpoint of theoretical reason and from the standpoint of practical reason. The image of a non-sensible, or non-empirical, standpoint for freedom which, as practical, is completely and ontologically distinct from that of theoretical reason would, for some of us at least, be virtually incomprehensible.

This incomprehensibility turns us to focus on a central, critical question of the limits of human knowledge. How we know that we cannot know freedom beyond the bounds of the territory of pure understanding (i.e., the island), where things – including human inclinations – are determined by nature, remains deeply problematic for the transcendental idealist who tries to hold onto Kant's two worlds without contradiction. This could be read as requiring a more complex metaphor, since the standpoint of freedom would have both to be located beyond the knowable world[39] and to be a 'fact' of pure practical reason. But can we have this knowledge, in order to think freedom?

Recall the quotations from Kant which were presented in the first section of this chapter. First of all, remember the contention that 'though I cannot *cognize* freedom … nevertheless, I can *think* freedom …' Second, keeping this first contention in mind, consider an additional and related claim: 'for morality I need nothing more than that freedom should not contradict itself, that it should at least be thinkable.'[40] Third, the space beyond what Kant has carefully mapped out as knowledge on the island of understanding might still support a claim to think freedom; and this could be imagined as 'the wide and stormy ocean' where many a 'fog bank' and 'swiftly melting iceberg' deceive. Kant's ambivalence on this is evident in that there is no way to know that (i) we cannot know freedom and that (ii) we can have no knowledge of the noumenal. Nevertheless, human moral experience shows us that we can think freedom.[41] This may not guarantee the absolute confidence of epistemological certainty, but it does place the confidence of ethical conviction in thinking freedom. Basically, it is not knowledge of, but belief in, human freedom that guides moral action.

The 'two-world' theorists may hold onto an ontological distinction between two worlds. Yet the history of the interpretation of Kant's spatial metaphors demonstrates the serious problems in conceiving two ontologically distinct worlds. As already argued, Kant himself draws on a philosophical tradition in which the island (whether identified as the land of truth or the territory of pure understanding) in his own writings has to be understood as having a history of interpretations. Kant's island imagery is most closely associated with Francis Bacon's *New Atlantis*.[42] The imagery refers implicitly to Bacon's island of truth; and Kant makes an explicit reference to Bacon in the epigraph to the first *Critique*.[43] In turn, Bacon's Atlantis imagery can be traced back to Plato, even though Plato's island has a very different location from Kant's or Bacon's. The myth of Atlantis has its own history in the philosophical imaginary; it may be that Plato made up the island metaphor of Atlantis as 'a lost … under water kingdom'.[44] Yet James Davidson, in an essay in *London Review of Books*, claims that some people today, especially scientists, historians and mythologists, still seek this lost island (Atlantis).[45] What is striking in the ambivalence associated with Kant's islands is that initially the island in his Transcendental Analytic is a secure location bounded by space: he is not – at least not immediately – in search of either greater knowledge or blissful pleasure.

Le Doeuff explores the source of Kant's island imagery in Bacon, whose work she knows well from her French translations of his *New Atlantis*.[46] Yet Kant himself does not go as far as to explore Bacon in imagining the sceptics in nautical terms at sea. Bacon's sceptics 'waver from one side to the other, like an orator speaking from a ship-deck, and they behave towards their idols like lunatic lovers who curse their loves but can never leave them'.[47] Yet the similarity of Kant's spatial metaphor to Bacon's remains in taking up the imagery of truth surrounded by a mighty ocean in which many an intelligence will drown in storms of illusion.[48]

Critically significant for Le Doeuff's structural analysis of the philosophical imaginary are the ways in which changes of the imagery can be evidence of evasion of certain philosophical pursuits. In fact, Le Doeuff's analysis of Kant uncovers his resistance to discovering a very different sort of island – that of perfect pleasure; the dangers of the sea and the security of truth tend to keep the knower on Kant's carefully mapped-out island. In this way, Kant's metaphor of the philosopher's island can support a conviction that dwelling on the territory of pure understanding is more secure than wandering elsewhere, especially if this requires a voyage on stormy seas. As Le Doeuff unfolds her analysis of the relationship of Kant's island-imagery to conceptual thought, she teaches philosophers a lesson about epistemic confidence.[49] But this lesson is only learnt by placing Kant's texts within the history of the philosophical imaginary. As she explains,

The promise of the island of the understanding is balanced by some terrifying dangers…one avoids the discomfort of the icy fogs but at the cost of renouncing the dream of discovery, the call of new lands, and hope.[50]

Le Doeuff's analysis of the ambivalence in the imagery from the first *Critique* is also supported by a similar use of imagery in Kant's 'Conjectural Beginning of Human History.'[51] In the latter, Kant claims that 'The existence of such yearnings proves that thoughtful persons [tire] of civilized life, if they seek its value in pleasure alone'.[52] With this historical and cultural background, Le Doeuff insists that the formation of Kantian thought is riddled with sacrifices and historically determinate tensions for the human subject. In her words,

> the subjectivity which finds pleasure in the passage of the *Critique of Pure Reason* is a subjectivity which is socio-historically determinate. The island…dates from the eighteenth century, and marks an epoch: philosophers had previously been in the habit of offering us more

joyful and directly desirable things at the end of the path of knowledge – holding out in their discourse a prospect of islands to which
we might more happily transport ourselves. In considering then, the
historical singularity of the Kantian island, one should also not for-
get the historical situation...of a dated historical formation which
strives to think...on questions which are those of an epoch, and of
a social category.[53]

Le Doeuff proposes, partly in light of the fact that Kant's passage is
known to belong to the earliest drafts of the *Critique*, that the metaphor
of the secure island is a 'dialectical presupposition of the theory'. As she
explains,

> The image of the northern isle is thus indeed a precondition of the
> Kantian theory: in one way it works towards the coherence of the
> system – we meet in it the major theses of the theory, even down
> to some of its details. But, in a contradictory sense, it reinstates eve-
> rything which the work of critique tends to empty or to disavow, it
> cancels the renunciations demanded by the theory. Decoding it, and
> reintroducing into the discourse its latent meaning, makes apparent
> the troubles of the system.
>   The island of the Analytic compensates for the recognition of the
> vanity of regrets of South Sea islands.[54]

Thus Le Doeuff finds in Kant a movement of repudiation and return:
'we will always return to metaphysics as to a beloved from whom we
have been estranged.'[55]

8.7   The relation of metaphor to concept

There is a significant sense in which the imagery which the philosopher employs unwittingly yet dogmatically forces the reader to agree,
stage by stage, with a certain philosophical relationship of metaphor
to concept. This dynamic, dialectical relationship is what has been
established by the philosophical imaginary. Yet questions remain. How
exactly does judgement move analogically from conceptual knowledge
to spatial imagery? How does a metaphor of spatial location map onto
reality? How does the image legitimate the confidence of secure knowledge on the island, while the unstable understanding due to reason's
constant striving in its pursuit of the unconditioned totality threatens
the loss or lack of epistemic confidence, in moving off the island? Le

Doeuff's implicit answer seems to be that reason's striving becomes the desire for the fulfilment of an ancient promise, of bliss where confidence is no longer an issue.

With this picture in mind, let us return to the Analytic of Principles in the *Critique of Pure Reason*, where Kant both reflects back upon what he has demonstrated in the Transcendental Aesthetic and Analytic of Concepts and looks forward to the Transcendental Dialectic to come. Notice the movement or development of Kant's thinking. First of all, he appears secure within the boundaries of his island.

> We have now not only traveled through the land of pure understanding, and carefully inspected each part of it, but we have also surveyed it, and determined the place for each thing in it. This land, however, is an island, and enclosed in unalterable boundaries by nature itself.[56]

Next, it becomes clear that he is not secure.

> But if the understanding cannot distinguish whether certain questions lie within its horizon or not, then it is never sure of its claims and its possession, but must always reckon on many embarrassing corrections when it continually oversteps the boundaries of its territory (as is unavoidable) and loses itself in delusion and deceptions.[57]

Finally, we are led to question, where exactly are 'the bounds of sense' for this empirical employment of the understanding? Can we understand boundaries?[58] As already stated, Kant would seem to demonstrate that human knowledge continues to extend its epistemic limits, while what is beyond the boundaries of the empirical employment of the concepts of understanding remains unknowable.[59]

Kant demonstrates the nature of the object of our empirical knowledge as follows:

> Now the object cannot be given to a concept otherwise than in intuition, and, even if a pure intuition is possible *a priori* prior to the object, then even this can acquire its object, thus its objective validity, only through empirical intuition, of which it is the mere form. Thus all concepts and with them all principles, however *a priori* they may be are nevertheless related to empirical intuitions, i.e., to *data* for possible experience. Without this they have no objective

validity at all, but are rather a mere play, whether it be with representations of the imagination or of the understanding. One need only
take as an example the concepts of mathematics, and first, indeed,
in their pure intuitions. Space has three dimensions, between two
points there can be only one straight line, etc. Although all these
principles, and the representation of the object with which this science occupies itself, are generated in the mind completely *a priori*,
they would still not signify anything at all if we could not always
exhibit their significance in appearances (empirical objects). Hence
it is also requisite for one **to make** an abstract concept **sensible**, i.e.,
display the object that corresponds to it in intuition, since without
this the concept would remain (as one says) without **sense**, i.e., without significance.[60]

It would seem to follow from the above that freedom and God have
no sense, since they are 'concepts' without empirical intuitions; that
is, we cannot make sense of them. Does this lack of sensibility, then,
contradict the idea, which has been implied in the earlier pages of this
chapter, that we can think both freedom and God?

Kant has already guided us to be able to answer this. With spatial
metaphors, we can think freedom and God, even if they are 'empty'
concepts which cannot be 'made sense' of! Kant is clear that concepts
need intuitions, and that both the concepts (of understanding) and the
intuitions (of sensibility) are necessary for empirical knowledge, that
is, cognition. So, he makes a critical distinction between thought and
cognition. As we have also seen, it is only from the human standpoint
that we can speak of space, as well as the limits and the boundaries
of parts of space. Central metaphors in Kant's texts suggest that parts
of space put a limitation not only on sensibility, but on the understanding's employment of concepts. In fact, sensibility is a boundary
which restricts the pure concepts of understanding to certain bits of
space. Nevertheless, for Kant, thinking is not restricted by sensibility.
It is helpful to bring in Arendt's account of 'enlarged' thought here. In
the next section, we will seek to discover how spatial metaphors can
enlarge human thought without claiming more, in Kant's terms, objective validity than is humanly possible.

8.8   Standpoint of 'enlarged' thought

The quotation from Arendt in section 8.5 (above) challenges the two-
world distinction in Kant. A close alternative to the two-worlds reading

is the two-aspect reading of Kant. The crucial difference between these two readings is that the former implies, while the latter resists, an ontological distinction between (the world of) appearances and (the world of) things-in-themselves. A two-aspect reading interprets this distinction as epistemological, reading the appearances and things-in-themselves as two aspects of the necessary and sufficient conditions for Kant's theoretical and practical philosophy. The island imagery points to a standpoint from which the human subject can recognize herself in space and time as an empirical object (or phenomena) just like any other subject of knowledge, while also assuming no knowledge of herself in her noumenal aspect, that is, of being a subject in herself. According to this, we can know what appears as an object in sensible intuition, but non-sensible ideas such as freedom cannot be known, even though they can be thought. In turn, such ideas of reason can enlarge our thinking insofar as they extend beyond appearances and guide (moral) action. This enlarged thought recalls the second of the three principles of human thought which Arendt draws out from Kant's third *Critique*; that is, to think from the standpoint of everyone else is necessary for 'an enlarged thought'. Roughly, enlarged thoughts can mean shareable thoughts.

After Kant, some philosophers insist that it is best to represent a higher point of view, that of enlarged thought, from the perspective of 'the detective', who, I suggest, is similar to Arendt's 'spectator' gathering from the particulars a general point of view. Or, in Hans Blumenberg's picture, this would be 'the shipwreck with spectator'.[61] Here we may think of Kant's imagery of the free subject ascending to a higher immutable realm of intelligibility; this ascension happens when the agent acts morally as she ought to do, and, possibly, when she acts freely and creatively, in making a reflective judgement of enlarged thought.

Although some philosophers continue to argue that there are two ontologically distinct worlds in Kant's philosophy, philosophers who argue against the two-worlds readings of Kant insist that 'world' must be a metaphor for expressing the two aspects which Kant must give to knowledge and to the subject of freedom. I have nothing new to add specifically to either side of the two-worlds and two-aspects debates about space in Kant. Instead, I am urging that the interpreters of Kant consider the bigger picture of the philosophical imaginary, in order to understand better the nature and function of spatial metaphors in Kant and in his relation to the philosophical tradition.

There remains a need to explain and to sort out misunderstandings between philosophers who fail to communicate to one another due to a lack of awareness of their own positioning in thought and in reflective judgement. Does the philosopher speak from the standpoint of sensible knowledge, of empirical concepts, of the securely mapped-out land? Or does she act from the standpoint of pure practical reason, where the agent is free to think her own freedom, but also unable to know (the standpoint of) freedom, or to avoid the inevitable transcendental illusion in the extension of conceptual knowledge? Or is she speaking from each of these standpoints, separately or altogether? As Kant himself explains, '[there] is an illusion which can no more be prevented than we can prevent the sea appearing higher at the horizon than at the shore, since we see it through higher light rays'.[62] By understanding the nature of the limits to human knowledge, the space of both the knowable and the unknowable, as well as the boundary between them, we are able to recognize this illusion as inevitable, without allowing it to undermine our ability to think freedom and to imagine new possibilities in the space(s) of reason.

8.9 Conclusion

In this concluding section, I return to Le Doeuff's subtle and insightful grasp of Kant's images and their significance for his philosophical 'utterance'. As she explains,

> between the writing subject and his text there is a complex negating relationship which is a sign that something important and troubling is seeking utterance – something which cannot be acknowledged, yet is keenly cherished. As far as I am concerned, taking an interest in images and enquiring into this sort of evasion are one and the same activity.[63]

Investigating the metaphor of the philosopher's island and related spatial imagery in Kant has taken us to the heart of the philosophical imaginary, exploring both isolated features in a philosophical text and imagery which appears to follow a significant pattern. Le Doeuff calls this an iconographic investigation in philosophy. Such an investigation reveals, in the case of Kant's island, that this image appears in the first *Critique*[64] along with a range of spatial imagery, including the two-worlds and the two-aspects points of view.[65] Similarly, there are references to the spatial dimensions of higher and lower, inner and outer, in Kant's *Critique of Practical Reason*,[66] and of northern and southern islands in his 'Conjectural Beginning of Human History'.[67] The latter essay speaks of the yearning to return to the South Sea islands, which Kant may imply is a sign of laziness and a failure to face up to the responsibility of reason. Nevertheless, Kant's own central critical metaphor of an island and its surroundings is definitely suggestive of something more than thinking freedom and morality. This includes both the possibility of a return to metaphysics and the enlarged thought of reflective judgement.[68]

Le Doeuff points out the danger of cognitive prohibition, which, she insists, remains in the first *Critique*. The aim of this chapter, to scrutinize the subtle and salient differences between boundaries (*Grenzen*) and limits (*Schranken*) in Kant, has been to expose the serious confusion of believing a limit is a boundary which would prohibit new knowledge, by blocking the genuine extension of a limit to new ideas. In response to such prohibitions, Le Doeuff herself helpfully describes the cognitive shock of analysing a philosophical text which can jolt a reader out of any blissful or dozing slumber, allowing her to see new possibilities for cognition and for reflection. Perhaps the final word on the question of understanding the function of spatial metaphors after Kant is found in the new spaces opened up by the creative power of reflective judgement, in moving from the particulars to a universal, or a shared thought. From a human standpoint, reflective judgement is the act of the imagination which, by analogy to the known, can open up possibilities for the enlargement of our understanding of the nature of space and the function of spatial metaphors in philosophical texts, especially in traditional Kantian and contemporary post-Kantian philosophies.

Notes

1. Lisabeth During (2000), 'Islands and Theatres', in Max Deutscher (ed.) *Michèle Le Doeuff: Operative Philosophy and Imaginary Practice* (Amherst, New York: Humanity Books), p. 230. Cf. Pamela Sue Anderson (2009) 'A Turn to Spiritual Virtues in Philosophy of Religion: "A Thoughtful Love of Life"', in J. Cornwell and M. McGhee (eds) *Philosophers and God: At the Frontiers of Faith and Reason* (London: Continuum), pp. 167–86.
2. For an interesting example of how the Kantian distinction between limit and boundary can be applied to human knowledge of life/death, see Paul Ricoeur (2009), *Living Up to Death*, trans. D. Pellauer (Chicago: University of Chicago Press), pp. 11–22.
3. On the inevitability of this transcendental illusion, see Immanuel Kant (1997), *Critique of Pure Reason*, trans. Paul Guyer and Allen W. Wood (eds) (Cambridge: Cambridge University Press), A 296–8 / B 353–5, pp. 386–7.
4. Francis Bacon (2008) *New Atlantis*, introduction and notes by Susan Bruce (Oxford: Oxford University Press); cf. Francis Bacon (1980) *La Nouvelle Atlantide*, trans.

Michèle Le Doeuff and Margaret Llasera, 'Suivi de '*Voyage dans la pensée baroque*' (Paris: Payot); *La Nouvelle Atlantide*, deuxième edition (1991), trans. Michèle Le Doeuff, complètement refondue, pour la collection Gallimard/ Flammarion. Also see Pierre Vidal-Naquet (2007) *The Atlantis Story: A Short History of Plato's Myth*, trans. Janet Lloyd (Exeter: University of Exeter Press); and Jean-Jacques Rousseau (2009) *Emile, or On Education*, Christopher Kelly (ed.), trans. Allan Bloom (NH: Dartmouth College Press).

5. Michèle Le Doeuff (1989; 2002), *The Philosophical Imaginary*, trans. Colin Gordon (London: Continuum).

6. Kant, *Critique of Pure Reason*, A 235–6 / B 294–5, pp. 338–9; also, for the second edition of this passage, see pp. 354–5. This passage is crucial for the metaphor of an island, or 'the land of pure understanding' which appears in Kant's 'Transcendental Analytic', book two: 'Analytic of Principles', chapter three: 'The Ground of the Distinction of all Objects in general into Phenomena and Noumena', *Critique of Pure Reason*, pp. 338–65.

7. Kant, *Critique of Pure Reason*, A 235–6 / B 294–5, p. 339.

8. Le Doeuff, *The Philosophical Imaginary*, pp. 8–20.

9. Le Doeuff teases out the role of prohibition in Kant in a novel manner with epistemological but also moral and political implications; cf. *The Philosophical Imaginary*, pp. 11–13. This topic is developed in Pamela Sue Anderson (2011), 'Michèle Le Doeuff's "Primal Scene": Prohibition and Confidence in the Education of a Woman', *Text Matters: A Journal of Literature, Theory and Culture* 1(1), 9–24. Also, see Pamela Sue Anderson (2010) 'Pure Reason and Contemporary Philosophy of Religion: the Rational Striving in and for Truth', *International Journal of Philosophy of Religion*, 68, 95–106.

10. See Miranda Fricker (2007) *Epistemic Injustice: Power and the Ethics of Knowing* (Oxford: Oxford University Press), pp. 17, 23–9 and 130–8.

11. See A.W. Moore (2006) 'The Bounds of Sense', *Philosophical Topics*, 34(1–2), 327–8, 333; 341 n3.

12. Le Doeuff, *The Philosophical Imaginary*, pp. 11–13; cf. Anderson, 'Michèle Le Doeuff's "Primal Scene."'

13. Immanuel Kant (1956) *Critique of Practical Reason*, trans. Lewis White Beck (Indianapolis: The Bobbs-Merrill Co.), p. 166. It has been argued that a contradiction in accounting for freedom from both a theoretical and a practical standpoint can be avoided by reading freedom as an 'absolute metaphor'; see Hans Blumenberg (1997) 'Prospect for a Theory of Nonconceptuality', in *Shipwreck with Spectator: Paradigm of a Metaphor for Existence*, trans. Steve Rendall (The MIT Press), pp. 101–2.

14. For an interpretation of Kant's 'boundaries' and 'the land of thought' as metaphors, see Hannah Arendt (1977) *The Life of the Mind*, one-volume edition (New York and London: Harcourt Brace & Company) Part One, especially pp. 103 and 109. For her fuller account of metaphor in philosophy, see Arendt, *The Life of the Mind* Part One, pp. 98–114.

15. Arendt, *The Life of the Mind* Part One, pp. 104f and 111. For additional background on Arendt's account of reflective judgement, see Paul Ricoeur (2000) 'Aesthetic Judgment and Political Judgment: According to Hannah Arendt', in *The Just*, trans. David Pellauer (Chicago: University of Chicago Press), pp. 94–108.

16. Le Doeuff, *The Philosophical Imaginary*, pp. 10–13.

17. Le Doeuff finds that 'the northern isle' in the passage from the first *Critique* is 'the island one must content oneself with, [it] has its symmetric antithesis in the island of the South Seas the seat of the Golden Age, which must be utterly renounced' (*The Philosophical Imaginary*, p. 9); cf. Immanuel Kant (1985), 'Conjectural Beginning of Human History,' in *On History*, trans. Emil L. Fackenheim (New York: Macmillan Publishing; London: Collier Macmillan Publishers), p. 68. Le Doeuff's original work on the philosophical imaginary demonstrates the necessity of imagery for expressions of conceptual knowledge. In particular, Le Doeuff's work on Kant's island imagery was a clever way to subvert the 'prohibition' placed on the young Michèle, who had been told by her philosophy teacher that Kant would be far too difficult for her to read! So she read him in her own way. Cf. Michèle Le Doeuff (2006) 'Each to her own primal scene', in *Hipparchia's Choice: An Essay concerning philosophy, women, etc.*, trans. Trista Selous (Columbia University Press), pp. 142–7, also 148–9. For the gendered distribution of the space of knowledge and learning, see Le Doeuff (2000) 'A Little Learning: Women and (Intellectual) Work', reprinted (2004) in Kelly Oliver and Lisa Walsh (eds) *French Feminist Philosophy*, Oxford Readings in Feminist Philosophy (Oxford: Oxford University Press), pp. 74–89, especially 80–4.
18. P.F. Strawson (1966) *The Bounds of Sense: An Essay on Kant's Critique of Pure Reason* (London: Methuen and Co. Ltd); and Moore, 'The Bounds of Sense', pp. 327–44. Cf. Kant, *Critique of Pure Reason*, B xxiv–xxix, pp. 114–16.
19. Anderson, 'Michèle Le Doeuff's "Primal Scene"', pp. 10, 12–17, 20–1.
20. I say 'near' because it may not be possible to locate these bounds exactly; see Strawson, *The Bounds of Sense*, pp. 11–12, 16, 24 and 44.
21. Kant, *Critique of Pure Reason*, B 44/ A 28, pp. 177–8.
22. A.W. Moore (1997) *Points of View* (Oxford: Oxford University Press), p. 251.
23. Kant, *Critique of Pure Reason*, A 236 / B 295, p. 354.
24. Kant, *Critique of Practical Reason*, pp. 166–7.
25. For a defence of a two-aspect reading of Kant instead of Strawson's two-world interpretation, see H.E. Matthews (1982) 'Strawson on Transcendental Idealism', in Ralph Walker (ed.), *Pure Reason*. Oxford Readings in Philosophy (Oxford: Oxford University Press), pp. 132–49; cf. Strawson, *Bounds of Sense*.
26. See Kant *Critique of Practical Reason;* (1952) *Critique of Judgment*, trans. with Analytical Index by James Creed Meredith (Oxford: Clarendon Press); and (1996) *Religion within the Boundaries of Mere Reason*, trans. George di Giovanni, in Allen W. Wood and George di Giovanni (eds) *Religion and Rational Theology* (Cambridge: Cambridge University Press).
27. For discussion of transcendental philosophy and its relation to naturalism, see Mark Sacks (2000) *Objectivity and Insight* (Oxford: Oxford University Press), pp. 172–7 and 198–218; and Joel Smith and Peter Sullivan (eds) (2011) *Transcendental Philosophy and Naturalism* (New York: Oxford University Press); here each of the contributors aims to understand the theoretical structures involved in transcendental explanation, and to assess the contemporary relevance of the transcendental orientation, in particular with respect to contemporary philosophical naturalism.

28. See Moore, 'The Bounds of Sense', *Philosophical Topics*, 327–44; also see Blumenberg, *Shipwreck with Spectator*; Le Doeuff, *The Philosophical Imaginary*.
29. Immanuel Kant (1996) *Groundwork of the Metaphysics of Morals*, trans. Mary Gregor, with an introduction by Christine Korsgaard (Cambridge: Cambridge University Press); and *Religion within the Boundaries of Mere Reason*, pp. 39–215.
30. Note that the 'imaginary' is not employed here in a psychoanalytic sense, especially not in the Irigarayan sense in which the imaginary is sexed as either male or female. For a much earlier introduction to this distinction between the philosophical and the psycholinguistic 'imaginary', see Pamela Sue Anderson (1998) *A Feminist Philosophy of Religion: the Rationality and Myths of Religious Belief* (Oxford: Blackwell), pp. 9–13 and 227–8.
31. Arendt, *The Life of the Mind*, p. 103.
32. See the three maxims of understanding, judgement and reason in Kant, *Critique of Judgment*, Paragraph #40, pp. 150–1. Also see Hannah Arendt (1982) *Lectures on Kant's Political Philosophy*. Edited and with an Interpretative Essay by Ronald Beiner (Chicago: University of Chicago Press), pp. 42–4; and Moore, *Noble in Reason, Infinite in Faculty*, pp. 87–9.
33. Arendt, *The Life of the Mind*, p. 94.
34. Arendt, *Lectures on Kant's Political Philosophy*, especially pp. 27–33 and 40–6.
35. Arendt, *The Life of the Mind*, p. 110.
36. See Howard Caygill (1989) *Art of Judgement* (Oxford: Blackwell); (1995) *A Kant Dictionary* (Oxford: Blackwell Publishers), pp. 267–8: Caygill claims that 'judgment provides the matrix of Kant's entire philosophy' (p. 267). Also see Robert Hanna, 'Kant's Theory of Judgment', in *The Stanford Encyclopedia of Philosophy* (online). Cf. Kant, *Critique of Pure Reason*, A 294–5 / B 350.
37. Arendt, *Lectures on Kant's Political Philosophy*, p. 44. Cf. Kant, *Critique of Judgment*, p. 18 (179).
38. Kant (2000), *Critique of the Power of Judgment*, trans. Paul Guyer (Cambridge: Cambridge University Press), p. 67 (5: 179); cf. Moore, *Noble in Reason*, p. 88.
39. Kant, *Critique of Pure Reason*, B 345 / A 289, pp. 381–2; also see A 253–6 / B 310–12, pp. 361–3; A 458–61 / B 486–9, pp. 492–3; and A 584–5 / B612–13, pp. 560–1.
40. Kant, *Critique of Pure Reason*, B xxviii and B xxix, respectively, p. 116.
41. Blumenberg, 'Prospect for a Theory of Nonconceptuality', pp. 101–2. Blumenberg attempts to argue that, as long as freedom is both necessary and practical in Kant, we can think it as an 'absolute metaphor'; it can never be made sensible/literal. Claiming to follow Kant, Blumenberg's reasoning is a bit strange, but it appears roughly as follows: (i) that freedom can be thought as a metaphor; (ii) that freedom must be a 'transcendental action of the understanding'; (iii) that freedom is theoretically incomprehensible, yet must be practical; and, (iv) hence, it must be thought as an absolute metaphor.
42. Francis Bacon (1974), *The New Atlantis* (Oxford: Oxford University Press). Cf. Le Doeuff, *The Philosophical Imaginary*, pp. 10–13.

43. Kant, *Critique of Pure Reason*, p. 91 (epigraph); and for the (Baconian) references to 'the land of truth (a charming name)', see Kant, *Critique of Pure Reason*, p. 339 and p. 354.
44. For the ongoing debates about the myth of a lost kingdom on the island of Atlantis, see Vidal-Naquet *The Atlantis Story* and the review of this text by James Davidson, 'Plato Made It Up', *London Review of Books*, 30(12), 3 and 6. Also see Pierre Vidal-Naquet (1992), 'Atlantis and the Nations', trans. Janet Lloyd, *Critical Inquiry* 18(2), 303.
45. Davidson, 'Plato Made It Up', p. 3.
46. See endnote 4 (above) and Le Doeuff, *The Philosophical Imaginary*, pp. 10–13.
47. Bacon, *The New Atlantis*, cited in Le Doeuff, *The Philosophical Imaginary*, p. 9.
48. Le Doeuff, *The Philosophical Imaginary*, p. 19.
49. Le Doeuff, 'A Little Learning', pp. 74–89, especially 80–4.
50. Le Doeuff, *The Philosophical Imaginary*, p. 12.
51. Kant's passage begins: 'Vain regrets for a golden age promise us unalloyed enjoyment of a carefree life, dreamt away idly, or trifled away in childish play. Such yearnings have been stimulated by stories such as Robinson Crusoe and reports of visitors to the South Sea Islands.' Cf. 'Conjectural Beginning to Human History', p. 68.
52. Kant, 'Conjectural Beginning to Human History', p. 68.
53. Le Doeuff, *The Philosophical Imaginary*, pp. 14–15.
54. Ibid., p. 17.
55. Kant, *Critique of Pure Reason*, A 850 / B 878, pp. 700–1.
56. Kant, *Critique of Pure Reason*, A 235–6 / B 294–5; pp. 338–9.
57. Kant, *Critique of Pure Reason*, A 238 / B 297; p. 340.
58. Moore, 'The Bounds of Sense', pp. 339–40.
59. Kant, *Critique of Pure Reason*, B 298 / A239, pp. 340–1.
60. Kant, *Critique of Pure Reason*, A 239–40 / B299–300, p. 341.
61. Blumenberg, *Shipwreck with Spectator*, pp. 7f, also 46, 74–9.
62. Kant, *Critique of Pure Reason*, A 297 / B 354, p. 386.
63. Le Doeuff, *The Philosophical Imaginary*, p. 9.
64. Kant, *Critique of Pure Reason*, A 235–6 and B 294–5, pp. 338–9.
65. Ibid., A 254–6/ B 310–12, pp. 362–3; B 345 / A 289, p. 381; A 458–61 / B486–9, pp. 492–3; and A 584–5 / B 612–13, p. 560.
66. Kant, *Critique of Practical Reason*, pp. 6–7, 162–7.
67. Kant, 'Conjectural Beginning of Human History', p. 68.
68. See Kant, 'Conjectural Beginning of Human History,' p. 68. Le Doeuff finds that 'the northern isle' in the passage from the first *Critique* is 'the island one must content oneself with, has its symmetric antithesis in the island of the South Seas [which appears in Kant's 'Conjectural Beginning' as] the seat of the Golden Age, which must be utterly renounced' (The *Philosophical Imaginary*, p. 9). Thus, her philosophical imaginary finds the necessity of imagery for our conceptual thought, even in the writings of Kant, whose difficulty was supposed to be blocked from her as a (young) woman.

References

Anderson, P. S. (1998) A Feminist Philosophy of Religion: the Rationality and Myths of Religious Belief (Oxford: Blackwell).

Anderson, P. S. (2009) 'A Turn to Spiritual Virtues in Philosophy of Religion: "A Thoughtful Love of Life"' in J. Cornwell and M. McGhee. (eds) Philosophers and God: At the Frontiers of Faith and Reason (London: Continuum).

Anderson, P. S. (2010) 'Pure Reason and Contemporary Philosophy of Religion: the Rational Striving in and for Truth', International Journal of Philosophy of Religion, 68, 95–106.

Anderson, P. S. (2011) 'Michèle Le Doeuff's "Primal Scene": Prohibition and Confidence in the Education of a Woman', Text Matters: A Journal of Literature, Theory and Culture, 1:1, 9–24.

Arendt, H. (1977) The Life of the Mind (New York and London: Harcourt Brace & Company).

Arendt, H., (1982) Lectures on Kant's Political Philosophy, R. Beiner (ed.) (Chicago: University of Chicago Press).

Bacon, F. (1980) La Nouvelle Atlantide, trans. by M. Le Doeuff et M. Llasera (Paris: Payot).

Bacon, F. (1991) La Nouvelle Atlantide, deuxième édition, trans. by M. Le Doeuff (Paris: Gallimard/Flammarion).

Bacon, F. (2008) New Atlantis, S Bruce (ed.) (Oxford: Oxford University Press).

Blumenberg, H. (1997) Shipwreck with Spectator: Paradigm of a Metaphor for Existence, trans. by S. Rendall (Cambridge, Mass.; London : MIT Press).

Caygill, H. (1989) Art of Judgement (Oxford: Blackwell).

Caygill, H. (1995) A Kant Dictionary (Oxford: Blackwell Publishers).

Davidson, J. (2008) 'Plato Made It Up', London Review of Books, 30, 12.

During, L. (2000) 'Islands and Theatres', in M. Deutscher. (ed.) Michèle Le Doeuff: Operative Philosophy and Imaginary Practice (Amherst, New York: Humanity Books).

Fricker, M. (2007) Epistemic Injustice: Power and the Ethics of Knowing (Oxford: Oxford University Press).

Hanna, R. 'Kant's Theory of Judgment', in The Stanford Encyclopedia of Philosophy (http://plato.stanford.edu/entries/kant-judgment/).

Kant, I. (1952) Critique of Judgment, trans. by J. Creed Meredith (Oxford: Clarendon Press).

Kant, I. (1956) Critique of Practical Reason, trans. by L.W. Beck (Indianapolis: The Bobbs-Merrill Co).

Kant, I. (1985) On History, trans. by E. L. Fackenheim (New York: Macmillan Publishing; London: Collier Macmillan Publishers).

Kant, I. (1996) Groundwork of the Metaphysics of Morals, trans. by M. Gregor (Cambridge: Cambridge University Press).

Kant, I. (1996) Religion within the Boundaries of Mere Reason, trans. by G. di Giovanni, in Allen W. Wood and George di Giovanni (eds), Religion and Rational Theology. (Cambridge: Cambridge University Press).

Kant, I. (1999) Critique of Pure Reason, trans. by P. Guyer and A. W. Wood (eds) (Cambridge: Cambridge University Press).

Le Doeuff, M. (2002/1989) The Philosophical Imaginary, trans. by C. Gordon (London: Continuum).

Le Doeuff, M. (2004) 'A Little Learning: Women and (Intellectual) Work' in K. Oliver and L. Walsh (eds) French Feminist Philosophy, Oxford Readings in Feminist Philosophy (Oxford: Oxford University Press).

Le Doeuff, M. (2006) Hipparchia's Choice: An Essay concerning philosophy, women, etc., trans. by T. Selous (New York: Columbia University Press)

Matthews, H. E. (1982) 'Strawson on Transcendental Idealism' in R. Walker (ed.) Pure Reason, Oxford Readings in Philosophy (Oxford: Oxford University Press).

Moore, A. W. (1997) Points of View (Oxford: Oxford University Press).

Moore, A. W. (2003) Noble in Reason, Infinite in Faculty: Themes and Variations in Kant's Moral and Religious Philosophy (London: Routledge).

Moore, A. W. (2006) 'The Bounds of Sense', Philosophical Topics, 34, 1 & 2 (Spring and Fall), 327–344.

Ricoeur, P. (2000) Reflections on the Just, trans. by D. Pellauer (Chicago: University of Chicago Press).

Ricoeur, P. (2009) Living Up to Death, trans. by D. Pellauer (Chicago: University of Chicago Press).

Rousseau, J.-J. (2009) Emile, or On Education. C. Kelly (ed.), trans. by A. Bloom. (NH: Dartmouth College Press).

Sacks, M. (2000) Objectivity and Insight (Oxford: Oxford University Press).

Smith J. and Sullivan P. (eds) (2011) Transcendental Philosophy and Naturalism (New York: Oxford University Press).

Strawson, P. F. (1966) The Bounds of Sense: An Essay on Kant's Critique of Pure Reason (London: Methuen and Co. Ltd).

Vidal-Naquet, P. (1992), 'Atlantis and the Nations', trans. by J. Lloyd, Critical Inquiry, 18, 2.

Vidal-Naquet, P. (2007) The Atlantis Story: A Short History of Plato's Myth, trans. by J. Lloyd (Exeter: University of Exeter Press).

9
Bird on Kant's Mathematical Antinomies

A.W. Moore

My aim in this chapter is to take issue with Graham Bird's treatment of Kant's mathematical antinomies in his recent commentary on the first *Critique*.[1] It is an imposing and magisterial commentary, running to over 800 pages, every one of which contains significant insights and displays admirable scholarship. My disagreement, in such a context, is minor. That said, at the end of the chapter I shall suggest, albeit very inchoately, a way in which this disagreement connects with some reservations that I have about Bird's fundamental project, which is to repudiate what he calls 'traditionalist' interpretations of Kant in favour of what he calls a 'revolutionary' interpretation. I subscribe to what (I am fairly sure) Bird would call a traditionalist interpretation[2] – though I admit to being altogether less clear about the contrast than he is.[3]

My focus, as I have already indicated, is Bird's treatment of the mathematical antinomies, which constitutes chapter 26 of his book. I have no special quarrel with his treatment of the details of the antinomic arguments. My concern is rather with his treatment, in section 3 of the chapter, of what he calls 'the character of the conflicts'.

As I understand it, Bird's conception of Kant's conception is roughly as follows. We are part of a physical reality which is largely independent of us. We can obtain knowledge of this reality, and of what pertains to it, such as our own psychological states, although we cannot obtain knowledge of anything else. All the knowledge that we do obtain relates to experience. But it also involves certain *a priori* concepts. And we can put these concepts to a further, independent use: to entertain the idea of an experience-transcendent reality, the reality of 'things in themselves' such as God. We cannot, however, obtain any knowledge of such a reality. We cannot even know whether things in themselves exist. But, once we have entertained the idea, it is irresistible for us to speculate about such things, and indeed to try to obtain knowledge of them, by pure reason. Moreover, in certain cases, we are subject to a powerful illusion of having succeeded. In the specific case of the cosmological questions with which the mathematical antinomies are concerned, our mistake consists in:

- starting with perfectly legitimate scientific questions about the structure of physical reality;
- using certain *a priori* limit concepts to address these questions;
- wrenching those concepts from that use;
- using them instead to raise questions about the experience-transcendent limits of physical reality itself;
- addressing these questions by pure reason;

  and

- fancying that we have answered the questions. (See, especially, section 3.1.)

There are two points in particular that Bird emphasizes as part of this conception:

(1) It is a mistake to think that we can settle issues about the character of the physical universe by pure reason (p. 671 and, a little more cautiously, p. 674).

(2) The particular issues about the character of the physical universe that we do think we can settle by pure reason we cannot settle at all: our attempts to settle them constitute 'an erroneous and undecidable' pseudo-discipline (pp. 674 and 680).

My own view is that there is a problem in ascribing (1) to Kant, and that, although he takes (2) to be true of the issues that arise in the dynamical antinomies, he does not take it to be true of the issues that arise in the mathematical antinomies. (This, indeed, marks one of the most important contrasts between the two sets of antinomies.)

Let us begin with (1). Before we can properly consider Kant's attitude to (1), we need to clarify what is meant by 'pure reason' in this context. If the term is used in the way in which Kant sometimes uses it – whereby to settle an issue by pure reason is simply to settle it *a priori* (B20, 480/B508, A712/B740, and *Prolegomena*, section 6) – then there is no question but that he would deny (1). For he would count what he achieves in the three analogies of experience (A176/B218 ff.) as a counter-example.

Come to that, he would count what can be achieved in pure mathematics as a counter-example (A157/B196). More often, however, and certainly in the passages that are most directly relevant to the antinomies, Kant uses the term 'pure reason' in such a way that not only must pure reason be free of any appeal to experience, it must be free of any appeal to intuition as well (e.g., A306/B363 and A750–1/B778–91). Then it is altogether less obvious what Kant would say about (1).[4,5]

Bird cites, in this connection, A409/B436. This is the passage in which Kant specifies a natural principle of pure reason: that, if the conditioned is given, then the unconditioned must be given also. This passage certainly highlights a mistake that Kant thinks we naturally make when we try to address issues about the character of the physical universe by pure reason, perhaps, indeed, the chief mistake: the mistake, namely, of taking this principle to be a truth about the physical universe.[6] But it does not suggest that the mistake is ineradicable; or, in particular, that the mistake cannot be eradicated by pure reason; or, crucially, that, once the mistake has been eradicated, pure reason lacks the resources to address the original issues.[7] It is quite compatible with what Kant says in this passage that we can settle issues about the character of the physical universe by pure reason.

Be that as it may, my concern hereafter will be with (2), which states that we have *no* way of settling such issues. That there is *something* awry with Bird's attribution of (2) to Kant is reflected in a crucial asymmetry between what Kant wants to say about the truth or falsity of the conclusions in each of the mathematical antinomies and what he wants to say about the truth or falsity of the conclusions in each of the dynamical antinomies. I do not mean the familiar point that he accedes to the falsity of both conclusions in the former case and to the truth of both conclusions in the latter case. I mean the less familiar point that he recognizes a modal contrast too. He says that the conclusions in each of the mathematical antinomies *must* both be regarded as false; and that the conclusions in each of the dynamical antinomies *may* both be regarded as true (e.g., A531–2/B559–60; see also *Prolegomena*, sections 52c and 53). The 'must' indicates that he does indeed think we can settle what to say in the former case: this is reflected in the pithy summary that he gives (A506–7/B534–5) of the argument for transcendental idealism from the reasoning in the first antinomy.[8] Bird, significantly, says merely that 'in the two mathematical antinomies both sides *can* be wrong' (p. 674, emphasis added); and, later, that 'Kant...*allows* the conclusions to the mathematical antinomies to be both false' (p. 681, emphasis added). This second quotation is not, admittedly, *in propria persona*; but neither is there any indication that Bird would demur.

What grounds this modal distinction? The answer is: another distinction which Kant draws in the 'Transcendental Doctrine of Method' (A740–1/B768–9). There he divides the misguided efforts of metaphysicians into two broad classes, according to whether their questions are ill-conceived or well-conceived.[9] Kant's idea is this. These metaphysical questions always involve some idea of reason, that is, some *a priori* concept of the understanding freed of whatever conditions allow it to be applied empirically. Such a question is ill-conceived if it involves a confused amalgam of an idea of reason with some concept that can be applied only to objects of possible experience. It is well-conceived if it involves ideas of reason without any such distortion. In the former case, the question has no answer. Or, rather, it has no answer *as intended*. Thus, if the question is which of two apparent contradictories holds, each involving the confused concept, then the answer is neither (A503–5/ B531–3). In the latter case the question has an answer, even as intended, but only at the level of things in themselves, which means that we lack the resources to ascertain what that answer is. The questions addressed in the mathematical antinomies are of the former kind: they are ill-conceived. The questions addressed in the dynamical antinomies are of the latter kind: they are well-conceived.

Although my principal concern in this paper is with the mathematical antinomies, I want to take a brief digression to discuss the dynamical antinomies. There is an issue about what exactly Kant takes the arguments in the dynamical antinomies to establish, once the illegitimate inference to how things are in themselves is separated off. Consider in particular the third antinomy. The question there is whether there is any such thing as freedom, and Kant takes the arguments to leave open the possibility that there is, at the level of things in themselves, even though there is not in physical reality. The argument for the antithesis is in this respect fairly straightforward. Kant takes that argument to establish just what it purports to establish: that there is no freedom in physical reality because 'everything [there] happens in accordance with laws of nature' (A445/B473). But what of the argument for the thesis? What Kant himself says, in his remark on it – and, unlike Bird (p. 693), I take Kant to be speaking in his own voice in his various remarks on these arguments – is this:

> We have really established [the] necessity of a first beginning of a series of appearances from freedom only to the extent that this is required to make comprehensible an origin of the world…But because the faculty of beginning a series in time entirely on its own *is* thereby proved (though no insight into it is achieved), now we are

permitted also ... to ascribe to the substances in [different series in the course of the world] the faculty of acting from freedom. (A448–50/B476–8, emphasis added)

What Kant takes this argument to show, it seems to me, is that there must be something uncaused grounding whatever happens in accordance with laws of nature. This relates to something else that I think Kant thinks we know: that there must ultimately be something unconditioned corresponding to whatever is conditioned (see Bxx). This is, of course, to be distinguished from the assumption cited above, which Kant certainly holds to be illusory: that there must be something unconditioned *and physical* corresponding to whatever is conditioned and physical. It is also, in my view, evidence of another error on Bird's part: the error of holding that Kant denies us *any* knowledge concerning things in themselves, even knowledge of their existence.[10]

To return to the mathematical antinomies: the questions addressed in these antinomies are, to repeat, ill-conceived. The question addressed in the first antinomy, for example, involves the concept of the physical universe as a whole. But this is a confused amalgam of the idea of unconditionedness and the concept of physical reality (A422/B450).[11] The physical universe as a whole, if there were such a thing, would have to be both physical and all-encompassing. But the only physical things that can exist are objects of possible experience.[12] And no object of possible experience can be all-encompassing. That is, no such object can encompass the whole of physical reality (*Prolegomena*, section 52c). The source of our mistake, when we conflate these concepts in this way, is a genuine item of knowledge that we have, the very item to which I just referred: that there must ultimately be something unconditioned corresponding to whatever is conditioned, and in particular corresponding to whatever is conditioned and physical. What we fail to appreciate, however, is that such unconditionedness must reside in things in themselves, which physical things are not. We naturally assume that some *physical* thing must be unconditioned, the very assumption that we have already seen Kant reject; or, to put it another way, that there must be such a thing as the physical universe as a whole, finite or infinite as the case may be. Once we drop this assumption, we can acquiesce in the conclusion that every physical thing is part of some other physical thing that is older and bigger – as the earth, for instance, is part of the solar system – though there is no one physical thing of which every physical thing is part ('Transcendental Dialectic', Bk II, passim, especially section IV ff.).[13]

How exactly does this account set me apart from Bird? There is, of course, the point that I, unlike Bird, allow us, on Kant's behalf, a minimal item of knowledge concerning things in themselves. But there are differences even apart from that. Bird again and again insists that in the mathematical antinomies we are, in Kant's view, addressing questions that are undecidable for us. I disagree. Kant stands by the correctness of the arguments in these antinomies, except, of course, for what he sees as their erroneous shared presuppositions (*Prolegomena*, section 52a);[14] and he takes them to show exactly how to decide the questions addressed. We have first to reject those shared presuppositions (A481–2/B509–10), then apply the arguments. Thus, the correct verdict in the case of the first antinomy is that it is false that the physical universe as a whole is finite, and false that the physical universe as a whole is infinite, because it is false that the physical universe as a whole *is* (A501–2/B529–30 and A506–7/B534–5).[15]

In the section beginning at A476/B504, Kant is explicit that we must not treat our failure to reach a satisfactory verdict on such matters as an excuse to say that they are beyond us. Bird refers to this passage. He mentions in particular Kant's objection to our pleading 'unavoidable ignorance' (A477/B505). 'What [Kant] objects to,' Bird comments, 'is not the fact of our ignorance but the failure to explain it' (p. 676). Yes, in the case of the dynamical antinomies. No, in the case of the mathematical antinomies.[16]

I want, finally, to fulfil the promise I made earlier, by relating this discussion to Bird's fundamental project. I shall say very little, however. The matter is far too complex for me to go into detail here. It would be nice for me if I could claim that only an interpretation of the sort I favour – a sort that Bird would call traditionalist – can accommodate Kant's insistence that there is no such thing as the physical universe as a whole. I do think that such an interpretation is particularly well placed to accommodate that insistence, because I think that it is particularly well placed to explain Kant's repudiation of experience-transcendent facts about physical reality, of which any fact about the physical universe as a whole would be an instance (cf. A503–5/B532–3.) It is particularly well placed to explain Kant's repudiation of such facts because it entails, in a fairly direct way, that there is, for Kant, nothing *to* physical reality beyond what is capable of being given in experience. But that is as much as I want to claim. I do not want to claim anything stronger, because an interpretation of the sort Bird favours can also, I believe, explain Kant's repudiation of experience-transcendent facts about physical reality, albeit more subtly. Indeed, I find the *position* in question – the combination of the broad view that Bird finds in Kant with a repudiation of experience-transcendent facts about physical reality – extremely attractive. The problem is that, great as my admiration for Kant is, not even a principle of charity allows me to convert my sympathy for the position into sympathy for the corresponding exegesis.[17]

Notes

1. Bird, G. (2006) *The Revolutionary Kant: A Commentary on the Critique of Pure Reason* (Chicago and La Salle: Open Court). All unaccompanied references to what Bird says will be to this book. All unaccompanied references to what Kant says will be to Kant, I. (1998) *Critique of Pure Reason*, trans. P. Guyer and A.W. Wood (eds) (Cambridge: Cambridge University Press), using the standard 'A'/'B' notation to represent the first and second edition respectively. References to the *Prolegomena* will be to Kant, I., *Prolegomena to any Future Metaphysics that will be able to Come Forward as a Science*, trans. G. Hatfield, in Kant, I. (2002) *Theoretical Philosophy After 1781*, H. Allison and P. Heath (eds) (Cambridge: Cambridge University Press). References to the third *Critique* will be to Kant, I. (2000) *Critique of the Power of Judgment*, P. Guyer (ed.), trans. Paul Guyer and Eric Matthews (Cambridge: Cambridge University Press).
2. See my (2012) *The Evolution of Modern Metaphysics: Making Sense of Things* (Cambridge: Cambridge University Press), ch. 5.
3. Part of my reason for being unclear about the contrast is that Bird takes P.F. Strawson to be an arch-exponent of a traditionalist interpretation. But I think that there are some critical respects in which Bird is as unfair in his reading of Strawson as he takes Strawson to be in his reading of Kant. One central issue is how close Kant is to Berkeley: nowhere near as close, in Bird's view, as Strawson makes him out to be (see, e.g., p. 8). It is certainly true that, for Strawson, 'Kant...is closer to Berkeley than he acknowledges' (Strawson, P.F.(1966) *The Bounds of Sense: An Essay on Kant's* Critique of Pure Reason (London: Methuen & Co.), p. 22). But Strawson never denies the really crucial differences: that Kant, unlike Berkeley, insists on the atemporality of things in themselves; that Berkeley, unlike Kant, acknowledges spiritual substances; and that Kant, unlike Berkeley, acknowledges material substance.
4. I should emphasize that my concern here is only with the exegetical issue. I do not deny that he *should* accept (1). It seems to me that it *is* a mistake to think that (substantive) issues about the character of the physical universe can be settled by pure reason. In fact, it seems to me that this is a mistake even on the first and less attenuated conception of pure reason (the only conception, incidentally, on which I take Kant to be guilty of the mistake, though that is not something that I shall argue in this chapter). Thus, contemporary cosmologists tell us that the infinitude of space and time themselves, never mind the infinitude of the physical universe *in* space and time, is, in part, an empirical matter – something that Kant would, of course, have strenuously denied. (In fact, many contemporary cosmologists take space and time to be finite.)

5. In view of what I say in this paragraph, I take it to be a slip on Bird's part when he refers to 'the questionable assumption that we can decide issues about the character of the physical universe by *a priori* reasoning alone' (p. 674). He surely means: '... by pure reason alone'.
6. At A 498–9/B526–7, Kant concedes that it is a truth about things in themselves. But then, of course, it is not relevant to (1).
7. Cf. in this connection A425/B453.
8. I note also that this argument for transcendental idealism seems to me altogether less secure on Bird's interpretation, though I shall not pursue that here.
9. This terminology is mine, not Kant's.
10. Not that it is by any means the only evidence: see, for example, Bxxvi and A696/B724 and the third *Critique*, 5: 196. I should emphasize in this connection that by knowledge of the existence of things in themselves I mean something extremely tenuous: knowledge simply that there is a way things really are. And I should also emphasize that I think Kant thinks we have such knowledge, not because I take him explicitly to say so, but, rather, because I take him to endorse the idea that there is a way things really are without any of the caveats that would be required if he were endorsing something that he nevertheless took to be unknown, for example, because he took it to be an article of faith.
11. Cf. also the passage from A420/B447–8, with which I think Bird struggles on p. 676.
12. Here it is important to remember that for Kant 'experience' is to be understood very broadly, as equivalent to 'empirical cognition': see B147.
13. This signals an interesting asymmetry between the thesis and the antithesis, at least in their temporal aspects. Although Kant holds both the thesis and the antithesis to be false, the latter is, so to speak, closer to the truth than the former. After all, Kant takes himself to have established in the second analogy that every event has a prior cause; and this means that there is a sense in which history is infinite. The point, however, is that it is a sense having to do with the *a priori* form of events, rather like the sense in which time itself is infinite. It does not yield a sense in which history – conceived as the contingent course of events hitherto – exists as an infinite unconditioned whole. (Here I think I am in agreement with remarks that Bird makes at pp. 692–3 about the relation between the second analogy and the antithesis of the third antinomy. I likewise think that Bird is right, on p. 675, to reject a suggestion that he finds in Jonathan Bennett about Kant's own position being indistinguishable from the antithesis. That said, I am not sure that this *is* Bennett's suggestion, or not in the form in which Bird finds it (see Bennett, J.(1974) *Kant's Dialectic*(Cambridge: Cambridge University Press), section 46 and 88); and, even if it is, it is not the preposterous suggestion that Bird makes it out to be, precisely because of the asymmetry.)
14. Kant stands by these arguments. He does not, however, offer them in a spirit of persuasion. He offers them in a spirit of descriptive rational psychology. He takes them (rightly or wrongly) to be arguments that ineluctably force themselves upon us as soon as we think about these issues (e.g., A339/B397 and A464/B490). This gives us licence, incidentally, to acknowledge idealist

elements in the arguments (e.g., in the argument for the spatial part of the antithesis of the first antinomy, at A427–9/B455–7), even though Kant uses the arguments in indirect support of his idealism. We need not worry that, in so doing, we are thereby imputing question begging to him. All that we, as exegetes, need to ask is how likely it is that Kant thinks that there are idealist elements in our thinking even before we have recognized them as such. It is extremely likely.

15. Does this conclusion not hold of what is ahead of us in time, as well as of what is behind us in time? Certainly it does. Why, then, does Kant explicitly decline to apply counterparts of the temporal arguments to the world's future (A410/B437; cf. A336–7/B393–4)?Well, he does not deny that such arguments can be constructed. He merely declines to construct them. This relates back to the point that I made in the previous footnote. Kant is concerned with arguments that he thinks ineluctably force themselves upon us as soon as we think about these issues. The arguments concerning the world's past do so, because of our urge to locate some unconditioned object of possible experience grounding what is conditioned. A thing's temporal conditions necessarily precede it; so our thoughts are ineluctably led backwards. But 'it is a matter of complete indifference' (A410/B437) to us what would happen if our thoughts took a similar route forwards. For further discussion see my (1992) 'A Note on Kant's First Antinomy', *The Philosophical Quarterly*, 42.

16. Notice that if Bird were right – if Kant held *both* that we are unavoidably ignorant in the case of the mathematical antinomies *and* that the thesis and the antithesis in each of them may both be false – then he (Kant) would have to allow for an incoherence in the concept of the physical universe as a whole which is beyond our ken. Not that that is in itself an objection to what Bird says. Kant does, indeed, think that we can be unavoidably ignorant even about what is possible (e.g., Bxxvi, n.). It does, however, add to the mystery of what sort of grasp Bird thinks that Kant thinks we have of the concept.

17. I am extremely grateful to Graham Bird for his comments on an earlier version of this chapter. These comments saved me from a number of errors, though no doubt from fewer than he would have hoped. Note: this chapter first appeared in *Kantian Review*, 15 (2011), a special issue devoted to Graham Bird's commentary, with replies by Graham Bird. I am grateful to the editors of *Kantian Review*, including the guest editors of the special issue – Sorin Baiasu and Michelle Grier – for permission to reprint the chapter here.

References

Bennett, J. (1974) *Kant's Dialectic* (Cambridge: Cambridge University Press).

Bird, G. (2006) *The Revolutionary Kant: A Commentary on the* Critique of Pure Reason (Chicago and La Salle: Open Court).

Kant, I. (1998) *Critique of Pure Reason*, trans. P. Guyer and A.W. Wood (eds)

Kant, I. (2000) *Critique of the Power of Judgment*, P. Guyer (ed.), trans. P. Guyer and E. Matthews (Cambridge: Cambridge University Press).

Kant, I. (2002) *Theoretical Philosophy After 1781*, H. Allison and P. Heath (eds) (Cambridge: Cambridge University Press).

Moore, A.W. (1992) 'A Note on Kant's First Antinomy', *The Philosophical Quarterly*, 42.

Moore, A.W. (2012), *The Evolution of Modern Metaphysics: Making Sense of Things* (Cambridge: Cambridge University Press).

Strawson, P.F. (1966) *The Bounds of Sense: An Essay on Kant's* Critique of Pure Reason (London: Methuen & Co.).

10
Space and the Limits of Objectivity: Could There Be a Disembodied Thinking of Reality?

Roxana Baiasu

> No one can be credited with an 'objective' model of the world if he does not grasp that he is modelling the world *he is in* – that he has a location somewhere in the model, as do the things he can see.
>
> (Gareth Evans)[1]

10.1 The question of objectivity and embodiment

Objective thinking is a mode of understanding which aims to leave behind local viewpoints or perspectival engagement with the world. The enlargement of understanding through objectification can be thought of as a gradual process of progressive detachment from specific perspectives on the world. In *The View from Nowhere*, Thomas Nagel refers to degrees of the objectivity with which we can approach some aspect of reality. For example, he contends that the 'standpoint of morality is more objective than that of private life, but less objective than the standpoint in physics'.[2] He compares the process of objectification and the corresponding layers of understanding with 'a set of concentric spheres, progressively revealed as we detach gradually from the contingencies of the self'.[3] Nagel refers to a classical picture of the process of enlargement of understanding: this process is taken to begin with the interaction between our *bodies* and the world which produces sensations and perceptions in us. Embodiment is constitutive of our relation to the world in a way which, to a large extent, brings in elements of perspective. For example, the kind of sensory–motor apparatus humans have is constitutive of a general human point of view from which we experience the world. Had we had a different kind of sensory–motor apparatus, the world would have looked significantly different to us.

Nevertheless, if we accept that things in the world exist independently of us, their true nature must be conceived as not depending on their perceptual appearance. This means that the project of thinking about the physical world objectively must transcend a general human perceptual point of view and must develop concepts, representations and theories which are, in principle, accessible to a rational creature with a different sensory point of view on the world.[4] But, however fruitful with regard to the production of successful theories about the physical world, this strategy cannot provide an appropriate account of the specific bodily viewpoints involved in perception, which constitute the starting point from which the enlargement of understanding begins, and which it leaves behind as theoretically irrelevant.[5]

Gradual detachment from particular locations and specifics of the subject leads to higher and higher levels of objectivity. The limit or extreme of this process of gradual detachment might be conceived as a grasp of reality which has left any perspective or particular standpoint behind. This would be, in A.W. Moore's terms, a grasp of reality formed through 'absolute representations'. In *Points of View*, Moore defines the notion of 'an absolute representation' as 'a representation from no point of view'[6]constituted by thinking 'about the world with complete detachment'.[7] He contrasts it with the concept of 'a perspectival representation', which is 'a representation from a point of view'.[8] Points of view are constituted by the multiplicity of ways in which our making sense of the world depends 'on how and where we are situated'.[9] A point of view is understood as a 'location in the broadest sense': it could take the form of a spatial location, a temporal location, a historical location, a cultural location, or some other kind of situatedness determined, for example, by our embodiment.[10]

An 'absolute conception of reality', as Bernard Williams calls it, or what, in Nagel's terms, is a thinking 'from nowhere', would integrate all objective representations of reality as well as the particular standpoints in which, in some cases, objective representations are rooted, and which they left behind through the process of objectification.[11] In Williams's view, the idea of an absolute conception of reality is a necessary presupposition of knowledge and objectivity, which has been a permanent problem for Western thought since Descartes. Williams takes the following epistemological point to be a fundamental one: if knowledge of physical reality ever attains its proper status and is what it claims to be, then it is knowledge of a reality which exists independently of any thought or experience (including that provided through the body). Knowledge is of 'what is there *anyway*'.[12] He thinks that a sophisticated argument can show how from this fundamental epistemological claim it follows that knowledge requires the possibility of a detachment from anything local and, at the limit, an absolute conception of reality. In *Points of View*, Moore further develops Williams's line of argument under the title of the Basic Argument, which is meant to support the main claim of his book, which is that absolute representations are possible.[13]

The epistemological significance of the issue of absolute thinking is manifold. Moore stresses that a negative answer to the question concerning the possibility of absolute representations about the world would be deeply troubling for those engaged in theoretical enterprises. Objectivity and, at the limit, absolute representations of reality are goals for scientific theories, especially in the natural sciences and, in particular, in physics. More generally, absolute thinking is a goal for understanding wherever there is an aspiration to comprehensiveness with regard to what one can make sense of, and an attempt to transcend what is local and perspectival. As has been mentioned above, in Williams's view, the idea of a neutral grasp of reality leaving behind any privileged point of view can be shown to be a basic presupposition of any genuine claim to knowledge. The inquiry concerned with such an extreme form of detachment from the specifics of particular locations and perspectives is, as Moore and Nagel note, relevant for an investigation into the limits of objectivity. These related concerns are important not only in relation to the natural sciences but also for those ethical theories for which ideas of rationality, impartiality or utility are central. Historically, absoluteness, understood as a form of objectivity, has been approached in the contexts of discussions of ideas such as a God's-eye point of view, the ideal observer, impartiality, neutrality, or what Nagel calls 'the view from nowhere'.[14]

The approach to the limits of objectivity proposed here starts from the assumption that absolute thinking, conceived as an extreme form of objective understanding, may be possible. Another starting point for the inquiry is the Kantian distinction between thinking about the world and the preconditions of that thinking. I inquire into certain spatial preconditions of absolute thinking about the world. I am thus concerned with spatial thinking. The discussion is not meant to offer claims about pure mathematical thinking or about absolute thinking that, say, a God-like being could have in relation to abstract entities, but deals with absolute thinking *about the world*. The inquiry into certain spatial conditions or limits of objective thinking is carried out in order to address the following question: Could objective thinking, and its extreme form, absolute thinking, ever be completely disembodied? In other words, the question is whether an absolute thinking about the world is available to a disembodied being. I argue that, if absolute thinking about the world is possible, it is available only to an embodied being. This line of thought develops certain elements which might be integrated into an argument against the existence of God, insofar as God is understood on a traditional conception as a disembodied, absolute intelligence who is capable of thinking about the world.

The question I am concerned with here can be also put in terms of a distinction that Moore makes between a representation's being *from* a point of view and a representation's being produced *at* a point of view.[15] A representation which is produced *from* a point of view is perspectival.[16] This means that its content depends on the standpoint of whoever produces it. For example, visual representations are produced from determined spatial points of view; their content depends on the perspective from which the perceiver looks at things. Representations which are produced *at* a point of view are representations formed by a thinking which cannot belong to a free-floating mind, but which is situated. Unlike God or angels (understood on a traditional conception), the being to which this thinking belongs must be located somewhere in the world. I argue that, if representations about the world can be formed that are not *from* any spatial point of view, they must, however, be produced by a mind which is *at* some *spatial location(s)*.

The present inquiry into the limits of objectivity is not primarily concerned with the attainability or with the possibility of an objective, possibly absolute thinking about reality. Nor is it concerned with the issue of whether we can know when we have reached and are in possession of such representations. These issues have a long history and have been much debated. Many realists, certain idealists (perhaps including Kant) and, at any rate, many philosophers in the Cartesian tradition have offered competing positive answers to these questions. Critiques of them, equally numerous and varied, have been put forward by relativists, sceptics, Nietzscheans, certain phenomenologists and feminists who have contended that any knowledge is from a point of view, and any thinking involves a perspective or a set of perspectives which cannot be transcended. The investigation here, however, does not engage with either historical or thematic aspects of these debates concerning the attainability or possibility of completely objective thinking. Rather, the question of this chapter is mainly a conceptual one: it concerns our conception of absolute thinking about the world and, more broadly, our conception of objective thinking. The question is whether objective, possibly absolute thinking can be understood as being produced by a disembodied mind. In other words, the question is whether it is possible to conceive adequately of objective thinking as completely separated from the body. As mentioned above, I argue that there cannot be any form of objective thinking about the world which could be understood as disembodied.

10.2   Spatial awareness

Two elements of spatial awareness are crucial for the argument, and for the answer to the question of this chapter. First, spatial awareness involves a sense of *proximity*, a grasp of the things one is concerned with as being *here*. For example, things that I (can) touch, see, or use are close to me in accordance with my current perceptions, cognitions, tasks or interests. Second, there is a sense of *distance* inherent to spatial awareness. This is a grasp of locations or places which are more or less remote in relation to others. For example, in relation to one's own place there are things which are over *there*, at more or less distant locations. The concepts of proximity and distance can be understood in terms of measurable spatial determinations, but they might also involve a phenomenological sense corresponding to one's involvement in the world. For example, the pen I intend to use to make a note might appear phenomenologically closer to me than the air between me and the pen – even though the air is objectively closer – in as much as I might try to pick up the pen but have no concern with the air. This example illustrates two senses in which proximity and distance can be understood: first in terms of magnitude, of measurable spatial determinations, and, second, in a phenomenological sense, referring to the way things appear to the subject in accordance with his or her concerns, actions or abilities. These two ways of understanding proximity and distance may be contrasted in certain cases, but they might also be interconnected in some other cases. The way in which some spatial aspect of the world phenomenally appears to somebody might guide and orient her interest in, and concern with, certain spatial determinations rather than others. In its turn, an awareness of relevant spatial magnitudes might inform a phenomenological sense of distance or proximity.

There is no need to develop in more detail the relationship between these two senses of the basic spatial elements discussed here.[17] The main point is that the sense of proximity and the sense of distance, of 'here' and 'there', inherent to spatial awareness are necessarily linked to one another. In other words, somebody's grasp of what is close, in accordance with her current concerns and thinking, is connected to her grasp of what is at more distant locations. For example, my sense of my being here, at my desk and writing this piece, or taking a short break to reply to an email, is connected to my sense of other people there in the world, who might read what I am writing. My grasp of the laptop which I am using at home is connected to my awareness of the University – through which I have email access – at some distant location. The sense of what is close is necessarily linked to the sense of distant locations in accordance with current concerns, attitudes, beliefs or knowledge. I shall come back to this claim of the necessary link between proximity and closeness, between 'here' and 'there', in the last section, which presents the argument answering this chapter's question.

10.3   Embodiment and proximity

This section is concerned with certain aspects of a phenomenological account of the body and its spatiality. On this phenomenological account, we have a sense of our own bodies – whether or not we are reflectively aware of it – insofar as we are concerned with, and engage in, the world through our sensory perceptions, movements or actions.[18] For example, I have a certain awareness of my hands as I am typing this sentence on the keyboard of my computer. The patient on a dentist's chair feels the pain in the decayed tooth as the drill strikes the tooth nerve. The woman in labour has a strong sense of certain parts of her body and of the pain affecting them, which indicates the approach of the moment of birth. Somebody can have a sense of his or her body in relation to another object, say, a bookcase's being on his or her left; or someone can have a sense of the whole body in motion in relation, for instance, to a car approaching as he or she crosses the street.[19] Although the first three examples do not mention the body as a whole, they are not meant to suggest that the individuals to which the examples refer would not have a sense of the other parts of their living, acting body, and that these bodily parts would be unaffected or inactive in the current context. The awareness of these is less vivid or manifest, but is connected to the sense of the affected or more active parts of the body, like the comet's tail to its head.[20]

In each case, the sense of embodiment is perspectival: it is constituted from one's own point of involvement in the world. Moore defines the notion of a point of involvement in terms of a perspectival grasp of the world, a grasp which is informed by one's concerns, interests, affects or values.[21] The sense of one's own body is formed from one's point of view in accordance with one's concerns and interests, and with one's physical endowment, sensibilities, abilities and dispositions to act. The perspectival character of the lived sense of the body can be understood in connection to a phenomenological notion of the ownness of the body. Considered phenomenologically, the thought of one's body as one's own has a non-trivial content. Two important aspects of the ownness characteristic of the living body need to be considered here.

A first general point about the sense of one's body as one's own is that it involves an awareness of the body as distinct from other bodies. This point can be illustrated by the examples above, but let us consider an extreme example which can be taken to refer to pregnancy, but which can also be construed as part of some science-fiction story. The example refers to a living being growing inside another. The individual, say a certain woman, in whom that living being develops has a sense of her limbs, eyes and so on as her own, whilst she is or becomes aware of the animate body growing inside her as a body distinct from her body, as a body which is not part of her own body. For instance, she is aware of the movements of that embodied being as movements which are not of her body; she grasps this being's development as a growth which is not of her body but of the other being.

Second, the awareness of one's own body involves a sense of the body as a centre of sensibility, perception and action. There are passive and active aspects of embodiment. Both Husserl and Merleau-Ponty stress in related ways the active side of the living body. In the *Cartesian Meditations*, Husserl discusses the notion of a 'central body' understood as something which is one's own in a fundamental sense.[22] On this view, the living body constitutes, through its multiple changes of orientation, a unified multiplicity of perspectives on nature. In the *Phenomenology of Perception*, Merleau-Ponty conceives of the centrality of the body in terms of the capability of the body to access the world. He writes:

> I am conscious of my body *via* the world, that it is the unperceived term in the center of the world towards which all objects turn their face, [...] the pivot of the world. [...] I am conscious of the world through the medium of my body.[23]

The awareness of the lived body (as related to the world) is thoroughly perspectival. It is essentially linked to 'my point of view upon the world',[24] which is constituted as a point of involvement in the world: 'having a body is to be intervolved in a definite environment' in accordance with one's tasks, concerns, interests.[25] My body is my own in the phenomenological sense that it is part of the scheme of my projects, actions or attitudes. My representations and sense of my own body have a place in the history and texture of my life which makes them essentially my own.

The passive side of embodiment can be understood in terms of physical endowment and of the capacity of the body to be affected, respectively. For example, we humans are predetermined to perceive things as our sensory apparatus enables us to perceive them; we cannot have the sensations elephants have. We cannot be affected by the world as elephants are. Moreover, bodily endowment which informs one's ways of being involved in the world differs between groups of individuals or perhaps even from individual to individual. The passive side of embodied existence constitutes specific ways in which one has or can have a sense of one's own lived body. Not only current tasks and projects of action, but also one's physical endowment and capacity to be affected, inform the perspectival sense somebody has of his or her own body. In each case, when something affects the embodied being it does so in accordance with that being's physical characteristics. For example, somebody has a certain sense of the toothache caused by the dentist's drilling as his own, or someone is aware of bodily suffering as she gives birth to her child as a suffering of her own body (and not, for example, of her child): this means that somebody else cannot *feel* his or her pain (although, of course, the pain can be represented or imagined by somebody else).

One might be tempted to object to this line of thought by raising the issue of the unshareability of the embodied perspective and the privacy of the sense of one's own embodiment. The objection would go like this. On the phenomenological account sketched above, it seems that the sense of someone's body as one's own is private, accessible only to him or her, and inaccessible to others. The sense someone has of his or her living body caught in action, or as it perceives and moves in the environment, can be formed only from the point of view of that particular individual. Somebody's awareness of her hands typing on the computer board, of her painful tooth, or of her body in labour can only be constituted from her own unique embodied perspective, and cannot be shared by somebody else. I could have the sense of the bodily experience that you have while you perceive something or are engaged in some activity only if I were you and had the experiences that you have from your perspective. But, the objection would continue, this is not possible. I have my experiences from my embodied perspective and you have your experiences from your embodied perspective. There is an unbridgeable gap between our embodied points of view. We do not and cannot share our embodied perspectives and the sense of our own lived bodies.

But, if embodied sense and perspective are unshareable, then they cannot be used to articulate an account of objectivity, such as that put forward by the dominant view of the objectification of understanding mentioned at the beginning of this chapter. This is because, according to this dominant account of objectivity, embodied sense and perspective are starting points in the objectification process, and if they are unshareable objectification is impossible. Let me explain this in some more detail. The objectification process is supposed to detach what one makes sense of from an embodied perspective from local, contingent aspects, in order to make understanding less and less dependent upon, and affected by, such local contingencies. Making understanding and its claims less dependent upon local contingencies in this way implies also making them more shareable. If, for example, someone's understanding of justice is no longer informed by his gender, then his claims about justice will no longer be gender-biased and, hence, they will more easily be shareable with those of a different gender.

Yet, if embodied sense and perspective were unshareable, then the distinction between necessary and contingent aspects of these perspectives would divide between various aspects in different ways for each different perspective. This means that one perspective would have certain necessary features, which would not be shared with those of a different perspective. Hence, no matter how far the objectification process attempted to go, the understanding starting from one or the other of these two perspectives could never become enlarged and approach objectivity. For a process can be one of objectification only if, by gradual detachment from contingent features, claims can capture more and more of the features of their object, features that are independent of any particular perspective and view on the object. Yet unshareable perspectives, no matter how much they were separated from their contingent features, would still lead to understandings and claims which would be dependent on them.

Nevertheless, the thought that there must be something unshareable about the sense of embodiment, corresponding to an awareness of the body as one's own, seems intuitively very sensible. But is this the embodied point of view, as the objection presented above claims?

I shall argue that it is not the embodied perspective, but, rather, it is a certain aspect of the space taken up by the lived body that is essentially unshareable; this does not affect the shareability of embodied perspective and thus the possibilities of objectification. The response to the objection mentioned above has two parts: the first is concerned with space and an unshareable aspect of embodiment; the second with the issue of the shareability of embodied perspective.

10.3.1   The absolute here

On the phenomenological approach sketched above, the living body is conceived as a centre of perception, action and motility and as a way of access to the world. In the *Cartesian Meditations*, Husserl calls the living body 'the zero body, the body in *the absolute Here*'.[26] In this view, the perceiving body in motion is 'inseparable from the absolute Here.'[27] In the *Phenomenology of Perception*, Merleau-Ponty contends that 'an absolute awareness of "here"' is required for an awareness of one's own body as a body moving and acting in accordance with current tasks and concerns.[28] In this account, the absolute Here of the living body is understood phenomenologically not only in terms of the immediacy of its givenness in action, motion or perception, but also in terms of the basic situatedness of the active body. Spatial situatedness constitutes a very primitive characteristic of the living body. In each case the body is situated spatially at some location or place – it is not, and cannot be, nowhere. This is not solely a matter of where the body is located, but that it is situated, and how it is situated. The living body is spatially situated in such a way that it enacts *'the first co-ordinates'* of 'the situation of the body in the face of its tasks'.[29] These first spatial co-ordinates of embodied agency constitute the fundamental framework necessary for any 'navigational' undertaking in particular environments in accordance with current tasks and interests.

The living body's absolute Here, understood in terms of basic spatial situatedness and the corresponding spatial framework for agency, thus makes possible the grasp of locations within an environment. By setting up certain spatial limits for embodied agency, the absolute Here is a condition of possibility of the awareness of particular locations. Somebody's awareness of a body's being at a location which is more or less close to her cannot be formed except in relation to the spatial co-ordinates set by her embodiment. Her understanding of what appears as the *nearest* thing to her requires a spatial sense of her body, a sense of it being here for her. So the awareness of one's own body enacts a limit for the sense of that which can be grasped as near, a limit of the sense of proximity.

So far, I have pointed out three interrelated ways of understanding the absolute Here of the living body: first, as basic situatedness; second, as constituting a basic framework or 'first co-ordinates' for action and perception; and now, finally, as a spatial limit. As we have seen, the first two are important as part of the account of the spatial limit enacted by embodiment. The claim according to which embodiment enacts a spatial limit of proximity constitutes one of the main premises of this chapter's central argument, explicitly formulated in the last section.

The absolute Here of the living body is in each case associated – even if only contingently – with a spatial location. The awareness of the latter can be understood phenomenologically as being informed by, among other things, one's concerns, abilities or cultural background; at the same time it might also involve objective spatial thinking concerning, for example, the body's spatial position in three-dimensional space. Both phenomenological and objective elements informing the awareness of the spatial location which enacts the absolute Here of one's lived body are, in principle, shareable. Nevertheless, the spatial location with which the absolute Here is in each case associated cannot be shared as the same time by distinct embodied beings. For example, I cannot share with anybody else my being here now sat at my desk writing this piece, or my having been at 10.00 a.m. on the dentist's chair enduring her drilling my tooth.

The awareness of the absolute Here corresponds to the phenomenological ownness of the body, the lived experience of the body as one's own, distinct from any other living body – a centre of sensibility, motility and action. The spatial situation of the living body in the moment of perception or action cannot be taken up by any other living body. I cannot share with anybody else the instantiation of my basic situatedness, constituting in each case the concrete first co-ordinates for action and perception and the spatial limit enacted by my body. There cannot be another body which can be situated at the same absolute Here enacted by my body.

10.3.2 Embodied perspective

I shall now turn to the second part of the response to the objection presented earlier. I shall support a view according to which embodied perspective is to some extent shareable. As mentioned earlier, embodied perspective is understood in terms of Moore's notion of a point of involvement, which refers to a grasp of the world informed by one's concerns, interests, affects or values.[30] To share a certain point of involvement is to share certain corresponding concerns, affects or values. It is possible to share these only against a certain common background of making sense of things. In phenomenological terms, this background is that of (embodied) being-in-the-world.[31] In Moore's terms, and in relation to certain perspectival representations, the background is that '*of shared sensibilities and values*'.[32] Examples of the perspectival representations Moore has in mind in this context are 'subjective representations involving concepts such as *chivalry* or *dignity*, concepts whose application is arguably unintelligible except against a specific background of shared sensibilities and values'.[33] To think of a certain comportment as manifesting dignity or as an instantiation of genuine chivalry, one must have certain sensibilities and must uphold certain values. One must also be able to act in certain ways corresponding to the ideas of chivalry or dignity or, at least, must have a sense of what is like to act in these ways. The sensibilities, capabilities and upholding of values at issue here are or can be made manifest in attitudes, actions, words or other forms of expression.

Another example relevant in this context is the understanding of one's own finitude and mortality. This understanding arises from one's own point of involvement with death. The point of view from which somebody grasps his or her own mortality is shareable insofar as there are, for finite beings like us, common, corresponding sensibilities concerning mortality and perhaps values of life. These sensibilities can find certain forms of expression such as, for example, 'the song, the prayer, the requiem'[34] through which one's sense of one's own finitude is shared or shareable. The awareness of one's own mortality is not a private state of mind inaccessible to others. Nor is the point of view from which it is formed essentially unshareable.

So to share a point of involvement is to share certain interests, concerns or affects, and this is possible if there is a common background of sensibilities, capabilities and values. This background makes it possible for the individual to respond in a relevant way to the situation in which she finds herself. Her response to that situation attests the shareability of the relevant perspective and of what is made sense of from that perspective. Now let us turn to embodied awareness, and the possibility of sharing an embodied point of view. Consider the example of two individuals who say 'My wisdom tooth hurts.' They might both feel disturbed or anxious, and they might both think that it would be a good idea to see the dentist. Other people might be able to tell this from these individuals' actions and from what they say or could say if they are asked about their dental problem. So they share the same concerns, interests and affects in relation to the tooth pain. In Moore's terms, they share the same point of involvement with tooth pain. A specific common background of sensibility and capability to react to pain makes it possible for them to be bodily affected and to respond in the way they respond to the situation. To take another example, two women in labour might have the same concerns, worries or fears, which are expressed by similar patterns of bodily movement, breathing, writhing in pain or crying. Since they share certain specific bodily concerns and affects, they share the same point of involvement with pregnancy. A specific background of embodiment, including a certain embodied sensibility and bodily capability, makes it possible for them to share their embodied point of involvement. Embodied sensibility refers here to the passive side of embodiment, for example, to sensitivity to pain generally, or perhaps even pain which only women can have. Bodily capability reflects the active side of embodiment and consists in a certain capacity to move and act. For example, pregnant women in labour might still be able to walk or to throw a ball, but they cannot run and certainly they cannot do mountain climbing.[35]

To conclude this discussion, an embodied point of view is shared or shareable insofar as there is a specific common background of embodied sensibility and capability to act. This can be ascertained by the possibilities of giving voice or enacting in behaviour the sense of one's own embodiment. If these possibilities are lacking, there is no way to know that there is a point of view there, or that any sense is made of things from that point of view.

The view that embodied perspective is shareable can now be used to respond to the objection mentioned earlier. The objection's point was this: any approach to the possibility of objectivity and of the enlargement of understanding which employs the account of embodiment proposed here is problematic; this is so simply because, as argued earlier, if embodied perspective is unshareable, objectivity is not possible. But I have argued that, on the account endorsed here, embodiment is *not* unshareable. Embodied points of view are not essentially unshareable or private. They are subjective but are not necessarily hidden from other individuals. Since, on the proposed account, embodied perspective is conceived as shareable, the objection mentioned earlier proves to be mistaken. It fails in its attempt to challenge an approach to objectivity which employs the proposed account of embodiment.

The discussion of the lived body and its spatiality has, however, noted an element of embodied awareness which is not shareable and which

perhaps gives the impression that embodied awareness as a whole cannot in principle be shared. This element has been identified as the
definite location with which the absolute Here of one's own body is
associated. But, as we have seen, this is not shareable only in the sense
that distinct embodied beings cannot be situated at the same time at the
same spatial location. Nevertheless, this result does not have a bearing
on the issue of the shareability of embodied perspective. The distinct
embodied beings might be placed at the location at issue at different
moments of time or, in some cases, they need not ever be at the same
particular spatial location in order for them to be able to share a certain
embodied perspective. The examples mentioned above illustrate the
possibility of sharing an embodied perspective and awareness which
is constituted from different spatial locations. In these cases there is no
need to transcend one's particular location in order to achieve a more
comprehensive view on some aspect of reality at issue. Furthermore, a
general claim can be made in relation to the absolute Here of the living
body: since it is a limit of spatial awareness, the absolute Here cannot, in
principle, be transcended. This claim should not be taken to imply that
embodiment cannot be transcended. This would be an unwarranted
argumentative leap, and requires further argument. The claim made
here is that a certain limit of spatial awareness which is enacted by
embodiment – but not embodiment itself – cannot be transcended.

10.4 Objectivity and distance

Objectivity is here considered as a characteristic of a certain mode of
understanding, of making sense of reality.[36] The sciences, and in particular natural sciences, are usually taken to represent the paradigm for
this mode of understanding, and its specific detachment from subjective
representations and particular perspectives on the world. As mentioned
earlier, an extreme form of objectivity could be conceived in terms of
absolute representations; as such, it characterizes a grasp of the world
from no point of view, from no location. The transcending or 'standing back'[37] from any definite, local perspective corresponds to a radical broadening of the understanding. Enlarged understanding includes
new representations of reality as well as an objective, detached grasp of
the local perspectives which constituted the starting point or intermediate stages in the process of objectification. Moore describes this process of the enlargement of understanding possibly leading to an absolute
grasp of reality, in terms of the comprehensiveness of content which the

sciences aim to achieve, and as motivated by the finite understanding's 'craving for infinity'.[38]

When we understand an aspect of the world objectively, from no definite location, we have a sense of things as outside ourselves. I take this to be a basic assumption, which I shall use as part of the argument concerning objectivity and spatial awareness. What is involved in our being aware of an object as outside ourselves? In the Transcendental Aesthetic of the *Critique of Pure Reason*, Kant contends that a certain awareness of space is required for something to appear to the subject as outside him or her. There are two senses of the word 'outside'(*ausser*) which G. Bird notes in *The Revolutionary Kant*, and H. Allison mentions in *Kant's Transcendental Idealism*: Kant uses the term to mean 'outer' and also 'other than, apart from'.[39] With regard to the second use, Bird distinguishes between a transcendental sense, in which things in themselves are 'apart from' sensibility, and the sense in which something is 'apart from' some subject's perception. Since I am concerned with objective thinking about the spatial world, I shall leave aside the former sense, and shall take over, in the current context of the discussion of objectivity, the other Kantian uses of the word 'outside'.

There might be an inclination to think of the second sense of 'outside' in non-spatial terms. It is possible to think of something as other than me or apart from me in terms which are not spatial. Bird draws attention to certain risks such a position faces: if one pursues this inclination the difficulty is that

> it encourages a Cartesian account of a mind as something which has spatial relations to other (spatial) things, but is not itself spatial. [...] Kant clearly rejects such a Cartesian account.[40]

I follow Kant's line of thinking in this respect; I shall come back briefly to Kant's position towards the end. What is at issue now is the spatial awareness informing objective thinking. I argue that somebody's making sense of something as outside himself or herself involves a sense of distance in relation to what he or she is concerned with. This claim can be understood in connection with the two senses of 'outside' laid out above (the sense of 'outer', and the sense of 'other than' or 'apart from'). First, to have an awareness of something as *outer*, part of the external world, a sense of distance in relation to it is required. The object is grasped as being at some location which is outer in relation to the subject; this is a more or less remote location. Even when the object is in direct contact with the subject, it is, however, possible, at least in principle, to sever it, and thus it is possible for it to be at some distance from the subject. Had the subject no sense of distance, it would not be possible for him or her to make sense of something as being out there, part of the world. Second, for something to be *other than* or *apart from* the thinking subject there must be some distance separating the subject and the object, or, at least, the possibility of such a distance. Otherwise one would not be able to make sense of the object as being there, distinct from consciousness; it would not be possible to distinguish between an object of consciousness – say, for example, something which might be a product of imagination – and a real object, something 'which is there anyway'.

I have started from the thought that the objective grasp of some aspect of the world involves an understanding of it as outside, as something out there and other than oneself. As we have now seen, to think of something as outside oneself is to have a sense of distance in relation to it. So, objective thinking of reality requires a sense of distance in relation to what it is concerned with. To think of an object as being *there anyway* is possible only if it is thought to be at some distance; only thus can it be understood as being part of a reality which is out *there* independently of our thinking.

What sort of distance is involved in thinking about the world objectively, in a possibly absolute way? I shall consider here three related characteristics of the sense of distance informing absolute thinking: indeterminacy, formality and its role as a limit of spatial awareness. In the case of absolute thinking, the aspect of reality with which it is concerned is in some sense 'there', part of the world, but is not grasped as being at any specific location. If someone were grasping it as being at a certain, determinate distance from him or her, the understanding would have been perspectival. Suppose somebody produces certain objective, possibly absolute representations about the satellites in the solar system. The moon, as it happens, is over 300,000 km away from Earth, but such a perspectival element is not involved in the objective, potentially absolute representation. The moon is not represented as being at over 300,000 km away from Earth, or indeed as being at any other particular distance away. Moreover, it might not even be explicitly represented as being 'there'. Nevertheless, I argue that a more or less implicit sense of it being 'there', distanced from the subject, is a precondition for the subject's objective thinking.

Objective, possibly absolute thinking does not occur nowhere. But, if this thinking is part of the spatial world, in what sense can it be said that it is placed in space? It is not produced *from* any particular, specific spatial locations, but can be produced *at* any location. In other words, no location determines or informs that thinking, which is, however, situated in the sense that it is produced at some location. The location at which the absolute thinking is produced can be understood as indeterminate and can be infinitely variable; and so is the corresponding distance in relation to the part of reality the thinking is concerned with. As such, distance has a formal character. This means that the distance informing absolute thinking about the world is grasped only in relation to possible location(s) rather than any actual place. The basic, formal sense of there being some distance between us and the world can, in each case, be instantiated in infinitely various ways, acquiring definite contents in accordance with the particular contexts in which one finds oneself. It thus makes possible an awareness of determinate spatial relations and distances. This means that it functions as a precondition of spatial awareness of the world, of one's making sense of worldly things and beings as outside oneself.[41] Given its indeterminacy and formality, it could be said that the sense of distance enacted by objective, possibly absolute thinking pertains to an extreme mode of the sense of space, which, however, does not transcend spatial awareness. This radical sense of the distance between us and the world constitutes a limit of spatial awareness. I call the 'there' of the world thus distanced from us 'absolute There'. The claim that absolute thinking enacts this limit of our sense of space is an important premise in this chapter's argument, the conclusion of which is presented in the next section.

Objective thinking conceived at its limit in terms of absolute representations is not an aerial, top-down view on the world encompassing it from a certain vantage point transcending any location. The view that there would be such a vantage point runs into certain serious difficulties. First, it is always possible to imagine that there is another, more objective vantage point – say, still to be discovered – from which one can think about the world, a vantage point transcending and encompassing current ways of making sense of the world. This line of thinking can lead to a regress to infinity.

The vantage point of objective thinking is conceived of, in some way or another, as determinate. So, second, this view cannot account for what I have referred to above as the indeterminacy and potentially infinite variability of the location at which objective thinking takes place. The position(s) corresponding to the vantage point of objective, possibly absolute representations are conceived not only as determinate in some way, but also as actual. Thus, third, if one adopts the view that objective thought is positioned at some fixed place in the world, and thus is both actual and determinate, it becomes very difficult to explain the fact that there are various *possibilities* for objective thought to be situated in relation to what it is concerned with. Finally, to conceive of objective thinking as produced from a vantage point with a determinate, actual position is to understand it as constituted from a certain perspective. The thinking at issue cannot, then, be objective in the full-blown sense of objectivity, that is, of an understanding which is independent of any perspective.

Nagel characterizes the objectifying Self which forms a centreless view on reality in the following terms: 'the objective self is *the last stage of the detaching subject* before it shrinks to an extensionless point.'[42] Nagel seems to suggest that the detaching subject is not a-spatial; the objective Self is at the last stage *before* it would become almost *a-spatial*. The subject exercising objective thinking still has a sense of being spatial, and I would like to argue that this is so even in a more substantial way than Nagel suggests when he talks about a Self on the verge of becoming an extensionless point. The location at which objective, possibly absolute thinking occurs is irrelevant for the operations of this thinking; its variability does not affect them. However, since in each case it has a location, this thinking is part of the spatial world; it is not nowhere. But its having a location in the spatial world might not be well-conceived on the model of extensionless points in space. I shall return to this below.

10.5   Can objective thinking be disembodied?

The previous sections have worked out the premises of an argument which can now help answer the question as to whether objective thinking can be disembodied. I have contended that objective thinking about the world requires a certain sense of distance in relation to the world. A limit or extreme form of objective thought has been considered which can be conceived in terms of absolute representations. These are representations of reality which are produced from no location. I have argued that they involve a grasp of the world which presupposes, however, a sense of radical distance and of an absolute There characterized as indeterminate and formal. This extreme form of the sense of distance belongs to spatial awareness, and can be understood as one of its limits.

The phenomenological analysis of embodiment and its space has attempted to show that somebody's sense of his or her own body enacts a limit of proximity corresponding to the absolute Here of his or her body. In Section 10.2, I have pointed out that proximity and distance are two necessarily interrelated elements of spatial awareness. Since the living body and objective, possibly absolute thinking enact two limits of spatial awareness, they are necessarily linked.

The point I have sought to make in this chapter can be illustrated by an image depicted in a passage from Milan Kundera, which Moore quotes as a motto of chapter two of *Points of View* (the chapter offering an account of the significance of the question of absolute thinking):

> First she placed her fingertips to a spot between her breasts, as if she wanted to point to the very centre of what is known as the self. Then she flung her arms forward, as if she wanted to transport the self somewhere far away, to the horizon, to infinity. The gesture of longing for immortality knows only *two points in space*: *the self here, the horizon far in the distance*; only two concepts: *the absolute that is the self and the absolute that is the world.*[43]

The longing for infinity and for an absolute grasp of reality is essentially connected to the very core of one's own embodied being, the sense of which is expressible through a gesture such as the placing of fingertips to a spot on the chest, near the heart perhaps, or between the breasts like the gesture that the feminine character in Kundera's text makes. There is no gap between the embodied Self and the objective Self. The Self does not leap outside the body in order to become objective.

This view, I argued, can be accounted for in terms of certain limits of spatial awareness: the absolute Here of the living body and the absolute There of the world's 'horizon far in the distance'. The horizon can be understood as that which delimits all the possibilities of reality as a whole, all the possibilities that an understanding being can make sense of in such a way that they can be integrated within a unitary 'absolute conception of reality'. Since the world's horizon is There, it is not nowhere. But the absolute There of the world's horizon is not a particular place or location; as we have seen, it is indeterminate and formal. As such, it is open, expanding infinitely, as it were, 'far in the distance'. The 'two points in space', or, more exactly, the two limits of space which can be understood in terms of the absolute Here and the absolute There, are necessarily linked – and so are the phenomena which enact them: the living body and absolute thinking.

This view develops a certain Kantian line of thought. As mentioned earlier, in the Transcendental Aesthetic, Kant contends that space makes possible the grasp of things as *outside* the subject. Bird stresses that this contrast between the subject and what is outside the subject is not a contrast between a non-spatial, disembodied consciousness and the space around it. Moreover, neither is this a contrast between subjects reduced to 'dimensionless Euclidean points with a spatial location and a spatial point of view' and other regions of space, but between an embodied location and other spatial locations. On this interpretation, 'for Kant, our actual position is embodied.'[44]

This line of thinking has been developed here beyond Kant's philosophy and by drawing on certain post-Kantian contemporary discussions; I have thus sought to show that absolute representations must be conceived as essentially related to embodied awareness, the living body's experiential sense of itself and of other things. Since absolute thinking and the phenomenological sense of the living body are extreme forms of objective understanding and embodiment, respectively, objectivity in general must be thought of as linked in some way or another to embodiment. Objective thinking and embodied awareness cannot be conceived as completely separated from one another. How are they linked to one another? This is a different question, which I have not addressed here. The conclusion of this chapter, as just noted, answers a more modest question.

Notes

I am greatly indebted to A.W. Moore and to S. Baiasu for their suggestions and comments on this chapter.

1. Evans, G. (1982) *The Varieties of Reference* (Oxford: Oxford University Press), p. 212.
2. T. Nagel (1986) *The View from Nowhere* (Oxford: Oxford University Press), p. 5.
3. This account does not imply that objectivity should always be pursued when we try to make sense of the world and of ourselves. Nagel draws attention to the danger of 'false objectification', which he says 'Nietzsche warned' us of, and to the fact that certain aspects of reality might be better understood from a subjective point of view. (*The View from Nowhere*, p. 4).
4. Nagel, *The View from Nowhere*, p.14.
5. Nagel, *The View from Nowhere*, p.15.
6. A. W. Moore (1997) *Points of View* (Oxford: Oxford University Press), p. 7.
7. Moore, *Points of View*, pp. 1–2.
8. Moore, *Points of View*, p. 7. A.W. Moore's terminology of points of view and points of involvement, rigorously defined in his book *Points of View*, is particularly relevant and useful for a discussion of the limits of objectivity in relation to embodiment. Moore is not, however, directly concerned with such a discussion, although he often refers, more or less explicitly, to aspects of embodiment which play a significant role in the formation of our grasp of the world.

9. Moore, *Points of View*, p. 3.
10. Moore, *Points of View*, pp. 3–6.
11. B. Williams (1978) *Descartes: The Project of Pure Inquiry* (London: Penguin Books), pp. 64–8,211–12, 239, 245–9, 310–13; (1985) *Ethics and the Limits of Philosophy* (London: Fontana), pp. 138–40; Nagel, *The View from Nowhere*, and 'Subjective and Objective', in T. Nagel (1979) *Mortal Questions* (Cambridge: Cambridge University Press).
12. Williams, *Descartes*, p. 64.
13. See especially Moore, *Points of View*, pp. 68–74.
14. Whether and to what extent these more or less related notions are adequate cannot be discussed here in detail.
15. Moore, *Points of View*, p. 12.
16. Moore, *Points of View*, p. 7.
17. In *Being and Time*, Heidegger notes the significance of closeness and far-ness for our making sense of the things we come across in everyday envi-ronments. Cf. M. Heidegger (1997) *Being and Time*, trans. J. Macquarrie and E. Robinson (Oxford: Blackwell); (1993) *Sein und Zeit* (Tübingen: Max Niemeyer), section 22.
18. Merleau-Ponty stressed this point. See M. Merleau-Ponty (2002) *Phenomenology of Perception*, trans. C. Smith (London: Routledge). Husserl also made this point, although in a different way, in the Fifth Cartesian Meditation; see E. Husserl (1960) *Cartesian Meditations. An Introduction to Phenomenology*, trans. D. Cairns (The Hague: Martinus Nijhoff).
19. For the second and the fourth examples, cf. Moore, p. 43.
20. Husserl used this metaphor in his discussion of internal time-consciousness. See E. Husserl (1964) *The Phenomenology of Internal Time-Consciousness*, trans. J.S. Churchill (Bloomington: Indiana University Press), p. 52; (1966) *Zur Phänomenologie des inneren Zeitbewusstseins* (1839–1917), Vol. X, Husserliana (The Hague: Martinus Nijhoff), p. 30. Merleau-Ponty employs the metaphor in relation to the body. He writes: 'If I stand in front of my desk and lean on it with both hands, only my hands are stressed and the whole of my body trails behind them like the tail of a comet' (*Phenomenology of Perception*, p. 100).
21. Moore, *Points of View*, p. 4.
22. Husserl, *Cartesian Meditations*, p. 123, emphasis added.
23. Merleau-Ponty, *Phenomenology of Perception*, p. 94. Although there is some continuity in the phenomenological approach to the body initiated by Husserl and further pursued by Merleau-Ponty, there are also important dif-ferences. For a discussion of certain significant disparities between them, see T. Carman (1999) 'The Body in Husserl and Merleau-Ponty', *Philosophical Topics*, 1999,27(2), 205–25. For Husserl's approach to the body and space, see also Zahavi's and Overgaard's chapter in this volume.
24. Merleau-Ponty, *Phenomenology of Perception*, p. 81.
25. Merleau-Ponty, *Phenomenology of Perception*, p. 94.
26. Husserl, *Cartesian Meditations*, p. 123(emphasis added).
27. Husserl, *Cartesian Meditations*, p. 123.
28. Merleau-Ponty, *Phenomenology of Perception*, p. 161.
29. Merleau-Ponty, *Phenomenology of Perception*, p. 115 (emphasis added).
30. Moore, *Points of View*, p.4.

31. Cf. Heidegger, *Being and Time*, especially chs II and III of Division One, and Merleau-Ponty, *Phenomenology of Perception*, especially Part I.
32. Moore, *Points of View*, p. 12 (emphasis added). The quote refers to what he calls radically perspectival representations. The conception of embodiment discussed here matches, at least in part, Moore's conception of the radically perspectival. For Moore's definitions of the radically perspectival, see *Points of View*, especially pp. 11, 15.
33. Moore, *Points of View*, p. 12.
34. Moore, *Points of View*, p. 3.
35. Cf. I.M. Young (1980) 'Throwing Like a Girl. A Phenomenology of Feminine Body, Comportment, Motility, and Spatiality', *Human Studies*, 3, 137–56; D. Chisholm (2008) 'Climbing Like A Girl: an Exemplary Adventure in Feminist Phenomenology', *Hypatia*, 9–40.
36. See Moore, *Points of View*, p. 24.
37. Williams, *Descartes*, p. 64.
38. Moore, *Points of View*, p. 23, p. 37 respectively.
39. G. Bird (2006) *The Revolutionary Kant, A Commentary on the Critique of Pure Reason* (Chicago: Open Court), p. 141 f. and p. 792, note 3; H. Allison (2004) *Kant's Transcendental Idealism* (New Haven and London: Yale University Press), p. 100 f.
40. Bird, *The Revolutionary Kant*, p. 792, note 4.
41. Cf. CPR, A 22 B 37, where Kant writes: 'By means of outer sense (a property of our mind) we present objects as *outside us*, and present them one and all in space. In space their shape, magnitude, and relation to one another are *determined or determinable*' (my emphasis). In the *Dissertation* he writes: 'I cannot conceive of *anything* as located *outside* me unless I represent in a space different from the space in which I myself am; nor can I conceive things as outside one another unless I place them in different parts of space' (my emphasis). See (1986) *Inaugural Dissertation* in *Kant's Latin Writings*, trans. L.W. Beck, M.J. Gregor, R. Meerbote and J. Reuscher (eds) (New York: Peter Lang), section 15.
42. (Emphasis added). It might be useful to consider here the entire passage to which the quote belongs: 'The idea of the objective self has something in common with the "metaphysical subject" of Wittgenstein's *Tractatus* 5.641, though I stop short of excluding it from the world entirely. The metaphysical subject is *the logical limit* we reach if all the contents of the mind, including its objective thoughts are thrown into the world as properties of TN [Thomas Nagel]. The objective self is the last stage of the detaching subject before it shrinks to an extensionless point. It also has a great deal in common with Husserl's transcendental ego though I do not share the "transcendental idealism" to which his phenomenology is committed (Husserl, sec. 41). Neither do I accept the solipsism of the *Tractatus*' (Nagel, *The View From Nowhere*, n. 3, p. 62).
43. Milan Kundera as quoted by Moore in *Points of View*, p. 21 (emphasis added).
44. Bird, *The Revolutionary Kant*, p. 142.

References

Allison, H. (2004) *Kant's Transcendental Idealism* (New Haven and London: Yale University Press).

Bird, G. (2006) *The Revolutionary Kant, A Commentary on the* Critique of Pure Reason (Chicago: Open Court).

Carman, T. (1999) 'The Body in Husserl and Merleau-Ponty', *Philosophical Topics*, 27(2), 205–25.

Chisholm, D. (2008) 'Climbing Like A Girl: an Exemplary Adventure in Feminist Phenomenology', *Hypatia*, 9–40.

Heidegger, M. (1997) *Being and Time*, trans. J. Macquarrie and E. Robinson (Oxford: Blackwell); (1993) *Sein und Zeit* (Tübingen: Max Niemeyer).

Husserl, E. (1960) *Cartesian Meditations. An Introduction to Phenomenology*, trans. D. Cairns (The Hague: Martinus Nijhoff).

Husserl, E. (1964) *The Phenomenology of Internal Time-Consciousness*, trans. J.S. Churchill (Bloomington: Indiana University Press).

Husserl, E. (1966) *Zur Phänomenologie des inneren Zeitbewusstseins* (1839–1917), X, Husserliana (The Hague: Martinus Nijhoff).

Kant, I. (1986) *Inaugural Dissertation* in *Kant's Latin Writings*, trans. L.W. Beck, M.J. Gregor, R. Meerbote and J. Reuscher (eds) (New York: Peter Lang).

Merleau-Ponty, M. (2002) *Phenomenology of Perception*, trans. C. Smith (London: Routledge).

Moore, A.W. (1997) *Points of View* (Oxford: Oxford University Press).

Nagel, T. (1979) *Mortal Questions* (Cambridge: Cambridge University Press).

Nagel, T. (1986) *The View from Nowhere* (Oxford: Oxford University Press).

Williams, B. (1978) *Descartes: The Project of Pure Inquiry* (London: Penguin Books).

Williams, B. (1985) *Ethics and the Limits of Philosophy* (London: Fontana).

Young, I.M. (1980) 'Throwing Like a Girl. A Phenomenology of Feminine Body, Comportment, Motility, and Spatiality', *Human Studies*, 3, 137–56.

Part IV
Time

11
Heidegger on Time

Michael Inwood

In this chapter I explore some of Heidegger's ideas about time. But one cannot consider Heidegger's thought without taking account of other philosophers who influenced him and against whom he is reacting. It is essential to Heidegger's thought that philosophers never deal with pure uncontaminated problems but always with problems as they have been handed down to them by other philosophers and obscured, as well as illuminated, by them. So I consider Heidegger in relation to three other philosophers: Aristotle, Kant and Husserl. The first of them, Aristotle, interested Heidegger for several reasons. One is the enormous influence exerted on German thought and culture by ancient Greece– the 'tyranny of Greece over Germany'.[1] Another is that, although Heidegger's philosophical positions often seem more Protestant than Catholic, he was brought up and educated as a Catholic. He was, therefore, steeped in the Aristotelian tradition of the Catholic Church. A third reason for his interest lies within the phenomenological movement itself. One of its pioneers, Franz Brentano, was a devoted Aristotelian. Heidegger tells us that the first philosophical work he read was Brentano's book, *The Manifold Meaning of What Is, According to Aristotle*.[2]

The second philosopher I want to consider, Edmund Husserl, was a pupil of Brentano and a teacher of Heidegger. In the 1920s the relationship between Heidegger and Husserl was extremely close. Heidegger, like Husserl, regarded himself as a phenomenologist. But there are also differences between them, of which I here mention two. First, for Husserl phenomenology requires that we suspend our everyday 'natural attitude' to things, whereas for Heidegger it is just our natural attitude to the world that philosophy should examine. Second, on Husserl's account philosophy is essentially unhistorical: Husserl is interested in the history of philosophy only insofar as he can find anticipations of his own views and methods in previous philosophers. More precisely, Husserl distinguished between 'worldviews', *Weltanschauungen*, and 'scientific philosophy'. Worldviews change over time and are historically specific, but they are of no interest to the serious philosopher. Scientific philosophy, what Husserl claimed to do, is unhistorical in the same way as mathematics; it can be done in principle at any time. So the history of philosophy is of no intrinsic interest to Husserl.[3] For Heidegger, by contrast, history of philosophy is integral to philosophy. The problems with which a philosopher deals are not timeless problems, but are determined by the specific position that he occupies in the history of philosophy.

Before I turn to consider a part of this history in more detail, I want to say more about Heidegger himself. About one-third of Heidegger's first major work, *Being and Time* [I have put the title in italics] (1927), deals with time. The lectures that he gave shortly after its publication, *Basic Problems of Phenomenology*,[4] also deal with time for a third of their length. Why is time so important? Why 'Being and Time', rather than, say, 'Being and Space' or, for that matter, 'Being and Nothing'? Heidegger deals with 'the nothing' in *Being and Time* and also with space. Space is built into the notion of a world. The world is a spatial world and to be in-the-world, as Dasein is, is to be 'spatial'. But neither of these notions, nothing and space, has the same prominence as time. One reason is this. Heidegger wants to answer the question 'What is being?' He believes this to be a question we have forgotten how to ask. It is not wholly clear when it was asked in the past – by Parmenides, perhaps, or by Aristotle – but this doesn't matter for my purposes. At any rate, since the time of the Greeks philosophers have asked the closely related question 'What kinds of entity are there?' 'What sorts of thing exist?' Time plays an essential part in their answers: 'Entities are grasped in their Being as "presence"; this means that they are understood with regard to a definite mode of time – the "Present".'[5] Heidegger means that past philosophers believed that an entity only genuinely exists if it exists now, at present: purely past entities and purely future ones are less than fully real. Related to this, time is used as a criterion for distinguishing the types of entity there are. There are, first, temporal things and events – things and events that last only for a time. Then there are atemporal, non-temporal entities – spatial and numerical relationships, for example. And, finally, there's a different sort of atemporal or supratemporal entity, one that lasts forever – God or perhaps gods. Because what is fully real must be present, and what used to exist and what will exist are less than fully real, some philosophers have gone further and claimed that only what is supratemporal or non-temporal, what lasts forever or is outside time altogether, is fully real. A transitory entity, one which once did not exist and one day will exist no longer, is less than fully real even at the time when it does exist. This tendency persists from Parmenides – near the beginnings of philosophy – down to Hegel. A good example of it is Plato's theory of forms, in which time is one factor, though not the only factor, at work. Helen of Troy was beautiful for a time, but if she lived long enough she grew old and ugly and then ceased to exist altogether apart from a heap of unattractive bones. By contrast, the form or idea of beauty, beauty as such, never gets old and ugly and never ceases to exist. It remains eternally the same, the perfect exemplar and source of all beauty. Now the long-dead Helen is not fully real. But even 3,000 years ago, when she was in her prime, she was less than fully real in comparison with the form of beauty. She belongs to a lower order of being.

This illustrates the role that, according to Heidegger, time plays in traditional ontology. There is clearly something to be said for Heidegger's view. However, one of his arguments for the claim that the Greeks 'grasped [entities] in their Being as "presence"', is flawed. It is this: To denote existence or what exists the Greeks often used the noun *ousia*. This derives from the verb *einai*, 'to be'. The noun is used more often by Aristotle than by Plato, and in Aristotle is usually translated as 'substance'. For Aristotle substances, as opposed to, for example, their qualities, are what primarily and indisputably exist. A particular man, Alexander, and a particular horse, Bucephalus, are each a substance, and they exist in a more fundamental way than their qualities: their courage, for example, or their swiftness. The verb *einai*, 'to be', enters into many compounds: by adding a prefix you get a new verb with a different meaning. *Suneinai*, for example, is 'to be, live, or associate with', *apeinai* 'to be absent' and *pareinai* 'to be present'. Each verb generates a composite noun with *ousia* as its root: *sunousia* 'association, intercourse', *apousia* 'absence' and *parousia* 'presence'. Heidegger selects one of these nouns, *parousia*, and argues that it means more or less the same as the core noun, *ousia*. On his view *ousia* means 'presence' and, because the Greeks use *ousia* for 'being', being is for them associated with presence.[6] There are two objections to this line of thought. First, *pareinai* and *parousia* do not especially denote temporal presence; they also denote spatial presence, someone's presence at a lecture, for example, in contrast to one's absence. Second, it is arbitrary to select one of the compounds, *parousia*, and to equate it with the root noun, *ousia*. Heidegger's conclusion is better than his argument for it. That time plays an important part in traditional ontology is quite plausible, but the etymological argument for it (like many of Heidegger's etymological arguments) is weak. Still, however weak the argument, Heidegger believed that time is traditionally and persistently important in ontology, both because being is taken to be or imply temporal presence and because time supplies the criterion for distinguishing different types of entity. So, when Heidegger attempts to deal with this traditional enterprise, time is important for him too.

However, Heidegger has at least two disagreements with this 'metaphysical' tradition. First, he disagrees with its conception of time and wants to replace it with a conception of his own. Or, more precisely, he wants to unearth a more fundamental conception of time that underlies the traditional conception. Second, on the basis of this new account of time, Heidegger disagrees with the traditional use of the notion of time to distinguish different kinds of entity. He mentions, for example, the familiar distinction between 'the "timeless" meaning of propositions and the "temporal" course of propositional assertions',[7] between, say, the proposition that 2 + 2 = 4 and the assertion of it on a particular occasion, a distinction not wholly dissimilar to Plato's distinction between beauty as such and particular beautiful things. Heidegger wants to undermine distinctions of this sort, and is, in general, hostile to the attempt to find true reality in some atemporal or eternal entity or entities, whether it be forms, propositions, truths, meanings or God. In this respect he resembles Nietzsche, though he was not much influenced by Nietzsche when he wrote *Being and Time*. In the rest of this chapter I neglect this second question, the relationship between time and types of entity, and concentrate on the first question, the traditional conception of time and Heidegger's disagreement with it.

I begin with what Heidegger calls the ordinary or 'vulgar' conception of time as it was formulated by Aristotle. Heidegger presents a simplified version, both in *Being and Time* and in *The Basic Problems of Phenomenology*, of the account Aristotle gives in Book Four of his *Physics*. Physics deals with things that move and change, and motion and change involve time. Aristotle begins with two questions: Is time real? and What is the nature of time? One of the problems he raises about the reality of time bears on the relation between being and presence. Only the present instant exists now. Past time used to exist and future time will exist, but neither of them exist now. So time seems not to exist, at least not now. To the objection that at any rate the present still exists now, Aristotle responds that the present is a durationless instant, a boundary between stretches of time, the past and the future, but not itself an extended period of time. So there is no time at all that exists now. Aristotle does not apply this line of argument to events or objects, but it could apply equally well to them. It is not just the long-dead Helen of Troy who no longer exists, but also the past me: the person who typed the beginning of this chapter no longer exists, nor the person who wrote the beginning of this sentence, nor the person who typed the beginning of this word. Similarly, the person who will write the end of this chapter does not yet exist, nor does the person who will write the end of this sentence. All that exists now is a durationless boundary between the past author and the future author. Aristotle's solution to this problem, if he provided one, is too complex to be presented here.[8]

Aristotle's second question is: What is the nature of time? His answer, in brief, is that it is the measure or number of motion with respect to before and after. Aristotle imagines us measuring the time taken by a change or motion against a clock, which may be a water clock, a sundial or the sun itself. But, as he says later, motion is also the measure of time: the motion of the clock, most fundamentally the heavenly bodies, is taken as primary and other motions and changes are measured against it. Time is an infinitely, or rather indefinitely, divisible continuum. Between any two nows or instants there is always a further now or instant. In this respect time is parallel to motion itself and to the line or distance which a moving body traverses. Between any two points on a line there is another point, and a body moving from one point to another will pass through an infinity of intermediate points. In doing so, it will also pass through an infinity of instants of time. But time itself is infinite in a way that most movements are not: it has no beginning and no end. Incidentally, since there is no time without movement, this implies that the motion of the heavenly bodies is everlasting. This, then, is roughly Aristotle's view of time and, in Heidegger's view, it has dominated our thought about time ever since. Hegel's account of time in his *Philosophy of Nature* is very similar to Aristotle's.[9]

Aristotle is engaged in ontology. In the *Physics* he is studying the general features of one type of beings, the things or substances that move and change. He recognized two other realms of beings. First, there are mathematical objects – lines, points, shapes, numbers, and so on– and these are simply abstractions from things that move and change, though there is much to be said about them independently. Second, there are the unmoved movers, the eternal immaterial entities that move the heavens and the planets but do not themselves move or change. He discusses these other types of entity in his *Physics*, but especially in his *Metaphysics*. In the *Metaphysics*, however, he asks not just about the general features of particular types of entity; he also asks: What is being as such? And what are the features common to all the things that are? These questions are similar to, or at least the ancestors of, the question Heidegger asks in *Being and Time*. But Heidegger's approach to the question differs from Aristotle's in an important respect. Heidegger does what Aristotle did not do. He starts by asking about the being of *Dasein*, roughly human being. (Aristotle did, of course, ask what a human being is, but he did not start out from this question or view all other questions from that point of view.) If we consider the human being rather than, say, external bodies, time will still be important. *Dasein* is temporal. At the very least, its states follow each other in time and it is aware of the passage of time. But, more than this, the contrast between examining *Dasein* and examining external things is a false contrast. *Dasein* is aware of and interacts with other things; it is, as Heidegger says, transcendent, so that in considering *Dasein* we will also consider other things, only from *Dasein*'s point of view.

The word '*Dasein*' deserves some comment. In ordinary philosophical German it means something like 'existence': Kant, for example, spoke of the *Dasein* of God. And the corresponding verb, *dasein*, means 'to exist'. It is formed from two words, *sein*, 'to be', and *da*, 'here' or 'there' (as in 'Here they come' and 'There they go'). So literally '*Dasein*' means 'being (t)here', and Heidegger sometimes emphasizes this by hyphenating it as '*Da-sein*'. In colloquial German it is similar in meaning to 'life' (as in 'That's my life'), and in earlier lectures Heidegger sometimes used '*Leben*', 'life', in contexts in which he later uses '*Dasein*'. There are at least four reasons why Heidegger uses '*Dasein*' as an abstract term for 'human being', or 'being human', and also as a concrete term for 'human beings'. First, he wants to avoid traditional vocabulary such as 'mind', 'consciousness' or even 'person' or 'man'. To use such terminology would, he believes, commit him to certain assumptions that need to be examined rather than passively accepted.[10] The word '*Dasein*' is, by contrast, neutral and non-committal. Second, Heidegger believed, in contrast to, say, Descartes, that a human being is essentially in the world or, as he puts it, 'in-the-world'.[11] A human being is necessarily 'there' in the world. Third, and relatedly, Heidegger believes that a human being has no definite nature apart from its relation to the world and apart from its own decisions about how it is to be. It cannot be detached from the world because without a world there is nothing for it to be. '*Dasein*' is thus not simply a non-committal term but also an *empty* way of designating a human being. Finally, a human being is not only in the physical place it presently occupies. It is out there, over there, with the objects and the people in its environment. We might suppose that, when I am aware of something at a distance from myself, I am aware of it in virtue of some state of myself, a mental or physical state that is over here where I am but which represents something over there at some distance from myself. This representative may be a sense-datum, an image, a thought, a proposition, or whatever. Heidegger rejects this doctrine. He holds that we are directly aware of objects and of other people without any intermediary representative state or entity. His view of our temporal awareness is similar. One might suppose that a person is here in the present and that insofar as I am aware of past and future events it is because some present state of myself– a memory or an expectation – represents past or future events to me. But, according to Heidegger, this is not so. I am directly aware of past and future events, I am back there in the past and away there in the future, as well as here in the present. From a phenomenological point of view, human beings are not confined to a particular spatio-temporal location in the way that other entities are. And that is another reason why Heidegger refers to them as *'Dasein'*. Unlike Kant, Heidegger does not want to draw a sharp distinction between subjective time and objective time.

Suppose now that we adopt Heidegger's point of view and start out from *Dasein*. What should we then say about Aristotle's account of time? The main thing is that time, as Aristotle describes it, is a theoretical construct and does not do justice to our primary awareness of time. We are not naturally aware of time as infinitely divisible or of the present moment as a durationless instant. Aristotle's account of time stands in a similar relationship to our ordinary awareness of time as Euclid's geometry does to our awareness of our spatial environment. Again, according to Heidegger, the measurement of time, which is the central focus of Aristotle's account, is a secondary matter. When I give a lecture, I measure the time it takes in a rough and ready way. I take off my watch and place it where I can see it. I look at it occasionally to make sure that I do not run over time. But all sorts of temporal experiences and assumptions are necessary if I am to do this. I assume that a lecture takes time. I assume that my audience has other things to do with their time, that they need time for other things. And so on. When I begin the lecture, I look at my watch and think 'It's about time to begin,' and I am not measuring time when I do that. Even before that, I ask myself 'What's the time now? Is it time to start?' and that thought does not explicitly introduce any numbers, times or dates. We have an experience of time that is prior to numbers and measurement.

What are we to say about this primary experience of time? One approach is to be found in Husserl's lectures on time-consciousness, which he gave in 1905 and which were published under Heidegger's editorship in 1928.[12] Husserl takes as his example our listening to a tune. How are we aware of time when listening to a tune? What we do not do, except in unusual circumstances, is to measure the time the tune takes. We just listen to the tune, letting it flow through our consciousness. We hear each note or phase of a note as it comes along. Husserl calls this 'presentation' or 'enpresenting'. And our hearing of each note as it comes along, he calls a 'primal impression'. To hear a tune we obviously need to hear the notes, but this alone is not enough. Suppose that when we heard a tune we heard each note as it came along but forgot it completely as soon as it was over. Suppose, that is, that our consciousness was confined to the present. Then at no time would we be aware of what tune we were listening to or even of hearing a tune at all. At each moment we would be aware only of a particular note, a note that is presumably shared by many different tunes. What we need at any given moment, if we are to hear the tune as such, is not simply a perception of the present note, but also an awareness of the notes that have already gone by and roughly of the order in which they have gone by. Husserl calls this 'retention'. The note I hear at present is a primal impression. When the next note comes, the first primal impression is modified: I am still aware of it, but now I am aware of it as just having been. And as the tune proceeds, and this first note recedes further into the past, it is modified still further, as having been some time ago. It is followed by other notes whose primal impressions are modified, but modified to a lesser degree of pastness. Retention differs from recol- lection. Recollection is something we do only sometimes, not always. Moreover, recollection interferes with one's present perception. If, as I lecture, you think I said something interesting four minutes ago and are trying to recollect or recall what it was, this will prevent you from taking in what I am saying now: your mind is wandering. But your retention of the words I have just uttered does not have this effect. You could not understand what I am saying now if you did not retain what I said up to, say, one minute ago, but also beyond that, only with a lesser degree of vividness.

Husserl also introduces a corresponding type of expectation, or 'pro- tention'. What he has in mind is not a definite expectation of what I am going to say in my lecture. That would be the futural counterpart of recollection and it would probably interfere with your understand- ing of what I am saying now. Husserl's protention is the counterpart of retention, not just hearing my present words and retaining my past ones, but expecting me to continue in some way or other, and not thinking that the words I am uttering now are the last words of the lecture. Naturally, protention is less definite than retention. You do not expect any definite continuation on my part, though there are fairly close limits on how you expect me to continue. You would be surprised, for example, if I, having lectured so far on Heidegger's account of time, were to continue by saying 'And that concludes what I have to say about the pyramids.' If you were not surprised, if you placed no restrictions on how you expected me to continue, this would mean that you did not really understand what I was saying earlier. You heard and perhaps understood each word taken separately, but you did not hear them as forming a coherent lecture.

This is an appropriate point at which to bring in another philosopher I have already mentioned, namely, Kant. For, although Kant preceded Husserl by more than a century, he anticipated much of Husserl's approach, and Heidegger developed his view of time by engaging with Kant. Kant held that our 'sensibility', or capacity for receiving 'intuitions', roughly sensations or perceptions, is necessarily subject to two 'forms', space and time. Space is the form of our 'outer sense', while time is the form of our 'inner sense'. Anything that I perceive as external to myself, a tree for example, must be extended or spread out in space. It must be perceived as lying at a distance from myself, and at a distance from, or adjoining, other things to which it is spatially related, such as bushes and houses. By contrast, my own conscious inner states are not extended in space or spatially related to each other. If I am, for example, silently counting from one to ten, it makes no sense to ask whether my thoughts of the numbers are in the same place or different places, or how far they are from my contemporaneous headache. They are, however, successive in time and each thought lasts for a time. Kant wavers on the question of whether the intuitions of outer sense are also in time in the same way as they are in space. This may be because he believes that, while our ascription of temporal duration and order to outer objects and events depends on the temporal order and duration of our inner states, our perceptions, the temporality of outer events does not directly mirror the temporality of the inner states by means of which we become aware of them: the fact that our perceptions of the different sides of, say, a house inevitably succeed one another in time does not entail that the sides of the house are not contemporaneous.

My perception of objects, whether inner or outer, requires a 'spontaneous' intellectual input from myself and not simply sensory 'receptivity'.

When I look at a painting, for example, I see the painting as a whole, not simply as a set of discrete square inches. This presupposes that I am a unitary self. My seeing the painting is quite different from several different people seeing different parts of the painting, such that, although the whole painting is seen, no one sees it as a whole.[13] The perception of larger objects, such as a landscape or a house, requires not only spatial 'synthesis' but also temporal synthesis. I cannot take in the object all at once; I need to look at different parts of it successively. This is where 'retention' (as Husserl, though not Kant, called it) comes in. If I am to see the house as a whole, I must retain my earlier perceptions of it as well as 'enpresenting' it in my present perception. In fact, even the perception of a small, two-dimensional object, such as a painting, requires retention. To perceive something for only a punctual instant, or for that matter only a millionth of a second, is not to perceive it at all. Nor, of course, could I perceive movement without at least some span of retention.[14] Kant argues that, in addition to retention, I need something else if I am to see a painting *as* a painting or a house *as* a house. This is the 'concept' of a house, a painting, or whatever. Without a concept of a house and its application to the sensory data, I cannot see the data, both retained and present, as presenting a house rather than as a series of unconnected items.[15] Moreover, I cannot know which of the data presented to me belong to the house and which do not. Suppose, for example, that a fly has settled on the house or on the painting. I do not regard that as a part of the object, and I can do so only in virtue of my exercise, however implicit, of the concept of the relevant object. This is apparent, too, in Husserl's example of listening to a tune. How do I manage to hear the sounds as constituting a single tune, and not as a series of unconnected noises, like the coughs of the audience? How do I manage to exclude such extraneous noises – coughs, chatter, car horns – from the tune itself? Only by having a concept, however vague, of what counts as a tune. I may even need a vague concept of *this* tune to enable me to exclude from it the sound of a different tune being played in an adjoining room.

Initially, Kant treats space and time as two co-ordinate forms of equal importance. Later, however, he assigns time a higher significance than space. In the 'Schematism', for example, Kant attempts to supply sensory criteria for the application of 'pure concepts of the understanding' (such as ground and consequent) to our intuitions, thereby arriving at schematized categories (such as cause and effect). It is noticeable that here, and later, the pure concepts are schematized in terms of time, but not space, making a category 'capable of representation only as a determination of time' (A145/B184). Causality, for example, is 'the succession of the manifold, in so far as that succession is subject to a rule' (A 144/ B 183). One might suppose that spatial considerations are relevant to causality as well as temporal considerations. If one event occurs long before another event, we are reluctant to say that the first event is the cause of the second, at least without some explanation of the delayed effect in terms of intervening events. But equally, if one event is distant from another event, we are reluctant to say that the first is the cause of the second, without some explanation of the spatial remoteness of the effect in terms of intervening events. Kant may, of course, have been influenced by the fact that gravity operates over a distance, with no apparent intervening events. But there are more substantial reasons for giving time priority over space. There is, in the first place, no spatial analogue of temporal retention. Our present awareness is restricted to a short span of time (the 'specious present'), and we are tempted to restrict it to a durationless instant. There is no similar temptation to restrict my spatial awareness to an extensionless point, or even to a small area. I can take in a wide area of space at a single glance. The exploration of larger areas and of three-dimensional objects requires several glances. But here it is temporal retention that is in play. I retain my view of the front of a house as I move on to look at its other sides. I need time to explore space. Second, since time is the form of inner sense, whereas space is not, it is conceivable that I should have experience that is temporal but not spatial. Usually, when I listen to a tune, I do so in a spatial context disclosed to me by sight, touch and kinaesthesia, and the sounds seem to come from a certain distance and direction. But it is conceivable that I should hear a tune, and more generally sounds, in the absence of any spatial context, rather as when I hear ringing in my ears. Whether such a non-spatial experience could be an objective experience is another matter. I can find out whether the ringing I hear is only 'in my ears' or not by asking someone else whether they hear it too or whether it is 'just me'. But I can only do this because I have contact with another person that is more than purely auditory. It is not easy to conceive of a condition in which I experience other people in an exclusively auditory manner, and yet those people are genuinely objective, distinct from myself, and not just voices in my own head.[16] But a purely auditory and non-spatial experience, whether objective or not, is at least a conceivable experience. By contrast, an experience without time, with no retention whatsoever, would be no experience at all. Finally, since time is the form of inner sense and yet the external objects and events that we experience are also in time, Kant faces the problem of how we get from one to the other. The temporal duration and order of our subjective experience of things do not mirror their objective temporal duration and order. I view the different sides of a house successively, but the sides themselves are contemporaneous. I view the varying positions of a boat moving downstream successively, and its positions are indeed successive. Boring encounters seem to last an eternity, whereas interesting ones pass by in a flash. How do we determine the objective duration and order of things? This is a problem that Kant attempts to solve in terms of the application of schematized categories. But (he may have thought) no analogous problem arises in the case of space, since space is the form of outer sense, and not of inner sense. Kant was no doubt wrong about this. My sensory representations of things, the ways things look to me, are not spatially related to each other in the way that they are temporally related to each other. But they nevertheless do not mirror the objective spatial location, dimensions and relations of things, the objective spatial order. The shape and dimensions of objects are not obvious at a glance. But, whatever the truth about the matter, Kant seems to have felt that space presented no such urgent problem as that presented by time.

From a phenomenological point of view, Kant's and Husserl's accounts of time are an improvement on Aristotle's. I can follow a tune or a lecture without timing it, measuring its duration. But I could not measure its duration if I were unable to follow its course in a rough and ready way, enpresenting, retaining and protaining, not the precise quality of the notes or words, but more or less the notes or words that belong to the tune or the lecture. Moreover, Kant provides some support for Heidegger's belief that time is prior to space.

But their accounts of time did not satisfy Heidegger. The main difference between them and Heidegger is this. Husserl, in his earlier writings at least, is concerned with the human being primarily as a knower, an observer, and an observer not primarily of artefacts such as tunes, but of natural objects such as trees and stones, or of artefacts, such as a die, but considered as if they were no more than natural objects, objects with a certain geometrical shape. Husserl's central interest was to provide the phenomenological foundations of the mathematical and natural sciences. Kant, too, accepted the view of time endorsed by Newton: 'Absolute, true, and mathematical time, of itself, and from its own nature, flows equably without relation to anything external,' while 'relative, apparent and common time' is a 'measure of duration by the means of motion'.[17] Kant does, of course, add the important qualification that time is 'ideal' rather than 'real', but time as he conceives it is nevertheless fundamentally Newtonian. Heidegger, by contrast, is interested in the human being as a doer, an agent, though, because everyday activity too requires a sort of knowledge or 'know-how', he tends to question the distinction between theory and practice rather than to emphasize one side of it. The objects that *Dasein* deals with primarily are functional objects – hammers, nails and workshops – and what *Dasein* does with them is not observe or contemplate them but use them to do things. The observation of natural objects is a secondary and derivative matter. This suggests that Heidegger will view time differently, that time will take on a more practical aspect. Time is not just a continuous flow but a matter of practical urgency. I need more time to say everything I want to say. But will there be enough time for questions afterwards? Will I have time to do some shopping before the shops close? We might put the differences between Aristotle, Husserl and Heidegger as follows. Aristotle fills up his sink with water, looks at his watch, pulls the plug out and measures how long it takes for the water to run away. Husserl also fills his sink and pulls out the plug, but he does not look at his watch. He just observes the water running away, enpresenting, retaining and protaining. Kant does this too, though he is more inclined to consult his watch as well. Heidegger, like most of us, fills the sink in order to wash. He wonders whether there is time to shave before the cab arrives, and whether it will get to the theatre on time.

This feature of time Heidegger calls 'significance'. Time is time for things, time to do things, just as a hammer is not just a thing or a substance, but is something to do things with. He discusses three other features of time that are not emphasized by Aristotle, Kant or Husserl. Time is dateable. This does not mean primarily that we can assign numerical dates to particular times, but that we can refer to particular times by attaching to them particular events: at the time when I gave my first lecture, when so-and-so was prime minister, when Napoleon became emperor, and so on. This recalls a view that Heidegger expressed in an early essay,[18] in which he argued that time as conceived by the natural sciences is smooth and homogeneous, whereas in historical studies time is punctuated by decisive events and articulated into distinct periods. The fall of the Bastille or the Russian revolution mark, as it were, breaks in time, 'after which nothing was ever the same again'. The Victorian era or the twentieth century have a significance beyond the mere number of years they contain. So it is, too, with the time of an ordinary life. It does not run on smoothly, but is punctuated by decisive events, such as first love, examinations, marriage, and so on. This would not be so if time were not dateable.

Another feature of time as Heidegger views it is 'spannedness'. Time is spanned, it stretches out. When we say 'now' we never refer to a durationless instant, but always to some longer or shorter stretch of time: 'now, while I am lecturing', 'now that we have computers', and so on. Aristotle was aware that 'now' is often used in this way, but for him this is not its primary use; 'now' refers primarily to a punctual instant, with no duration, and its other use is derivative. For Heidegger it is the other way about, as it must be if we are engaged in phenomenology and not mathematics or physics. In fact, even mathematicians and physicists use the word 'now' in Heidegger's way, when they are off duty.

Finally, time is public. We talk to each other about particular times, arrange to meet at a certain time, and so on. We can do this even though we date times by reference to different events. For me, now is the time when I am writing this chapter, while for someone else it is the time when they arrived in Corinth. But somehow or other we can, later on, successfully communicate about this time. In this respect Heidegger contrasts with Aristotle and Husserl. Aristotle does not, in this context, consider the publicity of time at all. Indeed, he is not, officially at least, concerned with people as observers or agents, but only with the time taken by physical changes and movements. Husserl is concerned with the observer, but it is in the first instance a single observer, myself, and only later does he raise the question of intersubjectivity, of whether and how different individuals can share the same world and the same time. For Heidegger, by contrast, other human beings are along with me from the start. I do not begin with a private world of my own and then later discover that there are also other people on a par with myself. The world is public from the beginning, and so, therefore, is time. Heidegger calls time of this sort 'world-time'. It enables us to engage with things in the world. Indeed, temporal awareness is necessary for our 'being-in-the world' at all. Without something like retention and protention, I would at any given time be aware only of the object of my present attention, not of the things *over there*, the things I used earlier or the things I shall need later on.

Heidegger is primarily concerned with *Dasein* as an agent, and from this point of view it is important that time, as it were, consists of or involves the past, the present and the future. This feature of time does not matter much if one is engaged in physics. To simplify: the physicist is concerned with such questions as 'How long does it take a stone to reach the ground if it is dropped from the top of the tower of Pisa?' and it does not matter to the physicist whether the stone is dropped now, or in the past or in the future. Since Husserl is concerned with the human being as an observer, the past–present–future aspect of time is important for him. What may not matter much to him is the fact that, while we know a good deal about the present and remember much of the past, the future is, as it were, open to a variety of possibilities and we do not know which will be actualized. Russell said that it is a relatively unimportant contingent fact that we know more about the past than we do about the future, that it could easily have been the other way about, with the past obscure and, as it were open, the future easily accessible and foreseen or precognized.[19] That would not matter much from the point of view of physics. It is harder to imagine how one would listen to a tune in such a condition. We would hear the tune before the orchestra played it. But then the orchestra would have to play the tune and we would have to listen to it, for that is what we precognized, and if it were not to happen we would not have precognized it. The real difficulties arise when we consider action, choices and decisions. It seems essential that the future be open to various possibilities. I can do x, y, or z; I can make A happen or B happen or C happen. Neither A nor B nor C has happened yet, and none of them is yet bound to happen. It is up to me which of them will happen, and I will decide which of them does by deciding whether to do x, y or z. Equally, it is hard to imagine deciding and acting without some awareness of the past, of what has happened already. If I had no retention or recollection of what I have written in this chapter so far, I would not have the faintest idea what to say next. I might start writing about Aristotle all over again, or even about the pyramids. Unless I had made careful notes on events as they happened, and continually referred to them for guidance, my conduct would become quite erratic and incoherent. But you, of course, would not notice this, since your own intellectual and practical operations would be equally incoherent. That is one reason why past, present and future –'ecstases', as Heidegger calls them – are important.

Insofar as they are concerned about past–present–future at all, Aristotle, Husserl and Kant assign priority to the present. In Kant's theoretical philosophy, focused on the natural sciences, the future is subordinated to the past: 'for the complete comprehensibility of what is given in appearance, we need the grounds, but not the consequences;'[20] we need to know about the past, that is, but not the future. By contrast, Heidegger assigns priority to the future. This depends primarily on his concern with *Dasein* as an agent. Agents make things happen later. I cannot decide what to do now unless I have a future-oriented purpose. Others cannot appreciate what I am doing now, unless they know my future-oriented purpose. We cannot understand a historical event unless we know something of its consequences. Indeed, Heidegger regards possibility, in the sense of a possibility for conducting oneself in a certain way, as prior to actuality. This is so even if *Dasein* is in a condition of 'average everydayness', doing the things it (or 'one') usually does without taking stock of its life as a whole. Even everyday *Dasein* is 'ahead of (*vorweg*) itself', wondering what to do next or, as we might say, 'up to something'. This is more obviously the case when *Dasein* is 'authentic' and 'resolute', capable of making crucial decisions in view of its life as a whole. Then it 'anticipates', or 'runs ahead (*vorlaufen*)' to, its own death, whenever this might occur; it returns to a correspondingly remote past – its own birth or perhaps ancient Greece – and finally recoils into the present, the moment of decision – now called the '*Augenblick*' in order to differentiate it from the present of Husserl and of inauthentic *Dasein*. An important point here is that *Dasein* is not simply an observer of time and of events in time, nor simply a user of time. It is itself temporal. We might put the point in this way. In *Being and Time* Heidegger introduces three 'modes of being', the 'ready-to-hand' (*zuhanden* – roughly, things considered as objects of use), the 'present-at-hand' (*vorhanden*– things considered as objects of disinterested observation), and *Dasein* itself. Aristotle, Kant and Husserl tend to regard time as present-at-hand. World-time, as Heidegger conceives it, is time for doing things and is therefore linked to the ready-to-hand. But now, Heidegger insists, there is a 'primordial' or 'originary' (*urspüngliche*) time that shares *Dasein*'s mode of being: *Dasein* itself is temporal. Because *Dasein*, and only *Dasein*, is 'ecstatic', stepping forth into the future, reaching back into the past, and rebounding into the present, *Dasein* opens up the world in its temporal dimension. This idea – that a human being involves the past, future and present in itself, as it were, contemporaneously – is already implicit in Kant, Husserl and, occasionally, Aristotle. But they made less of it. Kant did indeed believe time to be 'transcendentally ideal' rather than 'real', but not for the reason that it is human beings alone who 'reproduce' past time. Kant's own tendency is to suppose that the most fundamental human self, the 'I think', the self as it is 'in itself', is non-temporal, but somehow views itself through temporal spectacles in such a way that the 'empirical self', the self as it appears to itself through inner sense, is temporal. For Heidegger, by contrast, *Dasein* is temporal through and through, and thereby unfurls the time of the world. It does not, however, unfurl the infinite time of Aristotle, Newton and Kant. For even the most resolute *Dasein* cannot run ahead beyond, not at least far beyond, its own death. Primordial time is finite.

But what about non-primordial time? Did Heidegger, like Kant, regard time as ideal? There would be beings without *Dasein*, but no Being.[21] In the absence of *Dasein* there would be no world. There would be nothing to be aware of 'beings as a whole' or to sustain the significant inter-relationships that characterize the things of our world. (There might, nevertheless, be animals, but animals in Heidegger's view are 'world-impoverished', unaware of anything beyond the object of their present attention.) There would, in the absence of *Dasein*, be no authoritative perspective on things. A hammer, for example, is essentially a hammer, because we made it so. A mountain is essentially a mountain, a unitary mountain, because that is how we see it. But without us there would be nothing to make it a mountain rather than a collection of molecules, to give authoritative endorsement to one of the many possible descriptions of it. Things would be next to other things, but there could be no space with the significant contours that we confer on it: left–right, up–down, east–west–north–south, home–abroad. There could be no world-time, as Heidegger conceives it, no time for doing things. (Animal species have their times for things, but their times are far more parochial than ours.) There might, however, be 'ordinary' (*vulgäre*) time, as Aristotle conceives it, time as an infinite sequence of undifferentiated 'nows' or instants. Kant had a theological motive, as well as philosophical arguments, for denying the reality of even such an impoverished, homogeneous time: God is not in time, and his 'intuition' is not temporal.[22] Heidegger has no such motive, and shows no interest in Kant's arguments. He therefore has no reason to deny the reality of something like Aristotelian time.

Notes

I would like to express my gratitude to Roxana Baiasu, Fiona Ellis and Edward Kanterian for their valuable comments and suggestions.

1. E.M. Butler (1935), *The Tyranny of Greece over Germany: A Study of the influence exercised by Greek art and poetry over the great German writers of the eighteenth, nineteenth and twentieth centuries* (London: Cambridge University Press).
2. F. Brentano (1862) *Von der mannigfachen Bedeutung des Seienden nach Aristoteles* (*On the Several Senses of Being in Aristotle*), trans. R. George (Berkeley, CA: University of California Press, 1975).
3. E. Husserl (1956) *Erste Philosophie* (*First Philosophy*)(*1923/24*). *Erster Teil: Kritischer Ideengeschichte. Husserliana*, vol. 7 (The Hague: Nijhoff), trans. J. Allen (The Hague: Nijhoff, 1978).
4. M. Heidegger (1988) *The Basic Problems of Phenomenology*, trans. A. Hofstadter (Bloomington: University of Indiana Press).

5. M. Heidegger, *Being and Time*, p. 25. I adopt the pagination of the first German edition, which is printed in the margins of the translation, J. Macquarrie and E. Robinson's *Being and Time* (Oxford: Blackwell, 1962).

6. In ordinary Greek, *ousia* meant 'what is one's own, one's substance, property', as Heidegger notes at XXIV, 153; IM, 46/50.

7. *Being and Time*, p. 18.

8. See M.J. Inwood (1991)'Aristotle on the Reality of Time', in R.L. Judson (ed.) *Aristotle's Physics: A Collection of Essays* (Oxford: Clarendon).

9. In *The Basic Problems of Phenomenology*, Heidegger tends to reinterpret Aristotle's account of time in the direction of his own views as well as explicitly criticizing Aristotle. We are drawn from Aristotle into Heidegger with no clear idea of where the one ends and the other begins. Heidegger applies this technique selectively when dealing with other philosophers. He interprets Kant, for example, as a proto-Heideggerian and thus stresses his similarity to himself, but he tends to emphasize, indeed exaggerate, his difference from Plato and from Hegel.

10. Heidegger claims that the word 'man' ('*Mensch*', which in German applies to human beings of either sex) makes us think of the traditional definition of man as a 'rational animal'. This is manifestly not the case, as long as one has not read scholastic philosophy from childhood, and in lectures Heidegger often uses the word '*Mensch*' or the expression '*menschliche Dasein*' ('human Dasein') without apology.

11. The hyphens indicate, among other things, that if there were no Dasein in the world there would be no world, just things or beings that would not constitute a structured and significant world.

12. E. Husserl (1964)*The Phenomenology of Internal Time-Consciousness*, M. Heidegger (ed.), trans. J.S. Churchill (Bloomington: Indiana University Press).

13. This is the 'synthesis of apprehension in intuition' in Kant's *Critique of Pure Reason*, A 98–100.

14. This is the 'synthesis of reproduction in imagination' in the *Critique of Pure Reason*, A 100–2.

15. This is the 'synthesis of recognition in the concept' in Kant's *Critique of Pure Reason*, A 103–6.

16. In Chapter II ('Sounds') of his (1959) *Individuals: An Essay in Descriptive Metaphysics* (London: Methuen), P.F. Strawson constructs a purely auditory world, in which sounds are so arranged that they present an analogue of visual and tactual space, thus making possible a 'non-solipsistic consciousness'.

17. Quoted by H. Caygill (1995) in *A Kant Dictionary* (Oxford: Blackwell), p. 396, from I. Newton, *Mathematical Principles of Natural Philosophy*, trans. A. Motte (Chicago: Benton, 1952), p. 8.

18. M. Heidegger (1915) 'The Concept of Time in the Science of History', trans. H.S. Taylor, H.W. Uffelmann and J. van Buren, in J. van Buren (ed.) *Supplements: From the Earliest Essays to 'Being and Time' and Beyond* (Albany: SUNY, 2002).

19. B.A.W. Russell (1914) *Our Knowledge of the External World* (London: Allen&Unwin), p. 238: 'It is a mere accident that we have no memory of the future.'

20. *Critique of Pure Reason*, A 411, B 438.
21. *Being and Time*, p. 212:

> 'Of course only as long as Dasein *is* (that is, only as long as an under-standing of Being is ontically possible), "is there" Being. When Dasein does not exist, "independence" "is" not either, nor "is" the "in-itself". In such a case this sort of thing can be neither understood nor not under-stood. In such a case even entities within-the-world can neither be dis-covered nor lie hidden. *In such a case* it cannot be said that entities are, nor can it be said that they are not. But *now*, as long as there is an under-standing of Being and therefore an understanding of presence-at-hand, it can be said that *in this case* entities will still continue to be.
>
> As we have noted, Being (not entities) is dependent upon the under-standing of Being; that is to say, Reality (not the Real) is dependent upon care.'(Macquarrie and Robinson's translation.)

The last sentence refers back to p.183: 'Entities *are*, quite independently of the experience by which they are disclosed, the acquaintance in which they are discovered, and the grasping in which their nature is ascertained. But Being "is" only in the understanding of those entities to whose Being some-thing like an understanding of Being belongs.'

The first of these passages is discussed by W. Blattner (1999) *Heidegger's Temporal Idealism* (Cambridge: Cambridge University Press), pp. 238–46. Blattner argues that, according to Heidegger, time, even 'ordinary' time, is dependent on *Dasein*; Being is therefore dependent on *Dasein*; and, if we 'think away' *Dasein*, time and Being, then the question 'Do entities depend on *Dasein*?' can have no answer (ibid., p. 246). In my view, this clearly con-flicts with the second of the passages quoted above.

22. *Critique of Pure Reason*, B 71.

References

Blattner, W. (1999) *Heidegger's Temporal Idealism* (Cambridge: Cambridge University Press).

Brentano, F. (1862) *Von der mannigfachenBedeutung des SeiendennachAristoteles(On the Several Senses of Being in Aristotle)*, trans. R. George (University of California Press: Berkeley, CA, 1975).

Butler, E.M. (1935) *The Tyranny of Greece over Germany: A Study of the influence exercised by Greek art and poetry over the great German writers of the eighteenth, nineteenth and twentieth centuries* (London: Cambridge University Press).

Caygill, H. (1995) in *A Kant Dictionary* (Oxford: Blackwell).

Heidegger, M. (1915)'The Concept of Time in the Science of History', trans. H.S. Taylor, H.W. Uffelmann and J. van Buren, in J. van Buren (ed.) *Supplements: From the Earliest Essays to 'Being and Time' and Beyond* (Albany: SUNY, 2002).

Heidegger, M. (1962) *Being and Time*, trans. J. Macquarrie and E. Robinson(Oxford: Blackwell).

Heidegger, M. (1988) *The Basic Problems of Phenomenology*, trans. A. Hofstadter (Bloomington: University of Indiana Press).

Husserl, E. (1956) *ErstePhilosophie(First Philosophy)(1923/24). Erster Teil: Kritischer Ideengeschichte. Husserliana*, vol.7 (The Hague: Nijhoff), trans. J. Allen (The Hague: Nijhoff, 1978).

Husserl, E. (1964)*The Phenomenology of Internal Time-Consciousness*, M. Heidegger (ed.), trans. J.S. Churchill (Bloomington: Indiana University Press).

Inwood, M.J. (1991)'Aristotle on the Reality of Time', in R.L. Judson (ed.) *Aristotle's Physics: A Collection of Essays* (Oxford: Clarendon).

Newton, I.(1952)*Mathematical Principles of Natural Philosophy*, trans. A. Motte (Chicago: Benton).

Russell, B.A.W. (1914) *Our Knowledge of the External World* (London: Allen&Unwin).

Strawson, P.F. (1959) *Individuals: An Essay in Descriptive Metaphysics* (London: Methuen).

12
Time and Subjectivity: Heidegger's Interpretation of the Kantian Notion of Time

Françoise Dastur

The importance of Kantian ideas in Heidegger's thought is well known and, since the publication of his Marburg and Freiburg lecture courses as volumes in the complete works, one has been able to see that the *Kantbuch* of 1929 was preceded and followed by a background discussion, conducted by Heidegger throughout the course of his teaching, with the author of the *Critique of Pure Reason*. The Kantian thesis on Being forms the object of a substantial chapter of *The Basic Problems of Phenomenology*[1](the lecture course of the 1927 summer semester) and this was followed, during the 1927–8 winter semester, by a lecture course entitled *Phenomenological Interpretation of Kant's 'Critique of Pure Reason'*, which provides – and I cite here the remarks[2] of Ingtraud Görland, the editor of this volume of the *Gesamtausgabe* – 'a far more accessible way into Heidegger's intention in his interpretation of Kant', and which constitutes a more exact and detailed 'elaboration' of this interpretation than the book he devoted to him one year after and which was published under the title of *Kant and the Problem of Metaphysics*. And, after his return to Freiburg, Heidegger, during the summer semester of 1930, once again devoted to Kant the largest part of a lecture course entitled *Of the Essence of Human Freedom*.[3] However, these are not the only texts that Heidegger dedicated to Kant during the period immediately before and after the publication of *Sein und Zeit*. In his lecture course of the 1925–6 winter semester, delivered during the months in which he finished editing his master-book[4] and entitled *Logic, the Question of Truth*,one already finds the first interpretation of the *Critique of Pure Reason*, which by itself covers more than a third of a 417-page text.[5] Of these pages of this volume 21 of the complete edition, devoted to the analysis of the aesthetic and the transcendental analytic, and which make apparent the importance Kant accords to the problematic of temporality, the editor Walter Biemel writes in his postface that they make up 'the nucleus of the later work *Kant and the Problem of Metaphysics'* and that one can find in them specific analyses even more detailed than in this later text.[6] One finds there, in effect, an interpretation of the schematism of the pure concepts of understanding which is absent from the lecture course of 1927–8[7] and condensed into only a very few pages of the *Kantbuch*.[8]

It is certainly not my intention to undertake here a comparison of these three texts dedicated – respectively, in 1925–6, 1927 and 1929 – to the *Critique of Pure Reason*, or even to offer a detailed account of the 140 pages devoted to Kant in the 1925–6 lecture course, but, more precisely, to examine the reasons for the importance attributed to Kantian ideas in the framework of a lecture course dedicated to logic, of which the second section, greatly transformed from the original plan,[9] develops the question of truth in the Daseinsanalytical horizon of the problem of temporality.

It must be pointed out that the course of the 1925–6 winter semester, which devotes a long 'preliminary consideration' to the Husserlian critique of psychologism, and in the first part deals with the Aristotelian concept of *logos*, before focusing in the second part on the Kantian notion of time, thus presents, in startling summary, the group of the three philosophical figures who directly inspired Heidegger. The importance for Heidegger of Husserl and Aristotle is already attested to in the first courses at Freiburg and recognized by Heidegger himself when, retracing his development, he acknowledged that at the start of his university studies – that is, in 1909 – he expected from Husserl's *Logical Investigations* a stimulation decisive for understanding the questions raised by Brentano's dissertation on the problem of the manifold meaning of Being in Aristotle.[10] But the Kantian background, although it was present from the start – I recall that during the winter of 1915–16 the first works from the young doctor were devoted to Kant's *Prolegomena* and that it was again to 'Kant and German philosophy of the nineteenth century' that Heidegger devoted his lecture course of the following semester – will only appear in its properly phenomenological light after a long journey through neo-Kantianism, with which Heidegger will not break decisively until the start of the 1920s.

It has to be recalled that Heidegger began his first university work under the patronage of Rickert, whom he thanks in the foreword of his Dissertation for having guided him in comprehending the problems of modern logic. The opening lines of this first work were, moreover, in praise of the interpretation that Cohen, Windelband and Rickert gave of Kant, which, in stressing what constitutes the essential element of the *Critique of Pure Reason,* namely, the Copernican revolution, and in revealing the transcendental–logical dimension within it, opposed the psychologist conception of Kantianism which had dominated the philosophical scene for most of the nineteenth century.[11] And in 1916 it was again to Rickert that Heidegger dedicated his *Habilitationschrift* focusing on Duns Scotus. Nonetheless, a critical distance between him and neo-Kantianism was not slow in taking hold. In the lecture series of the 1919 winter semester, which focuses on 'Phenomenology and Transcendental Philosophy of Values', Heidegger briefly analysed the respective positions of Cohen and Windelband,[12] but, on the subject of Rickert, gave himself over to 'critical considerations', recalling, moreover, that he had already opposed Rickert in the same way in Rickert's 1913 seminar when Lask's *Theory of Judgement* had been discussed.[13] It is true to say that, beginning with the lecture course of 1925, *Prolegomena to the History of the Concept of Time,* Heidegger's judgement of the Baden School becomes unduly severe. There he evokes Windelband and Rickert's 'trivialization' of the initiatives given by Dilthey and the Marburg School. He explains that this trivialization consists in the fact that the structure of knowledge is no longer questioned from a transcendental point of view, that is to say, as giving an access to the real, but concerns itself solely with the question of the logical structure of scientific representation, the theory of science thus becoming an 'empty methodology'.[14] Heidegger goes on to analyse what he calls 'Rickert's misunderstanding of phenomenology and intentionality', demonstrating that in his book *Der Gegenstand der Erkenntnis,* published in 1892, the dogmas of the theory of knowledge bar his access to the true meaning of representation.[15] At Davos in the spring of 1929, responding to a question from Cassirer, Heidegger introduced his own definition of neo-Kantianism, demonstrating what there is in common between Cohen, Windelband, Rickert, Erdmann and Riehl: 'I understand by neo-Kantianism that conception of the *Critique of Pure Reason* which explains, with reference to natural science, the part of pure reason that leads up to the Transcendental Dialectic as a theory of knowledge.'[16] For Heidegger, the return to Kant which took place in the second half of the nineteenth century stems from the confusion in which philosophy, seeing the natural and human sciences overrunning the entire field of knowledge and no longer finding its own realm of knowledge elsewhere than in science, found itself at that time. It is precisely this situation that led one to see in Kant the theoretician of mathematico-physical knowledge; whereas, for Heidegger, 'Kant did not want to give us a theory of natural sciences, but rather wanted to point out the problematic of metaphysics, which is to say, the problematic of ontology'.[17]

For Heidegger, it is not a question of approaching Kant from an external perspective, from epistemological 'dogma', but, on the contrary, of approaching him from the problems themselves. It is, therefore, from the problematic of time that Heidegger, in the lecture course of the 1925–6 semester, turns toward Kant. For the uncertain character of the philosophical use of temporal concepts and determinations, and the crude way in which timelessness and temporality are habitually opposed, attest to the necessity of repeating the question of the temporality of phenomena. Heidegger sees in Kant 'the first and only one who got as far as groping in this obscure domain', yet without managing 'to penetrate the fundamental meaning of his attempt',[18] a judgement he will reiterate in *Sein und Zeit*: 'Kant is the first and only one who traversed a stretch of the path toward investigating the dimension of temporality – or allowed himself to be driven there by the compelling force of the phenomena themselves.'[19] *Zwang der Phänomeneselbst*, 'the compelling force of the phenomena themselves': here is that to which philosophy must submit, rather than trusting to its own faculties without having submitted them to critique, since it is exactly the definition that Kant gives of dogmatism in the *Critique of Pure Reason*: 'Dogmatism is thus the dogmatic procedure of pure reason, without previous criticism of its own powers.'[20] In the 1925–6 lecture course Heidegger congratulates Kant for having been able to open himself to the obscurity of phenomena without wanting to force them to surrender themselves prematurely to the light of an all-powerful intellect capable of explaining everything. He praises him for his modesty or reserve (*Zürückhaltung*) in the face of the problems, and for his prudence, which opposes itself to the violation of phenomena: 'When he encounters limits, he lets the problems stand, which is always more positive for research to come than the violence which consists in organizing half-clear judgements in an imposing system.'[21] This imposing system which thus opposes Kantian reserve and prudence is obviously Hegel's, of whom Heidegger says a little further on that his principle consists in 'taking us for the good God' and whom he will reproach for not having any sense of, or any respect for, the obscurity of the philosophical problems: 'For Hegel, on the contrary, everything is clear, because he is himself in possession of the absolute truth.'[22] It is Kant's proximity to phenomena which allows him to conceive far more concretely and in a more essential manner than Hegel what it is that space, time and nature are, because he has 'a freer position with regard to things', a position which still allows him to pose questions from the things themselves – which, for Heidegger, constitutes what is proper to Greek thinking. What is implicitly recognized thereby is Kant's proximity to the Greeks. According to Heidegger, there is in Kant an 'internal freedom of his philosophizing itself', which explains that he recognizes that 'human philosophizing encounters difficulties' so that philosophy stands at each moment before the possibility – to use a Kantian term – of having to pass through a turning upside down (*eine Umkippung durchmachen zu müssen*).[23] This exposure to an always possible wreckage of reason, which Hegel wanted to avoid with absolute knowledge, is in fact the touchstone of a thought faithful to phenomena and which allows its own law to be dictated by them.

This thought which is exposed to the danger of shattering against the hardness of 'the thing itself'[24] is phenomenology, the model for which – thanks to the thinker who has revived it in the modern era, namely, Husserl – Heidegger found in the Greeks, that is to say, in Aristotle. Kant himself is a phenomenologist who is, as such, unconscious of this, which explains why he is not wholly free of dogmatism – unlike Husserl, or at least the Husserl of the *Logical Investigations* and the period that preceded the transcendental 'turning', because, according to Heidegger, the Husserl of the transcendental phenomenology makes a return to neo-Kantianism and to dogmatism. As a matter of fact, Heidegger affirms that Husserl, in his first Göttingen lecture courses (this being probably an allusion to the *Phenomenology of Internal Time Consciousness* of 1905 and the 1907 *Lessons on Thing and Space*), goes much further than Kant in the investigation of the *a priori* structure of each domain of sensory(ial) data, which alone can serve to ground a genuinely scientific psychology.[25] But, in spite of the fact that 'Kant and all philosophy that precedes him lacked precisely this investigation' and that Kant 'did not explicitly see the phenomenological problematic', he nevertheless 'moved in it, as does all authentic philosophical research'. Heidegger wants here to underline the fact that phenomenology is not something particular, a philosophical direction or system, but simply 'the fact that, in philosophy, one does not only chatter, but rather discourses on the basis of the thing itself', which, Heidegger adds, 'is as easy to formally demand as difficult to fulfil'.[26]

For Heidegger, Kant is thus not a pure phenomenologist, since in a singular way he interweaves phenomenological and wholly dogmatic moments, that is, 'constructive' and 'argumentative' moments. It is for this reason that Heidegger emphasizes the fact that in order to study Kant – and not simply to read him with a view of cultivating oneself or passing exams – one must not only master the phenomenological problematic (Husserl's philosophy) but also grasp for oneself what, since its very beginning, comprises the basic problems of philosophy. One cannot, therefore, *begin* with Kant: one must at least have read Husserl and Aristotle, which is exactly the path followed by Heidegger in this lecture course. Nonetheless, after having thus opposed Kant to Husserl, Heidegger insists upon the fact that 'there is no pure phenomenology.'[27] Phenomenology is, in fact, always tarnished by presuppositions (despite Husserl having posited its principle as the absence of all presuppositions) because philosophy has something of the essence of human action, which can never unfold as a radical beginning, but necessarily has its source in the dogmatic, in the historical, in tradition: 'Every philosophical problematic has something behind its back that it cannot itself reach in spite of its supreme transparency, because it only possesses such a transparency to the extent that it ignores this presupposition.'[28] There is, therefore, something of the unmasterable in every philosophical project, and naïveté consists, according to Heidegger, in imagining, like Hegel, that the philosopher has eyes in the back of his head,[29] and in thinking that he can be in possession of eternal truth instead of trying to recognize upon what presupposition he inevitably founds his discourse. In Kant's case, the interweaving of the dogmatic and the phenomenological – which is, in fact, the case with all philosophy – has its foundation in his misunderstanding of the phenomenological problematic, which itself comes from his historical position, from his being distant from the Greeks and belonging to subjective idealism; on the other hand, however, this interweaving is essential and cannot be discarded by any philosophy, for which the point of departure is always historico-factual, constituting thereby its inalienable finitude.

It is this intertwining of phenomenology and dogmatism which, for Heidegger, explains the 'inextricable' obscurity of the transcendental aesthetic[30] on which his interpretation of the *Critique of Pure Reason*, in opposition to neo-Kantianism, puts great emphasis. Right from the beginning, Heidegger recalls this particular text from the end of Kant's introduction which says: 'There are two stems of human knowledge, namely sensibility and understanding, which perhaps spring from a common, but unknown to us, source. Through the former, objects are given to us; through the latter, they are thought.'[31] These two stems cannot be restored to unity, which, if it indeed exists, remains, as Kant maintains, 'to us unknown'. Not to respect their irreducibility is, therefore, to fail from the outset in the interpretation of Kant: this is, according to Heidegger, precisely what happens with the Marburg School,[32] which proposes a 'logical' interpretation of the *Critique of Pure Reason* that aims at reabsorbing the aesthetic into the analytic. Heidegger does, however, acknowledge 'the philosophical level' of Cohen's interpretation, which, in spite of its unilaterality and its violence,[33] dominates, far beyond its own time, every other interpretation of Kant. It has to be underlined that Heidegger recognizes in Cohen's interpretation a properly 'interpretative' and not only 'historicizing' level. Cohen saw in the transcendental apperception (in the Copernican revolution which places the subject in a 'constitutive' position with regard to the object) the veritable centre of Kantian thought, which itself constitutes an acknowledgement of Kant's thinking. But this is also what founds the unilaterality of his interpretation: Cohen tried to interpret the whole first *Critique* from the analytic, thereby depriving the aesthetic of its autonomy. In this way he was led to dissolve the properly receptive character of sensibility into the spontaneity of pure thought, without recognizing that it is not only categorial logic which constitutes knowledge, but also pure sensibility as 'creative receptiveness', the term 'creative' (*schöpferisch*) connoting pure intuition being used by Heidegger in the 1929 *Kantbuch*. There it is said: 'The pure receptive representing must give itself something capable of being represented. Pure intuition, therefore, must in a certain sense be "creative".'[34] Having failed to recognize the 'receptivity' inherent in the progress of knowledge, which is, for Heidegger, Kant's essential contribution, Cohen was at the same time led to break from that which, according to Heidegger, constitutes the very experience of thought: that is, the experience of a certain creative non-mastery, by which the one who receives must anticipate what thereby gives itself.

This is, then, the moment of givenness which is lacking in this 'logicalizing' interpretation of Kant, an interpretation whose secret complicity with Hegelianism can readily be made apparent. It is understandable, henceforth, why Heidegger could say that the interpretation of the Marburg School fails from the outset (*von vornherein*) in its interpretation of Kant: because it does not recognize, or wants to abolish, the opposition between receiving and thinking, it also fails to account for an entire tradition which, since Plato and Aristotle, distinguishes *aisthesis* from *noesis*, or, in Kantian language, the aesthetic from the logical. Kant begins without questioning this traditional distinction, without attempting to show in what the constitution of the human mind, of the *Gemüt*, is rooted. This contrasts with Heidegger, who, already in the same course of 1926, shows that *Dasein* as being-in-the-world is made up of irreducible but nonetheless non-isolatable existentials: comprehension and disposition, the relationship of which to the two Kantian roots cannot be mistaken.

For Heidegger, all the problems encountered by Kant in the first *Critique* come precisely from the far too abrupt separation that he makes between the two roots of knowledge, understanding and sensibility. He will thus be forced to look for a mediation between them and to find it in another faculty, the imagination, the hybrid character of which will remain largely unquestioned, so that he will finally give to the understanding the priority over sensibility. The Marburg School radicalizes this Kantian position (that of the second edition of the *Critique of Pure Reason*) by purely and simply dissolving sensibility into understanding, by considering the transcendental aesthetic as a 'remainder' from pre-critical philosophy at the heart of Kantianism, and by proposing a deduction of all that which is *a priori*, including pure intuitions. But, this done, the problem of the unity of the first *Critique* remains unresolved. It has, Heidegger gives it to be understood, perhaps not even yet been posed.[35] For Heidegger it is, then, a question of showing that the transcendental aesthetic is not something 'contingent' and that there is a necessity within the Kantian project to suppose an *a priori* intuition, which consists in doing justice to the aesthetic by allowing the unity of problematic of the *Critique of Pure Reason* to appear without arbitrary violence.

Now, what is essential to Heidegger's enterprise is that, conforming to the letter of Kantianism, it privileges the pure intuition of time in the transcendental aesthetic. Indeed, Kant himself underlines the fact that 'time is the formal *a priori* condition of all appearances whatsoever'[36] and not merely of internal phenomena from which, as the 'form of inner sense', time constitutes the frame. The reasoning, which is at the source of this primacy of time over space recognized by Kant, has to be recalled: all our representations, independently of their content, are temporal in as much as they are all, external as much as internal, situated in the 'flux' of consciousness. Time is thereby the immediate condition of internal phenomena and the mediate condition of external phenomena: all phenomena in general are thus 'in' time. It is effectively through the expedient of an 'interpretation of time' that the *Critique of Pure Reason* is approached by Heidegger in his 1925–6 lecture course devoted to logic and the question of truth. The question is then: What is it that leads from the question of truth to the question of temporality?

It is not possible to retrace here, even schematically, the whole of the route which Heidegger follows from Husserl to Kant by way of Aristotle. It has to be underlined again that the original plan of the lecture course[37] did not at the start envisage this sort of connexion between the problem of truth and that of temporality. The first part should deal with Aristotle and the beginning of logic; the second with the radicalization of the question of truth and the distinction between originary and non-originary truth, which is also the theme of section 44 of *Sein und Zeit*, which reveals the derivative character of the traditional concept of truth defined as *adaequatio*. It was not there a question of temporality. The lecture course actually delivered follows the original plan up to the second part, which came to be allotted an importance disproportionate in relation to the first (220 pages as opposed to 70). But, more importantly, this second part henceforth came to be given the subtitle: 'Repetition of the analysis of falsehood in relation to its temporality'. How does temporality appear in the context of the analysis of the question of propositional truth which was the object of the part devoted to Aristotle? This is the question that has now to be answered.

At the start of this second part, in section 15 entitled: 'The idea of a phenomenological chronology', Heidegger begins by citing one of Kant's *Reflections* which is also taken up in *Sein und Zeit* and which says this: 'The business of philosophers does not consist in giving rules, but in analysing the covert judgments of common reason.'[38] For Heidegger, this means that philosophy's concern consists in bringing to light the comportments which are the foundation of the everyday existence. It is in this sense that he understands the Kantian analytic: not only as the decomposition of something into its elements according to the chemical paradigm of analysis, but as the returning of something to its birthplace. The Greek term *analyô* – as Heidegger will recall much later in the *Zollikoner Seminars*, during the session of November 1965 – appears for the first time in Homer, in the second book of the *Odyssey*, to name what Penelope does at night when she undoes her day's weaving. It means to untie in the sense of setting free.[39] It is thus necessary to understand analysis as the bringing to light of the genesis of a phenomenon, the bringing to the fore of the ultimate conditions of possibility of the given. It is in this sense that Heidegger himself will speak of 'existential analysis' in *Sein und Zeit*.

Now, what constitutes the result of propositional analysis is not, as traditional logic will want (it being founded *after* rather than derivating *from* Aristotle), the idea that the proposition is the place of truth and that truth exists only in the enunciation and not in things; but, on the contrary, the idea that 'truth is the locus of proposition.'[40] Truth is no longer understood as a quality of judgement, but as a dimension of Being itself. Enunciation, which does not necessarily have the form of a judgement, thus adds nothing to what it uncovers, but simply *presents* it, makes it present. Being is thus the coming to presence of that which can be uncovered (truth) or recovered (falsehood) in a comportment. These are the theses which Heidegger reaches at the end of the first part: 'Being means presence (*Anwesenheit*). Truth means present (*Gegenwart*),' that is, present in the sense of allowing to come up against.[41] *Anwesenheit* and *Gegenwart* are characters of *Präsenz*, of temporal presence, and therefore modes of time, which implies that the analysis of proposition, of *logos apophantikos*, has to orient itself in relation to time, which necessitates a new task, that of allowing the time-character of logical phenomena to appear. Aristotle himself does not question the meaning of this identity of Being and truth, which he nonetheless brings to light; he sees, in other words, neither the temporal character of the presentation of what is enunciated, nor the temporal character of the determination of Being as presence. This is precisely why it is necessary to radicalize the question of truth by revealing its genesis in temporality.

Hence the project of a 'phenomenological chronology' which would constitute the analytic (as already strictly defined) whose task would be to let appear the temporal structure of phenomena. Heidegger uses here the Latin term *temporal*, and not the Germanic *zeitlich*, which he instead reserved to designate that which takes place itself 'in' time. For it is in no way a question, for Heidegger, of putting truth or Being 'into' time – which would be to fall back into the psychologism which has, once for all, been criticized by Husserl, who had strictly distinguished the timeless contents from the act of judgement taking place in time – but the question is, rather, of letting appear an understanding of the relation which truth and Being have to time.[42] Thus, it is there a question of proposing the task for philosophy as an inquiry or research revolving around time itself (*Erforschung der Zeit selbst*).

It is, therefore, within the framework of such an inquiry, of an analytic and genetic type of undertaking to which Heidegger here gives the name of 'phenomenological chronology', that the reading of the *Critique of Pure Reason*– a work whose exceptional character in comparison to all other philosophical conceptions of time has already been underlined – is carried out. What Heidegger here calls temporarily 'phenomenological chronology' must be thought of not in terms of a foundation of a new philosophical discipline which could be added to those already in existence, but as the redefinition of the entirety of the philosophical task, insofar as this task has remained, up until the present day, greatly uncertain in its employment of the determinations of time. In this respect, Heidegger, in section 6 of *Sein und Zeit*, underlines the surprising fact that the ontological function ascribed to time, its serving as a way of distinguishing different regions of Being, has not until now been questioned. The temporal, Heidegger recalls, is thus opposed to the timeless, that is to say, the spatial as the intrinsically non-temporal, to the atemporal, that is, the ideal as that which is without relation to time, and to the supratemporal, to that which is beyond time, to the eternal; as if all these distinctions were evident.

In which sense does this phenomenological chronology thus necessitate a background discussion with Kant? This is the last question to be answered. The task of phenomenological chronology should consist in the investigation of the *Temporalität* of phenomena, that is to say, not of their being-in-time, but of the fact that they are characterized by time and have thereby a temporal nature,[43] which is a question, as Heidegger subsequently makes clear, of considering time as no longer operating as a framework, but as a structure. This would necessary imply that a new conception of time be developed in which time should no longer be seen in terms of succession, that is, in other words, no longer situated within the traditional perspective, which, in an essential and unequivocal way, places it in relation to nature. The chronological problematic consists, in this regard, in bringing temporality to the fore not as a trait of the world, by which time would become something subsistent (*vorfindlich*),[44] but as a trait of the comportment of *Dasein* itself. This, nonetheless, in no way would mean a unilateral subjectivization of time. To say, as Heidegger does in 1924 in his lecture on 'The Concept of Time' to the Marburg theologians, that time is *Dasein* itself does not mean placing time 'in' the soul or in the subject, but consists in rendering it as singular as existence itself, in refusing to attribute to it a separate essence, in order, precisely, to think it in a temporal way.[45] It is necessary, as Heidegger emphasizes, if this new definition of time should not become a mere phraseology,[46] to bring to light the contrast between the apparent clarity of the vulgar comprehension of time, that is to say, of that which is the result of the understanding that *Dasein* has of itself in everyday life, and the obscurity of the temporal determinations of the existentials of *Dasein* that Heidegger proposes at this time to call *Temporalien*, 'temporals',[47] in reference to the history of the development of the concept of time. Such a history does not need to be traced in its entirety, but it is enough to confine oneself to the analysis of the crucial moments where the elaboration of the concept of time leads at the same time to attributing it an ontological meaning. The historical landmarks thus followed in the 1925–6 lecture course are the Hegelian interpretation of time (section 20) and the analysis of the influence of Aristotle on Hegel and Bergson (section 21), before coming back to the analysis of the Kantian position in relation to time (sections 22 to 36). As we can see, this synoptic history is finally resumed in *Sein und Zeit* in the long and famous footnote of section 82, where, above all, the names of Hegel, Aristotle and Bergson appear.

What is it, in the last analysis, that, for Heidegger, gives Kant such an exceptional place in the history of the concept of time? The answer, at least formally, is well known: it is in the theory of the Kantian schematism that Heidegger sees an essential approach to the chronological problematic, that is to say, an approach to a conception of time which is no longer that of a simple framework of the appearance of nature and of the objective world. For it is indeed a question of finding, in this 'art concealed in the depths of the human soul'[48] that is the transcendental schematism, the temporality of these comportments of *Dasein* that Kant names, in a language that remains traditional and Cartesian, 'transcendental apperception', 'I think,' that is, acts of understanding and consciousness. But this does not, according to Heidegger, allow us to think, as Hegel in fact does, that the relation established in schematism between understanding and sensibility, the timeless and the temporal, still remains external and not sufficiently 'dialectic'. It is, on the contrary, necessary to question, as Kant does, that which makes possible the determination of time, if this supposes the unification by understanding of the multiplicity of internal sense. Thus, in radicalizing the Kantian problematic, Heidegger does not hesitate to formulate the question through which, according to him, the entire Kantian problematic becomes comprehensible: what is the condition of possibility for a connexion between time in general and the 'I think' in general?[49]

In his theory of the schematism of the pure concepts of understanding, Kant has shown that understanding 'can in no way operate except in being essentially referred to time,'[50] since the mediating representations or schemes which allow the application of categories to appearances are *a priori* determinations of time. Kant has thus sensed, without truly being able to see it, the function assigned to time in all acts of understanding. And, if he was able only to sense it, it was essentially because of his conception of time, which he inherited from the philosophical tradition, in particular from Newton and Leibniz. This tradition goes back to Aristotle, who defined time as physical time, as time of the objective world. As long as one holds to such a conception of time, it remains impossible to see the intrinsic connexion of the acts of consciousness with time. Heidegger wanted to show that the fact that Kant defined time as internal sense in the transcendental aesthetic allowed him to have a presentiment of the intrinsic relation between time and mind. However, this does not mean that the self or subject is temporal in the sense of being 'in' time, but, on the contrary, that time itself has the character of selfhood. As an *a priori* intuition, time constitutes the possibility of seeing 'in advance' what can be received, the *a priori* being in itself a temporal determination and the basis of all possible anticipation of what can be given. It constitutes the capacity of the subject to be affected by external objects. Time has, therefore, to be understood as the originary and universal self-affection on the basis of which something like a self can be made possible. This is what no interpretation of Kant until now has been able to understand, but it is nonetheless what Kant explicitly said, at least in one passage of the transcendental aesthetic, which Heidegger takes as the basis of his own interpretation. In this passage,[51] Kant explains that the pure intuition of time is 'nothing else than the way in which the mind (*das Gemüt*) is affected by its own activity, that is, the position of the representation, therefore by itself, that is, a sense internal in its form'.

As Heidegger emphasizes, this capacity of pure self-affection constitutes the originary transcendental structure of the finite self as such, that is, of a self that has to receive external data. The mind (*das Gemüt*) does not exist before coming into relationship with something, but, on the contrary, this capacity of relating itself to something else constitutes mind as such. This means that time as pure self-affection is not something that can be separated from pure apperception, but already belongs to pure apperception as the ground of the possibility of selfhood. The fact that the 'I think,' as correlate of all our representations, remains the same does not mean that it is 'eternal', that is, without any relation to time, but, on the contrary, that it can remain 'stable' precisely because it is temporal, that is, finite. The 'I think' is not 'in' time, and this can also be said of time itself, which is not 'in' time, as Kant himself explains in the chapter on schematism, when he declares that 'time does not change' and 'remains the same'.[52]

Heidegger's interpretation of Kant's notion of time consists, therefore, in defining time as the root of transcendence itself, that is, of the possibility for the subject of having a relation to the object. But is this interpretation legitimate? Heidegger himself recognized later, in the 1973 foreword to the fourth edition of *Kant and the Problem of Metaphysics*, that in 1929 he had been inclined to go too far in his interpretation and that the problematic of *Sein und Zeit* was the very basis of his reading of the *Critique of Pure Reason*.[53] But, nonetheless, the question of the duality of sensibility and understanding that Heidegger tried to solve in 1929 remains the crucial question, however tentative, for the interpretation of Kant's first Critique.

This question, that of the unity of subjectivity, is also that which post-Kantian idealism had tried to resolve, without interrogating the presuppositions of Kant himself, by continuing in the same, that is to say Cartesian, direction as Kant, and by immediately putting the accent on the 'I think.' Heidegger goes even so far as to say that Hegel's philosophy remains incomprehensible if it is not situated within the horizon of this question of the unity of the sensible and the intelligible, and that the solution he gives to it is *'extremKantisch'*, ultra-Kantian, in so far as it is dialectical.[54] For Heidegger, the question is not of 'going beyond' Kant, but of letting appear that which is not elaborated in Kant's position, in other words, of extracting the 'phenomenological core' of his thinking from the Cartesian dogma which still covers it. It is, therefore, not surprising to find here a reference to the old method of Socratic maieutics: to render Kant to Kant, delivering him from his traditional and Cartesian shackles, is 'in some way to help him have an easy birth (*ihm zur rechten Geburt helfen*)'in coming ahead of him in dialogue.[55]

Such a dialogue which comes ahead of the one with whom one talks in order to help him be himself is, it has to be noticed, exactly what Heidegger calls *vorausspringende Fürsorge*, anticipatory concern or solicitude, which gives back to the other its own care and which thereby opposes an *einspringende Fürsorge*, a solicitude which substitutes itself for the other and in its place takes charge of its care.[56] The relation to the history of thought and to the thinkers of the past is thus similar to that which ties us to the other *Dasein*, and singularly to the *Dasein* of our contemporaries. One doubtless has there the sketch for a wholly other practice of interpretation than that which attaches itself only to the words of a thinker. It is necessary, says Heidegger, to refer ourselves in phenomenological interpretation to what 'Kant must implicitly have had in view',[57] which does not mean reading the words of the thinker as complete, as purely subsisting, and thus detaching them from the comportment of which they are the expression. This, in the last analysis, implies that the chronological problematic in the widest sense cannot solely be constitutive of the object of thought, of that which is thematically meant, but must also have an effect on the way in which one proceeds in philosophy. To 'chronologize' thinking, if I may be allowed this barbaric expression, or, more simply, to conceive of thought as chrono-logy, that is, as a *logos* which includes its own operation in the very 'object' that it deals with and which thinks its own temporaliza- tion instead of attaching itself only to its result, this doubtless is the path that it would be worth following. Such a method would permit us to reach the idea not of a 'subjectivization' of time, whether this be thought in the context of an absolute subjectivity of the Hegelian or Husserlian type, but of this strange 'identity' of *Dasein* and time, the presentiment of which Heidegger found in the Kantian schematism.

Time, space and body in Bergson, Heidegger

Notes

Second and augmented version of the paper by F. Dastur (1996) 'L'idée d'une "chronologie phénoménologique" et la première interprétation de Kant', in J.F. Courtine (ed.) *Heidegger 1919-1929: De l'herméneutique de la facticité à la métaphy- sique du Dasein*(Paris: Vrin), pp. 113–29.

1. Cf. M. Heidegger (1988) *The Basic Problems of Phenomenology*, trans. A. Hofstadter (Bloomington: Indiana University Press), pp. 27–76; (1975) *DieGrundprobleme der Phänomenologie* (Frankfurt am Main: Klostermann), GA 24, pp. 35–107.
2. M. Heidegger (1977) *Phänomenologische Interpretation von Kants Kritik der reinen Vernunft* (Frankfurt am Main: Klostermann), GA 25, pp. 434–5.
3. M. Heidegger (1982) *Vom Wesen der menschlichen Freiheit* (Frankfurt am Main: Klostermann), GA 31.
4. As the dedication to Husserl testifies, *Sein und Zeit*, published in February 1927, was finished in April 1926.
5. Cf. M. Heidegger (1976) *Logik, Die Frage nach der Wahrheit* (Frankfurt am Main: Klostermann), GA 21, sections 22–36, pp. 269–409.
6. Ibid., p. 417.
7. See again the remarks of the editor of GA 25, p. 435.
8. Cf. M. Heidegger (1990) *Kant and the Problem of Metaphysics* (Bloomington: Indiana University Press), sections 20–3, pp. 60–78; (1973) *Kant und das Problem der Metaphysik* (Frankfurt am Main: Klostermann), pp. 89–110.
9. Cf. GA 21, section 5, p. 21.
10. Cf. M. Heidegger (1972) *On Time and Being* (New York: Harper), p. 74; 'Mein Weg in die Phänomenologie', in M. Heidegger (1969) *Zur Sache des Denkens* (Tübingen: Niemeyer), p. 81.
11. Cf. M. Heidegger (1987) *Frühe Schriften* (Frankfurt am Main: Klostermann), pp. 3 and 5.
12. M. Heidegger (1987) *Zur Bestimmung der Philosophie* (Frankfurt am Main: Klostermann), GA 56/57, p. 140 ff.
13. Ibid., p. 180.
14. M. Heidegger (1992) *History of the Concept of Time: Prolegomena*, trans. Th. Kisiel (Bloomington: Indiana University Press), p. 17; (1979) *Prolegomena zur Geschichte des Zeitegriffs* (Frankfurt am Main: Klostermann), GA 20, p. 20.
15. Ibid., p. 35 (45–6).

16. Cf. M. Heidegger, *Kant and the Problem of Metaphysics*, Appendix II, 'The Davos Disputation between Ernst Cassirer and Martin Heidegger', p. 172; *Kant und das Problem der Metaphysik*, p. 247.
17. Ibid.
18. GA 21, p. 200.
19. M. Heidegger (1996) *Being and Time*, trans. J. Stambaugh (Albany: Suny Press), section 6, p. 20; (1927) *Sein und Zeit* (Tübingen: Niemeyer), p. 23.
20. I. Kant (1992) *Critique of Pure Reason*, trans. N.K. Smith (London: Palgrave Macmillan), p. 32; KRV, B XXXV).
21. GA 21, p. 201.
22. Ibid., p. 267.
23. Ibid., p. 269.
24. Cf. M. Heidegger (1992) 'Letter on Humanism', in D.F. Krell (ed.) *Basic Writings* (San Francisco: Harper), p. 246.
25. GA 21, pp. 273–4.
26. Ibid., p. 279.
27. Ibid.
28. Ibid., p. 280.
29. See the end of the Introduction to the *Phenomenology of Spirit*, where Hegel speaks of the conversion of consciousness into spirit, which allows it, so to speak, to have a look at what happens behind its back.
30. GA 21, p. 278.
31. CPR, pp. 61–2 ; KRV, A 15/B 29.
32. GA 21, p. 282.
33. Ibid., p. 271. Heidegger himself acknowledges the violence that is inherent to all interpretation as such in *Kant und das Problem der Metaphysik*(section 35, p. 196).
34. *Kant and the Problem of Metaphysics*, p. 30; *Kant und das Problem der Metaphysik*, section 9, p. 42.
35. GA 21, p. 272. On the Marburg School, see also GA 25, pp. 78–9.
36. CPR, p. 77; KRV, A 34/ B50.
37. GA 21, section 5, p. 26.
38. *Sein und Zeit*, section 1, p. 4.
39. M. Heidegger (1987) *Zollikoner Seminare* (Frankfurt am Main: Klostermann), p. 148.
40. GA 21, p. 135.
41. Ibid., p. 199.
42. Ibid.
43. Ibid.
44. Ibid., p. 204.
45. Cf. M. Heidegger (1989) *Der Begriff der Zeit* (Tübingen: Niemeyer), p. 26, where Heidegger declares that '*Die* Zeit ist sinnlos; Zeit ist zeitlich' ('*The* time is devoid of meaning, time is temporal').
46. GA 21, p. 205.
47. Ibid., p. 243.
48. KRV A 141/B 180.
49. GA 21, p. 309.
50. GA 25, p. 430.
51. CPR B 67.

52. Ibid., A 143, B 183.
53. *Kant und das Problem der Metaphysik* (Klostermann: Frankfurt am Main, 1973), p. XIV.
54. GA 21, p. 311.
55. Ibid., p. 313.
56. Sein und Zeit, section 26, p. 122.
57. GA 21, p. 313.

References

Dastur, F. (1996) 'L'idée d'une "chronologie phénoménologique" et la première interprétation de Kant', in J.F. Courtine (ed.) *Heidegger 1919-1929: De l'herméneutique de la facticité à la métaphysique du Dasein*(Paris: Vrin), pp. 113–29.

Heidegger, M. (1969) *Zur Sache des Denkens* (Tübingen: Niemeyer).

Heidegger, M.(1972) *On Time and Being* (New York: Harper).

Heidegger, M.(1976) *Logik, Die Frage nach der Wahrheit* (Frankfurt am Main: Klostermann), GA 21.

Heidegger, M.(1977) *Phänomenologische Interpretation von Kants Kritik der reinen Vernunft* (Klostermann: Frankfurt am Main), GA 25.

Heidegger, M.(1982) *Vom Wesen der menschlichen Freiheit* (Frankfurt am Main: Klostermann), GA 31.

Heidegger, M.(1987) *Frühe Schriften* (Frankfurt am Main: Klostermann).

Heidegger, M.(1987) *Zur Bestimmung der Philosophie* (Frankfurt am Main: Klostermann), GA 56/57.

Heidegger, M.(1987) *Zollikoner Seminare* (Frankfurt am Main: Klostermann).

Heidegger, M.(1988) *The Basic Problems of Phenomenology*, trans. A. Hofstadter (Bloomington: Indiana University Press); (1975) *DieGrundprobleme der Phänomenologie* (Frankfurt am Main: Klostermann), GA 24.

Heidegger, M.(1989) *Der Begriff der Zeit* (Tübingen: Niemeyer).

Heidegger, M.(1990) *Kant and the Problem of Metaphysics* (Bloomington: Indiana University Press); (1973) *Kant und das Problem der Metaphysik* (Frankfurt am Main: Klostermann).

Heidegger, M.(1992) *History of the Concept of Time: Prolegomena*, trans. Th. Kisiel (Bloomington: Indiana University Press), p. 17; (1979) *Prolegomena zur Geschichte des Zeitegriffs* (Frankfurt am Main: Klostermann), GA 20.

Heidegger, M.(1992) 'Letter on Humanism', in D.F. Krell (ed.) *Basic Writings* (San Francisco: Harper).

Heidegger, M.(1996) *Being and Time*, trans. J. Stambaugh (Albany: Suny Press); (1927) *Sein und Zeit* (Tübingen: Niemeyer).

Kant, I. (1992) *Critique of Pure Reason*, trans. N.K. Smith (London: Palgrave Macmillan).

13
Time, Space and Body in Bergson, Heidegger and Husserl

Dan Zahavi and Søren Overgaard

> In so far as I have a body through which I act in the world,
> space and time are not, for me, a collection of adjacent points
> nor are they a limitless number of relations synthesized by my
> consciousness, and into which it draws my body. I am not in
> space and time, nor do I conceive space and time; I belong to
> them, my body combines with them and includes them.
>
> (Merleau-Ponty)

In *Time and Free Will*, Bergson maintains that there is a radical difference between space and time. On his account, any attempt to spatialize
the stream of consciousness, any attempt to conceive of the temporality that is distinctive of consciousness in spatial terms, would lead to a
complete distortion of its proper character. Bergson's argument, however, relies not only on a particular understanding of time, but also on
a particular understanding of space. From a phenomenological point of
view, as we will argue, Bergson's conception of space – space understood
as a homogeneous medium – is questionable.

In sections 22–4 of Heidegger's *Being and Time* we find a phenomenologically more adequate conception of space. Heidegger's phenomenological account of space as it is disclosed in everyday experience
removes Bergson's principal argument for upholding a strict dichotomy
of space and time. Interestingly, however, Heidegger argues that the spatiality of the things at hand is conditioned by the spatiality of *Dasein*'s
being-in-the-world and that the latter must ultimately be grounded in
Dasein's temporality. In *Being and Time*, Heidegger consequently priori-
tized time (or temporality) over space (though obviously in a somewhat
different manner than Kant).

We suggest that this move is related to Heidegger's remarkable silence regarding the role of embodiment. If human embodiment were a fundamental feature of our being-in-the-world, then we would have a straightforward way of understanding the latter as spatial. But, because Heidegger is unwilling to make room for embodiment at the level of *Dasein*'s being-in-the-world, he has little choice but to view spatiality as something founded on the latter and, hence, ultimately founded on temporality.

In the final part of our chapter, we will briefly turn to Husserl in order to suggest that he (anticipating ideas in later French phenomenology) opts for an account that, in contrast to both Bergson and Heidegger, regards temporalization and spatialization as equiprimordial and interdependent.

13.1   Bergson on time and space

In his 1889 doctoral dissertation *Time and Free Will. An Essay on the Immediate Data of Consciousness*, Bergson articulates and defends a conception of time and space that sees them as radically opposed. On a common understanding, time and space are both homogeneous media. The main difference is whether their contents coexist or follow one another. On such an understanding, time can be viewed as a kind of line, and, if we try to visualize our stream of consciousness, we frequently think of it as consisting of a temporal sequence of conscious states, ranged alongside one another so as to form a discrete multiplicity. This multiplicity will be very akin to the multiplicity of spatial objects. Spatial objects are also perceived as distinct, isolated entities, externally related to one another. But time understood in such a fashion is, for Bergson, something utterly distinct from and alien to the lived time that is unique to and distinctive of consciousness, and which he terms *true* or *pure duration.*[1] Indeed, time conceived of as a homogeneous medium in which our conscious states are spread out so as to form a series composed of separate and distinct elements that stand in external relations to one another, like wagons in train, is for Bergson a spurious conception, one due to the transposition of the idea of space into the field of consciousness.[2] To think of time as a line presupposes a view from above, a view that, so to speak, takes it in all at once, but this merely reveals that simultaneity, and thereby spatiality, pervades such a conception of time. In fact, for Bergson, this conception of time basically betrays what is essential to time in favour of space.[3]

If, through a vigorous effort, we manage to isolate consciousness from the external world in order to intuit its true character, we will, according to Bergson, soon realize that true duration has nothing in common with space.[4] It is not quantifiable, and the moment we treat it as such and try to measure it we will do violence to it.[5] Indeed, in pure duration, conscious states are not distinct, but united. They are characterized by a dynamical self-organization, where they melt into and permeate one another without precise outlines. In fact, on this level, there is no real difference between the persistence of one state and the transition to another state. They intermingle in such a way that we cannot tell whether they are one or several. We cannot examine or approach them from this point of view at all without altering and distorting them.[6] To isolate one conscious state is consequently not like detaching one independent element from another, but rather like tearing off a fragment of material from a whole that is thereby left in tatters. Thus, rather than likening two conscious states to two wagons in the same train, it might be more appropriate to liken them to two waves in the same stream.

In reality, consciousness is nothing jointed; it simply flows. Rather than being a quantitative succession of separate bits, the stream of consciousness is a qualitative continuity without distinctions, where the different states are characterized by mutual penetration and interconnection.[7] However, unwittingly we will start to introduce spatial notions and categories into our understanding of experiential life. The distinctions we find among objects in the external world will be transposed and introjected into subjectivity. In this sense there will be an exchange between the inner and the outer.[8] To illustrate the problem at hand, Bergson asks us to consider the oscillations of a pendulum:

> As the successive phases of our conscious life, although interpenetrating, correspond individually to an oscillation of the pendulum which occurs at the same time, and as, moreover, these oscillations are sharply distinguished from one another, we get into the habit of setting up the same distinction between the successive moments of our conscious life: the oscillations of the pendulum break it up, so to speak, into parts external to one another: hence the mistaken idea of a homogenous inner duration, similar to space, the moments of which are identical and follow, without interpenetrating one another.[9]

A central tenet in Bergson's analysis is, consequently, that our conscious states reveal themselves in two radically different ways depending on whether we perceive them directly or through spatial forms derived from the external world. Bergson argues that the spatial forms distort and conceal the real structures of consciousness, and that our philosophical task is to do away with the forms in question in order to allow a disclosure of the true and ordinarily hidden nature of consciousness.

We need, according to Bergson, to distinguish two ways of regarding conscious life: a superficial and a more profound. To a superficial inspection, consciousness consists of a sequence of distinct conscious states. To a more profound investigation, consciousness reveals itself as qualitative continuity of mutually permeating states that form an organic whole.[10] Occasionally, however, Bergson also seems to suggest that there are superficial and more profound conscious states. The superficial states are those through which the ego is in touch with the spatial world, that is, states like perception or sensation, and, since they tend to acquire and take on the structures of that which they are about, they can to some extent be described in terms of spatial structures. But, as for the profound levels of consciousness, they cannot be quantified in any way whatsoever without altering their character drastically.[11] We are here dealing with structures so unique that they cannot be grasped by means of language or through any form of intellectual cognition. Reason can isolate, immobilize and spatialize the flow of lived experiences and thereby make them accessible to verbal description and analytic reflection. But the true life of consciousness cannot be caught in our conceptual network. It will always overflow our artificial demarcations and distinctions. Language as a whole makes us operate with sharp and precise distinctions, thereby imposing the same kind of discontinuities between our experiential episodes as exist between material objects.[12] But as soon as we introduce clear-cut distinctions, as soon as we isolate and identify a conscious state, we distort the processual character of our experiential life. Indeed, as Bergson writes, all that language is able to capture are lifeless shadows.[13]

Why are we constantly tempted into introducing distinctions taken from the external world into our inner life, thereby replacing the interpenetration of a constantly changing qualitative multiplicity for a fixed set of numerically distinct states?[14] As Bergson repeatedly asserts, when consciousness is broken into pieces that easily lend themselves to verbal expressions, it is far better geared and adapted to the requirements of *social life*. Given these demands, the self has everything to gain by assuming a form of self-forgetfulness.[15] Or, to be more precise, through socialization and language acquisition a second self is formed, one that Bergson in turn characterizes as a colourless shadow, as superficial and parasitic, and one that by necessity will obscure the deep-seated self.[16] As he writes,

> We generally perceive our own self by refraction through space, our conscious states crystallize into words and our living and concrete self thus gets covered by an outer crust of clean-cut psychic states which are separate from one another and consequently fixed. For the convenience of language and the promotion of social relations we have everything to gain by not breaking through this crust and by assuming it to give an exact outline of the form of the object it covers.[17]

As time goes by – if such a phrase is permitted – the link to the external world is increasingly solidified, and, as a result, our conscious states are not only broken off from one another and made into objects, they also break off from ourselves, that is, become alienated fragments.[18] Thus, on Bergson's account, we would be in a much better position to attain a correct self-understanding if each of us lived a purely individual life with no interference from society or language – though even in such a condition we would have difficulties escaping the entrapment of spatial thinking, given its insidious nature and our constant interaction with the external world.[19]

Although Bergson sought to overcome dualisms in his later works, in his doctoral dissertation he did operate with an absolute opposition and separation between inner and outer, between time and space, quality and quantity, freedom and determinism. The absence of a proper account of the body is also striking. Not only is there no reference to the body in Bergson's description of the inner world of the true self, but his account of pure duration also lacks any consideration of the role of embodiment.

There is much in Bergson's analysis that calls out for critical assessment. For one thing, the project he is engaged in seems confronted with severe methodological problems.[20] In this context, however, we will simply focus on his claim regarding the radical difference between space and time and on his insistence that a spatialization of consciousness amounts to a complete deformation of its proper character and structure. It is evident that his argumentation relies not only on a rather specific understanding of time, but also on a specific understanding of space. Bergson criticizes the idea that time is a homogeneous medium, but assumes without much ado that space is such a medium. But is that claim warranted? Let us move on to Heidegger and examine his reply.

13.2   Heidegger on space and temporality

Heidegger's analysis of space has its systematic location within his analysis of *Dasein*'s being-in-the-world. More specifically, Heidegger addresses the issue of space in the context of his analysis of one of being-in-the-world's three structural moments, namely, world (the other two constitutive moments being the *entity* that is in the world and the phenomenon of *being-in* as such). Heidegger rejects the claim that the world is to be primarily understood as the sum or totality of all objects. The world, understood in a phenomenological fundamental way, is the familiar context of meaning and signification that *Dasein* inhabits. World is consequently understood as an existential. It is a moment of *Dasein*'s ontological structure, a moment of *Dasein*'s mode of existence, and not a determination of entities that are present in the world. Only *Dasein* is characterized by being-in-the-world – only *Dasein* *has* a world, as we might put it. Other types of entities, by contrast, are 'within-the-world' or 'belong to the world', but the world is not 'there' for them; they have no world.[21]

In section 22 of *Being and Time* Heidegger raises a question regarding the spatiality of entities within-the-world. Not surprisingly, he is at first interested in the spatiality of the ready-to-hand, since his point of departure is the kind of entities that we first and foremost encounter. As Heidegger points out, the expression 'proximally and for the most part' (*zunächst und zumeist*) doesn't merely have a temporal but also a spatial connotation. That which we first and foremost encounter is that which is nearby. Given Heidegger's well-known rejection of the ontological primacy of the present-at-hand, nearness is not to be interpreted in geometrical terms, which apply to present-at-hand items. The spatiality of the ready-to-hand is manifest in our practical dealings with them, rather than in any detached observation or measurement of space. The ready-to-hand is nearby if it is *accessible* and *utilizable*. More specifically, the specific spatiality of the ready-to-hand, its place, is a question of its embeddedness in a specific context of use, where it belongs and has its functionality, and not a question of its physical location in a three-dimensional space. It is only within a pragmatic context that the utensil has significance, relevance and usability. Single pieces of equipment can never stand alone, but are always enmeshed in a network of references to other pieces of equipment. A hammer, for example, is a hammer only in the context of other equipment such as nails and boards. When we ask *where* something is, our question concerns this network. The spatial dimensions – above, beneath, next to, and so on– have such practical and concrete references.

Space, then, is primarily given to us in our non-thematic familiarity with the ready-to-hand. Space is a feature of the ready-to-hand, and not an empty container which can subsequently be filled with objects. It is only when our practical dealings are disturbed that we notice mere space; it is only when the flashlight is not there that we fully notice the drawer as a container.

Heidegger concludes section 22 by remarking that the ready-to-hand can only be encountered 'in its environmental space [...] because Dasein itself is "spatial" with regard to its Being-in-the-world'.[22] How is this statement to be interpreted? According to Heidegger, the spatiality of the ready-to-hand is a feature of its embeddedness in a worldly context of significance. But 'worldhood' can only be understood via an analysis of the being-in-the-world of *Dasein*. For this reason, an analysis of the spatiality of the ready-to-hand must necessarily include an analysis of the spatiality of *Dasein*.

In section 12 of *Being and Time*, Heidegger emphasizes the need to distinguish sharply between the *existential* 'Being-in' (*In-sein*) of *Dasein* and the *categorial* 'being in' (*Sein in*) of things. *Dasein* is not in the world in the same way that water is in a glass or a t-shirt is in a drawer. But the fact that the categorial spatiality of 'being-contained-within' does not apply to *Dasein*– which never simply occurs in space, but is always involved with its surroundings in some particular manner – does not mean that Heidegger thinks there is no sense in which spatiality belongs to *Dasein*.[23]

Heidegger continues this line of thought in section 23. Dasein is not something that is encountered 'within-the-world', and its spatiality must be understood in terms of *Dasein*'s being-in-the-world. What would a proper articulation of *Dasein*'s spatiality draw attention to? Heidegger focuses on two aspects in particular: 'directionality' (*Ausrichtung*) and 'de-severance' (*Ent-fernung*).[24] With respect to the former, Heidegger points out that *Dasein*'s being-in-the-world always has a certain direct-edness (perspective, interest). Our concernful dealings with the world are never completely disoriented. Or, rather, to the extent that a tempo-rary disorientation is a possibility, this is because *Dasein* is as such char-acterized by orientation and directedness. It is due to this character of *Dasein* that entities encountered within-the-world present themselves in perspectives and orientations: as something that is accessible in a particular direction; as something that is above or below, to the left or to the right, here or there.

Heidegger's choice of the second expression –'de-severance'– is an attempt to invoke the meanings of the two German words *Entfernung* (distance) and *entfernen* (to remove or take away). When he writes that *Dasein*'s being-in-the-world is characterized by de-severance, this should be understood to imply that *Dasein* removes distance in the sense in which you 'remove' the distance between you and your car as you approach it. That is, *Dasein* lets entities be *present* or *close*. This happens in practical dealings as well as in theoretical research. Heidegger writes that *'In Dasein there lies an essential tendency towards closeness'.*[25] But the closest is not necessarily that which is at the shortest 'objective' distance from *Dasein*. Rather, it is that which *Dasein* is concerned with, can reach out for, catch hold of, or see. To bring something closer is to involve it in the context of concernful dealings and use. Let us give a few concrete examples:

(1) Whereas, geometrically, I am closer to the ground on which I am standing, or the spectacles I am wearing, than to the painting I am looking at, a phenomenological description will claim that I am closer to the painting than to the ground or my spectacles.[26]

(2) Geometrically, the distance between Copenhagen and New Delhi is the same as it was 100 years ago.[27] Pragmatically, however, the distance has been reduced dramatically – at least for those of us who can afford the flight.

(3) When choosing one of two ways to achieve a certain goal, it is not always the geometrically shortest way that is pragmatically closest to the goal. If you have forgotten to bring your keys, and you are standing outside your locked front door, the geometrical closeness of the entrance hall does not prevent it from being pragmatically out of reach and hence remote. The moment you turn away from the front door and head for the unlocked back door, you are moving away from the entrance hall in geometrical terms, but moving closer in pragmatic terms: 'The Objective distances of Things present-at-hand do not coincide with the remoteness and closeness of what is ready-to-hand within-the-world'.[28]

(4) A town that is ten miles away may be within easy reach of a bicycle ride if the roads are good and the itinerary flat. As such, the town may be considerably closer than a rocky mountaintop a couple of miles away. 'A pathway which is long "Objectively" can be much shorter than one which is "Objectively" shorter still but which is perhaps "hard going" and comes before us as interminably long.'[29] In other words, measurements can be as exact as you like, without thereby

being relevant and useful when it comes to determining genuine spatiality as manifested in our experiences and pragmatic dealings.[30]

Heidegger's analysis has revealed two very different conceptions of space. On the one hand, there is the exact, three-dimensional space of Euclidean geometry. On the other hand, there is space as it unfolds in *Dasein*'s practical dealings with ready-to-hand entities. One might be tempted to suggest that geometric measurement gives us a neutral and objective description of space as it really is – space as it is *an sich*– whereas the conception of space that relies on criteria such as the ease and speed of access is subjectivist or, at best, anthropocentric. Heidegger, however, resists this suggestion. He maintains that it is precisely because space is accessible to us in a pragmatic context that it can be made the object of detached, scientific knowledge. In our concernful dealings with ready-to-hand entities, a need for more exact measurements may sometimes arise, for example, in the construction of buildings or bridges, or in the surveying of land. If one goes on to abstract completely from pragmatic interests, then space can become the object of mere observation and theorizing.[31] Unsurprisingly, however, Heidegger claims that such an exclusive focus on the geometry of space involves a neutralization of the originally given, pragmatically significant space. As Heidegger puts it, space becomes *'deprived of its worldhood'*.[32] The spatiality of the concrete context of concernful dealings is transformed into a pure dimensionality. Thereby the ready-to-hand entities lose their peculiar referential character, and the world is reduced from being a significant totality of equipment to being a conglomerate of extended things.

Therefore, the claim that 'objective', physical space is more fundamental than pragmatic space is the expression of certain metaphysical presuppositions. Moreover, Heidegger rejects the notion of a clear-cut division between an *an sich* reality and a subjective interpretation of it. As he writes in section 23, 'the Reality of the world at its most Real' is the reality as it is uncovered in *Dasein*'s being-in-the-world.[33] For the same reason, Heidegger distances himself from the Kantian conception of space as a subjective form of intuition:

> *Space is not in the subject, nor is the world in space.* Space is rather 'in' the world in so far as space has been disclosed by that Being-in-the-world which is constitutive for Dasein. Space is not to be found in the subject, nor does the subject observe the world 'as if' that world were in space; but the 'subject' (Dasein), if well understood ontologically, is spatial. And because Dasein is spatial in the way we have described,

space shows itself as *a priori*. This term does not mean anything like previously belonging to a subject which is proximally still world-less and which emits a space out of itself. Here *'apriority'* means the previousness with which space has been encountered (as a region) whenever the ready-to-hand is encountered environmentally.[34]

So far, Heidegger has offered a phenomenological corrective to the Bergsonian analysis of space, which we regard as, by and large, successful. As Heidegger shows, space is not simply the homogeneous medium Bergson thought it was. Towards the end of section 24, however, Heidegger suddenly seems to hesitate. He inquires which manner of being belongs to space, and replies that its being is neither that of the present-at-hand, nor that of the ready-to-hand, nor is it the being of *Dasein* itself. What, then, is its manner of being? Heidegger postpones his answer to this question, remarking that the analysis of space must remain incomplete until we have an adequate overview of the various types of being.[35] One might get the impression that Heidegger considers it possible that space may have its own unique and irreducible manner of being. Later in *Being and Time*, however, Heidegger returns to the question concerning the being of space – and this time he has a definitive answer. In section 70 – that is, within the framework of Heidegger's temporal reinterpretation of the analyses of fundamental ontology – he asks whether space does not constitute a limit to this temporal reinterpretation. Must we not accept that time and space are both equally fundamental characterizations of *Dasein*? Not according to Heidegger. Temporality is what makes possible *Dasein*'s being-in-the-world,[36] and so the latter must be understood on the basis of temporality. This also holds for the spatiality of *Dasein*: 'Dasein's specific spatiality must be grounded in temporality.'[37] Heidegger elaborates:

> Because Dasein as temporality is ecstatico-horizonal [*ekstatisch-horizontal*] in its Being, it can take along with it a space for which it has made room, and it can do so factically and constantly. [...] *Only on the basis of its ecstatico-horizonal temporality is it possible for Dasein to break into space.*[38]

This result ought not to surprise us. For it seems a natural outcome of Heidegger's analysis. First, he interprets the spatiality of equipment as based upon its being disclosed within-the-world. Next, this disclosedness within-the-world is characterized as an embeddedness in a context of pragmatic referentiality and significance. For Heidegger, this context of significance is made possible by *Dasein*'s existential structure. And this existential structure, in turn, is precisely what, in the second division of *Being and Time*, has to be reinterpreted in temporal terms. Thus, Heidegger's foundational story is this ('→' = 'founds'): Temporality → the existential structure of *Dasein* (care, being-in-the-world) → world → space. Clearly, then, Heidegger's answer to the traditional question whether time and space are on an equal footing, or whether one of them is more fundamental than the other, is unambiguous. In *Being and Time*, temporality is considered *the* most fundamental transcendental condition for the being of *Dasein*, and thereby for the world and space as well.

One might question whether there is any reason to consider this conclusion problematic. Perhaps Heidegger is simply right to emphasize time or temporality at the expense of space? Somewhat surprisingly, however, this is not the conclusion that Heidegger himself would finally reach. In his 1962 lecture 'Time and Being', he states: 'The attempt in *Being and Time*, Section 70, to derive human spatiality from temporality is untenable.'[39] Why would Heidegger retract the analysis of *Being and Time* on this crucial point? There are probably a number of different factors in play here. One reason, surely, has to do with Heidegger's famous 'turn' (*Kehre*) and the associated abandonment of the very attempt to offer a transcendental, foundational hierarchy.

Another reason might be that the idea that spatiality might be derived from temporality is very implausible. Bergson, surely, is right to warn against our tendency to grasp time in spatial terms. Spatial images (such as the flowing river) are just that: *images*; and if we take them literally we will be led astray. But it seems equally problematic to attempt to understand space in temporal terms. Our pragmatic spatial notions of 'here' and 'there' can hardly be adequately understood on the model of 'now' and 'then' (or any other pair of temporal notions). Just think of collaborative activities, in which it is often essential that several different things are done in different places but at the same time. It is important that you finish what you are doing over there at the same time as I finish what I am doing here, because I will need to attach your bit to my bit before the work can move on, and so forth. One does not need to adopt the questionable Bergsonian view that space is pure, measurable extension for it to seem highly implausible that spatiality can be made sense of in purely temporal terms.

But, if it is fairly obvious that such an account is implausible, then why does Heidegger nevertheless attempt to defend it in *Being and Time*? In the next section, we suggest that the answer to this question is intimately connected with a spectacular lacuna in Heidegger's thinking: the body.

13.3   Heidegger on the body

Earlier, when we discussed *Dasein*'s spatiality, and in particular the spatiality connected with *Dasein*'s pragmatic dealings with equipment, our discussion constantly presupposed something that we did not explicitly thematize: namely, that *Dasein* is *embodied*. There is, however, only one place in *Being and Time* where Heidegger explicitly mentions the body. This is in section 23, where Heidegger states that the spatiality of *Dasein* is connected with its 'bodily nature' (*Leiblichkeit*). He goes on to add, however, that the body 'hides a whole problematic of its own' that he will not address.[40] This silence on the body is remarkable, in particular considering how Heidegger's terminology – for example, the distinction between the ready-to-*hand* and the present-at-*hand*– draws constant attention to the fact that *Dasein* is embodied (e.g., has hands). And not only that: as already indicated, our previous discussion of Heidegger's account of the concernful disclosure of space has, in a sense, been all about the body. The closeness or remoteness of some place or entity has to do with its availability for use, the ease (or otherwise) with which it may be reached, and so on. All of this surely refers us to the working, grasping, walking – in short, embodied – subject.

It might be objected that it is simply obvious or self-evident that *Dasein* is embodied, and that an explicit analysis therefore is superfluous. After all, it does seem possible for Heidegger to offer analyses of space and of being-in-the-world without explicitly discussing the body. Indeed, it might be held that such explicit discussion ought to be avoided, as it might lead to a blurring of the distinction between the fundamental ontology of *Dasein* and a more anthropological or even biological analysis of the human being – and hence to a fatal misunderstanding of the former.

But surely these replies are too facile. As Heidegger himself emphasizes in the first section of *Being and Time*, in philosophy it is 'a dubious procedure to invoke self-evidence'.[41] And later, in criticism of Kant, he maintains that if a 'state of Dasein's Being is an obvious one, we are not thereby justified in suppressing the ontologically constitutive role which it plays'.[42] The very same criticism, it seems, could be directed against Heidegger himself for his refusal to elucidate *Dasein*'s embodiment.[43] This would particularly be the case if it turned out to be *Dasein*'s 'bodily nature' that makes impossible a temporal interpretation of space.[44] In addition, it can hardly be doubted that the analysis of *Dasein* as well as the phenomenological analysis of space become crucially enriched the moment an in-depth consideration of the body is included.

Our discussion so far has been limited to Heidegger's position in *Being and Time*. It is worth noting, however, that Heidegger does offer somewhat more extensive remarks on the body and embodiment elsewhere in his *oeuvre*. Of particular interest are two texts, the first of which is a lecture course pre-dating *Being and Time*. In this little-known text, Heidegger broaches the topic of embodiment in the context of a discussion of Aristotle's account of passions or emotions (*páthe*). Briefly put, Heidegger argues that a *páthos* is something that 'carries Dasein away',[45] and that this phenomenon of being carried away is misunderstood if taken to involve only a part of *Dasein*, such as its mind or soul.[46] As he puts it, 'Strictly speaking, I cannot say: the soul hopes, fears, feels compassion; rather, I can always only say: the human being hopes, is courageous.'[47] It is, in other words, the *whole* human being that is affected by the emotions or passion; and, as Heidegger repeatedly states, this also includes the body.[48] *Dasein*, 'as being in the world, insofar as it is affected by the world, *is also affected with regard to its corporeality*'.[49] Indeed, Heidegger emphasizes that 'the whole being of the human being [is] characterized in such a way that it must be grasped as the *bodily being-in-the-world* of the human being'.[50]

It is an interesting question why not a single trace of this insight is found in *Being and Time* itself, published only three years later. We shall suggest the contours of a possible answer to this question after a brief review of the second, much later text in which Heidegger touches on the question of the body. The *Zollikon Seminars* contain a series of seminars Heidegger organized together with the psychiatrist Medard Boss in the years 1959–69, as well as transcripts of a selection of Heidegger and Boss's conversations and correspondence. In an exchange dated 3 March 1972, Boss confronts Heidegger with the story of how astonished Sartre was to discover that *Being and Time* only contains six lines on the body. Heidegger replies: 'I can only counter Sartre's reproach by stating that the bodily [*das Leibliche*] is the most difficult [to understand] and that I was unable to say more at that time.'[51] A remarkable admission, not least in light of Heidegger's ability, a couple of years before composing *Being and Time*, to say a great deal more. What also makes this reply interesting is that it seems to suggest that, in the decades following *Being and Time*, Heidegger managed to give a more adequate treatment of the body. Yet, although the *Zollikon Seminars* do contain numerous remarks on the body, it is doubtful whether these remarks constitute a fundamental change in relation to *Being and Time*.

Let us give an example. Heidegger writes in the *Zollikon Seminars* that to interpret the body as a material, lifeless machine would be to misunderstand it fundamentally. For this reason, human embodiment should be sharply distinguished from the *corporeality* of something merely present-at-hand. But, as Heidegger adds, human embodiment can only be understood against the background of *Dasein*'s being-in-the-world. We could not exist in an embodied manner if we were not fundamentally characterized by being-in-the world. Heidegger illustrates this claim by repeating that *Dasein* is characterized by its direction and orientation. The reason we can distinguish between left and right, behind and in front of, above and beneath, is precisely that, in our very existence, we are directed. And, as he writes, it is because of this *Ausgerichtetsein* that we can have a body or be embodied. It is *not*, Heidegger emphasizes, our bodily existence that makes possible our distinguishing between left and right, and so on.[52] In brief, the spatiality of *Dasein* is expressed in its embodiment, but it is the body that is founded in being-in-the-world, and not the other way around. Clearly, this Heideggerian position does not differ fundamentally from the position advocated in *Being and Time*, according to which the spatiality of *Dasein* (including the body) was founded on its being-in-the-world, which itself was founded on temporality. In all essentials, this seems to be the position Heidegger still adopts in the *Zollikon Seminars*.

So why is it that, apart from a brief excursion in a 1924 lecture course, Heidegger seems consistently wary of conceiving of embodiment as a fundamental character of *Dasein*'s being-in-the-world? An exhaustive answer to this question would take us too far afield, but we would like to make the following tentative suggestion: Heidegger seems to have convinced himself that the notions of body and embodiment invariably promote conceptions of the human being as *composed* of various different types of entities. Concepts such as 'body', 'embodiment' and 'corporeality' tend, in the hands of philosophers, to evoke contrasting concepts such as 'mind', 'soul' and 'the mental'. To speak of the human body, then, is already to invoke the complementary notion of the human 'mind' or 'soul'; the notions of 'embodiment' and 'incarnation' seem to suggest that *something* (e.g., a 'pure ego') is embodied or incarnated, and so on. At any rate, this seems to be the worry that is driving Heidegger. In *Being and Time*, for example, he warns against philosophers' inclination to think that:

> Being-in in a world is a spiritual property, and that man's 'spatiality' is a result of his bodily nature (which, at the same time always gets 'founded' upon corporeality). Here again we are faced with the Being-present-at-hand-together of some spiritual Thing along with a corporeal Thing, while the Being of the entity thus compounded remains more obscure than ever.[53]

It is worth pausing to gauge the full import of what Heidegger is saying. To conceive of *Dasein*'s spatiality as founded on its embodiment or 'bodily nature' (*Leiblichkeit*) is *already*, so Heidegger seems to think, to operate with a spurious mind–body dualism (a 'being-present-at-hand-together' of a mental thing and a corporeal thing). But, if so, then it should start to become clear to us why Heidegger has to prioritize temporality over spatiality. For, given what we have just said, any attempt to grasp the directed being-in-the-world of *Dasein* in terms of *Dasein*'s embodiment is palpably hopeless. And that leaves us without any obvious way of interpreting the existential structure of *Dasein* in spatial terms at all. Therefore, the spatiality of *Dasein* must be founded on a (so to speak) 'pre-embodied' and hence 'pre-spatial' existential structure that, in turn, is interpreted exclusively in temporal terms.

To put it differently, if we are looking for a primordial spatiality in the being of *Dasein*, the structure of embodiment would be the most obvious candidate. However, on Heidegger's view, to invoke the body or embodiment is already to succumb to a questionable dualism. It is doubtful, therefore, whether there is any way to interpret *Dasein*'s being-in-the-world in spatial terms. Hence, only the temporal interpretation remains. This is, we believe, a plausible reconstruction of Heidegger's reasoning.

But, surely, the reasoning rests on a false alternative. We should simply refuse to accept the choice between a dubious mind–body dyad, on the one hand, and a 'pre-embodied' and 'pre-spatial' being-in-the-world, on the other. Heidegger is right to deny that the former is the correct way to think of human embodiment and spatiality, but he draws the questionable conclusion that embodiment must then be grasped as a secondary phenomenon, founded on some pre-embodied being-in-the-world. Although Heidegger occasionally suggests that the lived-body (*Leib*) differs fundamentally from a mere physical object (*Körper*), he never fully elaborates the difference. Also, despite the fact that, a few years before *Being and Time*, Heidegger had advanced the thought that our ecstatic and oriented being-in-the-world itself must be understood as an *embodied* being-in-the-world, it is a thought that he leaves underdeveloped and never returns to. And this is unfortunate, for it seems likely that this is the very thought that would have helped Heidegger avoid the implausible conclusion that space could be derived from temporality.

In the next section, we turn to a phenomenologist who did develop the idea of human existence as essentially embodied and who, as a consequence, pointed to a more fruitful way of understanding the relationship between temporality and spatiality.

13.4   Husserl on body, space and time

A central feature of Husserl's account of perception is his emphasis on the perspectival givenness of the perceived object. When something appears perspectivally it always appears in a particular *orientation*. That is to say, it presents itself from a certain angle and at a certain distance from the observer.[54] Hence no point of view is 'pure' and free-floating, and there is no view from nowhere. A point of view is essentially a situated and embodied point of view.

It is important to realize that Husserl's claim is not simply that subjects can only perceive and interact with objects in the world if they *have* a body. His claim, rather, is that perception involves an element of bodily self-experience. Suppose you are sitting in a restaurant, about to enjoy a sumptuous meal. The starters arrive, and so you pick up your knife and fork. What enables you to do so? In order to pick up the fork, you must know its spatial position relative to you.[55] Your visual perception of the fork, that is, must also provide some information about *you*; otherwise seeing the fork would not enable you to perform the act of picking it up. On the dinner table, the perceived fork is to the left (of you); the perceived knife is to the right (of you), and the perceived plate and wineglass are in front (of you). Every perspectival appearance implies that the embodied perceiver is himself or herself co-given as the zero point, the indexical 'here' in relation to which every appearing object is oriented. As a perceiving, embodied subject, you are the point of reference into which all your perceptual objects are uniquely related. You are the centre around which, and in relation to which, egocentric space unfolds.[56] In sum, every perceptual experience of some slice of the world is mediated and made possible by our embodiment.

But the body does not merely function as a centre of orientation. Its *mobility* is also of decisive importance, according to Husserl. As he writes in the *Crisis*:

> If we pay attention now purely to the bodily aspect of the things, this obviously exhibits itself perceptively only in seeing, in touching, in hearing, etc., i.e., in visual, tactual, acoustical, and other such aspects. Obviously and inevitably participating in this is our living body, which is never absent from the perceptual field, and specifically its corresponding 'organs of perception' (eyes, hands, ears, etc.). In consciousness they play a constant role here; specifically they function in seeing, hearing, etc., together with the ego's motility belonging to them, i.e., what is called kinaesthesis. All kinaestheses, each being an 'I move,' 'I do,' [etc.] are bound together in a comprehensive unity – in which kinaesthetic holding-still is [also] a mode of the 'I do.' Clearly the aspect-exhibitions of whatever body [*Körper*] is appearing in perception, and the kinaestheses, are not processes [simply running] alongside each other; rather, they work together in such a way that the aspects have the ontic meaning of, or the validity of, aspects of the body [*Körper*] only through the fact that they are those aspects continually required by the kinaestheses – by the kinaesthetic-sensual total situation in each of its working variations of the total kinaesthesis by setting in motion this or that particular kinaesthesis – and that they correspondingly fulfil the requirement.[57]

According to Husserl, spatial perception involves a tacit sense of oneself as bodily present in the perceived world. Moreover, when you look at something, you are not only in possession of an accompanying awareness of the present position of your body – you are also implicitly aware of an ordered system of movements that you are capable of performing. According to Husserl, in fact, your ability to perceive an object from a particular perspective presupposes that you are simultaneously implicitly aware of the various coexisting but absent profiles of the object. These absent profiles are related to the present profile in a very particular way. They are all profiles that will become perceptually manifested if you execute particular *movements*.[58] Whereas the present profile is correlated with your present bodily position, the absent profiles are all correlated with positions you could adopt, that is, they are correlated to what Husserl calls your 'kinaesthetic system'. If you were not in possession of this bodily self-awareness in the form of an 'I can' (move in such-and-such ways), you would be unable to intend the absent profiles of the object, and consequently unable to perceive spatial objects altogether.[59]

Let us illustrate Husserl's point with a concrete example. Suppose you are currently viewing your (open) laptop from a position in front of it. You are tacitly aware of this actually appearing profile of the laptop (keyboard, screen) as correlated with the present position of your body, and you are implicitly aware of a multitude of momentarily absent aspects of the laptop (the backside of the screen, the bottom, etc.) as correlated with other possible positions of your body – positions that you can realize, at least in principle, through self-movement. As Husserl puts this, the 'horizon' of absent but 'co-intended' profiles of the laptop is correlated with a 'kinaesthetic horizon', that is, with your capacity for possible movement.[60] An intentional if–then connection links the absent profiles with your kinaesthetic horizon. If you move in this or that way, then this or that aspect of the laptop will become visually or tactually present. The backside of the screen is only the backside of the same screen that you are facing now, because it can be brought into focus through the execution of a particular bodily movement.[61] The central point is not that we can perceive moving objects in space (although, of course, we can do this), but that our very perception of such objects is itself a matter of movement.

On Husserl's account, *perception* is thus closely intertwined with *action*. Perception is not simply a matter of passive reception, but crucially involves active exploration. The body is not merely our point of view, but also our point of departure.[62] As Gibson also stresses, we see with mobile eyes 'set in a head that can turn and is attached to a body that can move from place to place'.[63] A stationary point of view is merely the limiting case of a mobile point of view. For a recent formulation of such an enactive view of perception, consider the following statement by Alva Noë:

Perception is not something that happens to us, or in us. It is something we do. The world makes itself available to the perceiver through physical movement and interaction. All perception is touch-like in this way: perceptual experience acquires content thanks to our possession of bodily skills. What we perceive is determined by what we do and what we know how to do; it is determined by what we are ready to do. We *enact* our perceptual experience; we act it out.[64]

In ordinary experience, perception and movement are always united. I touch something by moving the arm. I see something by moving the head and eyes. That which is perceived is perceived as nearby or further away, as something that can be approached and explored. One might sum up Husserl's position by saying that perceptual intentionality involves movement that can only be effectuated by an embodied subject.[65]

Staying with the example of a visual perception of a laptop, let us note a very different, but equally crucial, point. If you move around the laptop in order to obtain a more exhaustive presentation of it, then the different profiles of it do not present themselves as disjointed fragments, but are perceived as synthetically integrated moments. A *synthesis of identity* is established, such that you constantly see new profiles of the same, unchanged computer. This process of synthesization is obviously temporal in nature and, as such, it cannot be fully accounted for by our awareness of it as correlated with a kinaesthetic movement. Or, to be more precise, in order for the 'constitutive duet'[66] of kinaesthetic movement and visual appearances to yield an awareness of a single, unchanged object being viewed from a series of different positions, it must be the case that our perceptual awareness reaches beyond what is given at the present moment. As Husserl explains, 'as soon as a new side becomes visible, a side that has just been visible gradually disappears from sight, becoming finally completely non-visible. But what has become non-visible is not cognitively lost to us.'[67] If it were 'lost to us', we would never have an awareness of what is now presented to us as another side of the same thing we were seeing the moment before. Nor, indeed, would we have any awareness of succession and duration – of anything beginning, ending, changing or staying the same. Since we are obviously conscious of such things, we must acknowledge that our consciousness, one way or the other, can encompass more than that which is given right now. Granted that we can be co-conscious of that which has just been and that which is about to occur, however, the crucial question remains: *how* can we be conscious of that which is no longer, or not yet, present to our consciousness?

One suggestion might be that we simply need to recognize that our perceptions (auditory, visual, etc.) are themselves temporally extended processes. Unfortunately, however, this suggestion will not do. If a perception has duration and temporal extension, it will contain temporal phases of its own. But, on closer inspection, it is obvious that a mere succession of such conscious phases will not, as such, provide us with the consciousness of succession. For that to happen, the succession of these phases must somehow be united experientially. The decisive challenge is then to account for this unification without giving rise to an explanatory regress, that is, without having to posit yet another temporally extended consciousness whose task is to unify the first-order consciousness, and so forth *ad infinitum*.

According to Husserl, the basic unit of temporality is – to use Jamesian terms – not a 'knife-edge' present, but a 'duration-block', that is, a temporal field that comprises all three temporal modes of present, past and future. Husserl employed three technical terms to describe this temporal structure of consciousness. There is (i) a 'primal impression' narrowly directed toward the strictly circumscribed now-phase of the object. The primal impression never appears in isolation and is an abstract component that by itself cannot provide us with a perception of a temporal object. The primal impression is accompanied by (ii) a 'retention', or retentional aspect, which provides us with a consciousness of the just-elapsed phase of the object, thereby furnishing the primal impression with a past-directed temporal context, and by (iii) a 'protention', or protentional aspect, which in a more or less indefinite way intends the phase of the object about to occur, thereby providing a future-oriented temporal context for the primal impression.

The concrete and full structure of all lived experience is consequently *protention – primal impression – retention*. Although the specific experiential contents of this structure change progressively from moment to moment, at any one given moment this threefold structure is present (synchronically) as a unified whole:

> In this way, it becomes evident that concrete perception as original consciousness (original givenness) of a temporally extended object is structured internally as itself a streaming system of momentary perceptions (so-called primal impressions). But each such momentary perception is the nuclear phase of a continuity, a continuity of momentary gradated retentions on the one side, and a horizon of what is coming on the other side: a horizon of 'protention', which is disclosed to be characterized as a constantly gradated coming.[68]

Retention is not a memory that re-presents the object in question, for retention provides us with an *intuition* of the just-past sense of the object.[69] Phrased differently, perceptual presence is not punctual; it is a field in which now, not-now and not-yet-now are given in a horizontal *gestalt*. This is what is required if perception of an enduring object is to be possible.

So, to sum up, our experience of the identity of the object across a multitude of changing appearances is made possible by what Husserl terms *time-consciousness*.[70] In fact, Husserl argues that, ultimately, temporality in the form of time-consciousness must be regarded as the most basic condition of possibility for the constitution of any object: 'In the ABCs of the constitution of all objectivity given to consciousness [...], here is the "A".'[71] Indeed, Husserl considers the analysis of temporality to be the bedrock of phenomenology, and he consequently claims that only an analysis of time-consciousness discloses that which is truly absolute.[72]

Husserl's detailed analyses of the body notwithstanding, the last few sentences make it look as if his position is ultimately very similar to Heidegger's. As Heidegger refers everything back to the temporality of *Dasein*'s being-in-the-world, so Husserl ultimately grounds the constitution of all objectivities in time-consciousness. Although this might seem a natural conclusion to draw at this stage, we nevertheless believe it is mistaken. First of all, even if Husserl on various occasions acknowledges the need for a distinction between various constitutive levels, and even if he regards time-consciousness as constituting the most basic and fundamental level, he never attempts to derive founded levels from this basic level. There is, in that sense, no attempt on Husserl's part to derive the structures of, say, perceptual intentionality from that of time-consciousness. Second, consider the following quote:

> If, now, time-consciousness is the primordial place of the constitution of the unity of identity or of an object like formation, [...], then we are still only talking about that consciousness which produces a general form. Mere form is admittedly an abstraction, and thus from the very beginning the analysis of the intentionality of time-consciousness and its accomplishment is an analysis that works on [the level of] abstractions.[73]

The analysis of time-consciousness is abstract in the sense that it only addresses certain formal structures of intentional consciousness.[74] But every experience, every concrete conscious episode, also involves a content. And the most basic content is provided by our sensuous affectivity.[75] This is why Husserl can eventually write as follows: 'We regard sensing as the original consciousness of time.'[76]

Our sensations, however, do not appear out of nowhere. On Husserl's view they are necessarily correlated to our kinaesthetic system and to our bodily sensibility.[77] But, if time-consciousness *de facto* requires sensuous affection, and if there is no sensuous affection without a lived body, we are ultimately led to the realization that temporality and embodiment must be understood in their interconnection.[78]

13.5 Conclusion

Let us take stock. Heidegger offers a phenomenological corrective to the Bergsonian account of space. The notion of space as a pure container of isolated, extended things has little to do with space as we experience it in our practical dealings with the world. But, when Bergson's account of space is rejected, we have removed his principal objection to the attempt to understand space and time as interconnected. And in Heidegger, indeed, we find such an attempt to conceive of space and time as connected. It is, however, one that views space as unilaterally founded in the temporality of *Dasein*'s existential structure. Yet, as we have suggested (and as Heidegger himself seems to realize eventually), it is hard to see how it might be possible to derive spatiality from temporality. This raises the question why Heidegger nevertheless makes the attempt in *Being and Time*. We have argued that this is intimately connected with Heidegger's refusal to address the body. It is because he does not believe there is any way of broaching human embodiment without introducing a problematic mind–body dualism that Heidegger chooses to remain silent with respect to the body. However, he thereby denies himself access to the most natural way of interpreting *Dasein*'s being-in-the-world in spatial terms. This leaves him with the temporal interpretation, and thus forces him to conceive of space as derived from temporality.

As this is a blind alley, we looked around for an account that avoided Bergson's strict dichotomy of space and time, while (*contra* Heidegger) conceiving the latter as equally primordial, interdependent phenomena. This, we have argued, is precisely the sort of account Husserl offers. On the Husserlian account, time-consciousness is fundamental in the constitutional hierarchy. But in isolation from sensibility – and hence the lived body – time-consciousness remains a mere abstraction. Every concrete consciousness is at once temporal and, *qua* embodied, spatial.

The story doesn't end here, obviously. Later phenomenologists, including Sartre, Merleau-Ponty, Straus, Derrida, Richir and Patočka, would in various ways continue Husserl's analysis and defend the view that temporalization and spatialization must necessarily be thought in their unity.[79] A discussion and appraisal of this subsequent development must, however, await another occasion.[80]

Notes

1. H. Bergson (1910) *Time and Free Will: An Essay on the Immediate Data of Consciousness*, trans. F.L. Pogson (Montana: Kessinger Publishing Company), p. 91.
2. Ibid., pp. 98–9. Ultimately, Bergson will claim that science cannot deal with time without eliminating its essential element. For the very same reason, sequential time, time understood as a sequence of separate, distinct and externally related events or episodes, has nothing to do with real temporality.
3. Ibid., pp. 91, 98.
4. Ibid., pp. 90–1.
5. Ibid., p. 106.
6. Ibid., p. 137.
7. Ibid., pp. 105, 107.
8. Ibid., p. 126.
9. Ibid., p. 109.
10. Ibid., p. 128.
11. Ibid., p. 90.
12. Ibid., p. xix.
13. Ibid., pp. 132–3.
14. When reading Bergson's descriptions it is difficult not to be reminded of Heidegger's discussion of *Ruinanz* or falling, that is, life's tendency towards self-forgetfulness, its inherent tendency to objectify and cover itself up. See M. Heidegger (1994) *Phänomenologische Interpretationen zu Aristoteles. Einführung in die phänomenologische Forschung* (Frankfurt am Main: Vittorio Klostermann), pp. 119, 121.
15. Bergson, *Time and Free Will*, p. 128.
16. Ibid., p. 138.
17. Ibid., p. 167.
18. Ibid., pp. 138–9.
19. Ibid., p. 137.
20. See D. Zahavi (2010) 'Life, thinking and phenomenology in the early Bergson', in M. Kelly (ed.)*Bergson and Phenomenology* (Basingstoke: Palgrave Macmillan), pp. 118–33.
21. M. Heidegger (1962) *Being and Time*, trans. J. Macquarrie and E. Robinson (Oxford: Blackwell), pp. 92–3.
22. Ibid., p. 138.
23. Ibid., pp. 79–82.
24. Ibid., p. 138.
25. Ibid., p. 140.
26. Ibid., p. 141.
27. Or, at any rate, only *marginally* different (due to the movements of the Eurasian and Indian continental plates).
28. Ibid., p. 141.
29. Ibid., pp. 140–1.
30. Husserl and Heidegger are in agreement on this point. The latter writes: 'Though these estimates [e.g., of distance] may be imprecise and variable if we try to compute them, in the everydayness of Dasein they have their *own*

definiteness which is thoroughly intelligible' (Heidegger, *Being and Time*, p. 140). In *Formal and Transcendental Logic*, Husserl writes: 'The trader in the market has his market-truth. In the relationship in which it stands, is his truth not a good one, and the best that a trader can use? Is it a pseudo-truth, merely because the scientist, involved in a different relativity and judging with other aims and ideas, looks for other truths – with which a great many more things can be done, but not the one thing that has to be done in a market?' E. Husserl (1969) *Formal and Transcendental Logic*, trans. D. Cairns (The Hague: Martinus Nijhoff), p. 278.

31. Compare Husserl's related considerations in 'The Origin of Geometry', in E. Husserl (1970) *The Crisis of European Sciences and Transcendental Phenomenology*, trans. D. Carr (Evanston: Northwestern University Press), pp. 353–78.

32. Heidegger, *Being and Time*, p. 147.

33. Ibid., p. 141.

34. Ibid., p. 146. It is important to bear in mind that Heidegger distances his position from that of Kant and emphasizes the difference between a sort of transcendental philosophy that operates with a notion of *das Ding an sich* and a critical transcendental philosophy, such as Heidegger's own phenomenology, which rejects this notion.

35. Ibid., pp. 147–8.

36. More precisely, temporality makes possible the structure that Heidegger calls 'care' (*Sorge*). 'Care' is his term for 'Dasein's primordial totality of being' (ibid., p. 227). Heidegger writes: 'the Being of Dasein means ahead-of-itself-Being-already-in-(the world) as Being-alongside (entities encountered within the world). This Being fills in the signification of the term "*care*"' (ibid., p. 237). To all except Heidegger scholars, this is bound to seem somewhat obscure. For present purposes, however, we may regard 'care' as picking out the same structure of being that we have been calling 'being-in-the-world', only in a somewhat more inclusive and elaborate way.

37. Ibid., p. 418.

38. Ibid., pp. 420–1.

39. M. Heidegger (1972) *On Time and Being*, trans. J. Stambaugh (New York: Harper and Row), p. 23.

40. Heidegger, *Being and Time*, p. 143.

41. Ibid., p. 23. Indeed, elsewhere he writes: 'But to philosophize precisely means to be fundamentally and constantly moved by, and directly sensitive to, the completely enigmatic nature [*Rätselhaftigkeit*] of that which common sense [*dem gesunden Verstande*] finds obvious and self-evident.' M. Heidegger (1976) *Logik: Die Frage nach der Wahrheit*, W. Biemel (ed.) (Frankfurt a. M.: Vittorio Klostermann), pp. 23–4.

42. Heidegger, *Being and Time*, p. 144.

43. Even as staunch a defender of Heidegger as Hubert Dreyfus is clear that the former's refusal to offer an account of the body is unsatisfactory. See H.L. Dreyfus (1991) *Being-in-the-World: A Commentary on Heidegger's Being and Time* (Cambridge, MA: The MIT Press), p. 137.

44. D. Franck (1986) *Heidegger et le problème de l'espace* (Paris: Les Éditions de Minuit), p. 56.

45. M. Heidegger (2002) *Grundbegriffe der aristotelischen Philosophie*, M. Michalski (ed.) (Frankfurt am Main: Klostermann), p. 197.

46. Ibid., pp. 122, 177.
47. Ibid., p. 197.
48. Ibid., pp. 203, 206, 207.
49. Ibid., p. 202.
50. Ibid., p. 199.
51. M. Heidegger (2001) *Zollikon Seminars*, trans. F. Mayr and R. Askay (Evanston: Northwestern University Press), p. 231.
52. Ibid., p. 232.
53. Heidegger, *Being and Time*, pp. 82–3.
54. E. Husserl (2001) *Analyses Concerning Passive and Active Synthesis*, trans. A.J. Steinbock (Dordrecht: Kluwer Academic Publishers), pp. 39–40.
55. See J. Perry (1993) *The Problem of Essential Indexicals and Other Essays* (Oxford: Oxford University Press), p. 205.
56. E. Husserl (1989) *Ideas Pertaining to a Pure Phenomenology and to a Phenomenological Philosophy. Second Book*, trans. R. Rojcewicz and A. Schuwer (Dordrecht: Kluwer Academic Publishers), p. 166. See also Husserl, *Analyses Concerning Passive and Active Synthesis*, pp. 584–5.
57. E. Husserl, *The Crisis of European Sciences and Transcendental Phenomenology*, p. 106. Translation slightly modified.
58. E. Husserl (1997) *Thing and Space: Lectures of 1907*, trans. R. Rojcewicz (Dordrecht: Kluwer Academic Publishers), p. 160. See also *Analyses Concerning Passive and Active Synthesis*, pp. 51–2.
59. Husserl, *Analyses Concerning Passive and Active Synthesis*, pp. 50–1.
60. Ibid., p. 52.
61. Husserl, *The Crisis of European Sciences and Transcendental Phenomenology*, pp. 106, 161.
62. Husserl, *Analyses Concerning Passive and Active Synthesis*, p. 50.
63. J.J. Gibson (1986) *The Ecological Approach to Visual Perception* (Hillsdale, NJ: Lawrence Erlbaum Associates), p. 53; cf. p. 205.
64. A. Noë (2004) *Action in Perception* (Cambridge, MA: The MIT Press), p. 1.
65. Husserl, *Thing and Space*, p. 148; *Analyses Concerning Passive and Active Synthesis*, p. 50.
66. Husserl, *Analyses Concerning Passive and Active Synthesis*, p. 52.
67. Ibid., p. 45.
68. E. Husserl (1977) *Phenomenological Psychology: Lectures, Summer Semester 1925*, trans. J. Scanlon (The Hague: Martinus Nijhoff), p. 154.
69. E. Husserl (1991) *On the Phenomenology of the Consciousness of Internal Time (1893-1917)*, trans. J.B. Brough (Dordrecht: Kluwer Academic Publishers), p. 43.
70. Husserl, *Analyses Concerning Passive and Active Synthesis*, pp. 601–2.
71. Ibid., p. 170.
72. E. Husserl (1983) *Ideas Pertaining to a Pure Phenomenology and to a Phenomenological Philosophy. First Book*, trans. F. Kersten (The Hague: Martinus Nijhoff), p. 193.
73. Husserl, *Analyses Concerning Passive and Active Synthesis*, p. 173.
74. Ibid., pp. 163–4, 174.
75. E. Husserl(1952) *Ideen zu einer reinen Phänomenologie und phänomenologischen Philosophie. Drittes Buch*, M. Biemel (ed.) (The Hague: Martinus Nijhoff), p. 11.

76. Husserl, *On the Phenomenology of the Consciousness of Internal Time (1893-1917)*, p. 112.
77. See E. Husserl (1973a) *Zur Phänomenologie der Intersubjektivität I*, I. Kern (ed.) (The Hague: Martinus Nijhoff), p. 292; and E. Husserl (1973b) *Zur Phänomenologie der Intersubjektivität III*, I. Kern (ed.) (The Hague: Martinus Nijhoff), p. 324.
78. For earlier interpretations of Husserl favouring a similar conclusion, cf. G. Brand (1955) *Welt, Ich und Zeit* (The Hague: Martinus Nijhoff), p. 47; and U. Claesges (1964) *Edmund Husserls Theorie der Raumkonstitution* (The Hague: Martinus Nijhoff), pp. 100, 143. For thorough discussions of Husserl's phenomenological analyses of embodiment and temporality, see D. Zahavi (1994) 'Husserl's Phenomenology of the Body', *Études Phénoménologiques*, 19, 63–84; D. Zahavi (2003a) 'Inner time-consciousness and pre-reflective self-awareness', in D. Welton (ed.) *The New Husserl: A Critical Reader* (Bloomington: Indiana University Press), pp. 157–80; D. Zahavi (2003b) *Husserl's Phenomenology* (Stanford: Stanford University Press); and D. Zahavi (2007) 'Perception of duration presupposes duration of perception – or does it? Husserl and Dainton on time', *International Journal of Philosophical Studies*, 15(3), 453–71.
79. See J.-P. Sartre (1956) *Being and Nothingness*, trans. H.E. Barnes (New York: Philosophical Library); M. Merleau-Ponty (1962) *Phenomenology of Perception*, trans. C. Smith (London: Routledge and Kegan Paul); E. Straus (1963) *The Primary World of Senses: A Vindication of Sensory Experience* (New York: Glencoe); J. Derrida (1984) *Margins of Philosophy* (Chicago: Chicago University Press); M. Richir (1989) 'Synthèse passive et temporalisation/spatialisation', in E. Escoubas and M. Richir (eds)*Husserl* (Grenoble: Millon); J. Patočka (1997) *Body, Community, Language, World*, trans. E. Kohak (Chicago: Open Court Publishing).
80. Thanks to Roxana Baiasu for helpful comments on an earlier draft of this chapter.

References

Bergson, H. (1910) *Time and Free Will: An Essay on the Immediate Data of Consciousness*, trans. F.L. Pogson (Montana: Kessinger Publishing Company).
Brand, G. (1955) *Welt, Ich und Zeit* (The Hague: Martinus Nijhoff).
Claesges, U. (1964) *Edmund Husserls Theorie der Raumkonstitution* (The Hague: Martinus Nijhoff).
Derrida, J. (1984) *Margins of Philosophy* (Chicago: Chicago University Press).
Dreyfus, H.L. (1991) *Being-in-the-World: A Commentary on Heidegger's Being and Time* (Cambridge, MA: The MIT Press).
Franck, D. (1986) *Heidegger et le problème de l'espace* (Paris: Les Éditions de Minuit).
Gibson, J.J. (1986) *The Ecological Approach to Visual Perception* (Hillsdale, NJ: Lawrence Erlbaum Associates).
Heidegger, M. (1962) *Being and Time*, trans. J. Macquarrie and E. Robinson (Oxford: Blackwell).

296 Dan Zahavi and Søren Overgaard

Heidegger, M. (1972) *On Time and Being*, trans. J. Stambaugh (New York: Harper and Row).
Heidegger, M. (1976) *Logik: Die Frage nach der Wahrheit* (Frankfurt am Main: Vittorio Klostermann).
Heidegger, M. (1994) *Phänomenologische Interpretationen zu Aristoteles. Einführung in die phänomenologische Forschung*. Gesamtausgabe Band 61 (Frankfurt am Main: Vittorio Klostermann).
Heidegger, M. (2001) *Zollikon Seminars*, trans. F. Mayr and R. Askay (Evanston: Northwestern University Press).
Heidegger, M. (2002) *Grundbegriffe der aristotelischen Philosophie*, M. Michalski (ed.) (Frankfurt a. M.: Klostermann).
Husserl, E. (1952) *Ideen zu einer reinen Phänomenologie und phänomenologischen Philosophie. Drittes Buch: Die Phänomenologie und die Fundamente der Wissenschaften*.M. Biemel (ed.) (The Hague: Martinus Nijhoff).
Husserl, E. (1969) *Formal and Transcendental Logic*, trans. D. Cairns (The Hague: Martinus Nijhoff).
Husserl, E. (1970) *The Crisis of European Sciences and Transcendental Phenomenology*, trans. D. Carr (Evanston, IL: Northwestern University Press).
Husserl, E. (1973a) *Zur Phänomenologie der Intersubjektivität I*, I Kern (ed.) (The Hague: Martinus Nijhoff).
Husserl, E. (1973b) *Zur Phänomenologie der Intersubjektivität III*, I Kern (ed.) (The Hague: Martinus Nijhoff).
Husserl, E. (1977) *Phenomenological Psychology: Lectures, Summer Semester 1925*, trans. J. Scanlon (The Hague: Martinus Nijhoff).
Husserl, E. (1983) *Ideas Pertaining to a Pure Phenomenology and to a Phenomenological Philosophy. First Book*, trans. F. Kersten (The Hague: Martinus Nijhoff).
Husserl, E. (1989) *Ideas Pertaining to a Pure Phenomenology and to a Phenomenological Philosophy. Second Book*, trans. R. Rojcewicz and A. Schuwer (Dordrecht: Kluwer Academic Publishers).
Husserl, E. (1991) *On the Phenomenology of the Consciousness of Internal Time (1893–1917)*, trans. J.B. Brough (Dordrecht: Kluwer Academic Publishers).
Husserl, E. (1997) *Thing and Space: Lectures of 1907*, trans. R. Rojcewicz (Dordrecht: Kluwer Academic Publishers).
Husserl, E. (2001) *Analyses Concerning Passive and Active Synthesis*, trans. A.J. Steinbock (Dordrecht: Kluwer Academic Publishers).
Merleau-Ponty, M. (1962) *Phenomenology of Perception*, trans. C. Smith (London: Routledge and Kegan Paul).
Noë, A. (2004) *Action in Perception* (Cambridge, MA: The MIT Press).
Patočka, J. (1997) *Body, Community, Language, World*, trans. E. Kohak (Chicago: Open Court Publishing).
Perry, J. (1993) *The Problem of Essential Indexicals and Other Essays* (Oxford: Oxford University Press).
Richir, M. (1989) 'Synthèse passive et temporalisation/spatialisation', in E. Escoubas and M. Richir (eds)*Husserl* (Grenoble: Millon).
Sartre, J. P. (1956) *Being and Nothingness*, trans. H.E. Barnes (New York: Philosophical Library).
Straus, E. (1963) *The Primary World of Senses: A Vindication of Sensory Experience* (New York: Glencoe).

Zahavi, D. (1994) 'Husserl's Phenomenology of the Body', *Études Phénoméno-logiques*, 19, 63–84.

Zahavi, D. (2003a) 'Inner time-consciousness and pre-reflective self-awareness', in D. Welton (ed.) *The New Husserl. A Critical Reader* (Bloomington: Indiana University Press), pp. 157–80.

Zahavi, D. (2003b) *Husserl's Phenomenology* (Stanford: Stanford University Press).

Zahavi, D. (2007) 'Perception of duration presupposes duration of perception – or does it? Husserl and Dainton on time', *International Journal of Philosophical Studies*, 15(3), 453–71.

Zahavi, D. (2010) 'Life, thinking and phenomenology in the early Bergson', in M. Kelly (ed.) *Bergson and Phenomenology* (Houndmills: Palgrave Macmillan).

Index

Printed in Great Britain
by Amazon

39104690R00176